THE BURDENS
OF
SISTER
MARGARET

THE BURDENS
OF
SISTER
MARGARET

by
Craig Harline

DOUBLEDAY
NEW YORK LONDON TORONTO SYDNEY AUCKLAND

PUBLISHED BY DOUBLEDAY
a division of Bantam Doubleday Dell Publishing Group, Inc.
1540 Broadway, New York, New York 10036

DOUBLEDAY and the portrayal of an anchor with a dolphin are trademarks of
Doubleday, a division of Bantam Doubleday Dell Publishing Group, Inc.

Library of Congress Cataloging-in-Publication Data
Harline, Craig E.
The burdens of Sister Margaret / by Craig Harline.
      p.   cm.
   Includes bibliographical references and index.
   1. Smulders, Margaret, d. 1648.   2. Franciscans—
Belgium—Louvain—Biography.   3. Franciscan convents—
Belgium—Louvain—History—17th century.   4. Louvain
(Belgium)—Church history—17th century.
I. Title.
BX4705.S6628H37   1994   93-42496
271′.973—dc20   CIP
[B]

ISBN 0-385-47395-8

10   9   8   7   6   5   4   3   2   1

IN MEMORY OF
MY GREAT-GRANDMOTHER,
HALLIE THATCHER,
WHO, BESIDES MUCH ELSE,
TOLD STORIES

CONTENTS

CONTENTS

FOREWORD

I FOUND MARGARET SMULDERS and the other nuns of Bethlehem because, like many historians nowadays, I wanted to get beyond lifeless generalizations about "the Reformation" and because I was lucky.

I wanted more individual faces, more emotion, and even some sound in my image of how both Protestant and Catholic Reformations went to work. Not that the unthinkable shattering of Roman Christianity during the sixteenth century wasn't already fascinating stuff: from Luther's toe-to-toe confrontation with the emperor Charles V to Luther's eventual split with Rome; from variations on the split by John Calvin in Geneva, Ulrich Zwingli in Zurich, or King Henry VIII in England to such implacable opponents of Protestantism as the Jesuits of Ignatius Loyola or the Most Catholic King of Spain, Philip II; from over a century of thunderous wars fought in the name of a new religion or the old—by such unforgettable characters as England's Queen Elizabeth or France's Cardinal Richelieu—to a flood of "definitive" councils that churches and states called to expurgate, formulate, and promulgate, there was plenty to enchant. Yet among the multitude of earthshaking events and consequences linked to the Age of Reform, most intriguing of all to me was a less celebrated matter: what happened in the hearts and minds of the untold faithful and not so faithful, especially after about 1565 when leaders of the rival confessions emerged from their respective council rooms and set out with greater precision than Europe had ever seen before to win, keep, and shape souls.

Once Lutheranism, Calvinism, revived Catholicism, and still other versions of European Christianity had laid down their distinctive ecclesiastical and doctrinal foundations, they turned with enthusiasm to the construction of visible communities of true believers—the very existence of multiple confessions now made urgent the task of building identities, of defining "good" Catholics or Lutherans. If searching for labels, we might call this contest for souls of the late sixteenth, seventeenth, and even eighteenth centuries "phase 2" of the Reformation, but the recent popularity of the subject has yielded names enough already. The Dutch say "Closer" or "Further" Reform, the French "Acculturation" or "Christianization," and various German and English speakers "application," "Confessionalization," or "Confessionalism," heavy terms with different meaning but the same lively impulse—to see Reformation in action, at every level of church and society. Despite unprecedented efforts at uniformity by the churches, reform clearly meant long, even bitter struggle, not only between confessions but within any one. Reform was more than the great laying down the law. It was more than Luther throwing inkwells at the devil, Calvin discovering the transcendence of God, Zwingli marching to the slaughter, St. Teresa in ecstasy, Ignatius limping gamely around Rome, or King Henry being rid of Queen Catherine. Mixed in as well, a million times over, were the desires and wills of such unfamiliar characters as Sister Margaret Smulders.

I came to know Margaret and her cosisters under most fortunate circumstances. Having decided to study the lesser-known Catholic version of reform, I had begun digging for information on assorted lay and clerical groups who lived in the old Spanish Netherlands, or roughly modern-day Belgium, an area which during the sixteenth and seventeenth centuries was at the geographic and in some respects spiritual front of the ancient religion. It was on my third trip to the Belgian archives, while wading through the deep records of female convents, that I miraculously saw—not quite in vision—the blessed bundles on Bethlehem. They had lain three centuries dormant in an archive so ill-ordered that until the 1960s (goes the rumor) manuscripts were located not with an inventory but an image of St. Anthony, finder of lost objects.

It wasn't simply the fatness of the bundles that hooked me—the reports by ecclesiastical visitors to this nunnery, though necessary and impressive, told a one-sided, official story. Besides, similarly hefty and one-dimensional stacks could be had for other convents, even during the Middle Ages. Besides again, I had seen hundreds of such files, more full of tedious formulas than information, more striking for the extra-wide margins and extra-large lettering characteristic of paid-by-the-line lawyers than for substance. And it wasn't fame that drew me in: Bethlehem was among the plainest of the two dozen monastic institutions in and around the old university town of Leuven. Street maps of the time fail even to mention the convent, or get its appearance and location all wrong. What rendered the documents extraordinary, I concluded as I excitedly thumbed through them, was that they contained more than the opinions of outside officials or the standard, well-ordered economic records that typified monastic files—here was page after page by the sisters themselves. To have found for the period before 1650 even one or two such detailed letters from the same house was rare, yet in my hands were dozens.

Instead of documents that grudgingly surrendered the occasional tidbit about the viewpoint of the sisters, instead of sterile generalities by official visitors that the house was devout or contrariwise, instead of a papal nuncio's thirdhand gloss that the sisters now had troubles or now lived in harmony, or the usual warm trail of normative prescriptions that led to the familiar cold trail of actual practice, here was breathtaking detail and passion from the sisters themselves. I marveled at the survival of these papers, their prolixity, the noise of a convent sworn to regular periods of silence, and again the diverse points of view revealed. Also surprising, since thick files are usually born of scandal or saintliness, and since nuns so often appear in literature and history as shadowy, mysterious figures, was that most of the documents had to do with positively routine aspects of conventual life, like unpolished, more heated, Flemish versions of Jane Austen—though as in any community the exotic surfaced in Bethlehem as well.

All this—the discovery, the rarity of the find, and the personalities that emerged from the letters—moved me. More than any high-sounding justification I can offer, in the beginning and in the end I wanted to tell this story because I liked it. But part of why I liked it was the chance, better than I had imagined possible, to bring flesh and blood (and of course soul) to that huge, potentially abstract question that motivated me from the start: how the Reformations were lived—in this case inside a renowned but little-understood institution of the time, the nunnery.

The thousands of female religious who dotted the map of Catholic Europe during the decades after 1565 made up a minority, yet a notable minority, numerically and psychologically, on the religious landscape. In places their total surpassed the male orders; by about this time there were perhaps 10,000 women religious in the entire Low Countries (approximately Belgium and the Netherlands taken together), triple the number of males. And their psychological influence is evident in the concerns that ordinary laypeople and ecclesiastical and municipal authorities frequently voiced over how religious should act. Lately scholars have learned more about these women, but since in history the exceptional often gets the ink, much attention has gone to the most provocative cases—the very good or very bad. If it's not the holy or the wicked under the spotlight, then it's one of the important new "active" orders (women oriented toward health care or the schooling of young girls), since they were supposedly more characteristic of the religious spirit of the age than traditional contemplative houses (women who stayed behind walls and prayed). Hence the few books about old-fashioned "garden-variety" nuns are necessarily painted in the broadest of strokes.

When it became obvious to me that between 1600 and 1650 Margaret Smulders and her generation of ordinary, cloistered, Franciscan, Grey Sisters confronted the major issues of the day, and in such recorded detail, I judged that their experience might help illustrate, in color, an important part of the Catholic panorama. More than what it told about this convent alone, here was a vibrant example—in some ways typical and others not—of the form of religious life that most in the Roman religion still regarded as the ideal for women, and which during the sixteenth and seventeenth centuries came under severe pressure to retrench and reform. In other words, convents were now being asked to do what the church had long demanded of religious women, with some seventeenth-century twists: observe cloister more strictly, sing more attentively, pray more furtively, work more diligently, dress even more modestly, love more generously, obey more speedily. Further, given the contact between these nuns and outsiders, I thought that we might learn as well about the larger religious world—how expectations from all sides touched life within, and, since Bethlehem was under episcopal jurisdiction, how processes in this little space might connect to processes in the hundreds of other communities over which bishops had charge.

My original plan to accomplish these ends was to compare "practice" with "theory." How did the women of Bethlehem measure up to the standards for female religious as prescribed by their particular order, and especially by the church's recent Council of Trent (1545–63), whose decrees were so wide-ranging and definitive that they remained in force for all aspects of Catholic religious life until Vatican II in the twentieth century? But this method seemed more and more inadequate as I became convinced that a universal standard, for any group within the church, was a myth. Trent's instructions were looser than I had thought—more guideline than blueprint. I also saw that the disputants, in Bethlehem as elsewhere, often disagreed about standards, and that accounts of practice often contradicted each other. By which standard was I then to measure practice, and on whose account of practice should I rely?

Given all this, the most useful approach proved to be one hardly invented by me: to concentrate on conflicting, subjective, unscientific perceptions and points of view; on the strenuous attempts by bishops, visitors, and sisters to shape standard and practice in the convent in the way that each believed was best and true; and on the roles in all this maneuvering of such mundane matters as personal interests and practical obstacles. This approach helped me to realize that the dynamics apparent in and around Bethlehem—between convent and episcopal palace, between episcopal officials, or between factions of sisters—were similar to patterns in other studies which suggest that religious life in this Age of Reform was shaped through lengthy debate among variously motivated groups and individuals, that it was regularly reshaped, and that it was variously perceived and enforced, rather than established forever by arbitrary proclamations from on high. In other words, Margaret Smulders fashioned religious life—in how she imagined and lived it—with as much energy as her sisters, mother superior, or bishop.

This shaping of standard and practice, most spirited in Bethlehem between 1625 and 1637 and highlighted by the unusually detailed letters of Margaret and the other sisters, is the centerpiece of the study; it was what attracted me initially, and it alone justified a fat book. Yet this debate became even clearer and more meaningful as I better understood the seemingly unrelated events that went before, events more about personal ties and antagonisms than the ideals of religious life and reform, and based not on Margaret's letters but inferred from a variety of other sources, such as a rare journal by a bishop. Gradually I became convinced that these messy details about relationships and the wider religious world were in fact wonderfully mixed up with the controversies over reform that followed. They therefore come first, in Book I, while Book II treats the debate itself, and Book III discusses the fate of debate in Bethlehem.

In short, I have tried to sketch a picture of conventual life and reform after Trent. It is admittedly set within a small space, includes a very few people, and treats a mere handful of the many decades affected by the famous Council—yet as with most close studies, composed in whatever medium on whatever topic, there are noticeable connections to bigger themes and movements. Since the chief points I wish to make about these connections are usually embedded in the narrative rather than explicit, I will state them briefly here so that there is no doubt as to my intent.

First, the events described in Bethlehem may in many particulars be unique to that place and time, but the general challenges evident in this convent dominated the experience of *most* female religious since the early Middle Ages and even extend to the present day. One can make a forceful argument that factionalism versus common love, dissent versus obedience, the rights of the individual versus the demands of the community, the drawing of the line between temporal needs and extravagance, or between being a product of the world while living separately from it, have always been the central tensions of monasticism.

Second, the experience of Margaret Smulders, and that of every other female religious before and since, was influenced in significant ways by the very fact that she was a woman. As noted by a number of scholars, the requirement of stricter cloister for women than men and the tradition of not ordaining women caused nearly automatic differences in material life among male and female religious during the Age of Reformation. Also important were less automatic differences between the sexes in regard to political and ecclesiastical influence, or forms of worship. This is not to mention the related difference, important in Margaret's case and time, that women—nuns not excepted—were believed to be more inclined than men to witchcraft.

Third, and in part to balance the last point, rivalry in and around Bethlehem was often not a case of clear-cut groups or cultures in competition. Sometimes it was visitor against visitor, or sister against sister, rather than simply the (female) convent against the (male) hierarchy— and this was all complicated by alliances with outside confessors and laypeople, as well as the fact that groups and individuals alike rarely hesitated to use the church's hierarchy against each other.

Closely connected, and fourth, the shape of religious life within a community, monastic or lay, was not simply the result of impassioned debate among the members of that community. It also depended on the will, temperament, and ability of the hierarchy above—its resources, number of officials, ease of communication, resolve, and tools to enforce. Questions of bureaucracy or administration are often less exciting than many others, but they bear considerable consequences for reform here and elsewhere.

Last and most generally I suggest—in the spirit of other studies but I hope in my own way—that instead of accepting such sweeping terms as "Catholic Reformation" as self-evident and then using the terms to define the ideas and actions of the players, it is more helpful to let the players, in all their glorious frailty and cleverness and inconsistency, breathe life into the terms. Many sisters of Bethlehem and sundry ecclesiastical officials disagreed on certain issues, and yet all considered themselves to be good, even reforming clerics and religious. Rather than try to compare practice to a slippery standard and inevitably conclude that the twain did not meet, I have tried to show that the standard was shifting; that a major part of practice during the Age of Reformation was to debate and hold up theory—however unsystematic and humble it may have been—according to one's own image. Moreover, not all debate or activity in Bethlehem or other communities was about reform at all; the eternal trials of female monasticism just noted often had little to do with reform. Of greatest interest and significance to me, therefore, has been to set the characters in motion, to see the shaping and reshaping of religious life by real individuals rather than incorporeal labels.

But enough of bald assertions and abstractions. I would rather devote the rest of the book to the more enjoyable task of illustration.

THE PRINCIPALS

Jacob Boonen (bo'-nun) – Archbishop of Mechelen from 1621 to his death in 1655; royal councilor; superior over Bethlehem.

Joost Bouckaert (yoast boo'-cart) – Head of the shrine at Scherpenheuvel; dean of Diest; bishop of Ieper from 1639 to his death in 1646; the loyal patron of Margaret Smulders.

Maria Coninxloo (all *o*'s pronounced as in low) – Veiled sister of Bethlehem from ca. 1619 to her death ca. 1670; major critic of Mater Adriana Truis and major supporter of Catharina Rijckeboer.

Henri Joos (yoas) – Confessor of Bethlehem ca. 1604 to his expulsion in 1618; later pastor of Mol; brother of Sister Maria Joos; died in 1638.

Maria Joos – Veiled sister of Bethlehem from 1609 to her death in 1660s; bursaress* from 1629; sister of Henri Joos; major supporter of Adriana Truis.

Barbara Noosen (no'-sun) – Veiled sister of Bethlehem from ca. 1595 to her death in 1625; Mater from 1619 to the end; unpopular with Adriana Truis, among others.

Catharina Rijckeboer (ryé-ku-booer) – Veiled sister of Bethlehem from 1617 to her death in 1635; vicaress* from 1626 on; unwilling leader of critics of Adriana Truis.

Margaret Smulders – Veiled sister of Bethlehem from 1606 to her death in 1648; excluded from the community twice (1616–18; 1624–35); major critic of Adriana Truis; and one of the most prolific letter-writers in early modern monastic history.

Adriana Truis (trouse) – Veiled sister of Bethlehem from 1605 to her death in 1668; bursaress from ca. 1613 to 1629; Mater from 1625 to the end; friend of Henri Joos.

Anna Vignarola – Veiled sister of Bethlehem from 1624 to her death ca. 1673; vicaress from 1635 to 1668; bursaress and novice mistress

---

*I add the "ess" to these titles because the sisters themselves did—they did so even for other less formal nouns referring to women.

after ca. 1650; Mater from 1668 on; major supporter of Adriana Truis and of Henri Joos.

Peter van der Wiel – Long archdeacon of the cathedral chapter of Mechelen and vicar-general of the archdiocese; a regular visitor to Bethlehem until his death in 1643.

LIST OF ILLUSTRATIONS

LIST OF ILLUSTRATIONS

Maps

NOTES ON USAGE

In rendering *clausura* I have used the word as it stands or the elegant "cloister," preferable to "enclosure," too easily confused with famous agricultural movements, or "claustration," which sounds like an ailment. In popular or even scholarly usage "cloister" often is used loosely to refer to all kinds of female religious institutions or to a convent as a whole, but I use it in the specific monastic sense: that part of a convent off-limits to outsiders and to which veiled nuns were restricted—usually the choir, dormitory, refectory, infirmary, workroom, and designated gardens.

All biblical references are to the King James version—perhaps an imperfect choice on various counts, but overall I find it the most poetic and moving English translation.

The official language today of northern Belgium and the Netherlands is properly called "Dutch" (*Nederlands*). To be sure, there are differences in how the language is used in each country, similar to the differences in the English of modern America and Britain, but during the seventeenth century variations of "Dutch" were even more striking than today, especially since there was no such thing as a "standard" tongue. Instead, people spoke a number of related dialects. The term "Flemish" was— during that time and beyond—often used by outsiders to describe the language of the entire area, but it more accurately describes the dialect of the County of Flanders, to the west, and not the centrally located Duchy of Brabant, where Leuven and the convent of Bethlehem were found. The nuns of Bethlehem rarely called the dialect of Brabant anything, but when they did it was "Duets" or "Diets." For the sake of convenience, I have usually used the term "Dutch" to refer to all dialects of the family, but the reader should be aware of the problem—and also of the complicating fact that residents of what is now southern Belgium and part of northern France spoke dialects of French.

I generally give place names in the polyglot Low Countries in the dominant language of the locale in question; thus the French and English "Malines" is dropped for the Dutch "Mechelen," "Louvain" is "Leuven," "Ghent" and "Bruges" and "Ypres" are "Gent" and "Brugge" and "Ieper." The only exceptions are Brussels and Antwerp, English renditions so common that it makes no sense to displace them.

It's well known that family names at this time were spelled at whim, so I have generally chosen a favorite version and stuck with it. Given names I have often left in the Dutch or French original, unless they are not easily recognizable or pronounceable; thus I have retained "Anna," "Adriana," "Maria," "Johan," and "Catharina," but have changed "Margriet," "Magriet," and "Margareta" to "Margaret," and "Petrus" to "Peter."

BOOK I

HOW JUST ABOUT EVERYONE CAME TO LOATHE SISTER MARGARET

1. REMEMBERING

A GUEST ROOM IN THE CONVENT OF BETHLEHEM, MAY 1628, THE MONTH OF MARY. When with the noon meal of soup and an egg there came through the grille news that visitation was imminent, the nun's first thought was of the usual maddening delays, but right behind was the rousing knowledge that the archbishop's men always did come eventually, so rather than wring her hands she would use every spare moment from now until they arrived to write about the foibles of her sisters, for oh the stories she could tell. She would not tell all because there wasn't enough ink and paper in the convent, and because she didn't want to ruin absolutely the reputation of her house, but she would divulge enough to show that the others had no business casting stones at her.

Not that she was without sin; in fact, she doubted whether hers could ever be forgiven. But if salvation was not for this one, then neither was it, she reasoned, for those sanctimonious hypocritical spendthrifts who had banished her to this guest room. Did any well-intentioned, grace-seeking middle-aged nun such as herself deserve the humiliation of being expelled from the cloister in which she had promised to live all her days? And to be thrown into a guest room right next door was worse than going leagues away, for the closeness sharpened the cuts of all the small humiliations that accompanied exile and reminded her daily of their loathing. Even the house confessor refused to comfort her—not that she would let him, mind you, but his public rejection piled on her disgrace, and the failure of a specially arranged Jesuit confessor to show up when promised added to her reproach. She wondered why, since she had shown no signs of her past troubles for three years now and since the others had also fallen into error of some kind, they should continue to despise her so and deny her another chance. Surely they would understand and forgive her failings if they would only recognize their own, which were legion.

She couldn't see much, but she was still allowed in choir, she had a dependable source of news from inside, and from her room-in-exile she could observe what seemed to be an endless stream of outside callers for all-too-willing nuns. Plenty of what she saw and heard went quite against the archbishop's two-year-old reforms for the house, and for that matter against centuries-old monastic standards. These transgressions

3

would have to be told, and this time in more enduring fashion and detail than she—or most any other nun—had ever attempted before. For the past two decades, in every interview with every official visitor who had come to Bethlehem, she had made the customary promise on her oath and conscience to disclose what she knew to be right or wrong in the place. But now she would go beyond the usual, brief oral testimony and add to it a written chronicle listing chapter and verse of the convent's ills. Something this extreme had to be done or their state would continue as before, in lukewarm mediocrity and worse. And there was of course her own unhappy situation to consider, a situation which might improve if the bishop were convinced that her sins were hardly greater than those of the others. She was no spiritual writer, like Teresa of Ávila writing her famous autobiography, or even the regionally revered author Maria Petyt of Gent, but she would prove herself an incomparable spiritual reporter.

After making arrangements with her only friend, Sister Catharina, for a fresh supply of paper, and as she fingered her secret relic and gazed at her new picture of St. Joseph, she began with little delay. There was no need or want for any grand scheme, or any notes, or any careful outline of points to be made or topics to be covered, for what she intended to say had burned long within. Searing memories and a bottomless reserve of unhappy anecdotes would carry her along for over a month, until in the end there would emerge thirty-two large, emotional, tightly spaced, winding pages—order, polish, and finery be damned. She cared not at all about catchy introductions, smooth transitions, simple sentences, or tight conclusions, but only that the archbishop should know the house's abundant problems, especially those caused by the woman only recently put in charge, Mater Adriana. What would he think of Adriana's lavishing unaffordable gifts on male and female friends, playing favorites, and alienating her second-in-command, the vicaress? The words spilled out: Mater "speaks so curtly and with such spite to her religious that I'm often amazed. . . . It seems that the vicaress and sisters are children who need to be muzzled. . . . It's as if she'd hauled us all—except her dear ones—right out of the muck." What of Adriana's continued cavorting at the grille with a former confessor? "I'm often amazed at Mater, how her heart lives when she may speak of him or hears talk of him. Such often begins innocently enough, but it inevitably ends with a bad smell . . . not that I suspect evil, but to avoid opportunity or cause in such matters seems more wise." If this wasn't enough, then what of her apparent weakness for workmen? "It's not right that Mater talks alone with [work]men, behind and before, above and beneath, early and late, sometimes talking with one man inside for an hour and talking of frivolous subjects which have nothing

A Grey Sister, anonymous, ca. 1650.
Note that the details of monastic dress varied not only between orders,
but even within. They also varied according to occasion—work,
choir, and so on. STADSMUSEUM LEUVEN.

to do with the work being done, but subjects which don't concern us. Standing and talking so long, from sunup to evening, even in the garden, is disgraceful."

Or what of Mater's pampered young protégée, Sister Anna? "Mater spoils [her] into the ground, but if there's any unrest about it, then Mater's all ablaze. . . . Mater and [Sister Anna] often walk with each other like fools in love; they take each other by the arm, fling their arms around each other's neck, walk hand in hand as if they're doing a dance in the churchyard, and think that no one sees them. . . . If she loved the rest even one-hundredth as much as she loves [Anna], it would be enough." How could the archbishop stand for Anna's preoccupation with the elaborate, expensive decoration of a stuffy choir so full of candles that wax residue covered the floor, her dangerous infatuation with a young chaplain who came to perform Mass, excessive devotion to the same confessor so esteemed by Mater, or for that matter her devotion to any outsider? "Whoever comes to visit, [Anna] is right there with them, religious, worldly, all sorts of people from whatever nation or quarter they come. Even if they speak with or see her only once, all want to be friends with her and be with her. We sometimes say among us that if a dog came off the street she'd be friends with it in a second."

Would any visitor be impressed with the convent's choir, where the services by the nuns were "done with such great haste, slovenliness, speeding past others, that it's more like a farce than a Divine Office. . . . Who slobbers most and fastest has the biggest prize and praise from Mater." Or with insolent Sister Maria, who barked like a dog at the vicaress? And what of the fact that the last member of Mater's special circle, a lower-status lay sister no less, went in and out at will, ordered around the veiled nuns, and shared distracting news from the outside world and disgraceful stories from the convent's past? Even as she wrote away, and also on days when she did not, she heard some of them clanging about downstairs, preparing to receive another special outside friend, cheating devotions and the common work.

Only Sister Margaret Smulders knew fully what distant and recent memories, what intense feelings, motivated her to write one of the most formidable accounts of routine monastic life composed by any nun of this era. Only she knew exactly where her hopes for a proper convent ended and her desire for revenge began. But the phenomenal length of her letter provides in itself a clue that there was more to the story than the casual narration of defects in monastic decorum, for even the most grievous faults were usually reported in a dense page or two. Fortunately, there are enough pieces from her past to tell us how she landed in this unenviable position outside the convent and why she began her watch as a lonely sparrow upon the housetop.

2. BEGINNINGS

THE YOUNG NUN FROM 1604 TO 1616. The murkiest part of Margaret's past is how she came to the religious life in the first place. As is the case with most sisters who entered the convent of Bethlehem, we know nothing of her childhood and adolescence except her place of origin—Stalle, near Brussels. We know nothing of her family except the names of her parents and that they provided her with a paltry annual income of 6 florins per year, suggesting an undistinguished status. Her age when she entered Bethlehem as a sparkling new postulant, twenty-one, gives no clue by itself, for it was fairly typical.

Only one scrap remains to suggest that she, like many others in these heady decades after the Council of Trent, was genuinely drawn to such a life, rather than forced into it by daughter-rich parents who preferred the cheaper convent dowry or by some nasty uncle-guardian who hoped to put her away and have her inheritance. At her interview for profession, the time to confirm her true motives, she expressed to the bishop's representative in April 1606 that "she had long had the inclination to enter this particular convent, even before she asked to be received," that no one had compelled her to do so, and that she desired to remain there all her days so as "better to serve God."

Others in Bethlehem spoke similarly, going beyond the formula required. One sister "felt the pull" of Our Lord and thus entered; a second, interviewed the same day as Margaret, entered "practically against the advice of her friends, and out of her own desire, which she regarded as a call from God"; a week later another "entered with great desire into this convent," a fourth "after mature deliberation," a fifth "to ensure the salvation of her soul," while a last "had the inclination to enter this convent since she was young." All seemed confident and hopeful, confirming to themselves and others that they came not because of family pressure, economic causes, or such "romantic" motives as reacting to an unhappy love affair, but for the purest of reasons. Perhaps this was all cliché. We rarely know. We can say only, with great imprecision, that there must have been a whole spectrum of emotions in play as a woman began the religious life, though the ideal of voluntary entry was certainly promoted by the decrees of Trent. Important for us is that Margaret, when given the chance, expressed the sentiment that the decision to become a nun had been hers.

We know still less about why Margaret ended up in this particular house and order. Even in an unassuming convent, even in these utopian times, it must have helped to have connections, especially if the ratio of applicants to entrants in Bethlehem was anything like the three to one in Pescia, Italy. We wonder what Margaret's connections were, how she came to know of such a place as Bethlehem, whether she knew one of the typical patrons who had somehow come to possess the right to nominate young women of their choice to a certain number of places in this house of around twenty sisters, and how keen the competition was. No evidence remains of laws to ensure that places were reserved first for candidates from Leuven, a popular requirement in many towns. Indeed, like Margaret, most nuns in Bethlehem were not from Leuven—some came from Brugge and Gent, more came from Brussels than Leuven. These origins suggest that the competition was not so great as to prompt Leuvenaars into complaining; but, given the distance which most sisters had to come, they also suggest that patronage mattered.

Another consideration in the choice would have been Margaret's less than impressive financial and social position. Among most postulants, one's own material resources often matched those of the convent and order one had in mind. In recent years Bethlehem had, with many other structures in the southern Netherlands, suffered from a decades-old war with the northern Netherlands. Once upon a time, the seventeen provinces that constituted all the "Nederlanden" (which simply means Low Countries) had been semiunited in their possession of a common ruler— first Charles V (1500–1558) and then his son, Philip II of Spain (1527–98). But during the 1560s many provinces rebelled against Philip, partly in the name of Calvinism, partly in the name of political liberty. This time of "Troubles," as it became known, signaled the beginning of lasting division in the Netherlands. By about 1585 the southern provinces had been retaken by Spanish armies and diplomacy, and thus became the "Spanish Netherlands." The seven provinces of the North, however, declared their independence and created the new Dutch Republic, a move that the Spanish would continue to dispute with arms until 1648. In any case, along with all the political and cultural consequences of these struggles, there came physical destruction as well, even in such obscure places as Bethlehem.

But war alone had not made Bethlehem humble; it had been so since the start, in 1402, when a certain Laurent de Vroede left a rundown dwelling in Leuven for "poor sisters of the third order of St. Francis." This first place included merely a garden, some utensils, and a small annual income. For decades the nuns were without a real church; a converted room somewhere in the structure must have served as a makeshift choir where the sisters could at least sing, pray, and hear

The Spanish Netherlands

Map 1. The Spanish Netherlands.

Mass. Even the house's location was a bit remote—inside the new walls but outside the old in one of the city's numerous "empty spaces"; a neighbor's house was part barn. At least there was room to grow from this typically modest beginning. The demand for entry and of course new resources from pious bequests allowed the nuns to have their own small church by the sixteenth century. Following a common pattern of evolution, the sisters steadily added on new houses bequeathed to them or built with donated funds. Still, the physical quality of the convent, the prestige of this branch of the Franciscan order, and the social background of most sisters long remained as plain as *plattekaas,* or the region's cream cheese. Unattractive to the great, Bethlehem appealed mainly to middling or barely middling sorts of families who sought a place for their unmarried daughters—or, at its most ideal, to young women who felt called to the way of St. Francis of Assisi. If Margaret had truly long hoped for entry into Bethlehem, as she claimed, then

9

perhaps the Franciscan style influenced her decision as much as anything else.

Christian women had been drawn to the idea of separation from the world—in various forms, but usually involving at least isolation, poverty, and chastity—since the quite male origins of monasticism in fourth-century Egypt, under the inspiration of Anthony and Pachomius. Such was the pressure from women for participation in this more rigorous lifestyle that the first monastic "rule," or set of regulations, designed specifically for them was eventually composed—by still other men—in the early part of the fifth century. Over the next millennium, many existing and new orders eventually instituted male and female sides of their particular family. Despites periods of very rough going, the female presence in the religious world had by Margaret's time not only dramatically increased but come to be taken for granted, even by detractors. Indeed, the variety of monastic families from which a woman might choose was by the seventeenth century so bewildering—despite a string of papal bulls over the centuries against proliferation of new orders—that fixing the provenance of a specific group or convent was no mean achievement.

Bethlehem belonged, as mentioned before, to the so-called third order of the Franciscans; but like every branch of sufficient age this one had undergone the usual grafting and mutation. Originally the third order consisted solely of laypeople—married or not—who were unable to literally forsake the world and join Francis's first (male) or second (female) monastic orders,* but who wanted to lead a more devout life while retaining their temporal cares. Such third or "tertiary" orders became fashionable in several monastic families during the late Middle Ages. The Franciscan version, from its roots in the thirteenth century to its continued flowering in the seventeenth, attracted great and small, who expressed devotion to Francis by the wearing of penitential clothing, adherence to a regime of prayer, periodic abstinence from food, regular confession, and the practice of humility, simplicity, and heroic almsgiving—all from one's own home.

But most in the medieval and early modern worlds still sought ultimate religious devotion in the traditional monastic style of the first and second orders: by accepting the three solemn and now standard vows of poverty, chastity, and obedience; by living in community under a normative rule; and, for women, by practicing strict cloister. Gradually these traditional forms of monastic practice began to show up in the third

---

*I use the term "monastic" broadly, to include all those separated from the world. Franciscan and Dominican "friars" were not "monks," neither were Augustinian "canons," but all were part of the professional religious world.

orders as well. Indeed, during the fourteenth century third-order Franciscans began buying up buildings for communal meetings, taking simple vows (the usual three monastic vows but of temporary rather than eternal duration), and establishing more specific requirements of behavior. Finally, in 1377, a "regular" or monastic branch of the Franciscan third order was even given its own distinguishing rule, replete with the traditional monastic characteristics of solemn vows, living in community, communal recitation of the seven hours of the Divine Office (the reading or singing of prayers and hymns at various times of the day), observation of silence, and a probationary novitiate. During the fifteenth century some of these regular female houses continued with the major identifying mark of the order: charity, especially care of the sick or the education of girls. But some of them became contemplative houses, practically indistinguishable from the Franciscan second order, by adopting the final monastic litmus test of the time: cloister.

The earliest houses of third-order regular women in the Low Countries appeared around the middle of the fourteenth century. Dozens more—most of them engaged in charity outside the convent—followed, including the house in Leuven in 1402. The women rapidly became a familiar sight, receiving names according to place: Cell Sisters, Sisters of St. Elizabeth, Daughters of Bread for God, Sisters of Lombardy, Soup Sisters, and so on. But because they usually wore grey habits and scapulars, these third-order women were most commonly known among the laity as "Grey Sisters." Most of the Grey Sisters in the Low Countries were by the late sixteenth and early seventeenth centuries still devoted to education or to care of the sick, despite bulls by Pius V in 1566 and 1568 that required "true" female religious to be cloistered. Indeed, by this time only one of the eight Grey convents in the archdiocese of Mechelen was strictly cloistered—and it happened to be Margaret's house in Leuven, after a roundabout journey.

The sisters in that city began with the trademark care for the sick. They continued nursing for over 170 years, until an outbreak of the plague in 1578 devastated the convent. Conversions to Calvinism around the southern Netherlands, and the subsequent Calvinist domination of Leuven and other towns during the late 1570s and early 1580s, forced the remaining two or three nuns into exile, in Cologne. When these few women returned to a reconverted Leuven in 1587, the archbishop decided to replenish their numbers by sending to them the dozen or so homeless Grey Sisters of Mechelen. Like many other religious of the area, the nuns of Mechelen had been forced into exile by a brief Calvinist takeover of their city, but when they returned they found "not one stone" of their fifteen-foot-high walls "left upon the other." Thus were two houses in need joined together, and with their joining the nature of the community in Leuven changed.

The convent itself was by the late 1580s as "small" and "mean" as ever, to quote contemporaries. It was a hodgepodge of houses, not yet architecturally unified as even convents of the simplest origins usually became. It went relatively undamaged during the exile, but one can't help wondering whether this was due to its unattractive plainness. The buildings were not roomy, and many were in poor condition due to natural disasters and want of maintenance; the sisters wrote in 1594 to plead for funds from the Council of State, noting that their miserable church, on the banks of a river, was sometimes inundated by "*grandes eaues,*" sometimes, they said for extra emphasis, "coming up to the high altar," where Mass was said and the Eucharist kept. Though it was hardly a pearl, the sisters from Mechelen came anyway—it was not as if they had enjoyed much better—bringing their privileges, remaining ornaments, relics, crucifixes, tabernacles, and annuities and foundations. In fact, the sisters of Mechelen came to dominate. They bestowed the name of their old convent on the new place, calling it Bethlehem; they took the leadership, as the sisters of Leuven were to "reverence" the Mater (or "Mother") of Mechelen as their own, and to put into her hands their properties and possessions. Perhaps it was their influence that in some small way forwarded the modest rebuilding, for in January of 1595 the remodeled church and its four altars were consecrated. And most important, since those in Mechelen had been cloistered, they brought cloister to Leuven as well. Such an imposition often provoked resistance, but with only two or three sisters left in Leuven the archbishop correctly calculated that this victory for newly emphasized monastic strictures would be an easy one. This is how Bethlehem came to be the only cloistered house of Grey Sisters in the archdiocese.

It was this poor convent of third-order, regular, cloistered Franciscan nuns to which Margaret came in 1604. She did not come emptyhanded. With her arrival or soon after there came four wimples of high-quality grey cloth; yards of material for work bodices, petticoats, and blouses; three dozen "nose-cloths"; eight pillowcases; ten aprons; a mattress; blankets, bowls, chair, cushion, kettle, candelabra, broom, small table, breviaries, stockings and shoes; and still other items recently bought or to be purchased soon (such as the six black veils she would need after profession). Yet most significant was the fact that Margaret came to Bethlehem with the intent to stay there the remainder of her days.

Perhaps she had traveled before, perhaps she knew nothing of the 750-year-old city of Leuven at all and caught her first glimpse of the five-towered skyline on that trip to enter Bethlehem. If she didn't know then, she would have learned later from the Leuvenaars themselves or

FIG. 15

LOVANIVM.

A View of Leuven, J. van der Baren, 1604.

Facing southeast. St. Gertrude's, the second large church from the left, is right in the middle of the panorama.
Bethlehem, though not distinct or mentioned in the key to this map, was just to the right of Gertrude's,
and at least partially hidden behind the fortress on the hill, in the foreground.

STADSMUSEUM LEUVEN.

*Two scenes in the city of Leuven, from a book
of sixteenth-century watercolors.*
*The Dyle River meandered through Leuven, breaking off and
coming back together more than once within the city's walls. No
known illustrations of the convent of Bethlehem have survived, but
recall that it was located next to the river and that it was humble.
The buildings to the right in the first picture are certainly humble
and may be monastic, though certainly many religious houses
were near the Dyle.* ROYAL LIBRARY BRUSSELS.

her sisters about its proud past—its great artists Bouts and Metsys; its having played host to countless counts, grand dukes, and other famous nobles, even breakfasting the boy Charles Habsburg, the future Charles V, when he attended their carnival in 1509; and of course its acclaimed university, which boasted such current shining lights as the famous philosopher Lipsius or such past ones as the controversial Erasmus. Darker moments shaped the city's identity too: the unsuccessful resistances against later Habsburg or Dutch impositions; the flooding of the city by its giver of life, the Dyle River; or the raging of the plague, which hit often during the sixteenth century. This disease, along with migration due to war, reduced the once-impressive population of 19,000 in 1525 to 14,000 by 1565, to the barely urban figure of 10,000 by 1600. But the Leuvenaars persisted. By the turn of the seventeenth century, the population included about 3,000 students at the flourishing university and nearly 1,000 male and female religious in two dozen religious houses (though even in the best of times it could never say, like Florence, that 15 percent of its women were in nunneries). Its chief industries of agriculture, viticulture, and brewing were doing well, and like any town it had its secondary industries too, such as tanning, stove-making, or marble-working. As Margaret passed through the gates, protected by triangular bulwarks designed to thwart any frontal assaults by besiegers (of whom the city had seen enough), she would have noticed the gabled, small-windowed, three- and four-story-high houses on both sides becoming gradually denser until they reached the city center with its marketplaces and magnificent Gothic town hall. Then left and through the Borgstraat-gate, owned by the university and used as a prison for unruly students or faculty, until they reached the street to Bethlehem and arrived there a few blocks later.

Bethlehem's chief claim to fame was a modest one: It possessed some relics of St. Renildis, a martyr from the region who, according to the nuns, was especially effective as a protector against all accidents to arms and legs. Unlike some of the renowned nunneries around Europe, Bethlehem produced no saints, housed no world-famous relics such as a lock of hair from one of the 11,000 virgins, a saint's tooth, or a thorn of Christ's crown. It could never match a big place such as medieval Cistercian Hertogendael with its seventy-seven sisters or the contemporary Cistercian Beaupré with its seventy-two, though its usual population of twenty-plus sisters was respectable; it didn't have sisters who went out full of zeal to establish branch houses and lead new monastic currents; it included none of the greats of society; it boasted no buildings of architectural significance; its choir was undistinguished; its handiwork was known locally at best; it had no great spiritual writers, not even a modest library, nor a competent illuminator of devotional works; unlike San

The Convent of the Annunciation Sisters, Leuven.
This convent, though no doubt more architecturally unified and
distinguished than Bethlehem, is probably not an unreasonable point of
comparison in size and appearance.   STADSMUSEUM LEUVEN.

Marco's in Florence it could never have afforded to hire such a celebrated painter as Fra Angelico to beautify its walls and cells; its nuns
produced no accounts of any marvelous spiritual visions and experiences, nor could they converse in Latin like women at legendary medieval nunneries. It was meaner than almost every other house of religious
in Leuven, too close to the street (wandering eyes could look from the
choir into the street and perked ears could hear most sounds), too close
to the river which flowed behind its rear walls, carried foul-mouthed
sailors, and occasionally flooded the lower rooms. It was undoubtedly
similar to most nunneries of the age in having but a local—perhaps
regional—function and reputation, and in owning the modest relics and
modest choir that it did. But, though a small glimmer in the monastic
constellation, Bethlehem could still take pride in belonging to an important elite in Catholic society as a whole. Specifically, the Grey Sisters of
Bethlehem practiced the form of religious life still regarded as supreme
for women: They were a solemnly sworn, chaste, poor, and obedient
community, whose members spent most of their time praying and sing-

16

ing to God, with periods of manual labor and study in between, forever shut behind walls and locked doors.

Whatever brought Margaret to this monastic family and these unassuming surroundings, she began the two-stage probation required by her order. This called for one year as a postulant, which meant the continued wearing of worldly clothes while living near the nuns to learn the cadences of religious life, especially choir. After this period of trial, the nuns voted to receive Margaret as a novice, which meant another year of trial, culminated by bestowal of the novice's habit, made of "common cloth" and excluding the scapular and cord worn by the professed nun. During this year she continued to live separately from the veiled nuns but was now instructed more vigilantly on how to become one of them. Perhaps it was during this year that she learned to read and write. She most certainly learned the order's rule and the house's statutes: to deaden the worldly desires within her; to be submissive and attentive in chapter, the weekly meeting for business and the correction of faults; to avoid private conversations with the professed nuns; to learn the Divine Office; to be reverent in choir, avoiding the temptation to smash little worms with her thumb and then smear them on the choir stalls, keeping instead her eyes fixed ahead or on the book rather than looking about with flying glances like a wild deer in the woods or a coarse peasant, pronouncing all words fully and devoutly rather than rushing through or raising her voice too high, and bowing with the whole body to the knee rather than merely nodding the head; to be kind to cosisters, alien to all contention, silent in the dormitory, sober at meals; to master her evil passions; to treat the convent's property with care; to be modest in movement, so that when one member of the body was used the others were rested, that when using any member it was in moderation so that in laughing her teeth did not show and in speaking she would not use her hands, grind her lips, move her head, lift her eyebrows, stick out her arms, or use her shoulders, and that in drinking she used both hands, without sighing, blowing out, smacking the lips (all signs of gluttony), looking around, or talking.

To encourage her to remain, Margaret learned stories of those who had come this far but then abandoned the path to the religious life. Several books included cautionary anecdotes: Two novices pleaded with their parents to return to the world, but then died from plague soon after returning. Another novice left his monastery, immediately went dancing, and then died when a tile fell from a roof and hit him on the head. A third novice was a well-trained singer who left his monastery thrice, but on the last journey he was punished by God with an ailment in the throat that left him not only unable to sing but dead. With examples like these floating around, one wonders just how free novices felt to leave, even in an age that insisted on true vocation. This is especially pertinent when we add to such stories the extra pressures put upon young women. Professor Geneviève Reynes has called Trent's requirement of voluntary entry into convents "timid, incomplete, and poorly enforced," particularly in regard to girls in their midteens who possessed more "reverential fear" for their parents than did young women of even slightly greater age. As many as one-third of the nuns who professed in France during the seventeenth and eighteenth centuries, Reynes estimates, did so against their own will and because they feared conflict with their parents. Such a statistic seems impossible to verify, but what was a young woman to say who had been told that it was in her family's best interests for her to enter the convent, who even if she exited the convent legally (before profession) faced likely social censure, and whose family would have to scrape together a new and more costly dowry for her now-difficult-to-arrange marriage? At the other end of the spectrum of motivations we mustn't forget courageous examples of those who defied their parents in order to profess, such as the famous Clare fleeing her seven brothers, or five-year-old Anne-Bathilde de Harlay of Paris who, after visiting an aunt in a local convent in 1616, was so drawn to the place that she refused to leave and professed at age eleven, causing anguish to her mother and father.

However free Margaret felt, she endured the novitiate and in 1606 desired to forsake the world and to profess. For this she had to undergo the interview mentioned earlier, which established not only her motives but her Catholicity, legitimacy, and general fitness for monastic life. In addition, Margaret had to receive the approval of the sisters. Mater presented Margaret's name in chapter three times, after which Margaret thrice came forward, fell prostrate, and humbly asked to be received; a majority voted to accept her, soon after her twenty-third birthday, a typical age in Bethlehem (of twenty-two nuns who entered between 1600 and 1640, almost all were between twenty and twenty-seven at profession, providing at least one piece of evidence that here young women were freer than their medieval or teenaged counterparts). Did Margaret have to wait weeks or even months for the ceremony to take place, as occasionally occurred when bishops and their deans were distracted? We know only that the ceremony took place that year, the same year as the great tempest in Leuven and much of the Spanish Netherlands. The storm's heavy winds, which knocked out even church bells, were still talked about decades later. Margaret and those around her may well have regarded the violent weather as ominous.

At some point before the ceremony, Margaret had her hair cut short, and also formally granted her worldly goods to the house. Some nuns in Bethlehem had brought major "gifts," namely the long de facto prerequisites of a generous dowry (for the convent) and an annuity (sometimes for the convent, often for the individual nun), and many entrants in later years would do the same. But most at this time—including Margaret—benefited from a recent decree of the Council of Trent that, like earlier councils, encouraged convents to abolish entry fees, railing against the notion that one had to be of certain financial security in order to take a vow of poverty. That such a decree had been issued before and would be again reflects that such idealism rarely lasted, but for now it was forceful enough in consciences to help Margaret.

During the ceremony itself, as Margaret appeared at the door of the choir, the dean anointed the scapular, cord, and veil, the final symbols of her new life. Before putting them on Margaret, he required her to make her profession in his hands: "I Sister Margaret swear to God Almighty, the Holy Virgin Maria, St. Francis, and all of God's saints, obedience to the archbishop of Mechelen and the mater of this convent according to the third order of our Holy Father Francis which was confirmed by Pope Leo X, and eternal chastity, renunciation of my possessions, and eternal *clausura* until death." Then came the draping of the scapular, the placing of the black veil over the grey wimple on her head, the pronouncement of the crowning glory of marriage with Christ, *"Veni sponsi Christi, accipe coronam quam tibi dominus praeparavit in aeternum,"* and the promise to her of eternal life if she fulfilled these vows. Mater and sisters led her to her place in the choir, whence came forth prayers and hymns of the Holy Spirit, the Virgin, and the stigmata of Francis, concluding with the exhortation of Francis: "May God bless and watch over you; show his works and mercy in you, submit your will to his, and may he give you peace."

There was one last step: the profession feast, which in Margaret's case must have been less fine than most, even by the standards of this house, but it was good enough for her and God. Thus at age twenty-three, much older than the typical nun from earlier medieval times, Margaret became a bride of Christ, legally dead to the world. She took her place in the nuns' dormitory, choir, chapter room, and refectory as a full-fledged member of the house.

For the next decade the archives give no hint that Margaret was anything but ordinary. Indeed, in light of her later difficulties she may even have looked back upon these early days with some fondness. But at some point things began to go terribly wrong, becoming far worse than Margaret had ever imagined when she first set out on the path of perfection.

3. DEMONS

THE PARLOR OF BETHLEHEM, SEPTEMBER 26, 1616. The first clear sign of trouble emerges from a document dated this day, a document that summarizes the interviews conducted by the archbishop's vicar-general during a specially commissioned visit to Bethlehem. The central purpose of his trip was this: to survey attitudes among the sisters on the impending return to the convent of Sister Margaret Smulders. It remains unclear when Margaret first left Bethlehem—perhaps weeks, months, or even years before. But whenever it occurred, this was a grave matter for a nun who had sworn never to go out.

Only nine of the fifteen or so sisters in the convent at this time were called to the parlor to express their sentiments to the vicar-general and his assistant. A few, knowing the rarity of such visitations, seized their chance and volunteered more information than merely the topic of Sister Margaret, such as violations of cloister or complaints about the "sober" regime. But always, from the other side of the grille, the visitors came back to the central question: Should Margaret return?

There was no debate, because almost all sisters were against the proposition, with the basic sentiment thus: If we must, on our oath of obedience, then we will, but given the choice, no thank you. Only Mater Judoca van Belle and perhaps Sister Barbara Noosen seemed willing to try. Several even suggested supporting Margaret at an outside location, a dramatic gesture in light of the convent's meager income. Two proposed to live solely "on bread and water" rather than see her return.

So much for the raw opinion poll. The explanations given for these sentiments offer further insight. One sister felt that it was in the interests of Margaret's "strength" to remain out, but most referred to spiritual rather than physical illness, vaguely noting the need for "peace" in the community. Mater Judoca believed that unity was greater now than when Margaret had been there, thanks to the diligent efforts of their good confessor; should Margaret be forced upon them, Judoca feared that all would be undone. Anna Marcelis "noted much hypocrisy" in Margaret; she implied that Margaret was eager to point the good monastic way to others but could not follow it herself. Then there were other vague references to "things past" and "past vexations" that upset the community and its benefactors.

The comments of one of the eldest sisters the vicar-general recorded

20

with earnest. "Agitatedly she urged" that Margaret not be allowed to return because she worried that the convent's outside friends would "not dare to visit" if Margaret was back. Further, the older sister continued, these friends would talk about Margaret and her problems with other outsiders. More vigorously than Mater Judoca, this nun feared that Margaret's return would vex their confessor—who had done so much to restore the peace of the community—which was no small thing given the difficulty of trying to "find another who would take up the care of the convent." Damage to relations with benefactors and confessor were obviously serious, but two of the last-interviewed sisters brought forward still more sinister explanations as to why Margaret should be banned.

Sister Anna Marcelis alleged that prior to Margaret's departure "images were scattered about" in the cells and that nearly every evening there appeared before the convent a strange dog, its head in the ground "so that it was hardly visible." Now that Margaret was gone, Anna stated, these events had ceased. The meaning of such claims could not have been lost on the vicar-general or the other sisters—cats, foxes, black sheep, bulls, spiders, vultures, bears, black pigs, and especially ferocious dogs were often associated with the devil and evil magic. Anna even recalled Margaret's saying that had Anna wanted to learn the "magical arts," Margaret could have easily taught her. Magdalena Remmens had a similar tale: When she and another lay sister* were sent on pilgrimage for the salvation of Margaret, they were terrorized at one point by strange, silent "dancing apparitions." Moreover, at night in the dormitory Magdalena and others would hear "great noise" and see that the shining rays of the moon—also associated with sorcery—caused the cell of almost every sister to glow with unusual brightness. Magdalena concluded, as had Anna, by noting that these events had stopped in Margaret's absence.

Obviously, there was serious resentment against Margaret. She made ever-necessary outside benefactors suspicious of the convent, and she broke one of the cardinal rules of monastic life by causing discord and upsetting the peace. But she struck at something more fundamental still, at the very essence of religion and humanity, when she was linked in the sisters' or visitors' minds to the feminine malady par excellence of the sixteenth and seventeenth centuries—witchcraft.

---

*"Lay sister" was the name given to those women who took no vow of *clausura* and thus were free to perform the convent's necessary outside affairs and errands. They did take vows, but of a lesser kind than the veiled nuns, and they were generally of lesser status, before and after entering.

The nuns of Bethlehem, like most people of this time, saw evidence of the usually invisible otherworld all around them. If God noticed every sparrow that fell and numbered every hair, and the devil was just as vigilant in opposing God, then nothing happened by chance. A comet, an earthquake, a miracle, an illness, sexual impotence, a pig that became lame, a cow that stopped giving milk, the birth of an ill-formed child— these were all interpreted as omens of God's displeasure and power or as manifestations of His opposite, Satan.

Both God and the devil worked not only by direct means—through angels and demons—but through human agents as well. God's grace could be found throughout Catholic Europe at numerous shrines, where the relics and divine powers of deceased holy people were made manifest, or they were present in future saints who still lived among the believers, healing and blessing. The devil was active too, in dreary or neglected places, and among humans in the form of witches or demoniacs. The crucial distinction between the two kinds of evil agents, a distinction developed only during the fourteenth and fifteenth centuries and not always cared about by nonexperts, was that the demoniac had been involuntarily possessed while the witch had entered willfully into a pact with the devil, becoming his servant in exchange for power over the elements. During the early modern period, as Professor Erik Midelfort has noted, it often seemed that the evil agents and spirits—be they witches or demoniacs—were more active than the holy. It wasn't that Satan was more powerful than God and His allies, but rather that God allowed Satan to act in the world as a result of the human proclivity to sin, or in order to illustrate His ultimately greater control by crushing evil spirits in very public rituals.

In this drama of supernatural evil during the Age of Reform, women were at the center, front, back, and sides of the stage. As if the whole of womankind had not already been burdened over the centuries with a long enough list of "ills caused," the systematic definition of witchery just mentioned would eventually leave them another: According to the celibate, male experts (such as the Dominican Inquisitors Heinrich Kramer and Jacob Sprenger, authors of the influential *Malleus Maleficarum*, or "Hammer of the Witches," first published in 1485), women were more likely than men to become witches. This, they explained, was largely because the female sex was more lustful and thus more easily enticed by the carnality of the devil, always one of his major lures. Women were not thoroughly evil, obviously, for enough among them had led lives of extraordinary holiness. But women were more extreme than men, tending to be very good or very bad—they were more likely to be saint, but also witch.

In spite of the *Malleus Maleficarum*, it's important to note that this specific connection between women and witchcraft was quite new. Belief in evil spirits had existed in Christianity from the start, but before this time, as far as can be determined, men and women had been about equally accused of dabbling in malevolent magic. By 1550 the notion that women were more prone to witchcraft had triumphed on the continent of Europe, while there is some evidence that this was less true in England. And, not surprisingly, the notion had become embellished—a female witch not only engaged in the usual exchange of her soul for supernatural power, but she became as part of the agreement the devil's sexual servant. By night the witch flew with her new powers to secret locations where the "Devil's Sabbat" was celebrated, a giant orgy of blasphemy, child-eating, and copulation between the devil and his eager servants—all obviously antihuman, anti-God, and antigoodness, as befitted the devil. Such a fantastic scene was not the product of the popular imagination, but had been developed by the hunters and definers of witches—theologians, lawyers, inquisitors, and other intellectuals. Yet the idea of the Sabbat caught on in wider circles as more and more people were brought to trial and as they heard the detailed accusations from their learned accusers. Roughly 80 percent of the tens of thousands of people charged with witchcraft during the sixteenth and seventeenth centuries were women; most people charged escaped execution, but among those who were put to death women again far outnumbered men. (Nine out of ten people burned in the Low Countries were female.)

It's necessary to know that, besides witchcraft, another possible contemporary explanation of Margaret's condition was possession. The question of whether women as a whole were also more susceptible than men to this affliction remains unanswered, although the experts agreed that certain types of women—including nuns, for reasons that will become apparent—certainly were. Indeed the most notorious examples of possession involved whole convents, as Margaret's coreligious knew only too well; these occurrences were scandalous in large part because of the high expectations people had of those in the monastic life. Between 1600 and 1650 entire nunneries in France and the Spanish Netherlands would experience wild, publicized bouts of possession, while other convents around Europe produced notorious witches. Alain Lottin has argued that during the seventeenth century there was an "epidemic of diabolical possession . . . among the female convents of the Low Countries." Whether a case involved witchery or possession, and whether there were any real witches or not (and Professor Norman Cohn thinks not), this was clearly a time of spreading fear. As scholars of the subject have shown, once a charge was made, it was hard to stop people from suddenly seeing the devil everywhere around them, and more accusations were sure to follow.

When the sisters of Bethlehem implied that Margaret was connected to the netherworld, in whatever frightening, unknown fashion, they were therefore not pulling ideas out of thin air. In fact, they had more than the usual dread, for they could draw upon events still closer to home than those just mentioned. Soon after profession or even before, each sister must have picked up the darkest bit of convent lore. In 1601, just a few years before Margaret and most of the current sisters had professed, one of the nuns of Bethlehem was executed for being a witch—hardly uncommon for the time or region, since the first fires were lit in the Low Countries toward the end of the fifteenth century and then burned brightest from the 1580s into the first few decades of the 1600s. But it mattered little to these anxious women that "their witch" was part of a larger trend and thus in retrospect might be considered "not that unusual." To them it was an ugly, extremely sensitive subject, perhaps explaining why no one referred explicitly to it during the 1616 visitation; but uneasy reference to it in other documents, one composed as late as 1672, confirms that the episode lingered in their hearts and minds. By poking around a bit, we can discover the distasteful event for ourselves.

The dismal story of the trial and execution of Marie Everaerts, including her alleged curses on assorted female religious, has been documented in a number of brief articles. But what has never been made clear before is that Marie herself was a Grey Sister. Her troubles began in 1599 when, at the order of the archbishop, she was imprisoned indefinitely in the convent of Bethlehem for *gravia delicta* ("weighty crimes"); this fact alone does not identify Marie as a nun, for various convents were known to have held lay prisoners on request or command. In the same year, thanks to a plea from her sister, the archbishop transferred Marie to her native Mechelen where she could be guarded by the Black Sisters of that city. There, in imprisonment, Marie supposedly did most of her dirty work, for less than two years later she came to trial at the ecclesiastical court, the charge now clear: witchcraft.

She confessed to the court that she had made the characteristic pact with the devil: obedience to him in return for supernatural powers. She also revealed that her victims were "certain religious." Because of this confession, because she showed no signs of remorse, and because the ecclesiastical court could not carry out capital punishment, Marie was turned over to secular authorities with the usual recommendation that she be strangled and burned. During several confessions, each more dramatic than the other and often interspersed with denials that were retracted upon threat of torture, Marie admitted that she had "sworn off the Christian faith, . . . had let the devil carry her away to a dance, eaten human flesh in the meeting of the witches, taken on a familiar, worshipped the devil with bowed knee as her God, engaged in carnal relations with him, even in holy places" and had "given different conse-crated hosts to the enemy." These admissions were quite standard by now, as we've seen, though Marie also mentioned the common "famil-iar" (usually a cat or other animal that served as intermediary between the witch and her master), and another devilish favorite, the blasphe-mous theft of consecrated communion wafers.

If such a confession was frequent enough, more relevant to our story was Marie's admission that through her fiendish power she "had trou-bled, tormented, and afflicted various religious in the convents of the Grey Sisters of Leuven and the Black Sisters of Mechelen, and had or-dered the enemy to break the neck of the vicar-general, a doctor of Theology, and the pastor of St. Peter's in Mechelen." Equally serious was Marie's assertion that she had *learned* the art of witchcraft from a nun of Bethlehem named Marie Switten, who had professed in 1597 and whose arts were not yet apparent to all. This came out during the usual postcondemnation search for accomplices, since it was assumed that an agent of the devil had not acted alone. Once, said Marie, when borne away by the devil to a tree near the Leuven-gate outside the walls of Mechelen, she had seen Marie Switten and Clara vander Zande (a Black Sister of Mechelen), or at least the devil in their images, dancing and offering up unholy sacrifices. She also insisted that she had long known and observed that Marie Switten was a witch, partly because of various marks on her body. Despite pressure for more names, Marie could tell them none. The executioner strangled her at the stake on February 27, 1601, and her corpse was burned immediately afterward. Marie Switten was punished as well, but for reasons unknown she was found to be less guilty than Marie Everaerts had asserted. Switten either volunteered or was forced to leave the convent in Leuven, for on June 1, 1602, the archbishop approved her removal to the city of Cologne, not to another convent but an unspecified "respectable place," where she was to try to retain as much of her religious lifestyle as possible.

That Marie Everaerts was herself a nun of Bethlehem becomes clear thanks to a couple of previously unconsulted documents. The first is a letter written by a mater of Bethlehem in 1624: "the story is still told that we had a witch here; it's been twenty-three years, but I hope to God that Sister Margaret isn't such a one." A second was composed by an episcopal official who wrote on Marie's case, in which Marie is posi-tively identified as a nun of Bethlehem. This connection and these broader ideas about witchcraft are important to know because they most certainly resonated in the collective conscious and unconscious of the

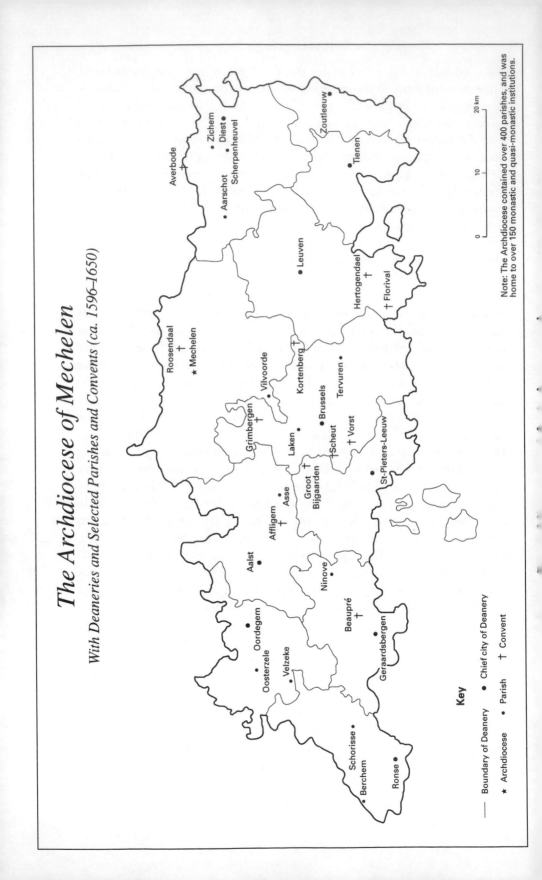

The Archdiocese of Mechelen

With Deaneries and Selected Parishes and Convents (ca. 1596–1650)

Averbode

Zichem
Diest
Aarschot
Scherpenheuvel

Zoutleeuw

Tienen

Leuven

Hertogendael

Florival

Roosendaal
Mechelen

Kortenberg

Vilvoorde

Tervuren

Grimbergen

Brussels

Laken

Scheut
Vorst

Groot
Bijgaarden

St-Pieters-Leeuw

Asse

Affligem

Aalst

Ninove

Beaupré

Oordegem

Geraardsbergen

Oosterzele

Velzeke

Schorisse

Berchem

Ronse

Note: The Archdiocese contained over 400 parishes, and was home to over 150 monastic and quasi-monastic institutions.

0   10   20 km

Key

— Boundary of Deanery   ● Chief city of Deanery

★ Archdiocese   ● Parish   † Convent

sisters of Bethlehem as they considered the case of Margaret Smulders. They couldn't help but see Margaret in light of them, and they certainly discussed them in private circles, despite their reluctance to raise the event with the visitor during the interviews of 1616. Besides the 1624 letter, another sister wrote as late as 1672 uneasily and vaguely of the ancient horror, telling how over the years the sisters repeated rumors among themselves that the convent had become infected while the nuns were in exile in Cologne during the 1580s and that while there several members of the house had supposedly learned the arts of magic. This persistence of memory helps us to understand better the vicar-general's 1616 discovery of worries about witchcraft and otherworldly events in Bethlehem. Certainly anxiety ran high among the nuns that if Margaret was allowed to return, demonic episodes would likewise resume. Few sisters would have cared at this point to look further and determine whether Margaret was a "true" witch, like Marie Everaerts, who had supposedly willingly allied with the devil, or a demoniac, involuntarily possessed in body. If secular and church judges often confused demonic possession with witchcraft and tended to focus on the latter, then how can we expect nonprofessionals to have bothered with clear distinctions? Even if they had, it's likely that at this time—based on the responses during the 1616 interviews—they would have leaned toward the more sinister of the two, witchery.

The archbishop heeded the fears of the nuns of Bethlehem; Margaret did not reenter the convent at this time. But there was more to the story of the demons, more details that Margaret had not yet told. These would emerge only over the next two years and would serve to galvanize feelings against her even more, to her unending frustration.

4. CONFESSORS

JUNE TO DECEMBER, 1618. Margaret never thought of herself as a witch, an active servant of the devil. Indeed, by the time she first left Bethlehem, before 1616, she doesn't even appear to have been sure that she was unwillingly possessed, a lesser condition that she would later admit to. More important, however, than exactly when Margaret became conscious of trouble with possessive demons is her insistence that they were not the cause of her exit. Rather, her departure was due to an equally scandalous reason, one that deepened her disappointment and embarrassment when most everyone refused to believe it. Margaret always maintained that she left the convent to avoid the sexual advances of the house confessor, the man who had done so much to restore peace in her absence.

There were at least two truths-universal about female monasteries: Every convent needed a confessor, and every confessor was male. Though religious women might serve as spiritual advisors, this was sanctioned by personal holiness, not hierarchically bestowed authority. Moreover, such a relationship was never sacramental, since nuns, though part of the professional church, lacked power to administer formal confession, perform Mass, or preach. For all of these functions—and for general advice and assistance—convents called in a priest. In houses under episcopal jurisdiction, this priest was sometimes appointed and in theory always approved by the bishop. Usually the nuns paid the confessor a salary, or even provided lodgings, to assure themselves of regular service.

How well the system worked depended, as ever, on the people involved. Some confessors were clearly satisfactory and served for years, but there were also those who neglected Mass, failed to preach, or were outright scandalous. The Council of Trent and the Provincial Council of Mechelen (the occasional meetings of the seven bishops who presided over the seven dioceses in the church province of Mechelen) tried to relieve built-in tensions by requiring that "extraordinary," or in other words "outside," confessors be sent two or three times a year to each house, so that no sister would feel "restricted" in case she didn't like the regular man.

With Henri Joos, their own chosen confessor, the Grey Sisters of Leuven long felt luckier than most convents. They had no complaints akin

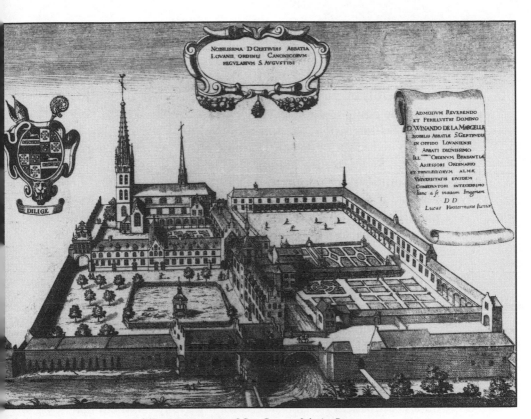

The Monastery of St. Gertrude's in Leuven.
From the monastery's church, Henri Joos served
the surrounding parish as the abbot's vicar.

to those made about the lightminded friars of Santa Chiara in Pescia,
Italy, or the confessors who for over three decades were "too familiar"
with the nuns of a convent in Nevele, near Gent. Unlike the confessor
of a house in nearby Aarschot, Joos wasn't accused of blabbing secrets
of the confessional; he wasn't called a constricter of consciences, as was
the Black Sisters' confessor in Leuven who so angered the women there
with his prohibition on speaking to any other confessor but himself that
they screamed in his face. Joos wasn't accused of hurrying confession, as
one sister in Bethanie of Brussels complained: "You're a murderer, you
button up my conscience, and you busy yourself in confession like you're
using a broom." No such charges were made against Henri Joos during
fourteen years.

Pastor Joos, originally from Balen in the eastern Spanish Netherlands,
had come to Leuven in the 1590s as a student at the university, where
he earned a bachelor's degree in theology. After completing his studies,

he somehow managed to win the attention of the abbot of St. Gertrude's, a convent of Augustinian canons in Leuven. Since Gertrude's church doubled as one of the city's five parish churches, it meant that the abbot was also parish priest; but because of his status and busy schedule he customarily chose a vicar to see to all parochial duties. In 1604 this respectable position of some 200 florins a year, plus a bit of beer and wood, plus fees for various services rendered, plus any fees one might earn if appointed rector of one of the numerous altars in the church, fell to Henri Joos. St. Gertrude's happened to be located near several other religious institutions, including the Small Beguinage (a group of houses owned by women who took temporary vows but who in the strict sense were not religious) across the street and the Grey Sisters around the corner. Contact with any would have been fairly routine, but when Joos arrived on the scene it was the Grey Sisters who needed help most, and it was he who provided it.

Given the poverty of their house during these years of rebuilding, and given the very recent affair with the condemned Marie Everaerts, it's no wonder that the sisters looked most favorably upon the condescension of Henri Joos to assist them, as one sister put it, "with compassion . . . and alms." He saw that they had no permanent confessor and little money to pay for one. Out of Christian charity, said some sisters, he practically volunteered to take on that position in addition to his other duties. Bethlehem's financial records, if we may call them that, say nothing, but it's possible that Joos received no annual fee, not unheard of in poorer convents. He diligently represented the convent when they sold an orchard or transferred a common annuity, he gave alms, and he said Mass and heard confession faithfully. His reputation beyond the convent was also good. Visitations to St. Gertrude's by the bishop's men were full of praise, beginning with the very first when the dean wrote "the pastor is commended" and "well liked by his parishioners," that there were "no scandals," and that "all commune."

But Henri Joos was no candidate for sainthood. Even without the accusations of Margaret we can discern this from his account books alone: Though required to keep such accounts by the Council of Trent, Joos's books were too tidy and detailed to reflect an intense longing for higher spheres. The deans regularly noted that his accounts were complete, something they could not say about entirely slothful priests or those preoccupied with pastoral concerns. These books reveal his command of temporal affairs, as well as time robbed from contemplation, prayer, and study. He lovingly noted the precious ornaments on the church's altars and reckoned to the last stiver his expenditures for jewels, green and red cloth, leather, and golden angels for his own Three Kings altar (added to his benefices in 1610), all tucked inside a neatly handwritten title page signed *"Pacificum Possessorem."* He showed his administrative acumen when he uncovered a fraudulent iron-caster and thereafter prudently kept the new one happy by granting him gifts of beer, along with drinking money for his servant. Certainly attention to temporal matters was necessary: Someone had to look after damage caused by the winds of 1606; someone had to care for ruined graves in the cemetery, repair the organ, track Easter contributions, buy a new confessional and a couple of tasteful new chairs for the vicarage (one green, one multicolored), and see that the roof was repaired. Such tasks didn't necessarily preclude profound spirituality, but Henri Joos relished the earthly too much for this.

St. Gertrude's itself hardly provided an atmosphere that might have spurred Joos on to loftier, more abstract pleasures. The monastery was known for its noble blood rather than devotion. Joos reported in 1604 that the place tolerated a "house of ill repute" right in its shadows. Another visitation some time after turned up disturbing stories of canons who ravished servant girls (once in the library no less), as well as maids who carried keys and went freely in and out of cells. Even more instructive is a suit that broke out after one of the canons swung a candelabra at the head of another during the noonday meal. The candle-swinger had long feuded with several members of the house, including the abbot, to whom he complained that food for private entertainments was too spartan; but what finally provoked him to violence was when another status-conscious canon proclaimed himself to be "ten times better" than the assailant. The point is that there was nothing about Joos's position in St. Gertrude's to goad him to be more than dutiful. So long as he fulfilled parochial obligations and oversaw the altars, he was satisfactory to his superiors.

To most of the sisters of Bethlehem, however, he had been much more. Indeed, perhaps Joos himself greatly enjoyed a place where he was clearly in charge and free of the requisite bowing and scraping owed the abbot. The sisters thought him the kind of confessor any place would like to have. Joos was so well regarded that there was no question at all of acceptance when he presented his sister and cousin for entry into Bethlehem back in 1609. But Margaret and at least one other felt significantly less enamored. In 1618 their story began to unfold; by the end of the year the man who according to most had done so much to restore peace in Bethlehem was unceremoniously removed.

Explicit charges by Margaret against Joos are almost nonexistent in the documentation of the affair. In line with much record keeping of the day (outside of actual trials), scandalous matters were often written about obliquely or evidence simply destroyed. Only a couple of the dozens of relevant documents specify that a sexual offense was at issue—and the most important of these is, not coincidentally I think, torn in key places. We can't determine exactly what happened, but thanks to a good deal of indirect evidence we can get a decent picture of the *perceptions* of those involved.

A key part of the puzzle is provided by Sister Lesken Nijns, who professed in Bethlehem just a year before Margaret and who in June 1618 became the first to level serious (but imprecisely recorded) accusations against Joos. Later mention by Margaret of Lesken's "affair," reference to the affair by other sisters angry at Lesken, and the fact that Lesken's case was tied to Margaret's, as we will see, all strongly suggest that sexual advances were involved. Lesken made her initial charges through a Pater Dhollander, no doubt a local Franciscan, who took her story to Archbishop Mathias Hovius in Mechelen. Given the sundry demands on Hovius, and the bouts with fever and fatigue which at age seventy-six not only made work increasingly difficult but also made him a favorite of the town's apothecaries, his involvement over the next six months reflects the case's gravity. Although no one can offer any statistics of such allegations or actual crimes by confessors, it's certain that when made public they always created a stir and contributed to an unflattering, often unfair stereotype of confessors among Catholic and especially Protestant contemporaries. That Hovius acted quickly in this and similar cases, in the midst of an officeful of other weighty matters, suggests that lecherous confessors were not common enough at this time to have been ignored by superiors, nor were they the norm.

By July 4 the archbishop had heard enough to instruct Mater Judoca secretly to ban Joos and his letters from the convent; he also sent a secretary to Leuven to deliver personally to Joos a notice of removal as confessor of Bethlehem. Such rapid action does not mean, however, that Hovius believed Lesken's story, only that he thought the charge serious enough to respond to. For at the same time this old but still-zealous bishop instructed his secretary to make Joos a proposition—would he come to Mechelen immediately and assume a position as lector, or "reader," in the diocesan seminary, one of the jewels of the archbishop's program of reform? Joos came the next day to accept, and although he then returned to Leuven, he implied that he would soon move for good.

What can we make of such an offer? When a situation warranted such, Hovius did not shy from harsh punishments or even defrocking. His proposal to Joos thus implies that he did not wholly believe Lesken—indeed, when in August Hovius permitted Lesken to come to the archiepiscopal palace to tell her story in person, he noted explicitly in his journal his impression that she was being less than truthful and his hope "that God would reveal the truth to him." Since in Hovius's

GENRE POURBUS

HOSPETAEL MAGDALENA 1562

A nun of the Magdalena Hospital in Brugge,
anonymous, sixteenth century.
Again, apparel varied, but this portrait offers
a sense of an ordinary religious woman.

33

mind the facts were vague, his primary concern became the avoidance of scandal. Thus he chose to kick Joos upstairs, which would get the man out of Bethlehem without giving offense to the faithful or propaganda-meal to the Protestants in Holland. Only Mater Judoca would guess the real reason, while the sisters were to imagine that their gifted confessor was upwardly mobile. At the same time Hovius also decided to send Lesken to another convent.

The plan turned out to be less simple than Hovius had hoped. Joos's parishioners in St. Gertrude's and his flock in Bethlehem both sent delegations to Mechelen to plead against the move. When Joos dawdled in Leuven instead of coming as rapidly as promised, and when Lesken Nijns left for her series of audiences with Hovius in August, the fiction began to fall apart. If Joos was still in town, the sisters must have reasoned, then why could he not come to hear their confessions, or at least visit? And why did Lesken Nijns, sworn to *clausura,* leave in the middle of all this? By August 25 the fiction was in pieces: The women of Bethlehem sent two lay sisters to deliver to Hovius written depositions about the character of Henri Joos. That they dealt with the question of character, rather than the question of Joos's transfer, reveals that the nuns were no longer fooled. As for Lesken Nijns, she told Hovius that she refused to go anywhere but back to Bethlehem. At one point, we learn from Hovius's journal, the archbishop grew impatient, Pater Dhollander muttered something about Lesken's "vileness," and Lesken stormed out of the room. Hovius now decided to send her away if only to punish her obstinacy, and by October he noted proudly that she was in a convent in Den Bosch, in the north of Brabant, near Holland.

If Hovius did not fully believe Lesken, neither did he fully believe Henri Joos. He told the abbot of St. Gertrude's that he had "suffered anguish" because of Joos and thought that Joos seemed a bit too untroubled by events. This, and the unraveling of the plan to cover the scandal, made Hovius regret having dangled the plum at the seminary. By the end of October Hovius's attitude toward Joos had soured completely; for the archbishop learned that just recently, despite the threat of excommunication upon Mater, Joos had been a guest in Bethlehem and that Mater had sent two sisters to wait upon him at his lodgings. Hovius ordered the dean to warn Mater "more gravely" and threaten her with removal from her office if necessary—and of course Joos was to blame as well.

It's likely that another reason Hovius became less enthusiastic about Joos over the months, and why he acted so quickly against him in the beginning despite suspicion about the story of Lesken Nijns, rested with the second part of the puzzle: Margaret Smulders. Remember that she had been out of the convent since at least 1616. She may well have spent this first exile with the Black Sisters of Mechelen, old friends of the nuns of Bethlehem since their days in the archiepiscopal city—for when Hovius called her to his palace on July 14, Margaret came straightaway. There is a chance that Hovius had spoken with Margaret before, but his journal begins only in November 1617 so we cannot be certain. In any case, his first recorded talk with Margaret was this one of July 1618, just after the accusations against Joos had gained momentum with Lesken. The timing may have been a coincidence, but we wonder why the busy Hovius would call to court, at this particular time, a quite obscure, long-exiled nun, unless he knew that Margaret had intelligence about a particularly sensitive and cloudy issue.

Hovius's notes from that meeting of July 14 are general but significant. At the first interview Margaret "acknowledged the hand of Mater," hinting that her exile was due partly to a clash of personalities and not merely the supernatural, and "said various things." A couple of other interviews took place, but the most important was the last, in mid-October, about the same time that Hovius decisively rejected Joos. Hovius noted that Margaret "affirmed by oath that the things which she had told me personally and written to me about were true." The archbishop made no more specific reference, as usual; but given the vague antecedents and that these conversations were being carried on at the same time that the stories of Lesken Nijns were being assimilated, we may reasonably imagine that they had to do with the conduct of Henri Joos.

Perhaps Margaret gave Hovius the same explanation she would give later in 1624, to another confessor, for the ears of another archbishop. "Everyone is of the opinion," wrote this confessor, that she left the convent in 1616 so that she might be freed from the demons that possessed her. But the real reason she left, continued the confessor, was to flee Henri Joos, who had "with carnal affection" so "often" importuned her. Margaret even maintained that the importuning and the possessions were connected. Enough words remain on this torn document that one of two things can be surmised about Margaret's opinion—the possessions happened *after* the advances of Joos, or *because* of them.

This is important not only because the charge against Joos was grave, but because in Margaret's mind, and by implication the mind of the confessor who was writing her comments, the supernatural events that surrounded her were to be understood as demonic possession rather than witchcraft—a critical distinction, because involuntary possession negated her complicity. Indeed, it put the blame not only on the devil but, by implication, on Henri Joos. If we consider contemporary ideas on the subject of how possession occurred, the possibility that Margaret attributed it to Joos is not as sensational as it might sound. Someone of her station would have been familiar with the assumption that evil spirits often entered into a victim at the direction of a witch—a human agent—rather than at the bidding of the devil himself. A woman called Spadens testified in February 1627 that nine years earlier, "a certain man had me by the neck, and blew into my mouth, and kissed my lips in three places leaving blue spots, and spoke certain words which I didn't understand." Ever since she had been ill and experienced mysterious accidents and sensations, so that she was stiff as a board and had to be clothed by others. (Such a catatonic state, incidentally, was not an uncommon symptom among the possessed.) According to modern scholars, it was also not uncommon for a victim to see a vision of the witch who tormented him or her, implying that the possession was caused, again, by a potentially identifiable human agent, rather than the less visible devil.

Margaret would have been in touch as well with the notion that those who removed demons could also invoke them, like undercover agents who, after living in a world of vice, embrace it. There were plenty of turncoat exorcists around. A dean's meeting in Antwerp in 1615 lamented that some clergy who had exorcised had become infested with demons themselves. The next year a Capuchin confessed to the ecclesiastical court in Mechelen that he had not only performed unauthorized exorcisms but gone over to the enemy and afflicted others with evil spirits. Was Henri Joos capable of such? Margaret apparently felt that he was and believed that his carnal advances were somehow related.

The latter point brings us to the sexual element in possession. Several historians have rightly noted that modern students of monasticism are too ready to find sexual fears and scandals behind every trouble. But the nature of Margaret's allegations, the Lesken Nijns case, the Spadens case, and the fact that the connection between sex and possession was not an unusual one in contemporary minds suggest that a sexual overture or act was indeed in question, however vague the charges. The scholar Jonathan Sumption has pointed out that "the idea of devils 'possessing' the sexually unchaste is particularly common in [medieval] monastic writing," a legacy that may have affected Margaret's seventeenth-century conscience as well and led her down the still well-traveled road of self-blame—in other words, that she somehow felt responsible for her unpleasant experience with Joos. If kinder to herself, she may have followed others of the time in questioning whether Joos had supernaturally inflicted her with unclean thoughts in an attempt to procure her willingness. The episodes of conventual possessions in the Low Countries, noted earlier, involved a strong dose of sexuality. And St. Anthony, that champion fighter of demons, was tempted always by two things when attacked: loss of chastity and acquisition of wealth. Clearly, possession was not merely about being taken over and frightened but involved sexual temptations as well.

Other cases confirm such a conclusion. A century before, in the town of El Provencio, Spain, a local exorcist named Garci Sánchez publicly expelled evil spirits from a woman named Ynés; right afterward, Sánchez took the woman to more private surroundings—namely his home—and seduced her. Eventually this exorcist's illicit behavior was uncovered: Witnesses testified that Sánchez boasted of his ability both to inflict and cast out demons; a number of women declared that when they sought out the man for help with their demonic afflictions, he had used his reputation and powers to seduce them, just as he had seduced Ynés; and Ynés herself recounted how for long she was confused about her condition, but thankfully she regained her senses and saw that Sánchez had deceived her.

Margaret was almost certainly aware of the notorious and more recent events in Aix-en-Provence, France, between 1609 and 1611. A teenaged Sister Madeleine among the Ursulines of Marseilles claimed that a confessor of that city had been intimate with her before she entered the convent. Indeed, she asserted that the man performed sorcery on her *in order* to seduce her. As a result of this accusation, she, like Lesken Nijns, was sent away to another convent; but at Christmas of 1609 Madeleine began to shake and have cramps. Further investigation revealed that several nuns back in Marseilles exhibited the same symptoms and were claiming that the confessor had cursed and seduced them as well. During the subsequent trial the accusers again went into convulsions, now recanting, now reaffirming their story, and even attempting suicide. Then, when the priest was convicted, the convulsions ceased. There was another famous episode, at Loudun, France, after Margaret's time, that also featured shocking charges by the sisters that the confessor had cursed them in order to have his way with them sexually. "The demons gave me very evil desires and feelings of quite licentious affection for the persons who might have helped my soul, so as to lead me to further withdrawal from communication with them," testified one of the lead witnesses. When the confessor was executed, the women were freed from the demons. In a last case, this time involving heavenly spirits, a young ecstatic in Spain, who had impressed King Ferdinand and various cardinals, accompanied her trances with bodily raptures and "spontaneous (some said lewd) dancing." One of the charges brought against her at a trial by her enemies was lascivious behavior. Thus even in a case in which the subject was deemed to be controlled by divine powers, we see the tendency to connect unusual bodily change and movement with sexuality and evil.

In sum, Margaret was quite up-to-date if she believed that an exorcist could also invoke demons. She was in good company in believing that where evil spirits were concerned, sinful acts or desires of the flesh were right behind. And she would not have been alone if her memory of what happened with Joos was vague and troubling, just as the nuns in Marseilles who alternately disavowed and confirmed, or the temporarily confused Ynés. Whatever Margaret told Hovius at this time, his subsequent acts show that he was more inclined to believe her than Lesken Nijns or Henri Joos. Initially, Hovius wanted Margaret to leave Bethlehem, as had Lesken; he promised to negotiate a place for her among the Black Sisters of Brussels. Like Lesken, Margaret refused, despite Hovius's monthlong exhortations. This time around, though, Hovius was not angry but sympathetic. He believed Margaret enough, thought her innocent enough, or perhaps merely found her poor enough that he returned her to Bethlehem. Writing to Mater Judoca on October 20, he not only reminded her of his ban against Joos, but ordered that she and the convent prepare to receive Sister Margaret "peacefully." This put Judoca into a dither. The events of the past couple of months were becoming ever more mysterious. When she saw that the archbishop was serious about keeping out their confessor, when she saw that Lesken was being sent away, and worst of all when she saw that the bishop was insisting on the return of Sister Margaret, she immediately wrote to Hovius asking for an audience—clearly she did not yet know all the details herself.

On November 2 Hovius "revealed the whole affair" to Mater, in person. She remained three days, returning to Bethlehem with more certain knowledge and with letters from Hovius to the Franciscans of Leuven asking that they provide pastoral care to the Grey Sisters until a new confessor was named. This informing of Mater Judoca at first seems important, for it makes us wonder what she told the others upon her return—from her warm opinions of Joos during the 1616 interviews, we know that she was probably a supporter of him. Yet in the end it may not have mattered at all what she said, for the sisters began to develop their own versions of events, a version that would crystallize over the years and make up the third part of the puzzle of Henri Joos. The clearest statement of this version was made in 1672 by the elderly Sister Anna Vignarola, who was characteristically sure that her favorable opinion of Henri Joos was the right one and that his two accusers were telling monstrous lies.

According to Anna's story, Joos had served the convent generously for years. Unknown to him, two "daughters" then entered who seemed capable enough to be allowed to profess but who in fact were "evil." Soon after profession—which would have put Margaret's and Lesken's problems closer to 1606 than 1616—the house was wracked night and day by noise and desolation. Only Joos, as confessor, knew the source, and he was not allowed to break the confidentiality of the confessional. Out of the goodness of his heart, Joos read exorcisms over these women "in secret." (Just the type of scenario which prompted the diocese of Antwerp in 1615 to reaffirm that in casting out devils at least two faithful persons should be present, besides the priest, to avoid scandal and rumor. This scenario is also our only clue that Lesken was linked to demonic possession as well, which suggests that, like Margaret, she blamed the problem on Joos.) But through their "evil instruments and jealousy" they told rumors about the man and brought him to "ruin." Eventually Joos was "scandalously removed from the community" by Archbishop Hovius. Anna claimed that Hovius had been "poorly informed" because the charges were brought "too late." The goodness of Joos was thereby repaid with evil, wrote Anna, for the devil despised him no end.

Unfortunately, we will never know for sure who was right about Henri Joos—a conclusion all too familiar to moderns acquainted with similar cases. But given Anna's depth of feeling and unflagging passion about her version of ancient events, even in 1672, as well as the equally impressive insistence on a contrary version by Margaret, Lesken Nijns, and at least a couple of others, we can say that this was the single most important question in Bethlehem for decades. *It defined almost everything*—for those who liked Joos and those who did not (though it's crucial to know that most sisters remained loyal to him throughout). Certainly the question of the timing of the possessions is important. To Anna, the possessions came first and Joos then tried to free the women. To Margaret and Lesken, the possessions followed private sessions. But while the truth will, again, remain uncertain, more important for the women of Bethlehem was what they believed happened and how they repeated it to each other. To the majority it was clear that the popular Joos was gone and the feared, infected Margaret was to return. No less clear to Margaret was that she had been misunderstood and Joos wrongly exonerated. Neither side would forget.

With the rumors that Margaret must have known were flying in Bethlehem, it's no wonder that she was reluctant to go home, even as she remained resolute about going nowhere else. On November 23, 1618, Hovius called Margaret to him and "exhorted her to return promptly." Three weeks later Hovius again ordered Mater Judoca to receive Margaret, who would be reintroduced by Pater Gummarus, probably their new Franciscan confessor. We don't know exactly when Margaret returned—records on the topic don't exist—but return she did, probably in December 1618, having been away more than two years. One imagines that her reception was hardly pleasant.

Mater Judoca died soon after the return, between February and May 1619, presumably still a believer in Joos and asking Hovius before her death that "all papers be burned," which explains why so few documents about the affair remain. Hovius and his vicar-general came in May to oversee the election of a replacement, apparently to be sure that the balance of power within the convent did not remain with Joos's supporters. As expected, when the secret ballots were cast, in an obvious sign of protest, Henri's sister Maria was elected Mater. The nuns didn't learn the official result, for after seeing the outcome Hovius decided to ask whether they wouldn't accept the candidate of his choice as their superior. The women, many of whom must have been suspicious, consented. Hovius settled on a woman whom he knew at least sympathized with Margaret and who was neutral toward Henri Joos: Sister Barbara Noosen.

Perhaps due to the distasteful affair with Joos and the headache of the election, Archbishop Hovius soon grew weary of the house. By late 1619 he tried to relinquish jurisdiction to the male Franciscans, but his cathedral chapter, which apparently possessed some bit of legal influence in Bethlehem since the old days in Mechelen, disallowed it—no chapter gave up any piece of turf easily. Hovius likely felt too tired to fight them over the matter; he wrote with such difficulty now that he usually relinquished the quill to his secretary. In May 1620 he died, with episcopal control over Bethlehem indifferently intact.

And what of Joos himself? Hovius told him in December 1618 that the position at the seminary was no longer available. The archbishop also sent several negative messages about Joos to the abbot of Gertrude's. This must have increased Joos's sense of discomfort in Leuven, though he remained at Gertrude's a few more years, saved from further episcopal pressure by Hovius's death. By the summer of 1623, thanks to family connections, Joos was put forward for the pastorship of Mol, about a day's walking northeast of Leuven in the diocese of Den Bosch, and adjacent to Joos's family and place of birth. The parish did not have the prestige of St. Gertrude's, but there were attractive compensations: It was large and respectable, the salary was good, he would have no abbot over him and a vicepastor beneath him, and there was the chance at a fresh start among people to whom he was not a complete stranger but from whom he had been gone long enough—and in a lucrative enough position in Leuven—to add to his mystery and stature. After much wrangling about distribution of tithes, after asking his new patron to keep the negotiations secret from the abbot of St. Gertrude's, and after the intervention of some Jesuits at one crucial juncture, Joos was at last appointed to the position in Mol and relinquished his post in Leuven. The document of nomination, composed far from Leuven, offered much praise for Joos's twenty years of service in that city and made a sentimental note that he desired to return to the area of his birth.

In what must have felt to Joos like a parting blow, the abbot of St. Gertrude's asked him to compile a full account of temporal dealings from beginning to end. (This despite the fact that Joos had already submitted annual accounts regularly; was there some suspicion in the abbot's mind?) Thus Joos put together at the end of a six-by-eight-inch leather-bound notebook a well-ordered list of his own expenses and credits, showing clearly "that he had spent more than he had received." And what language for a tedious account book, with familiar Latin epigrams on the final page: "That which you do, do prudently and think of the end; the end crowns the work." His last words, however, provide a more fitting conclusion to the question of whether he had behaved unseemly with certain sisters of Bethlehem: In this, and presumably in all things, he desired "no other compensation for my labor than the reward I expect from God almighty."

Besides Margaret and Lesken, who else was in a position to determine his just recompense?

5. DESPAIR

BETHLEHEM, JANUARY 17, 1624. The matter of the demons and the episode with Joos take us far toward understanding Margaret's unhappiness in 1628. But there was still more to the story; these same old afflictions and resentments would regularly reappear and intensify, and many new players would try to help or foil her. The paper trail picks up again in January 1624, the low point of Margaret's entire life. Not only had the demons come back, but persecution from the other nuns affected her so acutely that she attempted suicide.

On January 16 Margaret, at the request of a new archbishop who was trying to get to the bottom of her case, told the dean of Leuven that she was terrorized by "great noises" at night: Objects were thrown down and dashed to pieces and coverings on the bed ripped off. Though petrified, Margaret did not dare mention this to anyone else, or ask for another religious to sleep in her room for fear that suspicions about her would be renewed. To be moved to "another place"—presumably still within the nuns' dormitory—was all she asked. Despite Margaret's caution, there were already suspicions enough among the sisters, so that the house's Franciscan confessor, apprised of the latest sentiments, refused to minister to her, rendering her more disconsolate still.

Not content with this barest of accounts that she conveyed through the dean, Margaret sent also her own letter of explanation to the archbishop—the first of her many marginless, pleading, and rambling missives that would land on his table. Margaret wrote in this first letter that it was hopeless to try to describe in such a short space the afflictions that came over her at night, "for a very long time is necessary to do so, so complex is the matter." Margaret's sufferings were so difficult and sensitive that she had spoken to no one on the subject for eighteen months, but she could no longer contend alone. What she really hoped for was an audience with the archbishop, since explanation came easier in person, and there was the worry of who might read her letter on its way to the episcopal palace, or how many people might become involved in her affair. Could the archbishop not speak with her, Margaret pleaded, or appoint someone to the task? "I am prepared to talk to your reverence or his vicar at any time you may name . . . even about its origins." She did have a specific someone in mind, someone besides the dean—specifically, a Capuchin called Johan Evangelista, a man with whom she had once spoken "as openly as if she was in the presence of the Lord." But she had learned that he lived in Antwerp, too far to deal with her regularly. "Had the matter been pursued by him, I daresay that I'd already be freed from all burdens, for it's a very discreet man, much experienced in these things."

Until she could speak with Evangelista or the archbishop personally, Margaret wrote only that she was "marvelously afflicted." The community had such "evil suspicions" about her from the past and now from a much more recent event as well. Some items had gone missing from the cell of a troubled postulant, against whose entry into the convent Margaret had cast her vote. A few sisters blamed the theft "on me," Margaret continued. "Others say that I give the devil power to do it." The sisters also blamed Margaret when other things were lost or when food disappeared from the larder, which "I've never done or even had the desire to do or to have done, I take God as my witness." Margaret did not deny that she had been tormented, but if these recent events were the work of evil spirits or of humans, God only knew. The "accusations consume my flesh and blood, and I suffer so day and night from the devil and his sinister instruments, that it is often almost impossible for me to endure it all, and I fear that I might succumb, although I am by nature stubborn, which comes by the grace of God." She implored the archbishop to intervene, before her resolve collapsed, "or it is to be feared that it will go badly with me, through the constant temptation. . . . I desire with all my heart to be able to live as a religious ought." Don't delay, she beseeched, "for I'm now in a perilous state, having made no confession since New Year's" and having no desire to confess until the affair was settled. "It will be damnation to the community on the one hand and me on the other, through hate and envy."

It was on the night of January 17–18, perhaps the very night when she composed her petition for help and despaired that things would get any better, that Margaret took a knife to her stomach in an attempt to end her life. Mater and one other sister besides Margaret mentioned the event to the archbishop; Mater wrote that Margaret was "miraculously healed" on St. Paul's day, January 25, with no further clues about the wound or cure. No other sister ever mentioned the event, though it seems impossible that Mater, assuming she wanted to, could have hushed it up. But whether the rest of the sisters knew of the attempt or not, they had reasons enough to continue to plead with the archbishop for a solution.

JANUARY 27, 1624. Barbara Noosen was now lamenting her elevation as Mater five years before. Archbishop Hovius had hoped that an appointment in Bethlehem, rather than a faction-dominated election, would bring peace to the community, but in fact the disadvantages of Barbara's appointment were twofold. Her very want of popular election caused resentment, and under the circumstances of the appointment she could not help but be seen as an opponent of Henri Joos—a position clearly out of line with the majority of sisters in the house.

Though her installation had been memorable, with the archbishop handing her the keys of the convent and placing a crown on her head with much singing and bell-ringing, her only consolation since had been that her reign was good for her soul: She had learned empathy for other maters. If she didn't know the story about Mater Jacqueline of the Grey Sisters of Comines, in the western Spanish Netherlands, she would have appreciated it. The deceased Jacqueline appeared to a lay sister on All Saints Day in 1590 and told the girl that she had been in the flames of purgatory for six years as expiation for sins committed while mater.

Nineteen of the twenty veiled and lay sisters (everyone but Margaret) approached Mater Barbara on this day for permission to send to the archbishop a petition about their troubles. All knew that such a step was risky. Since each sister had the right to correspond privately with the archbishop individually (all other letters, in and out, had to pass through Mater's hands), the archbishop might regard this public, group request as a demand. That they were prepared to send it anyway was a measure of their desperation; according to one sister, they "thirst for nothing else than to have [Margaret] out."

Sister Adriana Truis, the most determined opponent of both Margaret and Mater Barbara, had composed the twenty-five lines of the petition in her square letters, leaving the customarily wide left margin for the reader's notes. She pleaded "once more" that the archbishop put an end to this problem about which they had made known their desires "with one voice" at the last visitation. Now "this matter seems daily to grow worse instead of better," for only two days before, while the community was saying morning prayers, the coverings on the bed of the postulant Barbara Beli were torn off and her clothes thrown out the window. The sisters weren't upset merely about soiled clothes. Without stating any suspects or causes, the petition implied that something or someone sinister was behind it all. Like other religious, these women of Bethlehem believed that the devil made the desecration of religious clothing a favorite pastime. To soften the impact of their request for help (and mysteriously making no mention of the even more upsetting attempt at suicide, which was another sure sign of demonic possession), the sisters of Bethlehem entrusted themselves to the archbishop's fatherly care and made the usual promise of prayers for his soul if he helped them.

After reading the piece, Mater Barbara was asked not only to approve but to put her name to it, placing her in a most difficult position. To sign would be to incur the displeasure of the archbishop. But to refuse would win the wrath of her flock, with whom she had to live and eat and pray and work and breathe, and without whose tacit support the hardships of monastic life would be rendered harder still. So she contrived a plan to placate both. First, she went ahead and signed the petition, positioning her "Sister Barbara Noosen, Mater Unworthy," somewhere in the middle. Those standing by pointed out that as Mater, her name should appear at the head of the list. Perturbed, she crossed out, then signed again. She watched as the names of the remaining sisters were added beneath hers, according to date of profession, oldest first. Half couldn't write at all, a few wrote barely legibly, but no matter— Adriana Truis and Maria Joos were more than willing to help. A couple put an "X" beneath their name, others simply permitted their names to be signed by Adriana and Maria. It was a formidable document, and except for the X's, neatly put together.

The petition entrusted to her care, and the sisters now gone, Mater Barbara executed the second part of her strategy: the rapid composition of a private explanatory letter to be sent along with the petition. As common sister and as mater, Barbara had been willing to give Margaret the benefit of the doubt—but toward Adriana she was less kind. For instance, while the 1616 visitation ordered by Archbishop Hovius was primarily about Margaret, Barbara had during her interview diverged to complain more forcefully about the meager food, drink, and clothing provided by the bursaress, who was none other than Adriana. She also noted Adriana's tendency to be so frequently at the grille, the barred area in the guest house where one could converse with outsiders.

Now, in her characteristically perfunctory fashion, hopping from one thought to the next, ignoring punctuation, and spelling most irregularly even by the standards of the age, Barbara wrote that the community was understandably upset—for the occurrences of late were troubling indeed. But the petition had gone too far. She had allowed the sisters to send it, Barbara stated, only to "make them content." The sentiments and actions of the sisters were in her opinion "instruments to bring the afflicted one to desperation," and experience had unfortunately proved her right, as evidenced by Margaret's attempt at suicide. The events surrounding the postulant, which were described in the petition and had happened on the same day as the healing, only made Margaret ill again, as now the rumor circulated that she was behind all "or at least gives the enemy power to do it." Barbara had all she could handle in trying to prevent the despondent Margaret from making once more "the same attempt" on her life. The sisters could "fill up each others' heads" and then walk away, concluded Barbara, while she had to "hear and

45

suffer all this noise and keep silent, or there would be no peace." Salvation, "on both sides," was in great peril.

At the same time that Mater Barbara was writing, her friend and supporter Sister Catharina Rijckeboer also retired to scribble a brief note to the archbishop. Catharina, perhaps because she was one of the younger nuns, was among the few to support Mater Barbara on most issues in the house, and the only one to treat Margaret in a manner that approached friendship. Catharina did not condone indecorous behavior, but neither was she blindly against Margaret like the others. Thus she too wanted to explain the petition and why she had signed it. Using every inch of her short sheet and writing with more sophistication than Barbara, Catharina recounted how from "both sides" she was deluged with requests for help, a comment which suggests that Catharina was already occupying, or wanted to occupy, a position as a dispassionate, reliable source in Bethlehem. From one side, she said, came the pleas of Sister Margaret, which deeply moved her heart as the woman "promises me earnestly that she'll do her best" to once again lead a regular monastic life. But from the other the community begged her to "help us in our time of need." There would probably be no peace from them, she guessed, until Margaret was out for good, for "it's gone on so long, and is now worse than ever." If this "tempest was on account of [Margaret], then perhaps we need throw her into the sea with the prophet Jonah," but only God knew. As far as Catharina was concerned, she would remain neutral and seek the will of God. She added almost as an afterthought, but it punctuated all else she had said, the news of Margaret's attempt on her own life. She folded the letter, then secretly gave it to the same messenger bearing Mater Barbara's.

MECHELEN, THE ARCHIEPISCOPAL PALACE, LATE JANUARY 1624. Jacob Boonen was already renowned in the archdiocese as the "almsman of the poor." During his four decades as bishop there and elsewhere he would not only render his considerable prestige to countless causes, but offer his plentiful florins too. The means to do so came not from his episcopal benefices, for his archdiocese, in rank the first of the seventeen bishoprics in the land, was one of the worst endowed. Before 1559 only three bishoprics had existed in the Low Countries; the erection of the other fourteen all at once brought serious questions—and few answers—about how to raise and equitably divide the temporal goods necessary to support a well-run, respectable diocese. Most of Boonen's money came from his mother, Gertrude, who was heir of the merchant Van Heetvelde's of Leuven. Most of his empathy probably came from his mother as well, as she was renowned for her piety. When Jacob was but six, and his two sisters not much older, Gertrude was presented with the news that her husband had been poisoned and executed by the Dutch. Sought out some time later by the penitent assassins, now kneeling at her feet, Gertrude readily forgave them.

If he owed virtue and wealth to his mother, he could thank his paternal family for a headstart on fame. Father Cornelius and grandfather Jacob had both sat on the highest council of state in the Spanish Netherlands, a career for which young Jacob also seemed destined. At age twenty-two, after graduating with distinction from the University of Leuven, he began work in the eastern Netherlands as a lawyer specializing in Dutch affairs. But upon moving back to his home town of Mechelen, he set out on the high-church road to influence—not for convenience or power (for he had access to either, in greater measure, without a clerical collar) but because of vocation. It was in Mechelen, in an emotional moment of prayer before the miracle-working image of Our Lady of Hanswijk, that he vowed to enter the clergy. He was rapidly appointed to a host of ecclesiastical offices, until in 1611 at age thirty-eight he was ordained and in 1616 became bishop of Gent. His old patron Mathias Hovius nominated him "above all others" to this post, calling him "a man of great valor and integrity."

When Hovius lay dying in May 1620, it was Boonen who rushed to his side with the last sacraments, and it was to Boonen whom the Archdukes Albert and Isabella (corulers of the Spanish Netherlands from 1598 to 1621) wrote asking suggestions for a replacement. The following year Boonen moved from Gent to become the fourth archbishop of Mechelen. For over three decades he was *primus* not only in the church province of Mechelen with its seven Dutch-dialect-speaking dioceses, but in the entire Spanish Netherlands, prompting one famous devotional author to compare him to Moses, leader of all the land, while a local Jesuit drama compared Boonen to the famous reforming Italian bishop, Carlo Borromeo, of the diocese of Milan. Thanks to his new position, Boonen would also sit in the Estates (or provincial assembly) of Brabant and display the old family talent for politics, talents that made him a member of Archduchess Isabella's Council of State and eventually a major envoy.

But this involvement in the political world did not make Boonen a throwback to the old medieval or contemporary prince-bishops who cared more for war and intrigue than for their flocks. We find him regularly at lesser monasteries and at ordinary parishes, and writing attentive reports about them. We see him personally investigating candidates for ecclesiastical posts as well as complaints about the clergy's underpreaching, overdrinking, incontinence, and petty rivalries. We sense his concern over the report of a chaplain that in Brussels there dwelt a multitude of people who were unaware that Christ was the Redeemer,

Jacob Boonen, seventeenth century.
KONINKLIJK INSTITUUT VOOR HET KUNSTPATRIMONIUM, BRUSSELS.

over people suspected of magic, and over Dominicans in Leuven who went alone to visit beguines. We can feel his disappointment with the students of the archdiocesan seminary, with convents and confessors who haggled, with "temptresses" in Brussels, with his own household for whom he proposed reforms in regular hearing of Mass and sermons, or with the indolent bishop of Arras, to the south, who never left his rooms or preached. Perhaps at this early date Boonen was not yet the archetypal archbishop, as was Borromeo or another Italian, Matteo Giberti in Verona, but he was very conscious of that ideal and strove after it eagerly. By his death in 1655 he would leave a mark as one of the great Counter-Reformation bishops in the Low Countries.

In spite of his zeal, at the episcopal palace of Mechelen even the most compelling affairs of a nun in Leuven could be drowned out in a roar of requests for his abundant expertise and charity. Margaret's problem, though serious, was no doubt from his viewpoint secondary to more pressing concerns: the threat of invasion from the Dutch, recovering the remains of the medieval mystic Ruysbroeck, establishing a home in Brussels for penitent women, and trying to get the common catechism for the whole church province into print and usage. Sister Margaret of the Grey Sisters was one of many squeaky hinges—annoying, clamoring for repair, but hard actually to get around to fixing. Most of the time Boonen's aides handled such cases, but when he deemed a case important enough, he got involved himself.

Examining all the documents, Boonen was confronted with obviously disturbing facts and gaps. Who could have ransacked Barbara Beli's room? There were a number of this-worldly explanations: Margaret attempted suicide on the night of the seventeenth, but Mater wrote that she had been healed on the twenty-fifth, the day of the ransacking. Was Margaret healed enough to have risen while the others were in choir? And why would she have done it? As an act of desperation to win back credibility, to make it look as if the source of evil was the postulant rather than herself? Could Beli have done it, to somehow get back at Margaret, perhaps having that Margaret had voted against her entry? Yet Beli was supposed to have been in choir with the others.

Boonen also couldn't ignore the fears expressed by the sisters about otherworldly explanations, though he had sat on too many tribunals to believe every suspicion about sorcery. In a decade or two he would undoubtedly have echoed the opinion of a vicar-general who stated that accusations of possession or witchcraft should not be made lightly. This was especially true, said the vicar-general—citing a common opinion among the experts of the day—"when it comes to women, for they often give evidence of great powers of imagination." But neither did he disbelieve in evil spirits; he took care in the diocesan pastoral handbook

49

to personally amend one of the formulas against demonic infestation and to add five new formulas against possession. And as an educated man he was certainly aware of the famous scandals involving evil spirits in France and the Low Countries. Perhaps they were at work in Leuven too.

A clearer understanding of Margaret's case would emerge only months later. For the moment, lacking as much information as he would have liked and knowing that Margaret distrusted the dean, Boonen took the safe path of calling in an expert—the man whom Margaret claimed would be able to cure her, if only given the chance.

6. THE SPECIALIST

LEUVEN, THE CONVENT OF THE CAPUCHINS, FEBRUARY 23, 1624. Margaret was mistaken about the dwelling place of her ideal confessor, the second distinguished figure on the Belgian religious scene to enter her life at this time. In fact, he lived only blocks away from Bethlehem in the new—and according to some brothers overdecorated—Capuchin monastery.

The Capuchin order (so-called because of the pointed hoods worn by its members) was established in 1528, in Italy, to resurrect strict observation of the Franciscan rule and to promote preaching. The movement gained popularity and spread north, so that by the late sixteenth century Bishop Torrentius of Antwerp could write that the Capuchins edified "everyone." The first convent in Leuven took shape during the 1590s, surrounded by the usual litany of miracles. On part of the grounds intended for the new building stood a house owned by a woman who refused to sell or trade up, despite generous offers from the friars. Within six months, however, God, who according to the chronicler did not forget his friends, struck the woman with an incurable disease and in another six months "she was a corpse." Soon after, the deceased's daughter declared, like Pharaoh, that she was ready to let the house go. Thus the convent was built and, by 1619, remodeled and enlarged.

From within one of the convent's thirty-five cells, the friar, who had been sent to Leuven to head up the novice-training but who was now called upon for much more, gazed into the garden below and pondered his past and recent experiences with the nun of Bethlehem. He was willing to report his sentiments on her situation, as the archbishop had requested, but doubted that he could do much good. This, though, was modesty, for he was no ordinary Capuchin. Gerardus Verscharen van den Bosch professed in 1614 at age twenty-five, taking the religious name Johan Evangelista. Since 1623 he had been Guardian, or superior, of the Capuchin convent in Leuven, and in 1624 his name was tossed about for the destitute see of Roermond, where only someone like a poverty-loving Capuchin could cope. Beyond these and other positions he held until dying of the plague in 1635 at age forty-seven, he also left his mark with three tracts on the inner life. Evangelista's writings circulated privately among monks and nuns while he lived, and when published later they caused scholars to name him one of the three great Capuchin writers of the Low Countries.

In addition to his leadership and writings, Evangelista's personal habits were said to have been exemplary. He lived in a manner marked by rejection of this world and pursuit of the next; meditation, two hours of sleep a night, and assiduous prayer and study were the basis of his daily routine. This all came to be reflected in the heaven-looking, mercy-seeking hagiographic portrait of Evangelista that now hangs in the Capuchin convent in Antwerp. In life as well as death Evangelista was renowned as an authority on matters spiritual, especially in regard to the professional religious. This reputation, along with his past promising meetings with Margaret, brought him to Boonen's attention.

How many times had he walked through his own front gate with the inscriptions of St. Augustine and the scenes of the Passion, then over the bridge and on for a few blocks to the convent of the Grey Sisters? Margaret's afflictions, he knew after two years of correspondence with Mater Barbara on the subject, and after his own visits with the patient herself, were "most perilous and grave," to her and to the community which she had single-handedly brought into tumult, he wrote to Boonen. At his very first visit, he continued, Margaret instantly revealed the depths of her heart to him, something she was loath to do with the house confessor. From this it became obvious that, as Margaret had said herself, the troubles were "most intricate."

These intricate problems must have included Margaret's account of strange noises and lonely nights, for Evangelista went on to review for Boonen his attempts to exorcise the poor woman. If their first sessions were marked by Margaret unburdening her soul, then much time after was devoted to this ritual. At one critical period that extended over several weeks, he visited her daily, sometimes twice per day, "reading some exorcisms." Evangelista had become convinced that Margaret was certainly not a witch, but he could not deny the presence of demons.

In arriving at this conclusion, how influenced by previous diagnoses had he been? Similarly, to what extent was Margaret's own view of herself as a victim of evil spirits shaped by earlier cases? Studies of witchcraft, possession, sainthood, and even travel accounts show that precedent prejudiced victims and observers alike. A person in a given situation tended to imitate the type laid down by predecessors, and was thus perceived similarly. Even the astute Evangelista must have been influenced in this way. As the historian Joseph Klaits has noted in his *Servants of Satan,* "Those assigned to counsel the possessed were usually religious personages who interpreted the sufferer's behavior in accord with their previous knowledge of demonic possession. They began their sympathetic therapy by reinforcing the suggestible victim's fear that he

V. P. JOANNES EVANG. SYLVÆD.

Hagiographical portrait of Johan Evangelista, anonymous.
CAPUCHIN MONASTERY OF ANTWERP.

or she was suffering from a supernaturally induced disorder." This is not to say that the woman or her advisor fabricated the possession, or that it was any less real in their minds, but rather—according to D. P. Walker, who has studied possession as much as anyone else—that "their knowledge of [other cases] will to a considerable extent condition their behavior." In 1599 a woman in France conceived of the idea to fake possession after hearing the many explanations given her by others as to the cause of her various ailments. Aware of widespread rumors regarding witches, this woman allowed herself to be persuaded that "her behavior and troubled mind were the result of being poisoned and bewitched." In a similar case in the Spanish Netherlands in 1629, a confessor told a beguine that the devil had her around the neck; she left the confessional without absolution, and the next day fell into a great faint so that she "lay there without speaking for five or six hours," a state known to be common among the possessed. Certainly Margaret, her sisters, and her spiritual advisors knew about the characteristics and prevalence of possession at this time. Indeed, it would not be surprising if either Henri Joos or a cosister had been the first to suggest possession to her.

At this date, Evangelista or anyone else might have drawn from the plenitude of well-known cases of possession a list of its chief manifestations: (1) ability to speak and understand exotic languages (usually Greek, Latin, or Hebrew); (2) clairvoyance; (3) unnatural body strength; (4) horror and revulsion at sacred things; (5) attempts at murder or suicide; and (6) long "swoons" or faints. Symptoms 3 and 4 were arguably the most commonly cited and were demonstrated usually by bodily and facial contortions and acrobatics. The French woman just described became visibly disturbed during exorcism, her face turned black, her tongue protruded the length of four or five fingers, her eyes rolled back, her mouth gaped, she arced her body and leaped and twisted in different directions; while it ultimately emerged that she had faked these possessions, it's significant that she obviously knew what the investigators were looking for. Cases in the convents of France recorded similar scenarios. As for Margaret, in addition to the external disturbances around her and the attempt at suicide, Evangelista recalled that on several occasions he had been waiting for her in the parlor when Mater came to inform him that Margaret was lying in a great swoon. Later another confessor noted Margaret's strange visage and her revulsion at his presence.

Yet even in cases such as this, when many of the usual signs were present, Evangelista knew that detection was a tricky matter. The best minds of the day disagreed over how to determine false and real infestation; even the early spiritual advisors of the famously visionary St. Te-

resa called her ecstacies demonic delusions. Moreover, said other authorities, some sufferers were all too ready to think themselves full of
demons, when in fact they were afflicted only with "natural" ailments
of the flesh. These people would have done better, continued experts, to
consult a physician for their epilepsy, hysteria, and melancholy. Yet, to
complicate things, it was also common knowledge in medical circles that
one had to be on guard against melancholy especially, lest it *lead* to
possession. Catharina Rijckeboer would later mention such a connection
to Boonen, and a tract by Johannes Wier, a German physician who
opposed witch-burning (*On the Deeds of Demons,* published first in 1563)
argued that one's chances of being possessed were greater if one suffered
from deep melancholy. It wouldn't have surprised Catharina or the
archbishop at all when in 1641 Catherine Janssens confessed that from
a young age she had been "very desperate and despairing of the mercy
of God, to such a degree that from then on she was possessed by the
evil enemy." The best medical opinion of the time even concluded that
especially nuns over forty, who were obviously long celibate and consequently of drier "humor" than younger women, were prone to melancholy and thus most susceptible to possession. (It had been believed since
ancient times that the balance or imbalance of the body's four humors,
or fluids, determined one's physical and emotional state; to be dominated by "dry" humors was to risk melancholy.) In fact, celibacy at any
age made possession more likely than otherwise. Evangelista knew also
that a person brought to melancholy not merely by age or unsettled
humors but by loneliness, obviously evident in Margaret's case, was a
strong candidate for possession. So was someone with serious financial
trouble, which he had just recently learned also applied to Margaret; she
owed 40 florins and change (nearly a year's support) to "someone" outside the convent, a debt originally contracted after she left Bethlehem in
1616. Since she had possessed no noteworthy private income to take
with her on that trip and since a new house would have been reluctant
to take her in for nothing, Margaret probably had borrowed money to
support herself—and her debt remained.

In addition to these many preconditions or causes of possession was
one more factor, perhaps most common of all: sin. It was elementary to
Evangelista that demons invaded with the permission of God, who
wished to punish disobedience or publicly prove His power in casting
out demons. But since in Margaret's case all publicity was avoided, and
since most cases focused on the sinfulness of the victim, we must assume
that those involved in Margaret's affair believed God was chastising her
for her sins. One possessed girl of Mechelen had demons enter her after
a full day's dancing, which was trouble enough, but that she danced on
the Sabbath made it a double dose of sin, implied the chronicler of the

case. And Sister Anna Vignarola, remember, called Margaret and Lesken "two evil daughters," suggesting they did something to deserve possession.

The thought must have also passed through Margaret's mind, and Evangelista's too. Perhaps Margaret was burdened by an uncertain, self-abusive, and vaguely guilty memory of what had occurred with Henri Joos. Perhaps she blamed herself for having given audience to the devil at all, through succumbing to melancholy. When she wrote elsewhere of possession as "temptations," she probably meant in the sense of being tempted to yield to discouraging moods; and there was temptation in that she might willingly surrender to the devil and be enticed into a more voluntary and sinister relationship with him, replete with the mysterious orgies and upside-down sabbaths of full-fledged witchcraft.

Evangelista was fully aware of the standard signs, causes, ploys, and counterploys as he formed his conclusions about Margaret. And he was unaware of later psychological interpretations, such as the notion that possession was common in monastic environments because it signified desperate resistance to discipline and repression. One of the many proponents of this theory has written that "to be the victim of possession was a means of expressing forbidden impulses and attracting the attention of otherwise indifferent or repressive superiors." In this situation, or for that matter whether involving a religious or a layperson, the "victim" of possession could shout out statements and engage in behaviors that, under normal circumstances, would have resulted in punishment or alienation, but that, when blamed on the devil, were virtually ignored. Other scholars have employed psychology to suggest that possession was the result of guilt over one's inability to live perfectly, for in an environment such as the convent, where goals were clear and high, and everyone knew the foibles of others, there was greater inclination to shift responsibility for one's shortcomings onto outside agents, such as evil spirits. Last, there is the provocative modern theory that an admission of possession would not only place blame on outside forces but would clear one from the more sinister charge of outright witchcraft, while also providing the demoniac with an explanation that was acceptable in the context of the time. These theories aid moderns who wish to understand spiritual troubles, but Evangelista could interpret Margaret's condition only with the tools of the time. Thus did he decide, he related to Boonen, that it was in fact appropriate and necessary to give this woman the supernatural help of the church.

He had therefore donned surplice and vestments, readied his crucifix, holy water, incense, candles, and books of scripture and ritual. Thus prepared, he began to read exorcisms over her. The knowledge that it was God who allowed possession implied that God was mightier than the ills. Ways to remove them were many, even in this time of increasing uniformity. Evangelista would have avoided the more spectacular, such as seating the patient in a chair, binding her fast to it, and making her drink a strange potion, "nauseating and intoxicating." Instead he recalled in his best clear voice the transcendent powers of Christ that had been shared with his apostles, including the power to withstand serpents and to cast out unclean spirits. He prayed that like power would be brought to bear against these forces that vexed this friend of the Lord. Blessed be the Father, Son, and Holy Spirit, he repeated often, crossing himself regularly as he went, and believing as most others that the very sound of the words and appearance of this sign could drive the foes out.

He turned to miracles from the Gospels, first pressing the book to his brow, mouth, and chest, then to the brow of Margaret, as if the printed words themselves had power. While positioned before her, he read from Matthew the story of the boy whom only the master could cure, then from Mark Jesus' promise that his disciples would have the power to cast out demons, then from Luke the account of the man cured in the synagogue, and from John the assurance that the Evil Prince of this world would be overcome. Again the book to Margaret's head, the sign of the cross on her brow, pronouncement against this unclean spirit, enemy of humankind, bringer of death, ravisher of life, enemy of justice, root of all evil, seducer of men, mother of envy, cause of discord, father of poverty—all through the power of He who cursed Lucifer to crawl on his belly, revived Lazarus, was sacrificed in Isaac, sold in Joseph, slaughtered in the lamb, and crucified in human kind, who showed his power in Job, cursed Pharaoh, shut the mouths in the lions' den, conquered with David, and damned Judas Iscariot.

Holding up the crucifix, Evangelista commanded the demons to behold the wood of the most holy cross, urged Margaret to look as well, and implored her to try to say with him "We adore you, Christ, and we bless you, because by your holy cross you have redeemed the world." He chanted the Kyrie eleison, Our Father, and other Orations, repeating formulas and prayers again and again. He called upon the God of the Angels, of the Archangels, of the Prophets, of the Martyrs, of the Saints (especially devil-fighting Anthony), of the Virgins, of the Sabbath, the God of Adonai, God omnipotent, the God who turned Sodom and Gomorrah to ash, the God baptized in Jordan. He would have recalled the power given to Paul and Peter and other saints, and the blood-soaked martyrs and the power of the holy sacrament against the persecutor of the innocents. And he blessed with the water on which sailed the ark of Noah, which sprang from Jacob's well, which had been parted by Moses, which flowed in Jordan, which turned to wine in Cana, on which Christ had walked.

Around these sessions, or as time went on, they must have talked about the inner life in which he was so experienced and she—despite twenty years as a nun—quite naïve. He may well have reviewed with Margaret the pattern laid down in his easy-to-follow, simplified devotional works: *The Kingdom of God in the Soul,* on meditation and prayer, and *Eternal Life,* on preparing for and receiving the Eucharist (a topic characteristic of the frequently communing Capuchins of the Low Countries). Like so many devotional works of the Flemish-Rhineland tradition, *The Kingdom of God* urged the reader to look for God within the soul, a task accomplished through prayer, meditation, and the exercise of virtue. This was as frightening and exciting as a first journey at sea, for it required one to leave the safety of familiar ground and ride strange, unsteady waters. Once embarked, the book advised, learn to unfurl your sails and catch the wind of God, to read the state of your soul like the skipper reads the sea floor, compass, or stars. Do not despair at times when you feel alone, when sorrow finds a place within you and tells you that you are empty and useless and without any special light from God.

In counseling Margaret, Evangelista may have concluded that she was among those many religious who were content with merely being a religious in name—not necessarily evil, but too interested in worldly necessities and ways, "like sniffing dogs, sniffing curiously into what goes on here and there," as he put it in *The Kingdom of God.* Too few were willing to go farther, to sell all they had to buy the pearl of great price within themselves, so few that if Evangelista had not "seen it himself he never would have believed it." Daily there were books published, he continued in his own work, "which tell us that the end and perfection of this life lies in a union with God," but most religious had "no more appreciation for such than a horse or cow for gourmet food."

Whatever had marked the discussions between Margaret and Evangelista, or his conclusions about her, his efforts proved of little consequence, he confided to Boonen, "because of various vexations" from the house confessor, her sisters, and that demon. Soon after Evangelista's sessions with Margaret, everything restored for a moment by the exorcisms was reversed. Losing hope, he told Boonen how he had ceased his "simple and imbecile" methods, insufficient for such an "arduous business." This may actually have been Evangelista's way of putting the burden for Margaret's cure back on Boonen. Indeed, since he had heard that Boonen was thinking of other methods to help her, he urged Margaret to submit herself totally to the archbishop's "paternal tutelage." Fortunately she was well disposed to this exhortation, and Evangelista expressed his confidence that His Illustrious Reverence would triumph and "free the dear little woman from the jaws of the most wicked wolf."

Before relinquishing responsibility, however, Evangelista had one suggestion of his own for Boonen and two pieces of opinion from Margaret.

Among the "vexations" and the "impediments" to Margaret's recovery, one of the most damaging, he argued, was the constant slander against her. For this reason, Evangelista doubted that she would ever be fully cured if she remained in Bethlehem—a sentiment, he wrote, that he knew Boonen had come to share. As for where she should go, Margaret was willing to do the archbishop's bidding, but she desired the guidance of a man to whom she could open her soul; for, as Evangelista noted, the "age-old tricks and machinations of the devil" would continue. Margaret's problems "require the total man," he decided, someone who could give more than he. A recent warning from his order against spending excessive time with female religious, her heavy needs, and his massive responsibilities simply did not mesh.

Evangelista concluded with Margaret's own opinions of her condition, which he thought the archbishop might find useful, since her recent request to come speak with Boonen had been denied. There were two points. First was her explanation of the old Henri Joos affair, already reviewed in chapter 4: If possession had occurred then it was Joos's fault. Evangelista was a bit puzzled as to why she would bring this matter up now, unconnected as it was with "the present business." Perhaps, he guessed, Margaret was merely trying to say that she had never been fully freed from the demon, a position that the others in Bethlehem certainly held. Or perhaps she wanted only to explain to the uninitiated her version of how the troubles had all begun.

The "present" (and second) business was not the affair with Beli or any other recent drama in Bethlehem, but a situation discussed in no other document: namely Margaret's old debt of 40 florins. After returning to Bethlehem in late 1618, Margaret was long pestered by her creditor to pay up. Finally she "found no other means" to repay the debt than by contracting another. She therefore asked "that wizard (*magus*) who frequently came to her" whether he would satisfy it in her name, which, at some unknown date, probably in 1623, he did. In so doing, however, he took care to obtain from her one condition: that if she didn't pay back this new loan by the coming Easter (1624), then she would have to consent to that "filthy act" that he had already and for so long required (*in turpem actum ad quem illam iam diu requisivit*). Margaret pleaded for help, pleaded to be free "from the rule of that man."

Was Henri Joos "that wizard" who had demanded a "filthy act"? Evangelista's statement that the past and present business were unconnected did not necessarily mean that the persons involved were different, but rather that two different episodes were in question. Moreover, if Margaret did blame Joos for her possessions, as I suspect, she would not have hesitated to call him "that wizard," a man who dealt with the supernatural. The absence in Evangelista's letter of a clear antecedent, as well as the lack of any other names besides the earlier reference to Joos, is also suggestive. Finally, apart from Margaret's remark about Joos's frequent importuning, there is no record of anyone else having pestered her about a "filthy act"—though obviously want of such evidence doesn't prove conclusively that Joos was the man.

Along with the indirect suggestions in this letter from Evangelista to Boonen, there is a final matter to consider: from whom else could Margaret have gotten such a loan in 1622 or 1623. The question is especially pertinent when we consider that she knew few people in Leuven and seems, unlike many other nuns in Bethlehem, rarely to have been visited by family or friends. The Mont de Piété, or pawnshop, was not an impossible source of money, but what did she have to pawn? Later when she needed money she would turn to Boonen—but not yet. The *magus* was almost certainly from Leuven, since her first debt was satisfied there and Joos was still in that city. Whether she liked him or not, she was desperate and had opportunity with him more than with anyone else to ask such a thing, for even after his expulsion Joos continued to visit Bethlehem. Boonen was still quite new to his position at this time, and had either been unaware of Hovius's old ban or found it unreasonable, at least before now, to exclude a man from a convent where he had a sister and cousin and to which he still gave much-needed alms. Whether the *magus* was Joos or someone else, there certainly occurred a pathetic but classical scene in which the humiliated Margaret, as the wretched debtor, seeks out the notorious, opportunistic creditor who extracts from his victim a suitably desperate promise. Whoever her tormenter, Margaret was still clearly in trouble by February 1624.

Finally, after mentioning Margaret's debt and the "*magus*," Evangelista closed his letter, hoping that Boonen had a fair idea of how he saw the case. Upon receiving the missive, Boonen made note of several parts, including the assurance that demons were involved, that Evangelista could no longer care for her, and that debt and a *magus* were involved. Not long afterward, the archbishop made his decision.

BETHLEHEM, MARCH 14, 1624. Boonen's response could not come quickly enough for the nuns of Bethlehem, who saw Margaret's "sorrow and desolation" continue. And the daily visits of a man such as Evangelista, after all not the house's confessor, must have confirmed to many sisters what they had long suspected. Sympathizing with this "miserable patient," Catharina Rijckeboer wrote secretly to Boonen that one root of Margaret's sorrow was, put in the gentlest possible way, the failure of the archbishop to send instruction. Margaret had lamented to Catharina, with tears streaming down her face, that she had been so open with Evangelista and allowed him to write Boonen about the "depths of her heart." She couldn't imagine that the letter had actually reached Boonen, for he had "carefully answered" all her previous requests. Now not only did Evangelista know her plight, but she feared that some stranger between Leuven and Mechelen or some cleric at the episcopal palace might have read about it as well. From this thought Margaret "tasted extraordinarily great" shame, not to mention reproach "from the enemy and his evil instrument."

Such fears were not unfounded. Even the great worried about lost letters and the risk involved in committing messages to paper. This disquiet contributed to Margaret's remaining unconfessed since New Year's, which "burdened her conscience" and scandalized the convent, since "not one hour of life is certain" for any human being. Catharina continued that they all awaited a remedy from the archbishop, for if things continued, "they would be worse than before." She fretted again at Boonen's lack of attention: "it would be a pity to again waste her goodwill and intentions," Catharina suggested, "which she has demonstrated recently." In concluding, Catharina requested that Boonen please send Margaret a brief word, if on nothing else but the safe arrival of the Capuchin's letter.

Finally there was news to confirm that Evangelista's letter had been received—but that worry was now quickly forgotten. For Boonen sent not only money to relieve the onerous debt to the *magus*, but an unusual and arousing plan that reflected the desperateness of the situation. Margaret, accompanied by her only friend Sister Catharina, was to leave the monastery once again and this time seek her cure at the miraculous shrine of Our Lady of Scherpenheuvel.

7. PILGRIM

SCHERPENHEUVEL, LATE MARCH TO NOVEMBER 1624. Though it could be done, as we have seen already with Margaret and Lesken Nijns, departure from a convent by a veiled nun who had sworn to observe *clausura* was no routine affair. Archbishop Hovius rejected more than his share of petitions, even when they included such compelling motivations as the need to care for dying parents. And when a sister of Bethlehem asked Boonen in December 1624 whether she might travel to a famous shrine at Laken, near Brussels, where she "had a devotion" and where she hoped to have a cure for headaches that caused her to "tear her eyes out," he refused, stating that a dispensation to leave cloister should be granted only "with great scrupulousness"—a decision praised by both the dean of Leuven and Catharina Rijckeboer, who hoped it would discourage others.

In light of such resistance, we may see the plan to send Margaret on pilgrimage as another sign of the frustration felt at all levels over the lack of a cure and over the turmoil in the community. Clearly Boonen had little to lose. He also had a good deal of confidence in the able man who directed the complex at Scherpenheuvel, and of course he didn't negate the potency of the shrine itself, which offered another means besides exorcism in the dispossession of odious spirits.

All such shrines in Catholic Europe had as their chief function healing, both of the body and the spirit. In the Low Countries, Scherpenheuvel, about 40 kilometers northeast of Leuven, was now the rage. If Margaret had not read the new, popular collection of miracles there—"only the confirmed, sworn miracles, not those based on mere rumor"—she certainly knew of them. The lame, the blind, or those with withered hands all found their cure at Scherpenheuvel, while (in less beneficent displays of power) those who ridiculed the shrine were suddenly maimed. Margaret would have known especially about the female religious who had experienced marvelous effects—including women from Leuven. Catharina Tserraerts of the White Ladies had a left leg that was shorter than the right by five or six thumbs, but this difference miraculously disappeared after she finally won permission to travel to the shrine with a patron. Sister Anna Laureys of the Annunciants one day overexerted herself in choir, causing something in her head to pop, so that for eighteen years she suffered a terrible ringing in her ears.

Though she was not allowed to leave the cloister, she was healed soon after in a replica of the chapel of Scherpenheuvel, built for her in the garden by her sisters. And there was Margaret van den Perre, a Grey Sister of Antwerp, who had so much pain from a "cancer in her breast" that she could not travel overland but had to come a roundabout way by water and foot, and who during one of the services at Scherpenheuvel felt a hand yank the cancer out.

Margaret knew that not only bodily ailments could be cured at shrines, but spiritual maladies such as hers. Engravings of dramatic exorcisms around these holy places were common, as were written accounts: At the shrine of Our Lady of Hanswijk in Mechelen, a possessed girl of twelve was healed by a quick-thinking young boy who recognized the demon, saw that it was near the girl's navel, made the sign of the cross at that spot, and gradually led the beast up the body so that it finally came out her mouth in the form of a hairy worm. Or Margaret could have read in Thieleman's *Lives of the Franciscan Saints* how possessed persons who visited Francis's favorite church of Portiuncula were immediately freed of their demons.

No wonder that when she heard the news from Mater Barbara, Margaret was overjoyed, in the best spirits we have seen her. The thought of leaving Bethlehem was no doubt liberating, and heightening her anticipation was knowledge of the powers at this particular shrine. In a new letter she thanked the archbishop profusely for his "genuine fatherly care" and begged forgiveness for the trouble she had caused—yet pleaded "please don't forget me," as he had recently in taking so long to respond to her, "for I cannot help myself." There was also the problem of money. Though grateful for the funds Boonen sent to discharge her debt to the *magus*, "so that he would have no more cause to harm me," she needed more to go on pilgrimage. Her paltry annuity of 6 florins wasn't due until August. "I wish I had it now," Margaret wrote, "for I would gladly use it [for the trip] and rather live in poverty all my life in order to have a good soul." Many thanks she repeated to Boonen, for all he had done for unworthy her; "if it will go better with me, then I'll earn [your kindness] with a virtuous life and will pray all my life long for your reverence." There was one last kindness Margaret requested: that the archbishop please send a document, "written and signed in your own hand," ensuring that "without a second thought I may stay away for a time, for I know that they'll do all in their power to keep me from coming back." Her assessment would prove only too true.

Joy among the rest of the sisters at the prospect of Margaret's departure was no doubt widespread, but the only remaining response we have is the negative one of Mater Barbara. It was not that she disputed the bishop's wisdom or the efficacy of the shrine, or even that she thought Margaret's condition hopeless. Rather, she feared the scandal that might befall the convent "once again" if Margaret went to this very public place. How Mater wished that the "incantations could occur secretly in house, for when they're about to begin Margaret is often not herself, the enemy puts her into a trance or cripples her, so that she can't reach the place where the rites are performed." She had hoped that it could all be kept secret, "which simply isn't possible there, because all the world will see and hear, and it will be a travesty for our convent." Here was a public relations problem that would rise again and again in this convent and others: Knowledge that a house contained a possessed nun might drive away badly needed alms or, more abstractly, blemish its reputation.

As for the costs, they were too great for such a convent "in decline," and besides, how was Margaret to get there? Evangelista had advised against her riding in the public wagon, for fear of scandal, but who would provide a private coach? The only offer Mater could make to Boonen now came too late—keep Margaret at home and put her for the time being in a guest room, where Evangelista would have easier access to her. But if his reverence insisted that Margaret must go, then Mater would cooperate. But to make things easier, she asked, like Margaret, that Boonen write a note—in Dutch rather than Latin, please—saying that she had his permission to leave, and thus by implication to return. At the end of this letter Barbara informed Boonen that the story of their sorceress, Marie Everaerts, was still making the rounds.

Despite Mater Barbara's opposition, and though details have not survived, it is certain that Margaret and Catharina soon set off. Along with anticipation might have gone a sense of fear; besides the usual threat of bandits, Margaret knew that evil spirits and demons had a liking for out-of-the-way places, such as along the road from Leuven. Remember that the nuns sent on pilgrimage on Margaret's behalf years before had along their lonely way encountered strange sights and sounds. Only a few years later another woman accused of witchcraft would claim that her initial contact with the devil occurred on the road to Scherpenheuvel. The devil's sabbath itself was said to occur in remote locations: a large field, woods, a mountain, amid ruins, dunes, or at crossroads. But Margaret and Catharina passed through unscathed and arrived at their destination. The two Grey Sisters may have lived briefly in Diest, near Scherpenheuvel, with a "widow" mentioned by Mater, but eventually Margaret spent most of her time among the Hospital Sisters, a less private but probably cheaper place. She was to remain in the area for much of the rest of the year, with Sister Catharina by her side until late August.

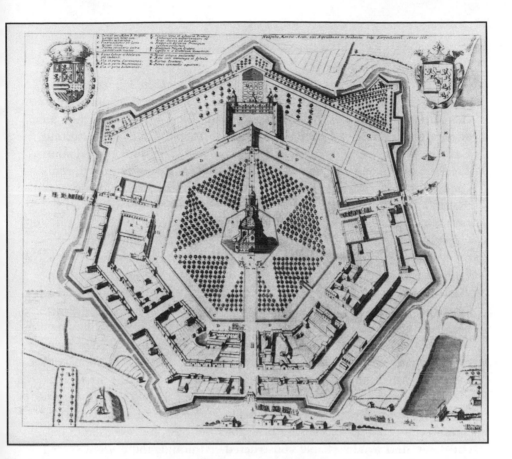

Plan of Scherpenheuvel, engraving by C. Lauwers.
(an eighteenth-century work reprinted many times)

FROM SANDERUS, *CHOROGRAPHIA SACRA BRABANTIAE.*

Rising abruptly out of the hilly region east of Brussels, the "sharp" or steep hill (*scherpen-heuvel* in Dutch, *mont-aigu* in French) at first appears to be another one of those remote places so eagerly frequented by the devil and his minions. Though holy sites also were found in such places—indeed God did many miracles on mountains—one chronicler of the miracles that occurred on the Scherpenheuvel considered it a "wonder that the Mother of God would choose this raw and wild little mountain, in the area of a very poor and common city," near the border with the rebellious and heretical Dutch. It was another in a series of divine surprises, demonstrating that the godly was greater than the sinister, for here was triumph in the devil's backyard. The remoteness added only further to the spiritual intensity of the journey, since from almost anywhere one began, the trip was a formidable one. Moreover, in contrast to one's ordinary home parish, the psychological otherness of the shrine was pronounced.

But it was more than distance or variety that made Scherpenheuvel stand out; it was the sacredness of the place that mattered. Some centuries before, at the top of this uninhabited hill, there had appeared on an ancient oak a miracle-working image of the Virgin. Like others around Catholic Europe, this image exuded grace and performed miraculous deeds on and from that spot. Whenever the image was removed, it always returned, a miracle in itself, making evident to all that it was here that intercession with the divine was to occur and confirming to all the common knowledge that grace was attached to place.

For many years, until the late sixteenth century, the shrine at Scherpenheuvel was but one of many local Marian shrines around Europe, visited for quite ordinary problems. Mary was long the single most popular saint to whom a shrine might be erected, partly because of her "general" abilities to cure and comfort—as opposed to more specialized patron saints—and partly because of her infinite benevolence. Nonetheless, whether a shrine honored Mary or any other saint, it needed more than ordinary miracles and backers to stand out. After 1587 more and more Spanish soldiers visited Scherpenheuvel, in 1602 the first organized pilgrimage was made, and soon Archbishop Hovius began to patronage the site, authenticate its miracles, and organize its setting. For instance, to promote and ensure the spot's holiness, he had the old oak cut down and a new chapel constructed. Although there were sacred oaks in Holy Scripture, such as that under which Jacob buried pagan gods, Hovius wanted to preempt any confusion about whether the tree or the image was the source of power.

But true fame waxed only with the enthusiastic, full-coffered support of the pious Archdukes Albert and Isabella, who attributed progress against the Dutch to the powers of the new shrine. When in September 1603 the Dutch ended their siege of the city of Den Bosch, the grateful archdukes soon afterward made their first pilgrimage to Scherpenheuvel. In July 1604 Hovius dedicated the new chapel. In September, as if the Virgin were expressing thanks for the new structure, the Dutch garrison in the important coastal town of Oostende capitulated. To the archdukes and others, there was a clear connection among all these events. The Virgin of Scherpenheuvel became an object of their deepest devotion; it surpassed other favorite Marian shrines of the area such as at Cambron, Chièvres, Our Lady of Hanswijk in Mechelen, Lede near Aalst, Scheut near Brussels, or even Laken and Halle, to become *the* shrine of the Spanish Netherlands. In order to emphasize this, a new shrine was to be erected, set squarely in the middle of a larger, more dignified church atop the lonely hill, while around it would be constructed from the ground up an entire city, conceived of by the arch-dukes themselves. The villagers who arrived by November 1605 to begin this new city received the same royal "privileges," or rights, enjoyed by its new and unlikely spiritual cousin: the distant, worldly city of Oostende. They laid the first stone of the church in July 1609, only months after the enemy Dutch had agreed to a Twelve Years Truce—again no coincidence—and the first pastor came in 1610, along with numerous underpastors to aid in preaching and hearing confession. Accounts of miracles now poured in, confirming the rightness of the decision.

When Margaret approached the still-unfinished place in 1624, she may have engaged in rituals typical of pilgrimage, such as walking barefoot for part of the trip, or climbing steps on her knees, or mortifying her flesh. In whatever manner she came from Diest, she would first have seen the nearly completed Baroque, round, domed church, fifty meters high, then the incomplete surrounding wall, begun in 1620, in the form of a septagon, representing the sacred, magical number seven but more important the seven points of a star, the symbol of the Virgin. She might have seen workmen on the wall, or children making holes in it to the irritation of authorities. Entering through the main gate opposite the front of the shrine, or one of the several side gates accessible by steps up the hill, she would have readily grasped that the interior of the city continued the star motif of the walls, with the still-earthen streets and houses laid out in seven clear sections. Beyond the rows of houses came a seven-sided wall surrounding an enclosed, seven-pointed, star-shaped, sapling-filled garden around the star-covered church.

Just outside the garden wall stood peddlers of sacred and not-so-sacred objects. Irish soldiers from the garrison at Zichem also frequented the town, on pilgrimage to the shrine or just as likely to the cafés that served the strong beer of Diest. As Margaret passed through, she probably moved with eyes down to avoid distraction, as was recommended for the nuns of her order and as hoped for by Mater Barbara. Or perhaps she fixed on the church, oblivious to the other pilgrims, who came from nearby or as far away as Italy, borne on stretchers, either crippled or, like her, spiritually ill. The crowds increased in size according to the season. This was a busy time of year but less so than summer. The temptation to be distracted did not cease once at the threshold of the church, for some tried to sleep there, others milled around the large door, workers continued construction, and beggars from all corners looked for money or pillaged the offering boxes during services, often putting wax across the openings to catch coins before they fell through.

She recognized the four evangelists above the entry to the church and then went inside, noticing first the unfinished but chalk-white star-filled

Our Lady of Scherpenheuvel. The sign reads: "I love those who love me."
FROM SANDERUS, *CHOROGRAPHIA SACRA BRABANTIAE.*

ceiling. The interior was much barer than today, but there was still plenty to see, and given the circular form you could see almost every-thing at once: the brand-new white marble high altar with the initials of Albert and Isabella prominently inscribed, the freshly painted Ascen-sion of the Virgin above it, the red flagstone, the surrounding confes-sionals, the seven alcoves in the wall housing images of Old Testament prophets, the rows of silver candelabra and hanging lamps, the finely crafted baptismal font, the side altars and chapels, all to be dedicated to different saints and filled with a couple of dozen relics from twenty other saints, and the pile of ex-votos, little wax models of parts of the body sent to the church in thanks by those who had been cured. At some point her eye would have rested on the object she and everyone else had come to see. In a silver alcove above the altar was the oaken Virgin, 30 centimeters by 11, infant Jesus on her left arm, scepter in her right hand, clothed in proper liturgical colors in one of the many sump-tuous gowns sent to the shrine by grateful donors.

Margaret would have witnessed these scenes frequently while at Scherpenheuvel. To what extent the shrine alone aided her cure is un-known. More certain is that here or in Diest she and Catharina would have met the man who directed the shrine and gave it his stamp—the third of the prominent religious figures to come into her life in 1624 and the one who would exert the most lasting influence. Indeed, while the shrine was important, Boonen's trusted friend Joost Bouckaert may have been the real reason for his decision to make Margaret a pilgrim.

Bouckaert was the man who had arrived in Scherpenheuvel in 1610 as its first pastor, and he eventually became bishop of Ieper—but most important for us, he was the chief patron and counselor of Margaret Smulders. Renowned for his benevolence, he could also be tenacious, especially in begging and pleading and fighting for funds to complete his shrine. In spite of chronically poor health, he never ceased in his efforts until Boonen finally dedicated the church of Scherpenheuvel in 1627. For years he reminded the Council of State to compel pledge-breakers to pay up. He also pestered the Council for a monopoly on the sale of sacred images, arguing that the shrine alone should be allowed to make and distribute these, partly because they needed the funds and partly because competitors were often unscrupulous heretics who fash-ioned marionettes out of the Virgin and then made money from their sacrilege. This was the man who labored more than any other for the place, who determined to make it a "church for the entire fatherland," who dogged the local magistrates for capable guards, yet who convinced Isabella never to garrison soldiers in the town, and who always said the Mass solemnly, for small and great alike. Clearly the shrine hadn't risen up or achieved its fame by accident.

Joost Bouckaert, seventeenth century.

KONINKLIJK INSTITUUT VOOR HET KUNSTPATRIMONIUM, BRUSSELS.

Margaret certainly felt herself fortunate to be entrusted to this zealous but kind man. With the religious life he was familiar, since besides being pastor he was dean of Diest, a position that required him to visit female houses regularly. We don't know what he thought of Margaret at first, though over the years he was clearly sympathetic. We don't know details of her eight-month stay or even whether things were as public as Mater Noosen had feared. But we do know that from April to November she would have spent significant time under the influence of this shrine and its framer. One witness later commented on Bouckaert's expertise as a theologian; but an early historian of the church in the Spanish Netherlands noted that above all his ecclesiastical positions and academic degrees, Bouckaert was a shepherd of souls.

The inner life, so important to religious, would have occupied the centerpoint of her healing and their discussion. Among the ideas that Bouckaert could have introduced in his attempt to heal Margaret were familiar ones, such as Evangelista's lessons on how to prepare for the Eucharist, his three ways to know that her soul was on the path to God, and his four ways to achieve the Kingdom of God within. They also could have gone beyond Evangelista quite easily, now that there was time, inclination, and more works of devotion available than ever before. The popular little book on meditation assembled by the Spanish Franciscan Alcantara and immensely influential upon Teresa offered specifically for religious two weeks' worth of nuggets for thought: during the first week, consider personal sins on Monday, misery and the brevity of life on Tuesday, the hour of death on Wednesday—which Alcantara promised would make one run to confession and communion—the last judgment on Thursday, the pangs of Hell on Friday, the peace of eternal life on Saturday, and the benevolence and grace of God on Sunday. The second week discussed the period from the Last Supper to the Ascension, vividly reminding the reader that some doctors of theology believed Our Lord's crown of thorns to have been so enormous that the only way for his enemies to get at the robe was to rip the crown from his head, turning his body into one big, bloody wound. There were plenty of systematic, even mnemonic techniques for meditation, including Balbano's *Seven Meditations,* the Jesuit Androtius's relentless *Devout Memorial of the Passion* with its twelve mysteries, each with five meditations and each meditation with 5 submeditations, and the famous Vervoort's popular *Wilderness of the Lord,* which provided forty days of meditations and prayers with a woodcut of a holy scene for each. There was the synthesis by Madrid, the *Golden book to learn the art of serving God sincerely,* which the author assured outpaced all the others because it showed how to put the others to work, warned that it "wasn't as heavy as it looked," and cautioned that reading it once wouldn't suffice in learning the two ways to serve God, five steps to come to God, and three steps to holy and perfect love.

Bouckaert could have given Margaret books of comfort, such as Spoelberch's reassurance that God's love was so great that He granted a special angel to watch over each person, even great sinners, even anti-Christs. It's this angel who helps you fight against the devil in all temptations, Spoelberch assured. Think that God is prepared to forgive in an instant even great sins. Think also that God doesn't punish twice for the same fault. Think that God doesn't overwhelm anyone above her power to be tempted—all of which would certainly have been soothing to Margaret. Other possible books included various *Lives of the Saints*, or accounts of miracles in evocative, faraway places such as Palermo, Sicily, or the more recent drama of the closer martyrs of Gorcum.

There were more basic works, also specifically for religious, including Ferraria's treatise on the three monastic vows. Was she truly poor, or too covetous of worldly possessions? Was her breviary too well decorated, could she leave her cell open for thieves rather than lock it to protect that which would turn to dust? Was she obedient, or did she anger Mater Barbara in not being enough of a dumb mule, in resisting burdens or doing as she was told? The rule of her order reminded her that the "highest religious perfection lies in the conquering and sinking of self-will. . . . The children must give themselves wholly to obedience, and when they hear their superior's voice they'll obey as if it were God's." Was she chaste, and did she love enough the three remedies against lust? And there were plenty of other works from Balsamo's recommended list of twenty-seven books for every religious.

Even simpler writings would have been appropriate, such as the pithy, self-deprecating *Contemplations of an Idiot*: Live purely, Consider your smallness, Be alone gladly, Keep peace with others, Think on the day, That passes no one by. She could have benefited from reading the *Spiritual A.B.C.* of St. Bonaventure, or from such elementary but profitable exercises included at the back of her Book of Hours as pondering the ten commandments; the three divine virtues of faith, hope, and charity; the four cardinal virtues; the seven gifts of the Holy Spirit; the twelve fruits of the Holy Ghost; the eight steps to salvation; the seven deadly sins; and the four extremes (death, judgment, hell, heaven). If Margaret felt primarily blame and guilt for her troubles, as she hinted elsewhere, then the seven penitential psalms would have been fitting: *Have mercy upon me, O Lord; for I am weak: O Lord, heal me. . . . My soul is . . . sore vexed. . . . I am weary with my groaning; all the night make I my bed to swim; I water my couch with my tears. . . . For mine iniquities are gone over mine head; as an heavy burden they are too heavy for me. . . . Mine enemies are lively, and they are strong: and they that hate me wrong-*

fully are multiplied. . . . Mine enemies reproach me all day; and they that are mad against me are sworn against me.

Precisely which writings and impressions were involved cannot be said, but clearly Margaret worked at being healed, and the ways to do so were almost as numerous as the stars at Scherpenheuvel. At some point she did confess to Bouckaert, and then communed, something she had not done for months. That alone was a sign of improvement. She seems to have begun to feel at home at the hospital in Diest, so much so that Mater Barbara and even Catharina began during the summer of 1624 to talk of Margaret's staying on for good, while wearing her Franciscan habit under the new one and observing her original vows and obligations as much as possible.

Despite all these hopeful signs and any possible rumors that may have reached the nuns at Bethlehem about Margaret's convalescence, what the other sisters most surely would have remembered were Margaret's troubles. Indeed, while Margaret was gone, the nuns of Bethlehem continued to rage furiously against her.

8. FULMINATIONS

BETHLEHEM, JUNE 5 TO NOVEMBER 1624. Mater Barbara could not long enjoy the peace that came with Margaret's lengthy absence. Within a couple of months of Margaret's departure, one of the women of Bethlehem told a most unsettling story to the house confessor, who called in the dean of Leuven, who called in the seasoned vicar-general to come and hear for himself.

When the nuns sent in January their petition about strange events in the cell of a postulant, they had strongly implied that Margaret and something supernatural were involved, but no one had clear proof. Now the young victim came forward and privately offered to the vicar-general her disturbing version of those events.

Twenty-year-old Barbara Beli had entered Bethlehem in June 1623, thanks to the patronage of a beguine in Brussels. She testified that her stay in the convent had soon become unpleasant, reaching a nadir at Christmas when a hairshirt and a "discipline" (an unspecified instrument of mortification) were taken from an unlocked chest in her room. Shortly after this, she discovered on two different occasions a "rod" (probably a switch), on top of her bed, and once a rod between the blankets. Then three times within a short period her clothes and linens, which had been placed neatly in the chest, were scattered all around. On the third occasion she caught the culprit red-handed. Returning from the noon meal, Beli found Sister Margaret Smulders standing next to the just-emptied chest.

Immediately, she continued, Margaret began to threaten, forbidding her to tell anyone, confessor or sisters or outsiders, or "she would not escape alive." Margaret even exacted an oath of silence. For months the postulant had dared not speak of the confrontation, but now, perhaps remembering that the oath had been made under duress and also that Margaret was out of the convent, she decided to tell all. Indeed, there was more to the terror. Occasionally during Mass, Barbara alleged, just after the elevation of the host when faces were on the ground in reverence, Margaret would kick her in the head. Mater finally noticed and promised to deal with the matter privately, but warned Beli not to tell anyone else lest her chances of advancing to the novitiate be jeopardized. Beli declared that she was prepared to swear to the truth of her story to

74

anyone in the hierarchy who was interested, but she promised the vicar-general to keep it secret from her sisters in the convent.

In examining this testimony, it seems quite puzzling that Mater Barbara would order Beli to keep quiet. Perhaps Mater did not think Beli so innocent as she presented herself to the vicar-general, or perhaps she feared that the sisters would somehow connect Beli to Margaret and therefore ruin her hopes for entry. In any case, the story must have remained hidden, for Beli succeeded in being advanced to the novitiate in July, only a month after the interview. But, for reasons unknown, within weeks of her advancement Beli decided to tell the other nuns her unpleasant tales about Margaret. Perhaps she did so to ingratiate herself, since she knew virtually all disliked Margaret. Perhaps she did so after rumors had reached Bethlehem during the summer that Margaret was on the mend, and everyone, especially Beli, wanted new evidence to keep her from returning when she became whole. Or perhaps Beli started in so as to preempt stories that she and Margaret were somehow partners-in-sorcery. Beli knew that if the events of the past January were ever seen as demon-connected, Margaret-connected, *and* Beli-connected, she would have no chance of being allowed to profess.

Whatever the motivation and timing, Beli's decision to talk brought about the result that Mater Barbara had feared: Blame was not at all transferred from Margaret. Instead, the nuns merely added Beli to their list of undesirables. The chances of their allowing a sister into the convent who might prove as vexatious as the dreaded Margaret were about as slight as the most ascetic Franciscan nun. If this disobedient novice wasn't trouble enough, more came literally knocking at the door.

On June 25, two days after the profession ceremony for the promising Anna Vignarola, there arrived a message from the local Franciscan Guardian. In it he informed Mater of a recent decision taken by the order's provincial chapter, or council: namely, within three months the friars would stop performing services at all convents of the third order not directly under Franciscan jurisdiction. Of course this included Bethlehem. If the archbishop relinquished authority over the convent, then they would gladly continue. Important for our story is that this provincewide decision did not germinate spontaneously: Certainly the headaches caused by Margaret had their effect.

Just as there was a long tradition of confessors in nunneries, so was there a long tradition of confessors threatening to quit. During the boom years of the late Middle Ages, most confessors in female houses came from the male side of the monastic family. But enthusiasm among these men soon wavered. The Norbertines not only broke up their unique double houses (men on one side, women the other) but ended the female branch altogether. The Dominicans ceased ministering to religious women soon after Dominic's death, though they eventually resumed their services. The Carthusians concluded that the five female monasteries under their care were the five wounds of the order. Francis himself by the end of his life rarely visited Clare and her Poor Ladies of San Damiano. Over the centuries the male Franciscans generally came to regard the female second order, as well as the whole of the third order, as sources of embarrassment and trouble. Hence the Franciscans of Leuven, in their recently enlarged house south of Bethlehem, proud home to the tombs of the famous artist Dirk Bouts and the renowned scholar Lipsius, inherited a long legacy of suspicion about nunneries. Recent events also had not helped; the threatened return of Margaret only added ammunition to the friars' already well-stocked arsenal of misogyny.

Such feelings were of course not universal. Some recent studies have shown that confessors were always eager to be associated with a holy woman. The Franciscan-cousin Capuchins and the Jesuits were active in caring for women, and some confessors and houses seem to have mutually enjoyed their association. But for many males, female houses were often nuisances or, at worst, full of tempting objects. By the seventeenth century women were still considered not only more likely than men to become witches or demoniacs, but more lustful and seductive. Think, said experts, upon Adam and Eve, Samson and Delilah, David and Bathsheba, Solomon's pagan wives, and ad nauseam. Another consideration was that care for nunneries detracted from other, higher-profile activities, such as preaching and missions. Preaching was easier than steady, patient ministering to any community, and both preaching and missions were more dramatic than long-term care. Yet most important of all was the question of control. Partly because the friars wavered in their commitment to serving them, and partly because bishops were vigilant, many convents came under episcopal or "ordinary" jurisdiction. But when these houses could not afford a confessor of their choice, a bishop often asked the friars to serve as confessors—under his thumb. If the friars consented, they quickly grew frustrated when the nuns ran to the bishop to appeal unpopular advice or confessors. If we must confess nunneries, argued the friars, then grant us full control to enforce our will.

Bethlehem was a perfect example. Henri Joos had been needed in 1604 because somewhere along the line, the friars in Leuven became unwilling to serve merely as confessors. When offered the chance again in 1618 to take up care—but not jurisdiction—of Bethlehem, the friars agreed, perhaps because of increasing competition for souls, but probably because the house was so obviously in need. So the Franciscans arranged a system for Bethlehem in which the task of being confessor rotated annually among members. Soon all parties were unhappy. Arch-

A Grey Sister, Franciscan friar, and Capuchin friar,
anonymous, from an eighteenth-century costume book.

bishop Hovius complained that the first man was "wholly" unlearned. Maters protested that the friars weren't fulfilling their duty. As for the friars themselves, they complained that they had no real control—their words were by definition advice, not law, and some sisters were already agitating to carry out the friars' nightmare of running to the Jesuits. The declaration by Pope Benedict XV in 1623 that *all* confessors of female religious, even the male religious of the same order, must be approved by the local bishop, together with old pronouncements against visiting female convents, probably made the friars even more reluctant to serve any house over which they had ever less control.

This background is important not only to make clear the role of confessors in nunneries, but to help put our particular story in context. When the friars complained about control, they especially had in mind the troubles caused by Margaret and Barbara Beli and the inability of the archbishop to solve them. It was no coincidence that they flung down their gauntlet about complete jurisdiction at the same time that Beli was relating her tale and reports of Margaret's improvement and possible return were in the air. Indeed, the Franciscans were already voicing to the sisters the same campaignlike promise they would repeat many times over the months and years: Lobby the bishop to grant us jurisdiction and your problems will be solved.

Mater Barbara must have found the timing of the friars rather unsporting and their sloganizing cheap. But she did pass on the Guardian's message to Boonen, along with her own request. She simply and tactfully asked the archbishop to decide quickly, one way or the other, since they had been without a real confessor for six years. Boonen, taking no visible offense, decided to poll the sisters of Bethlehem about their feelings on the topic of jurisdiction and, as usual by now, on Margaret.

Even before the archbishop's representative arrived at the convent, Maria Joos and Anna Marcelis hurriedly wrote secret, impassioned pleas against relinquishing jurisdiction. Both noted that the friars were notorious for "constricting consciences," or in other words for prohibiting sisters from using non-Franciscan confessors. This constriction caused great inconvenience if one needed a confessor right away or if one just didn't like the friars. Maria told of a sister who had been forced to wait with a burdened conscience for three days because the friars were busy elsewhere, while Anna wrote from personal experience that she had asked for a Jesuit confessor through the dean of Leuven, "who saw me in such great pain, weeping bitterly, and who went to the Jesuits himself to seek help for me," in spite of the prohibition against them. Maria even claimed that "only four or five" sisters really favored a switch to Franciscan jurisdiction, and these same women whispered to the friars the names of those who opposed it—which led to even less freedom in the confessional and still more tension in the house.

Archbishop Boonen's dean in Leuven, Peter Lucius, arrived at Bethlehem on August 20 to investigate the question more systematically. From his notes we see that Maria Joos was wrong that only "four or five" sisters supported the switch. Out of twenty—Catharina and Margaret were still away—sixteen favored granting complete jurisdiction to the friars, three were for retaining them as confessors only, and Mater Barbara would do as the archbishop desired, though she was inclined to oppose reorganization. Significantly, given later events and alliances, Maria Joos now changed her mind and went over to the Franciscan camp. If the sisters were all aware of the friars' reputation for strictness—and they probably were—then the overwhelming desire in Bethlehem for a fixed confessor to help them solve their problems outweighed any fears about style. Some argued that nuns were more appropriately served by regular (monastic) rather than "secular" (parochial or episcopal) clergy, others that a secular confessor was too costly. But clearly the chief reason for their desire to change was that Boonen was too busy to solve their numerous problems. The archbishop's other affairs prevented him from watching out for this convent, the Franciscans were "closer" and thus better able to serve them, and, said eight sisters, the friars would bring about a better "reformation" than the archbishop. Adriana Truis, Maria Joos, and Lesken Joos—three of the five future leaders of Bethlehem—preferred the Franciscans specifically because the archbishop had failed to solve the problem of Margaret. Their language was even the same, suggesting that Adriana and Lesken had persuaded Maria to take their side.

Boonen characteristically put off a decision on jurisdiction and confessors, though he did check with two secular priests about serving as confessor in Bethlehem. (Both pleaded overwork.) As a result of indecision and reluctance, the problem would go on to haunt the convent for decades. However, of chief importance for us is that the issue of ecclesiastical jurisdiction came up precisely when Margaret's problems, and Beli's related troubles, were at their peak.

That brings us to a second topic of the interview by Dean Lucius: whether Sister Margaret should be allowed to return. Just before his visit, the sisters learned the definite and alarming—or depending on one's fountain of mercy, hopeful—news: Margaret was healed and ready to come back.

If return she absolutely must, then the first thought on the sisters' minds was to establish proper penance. One sister opined that for the remainder of her days Margaret should be the "last" of the convent—in other words, that she should be seated in the most junior place in choir, refectory, or chapter, stand last in line, and so forth, an obviously humiliating position in the seniority-conscious world of monasticism. Barbara wasn't averse to the punishment, but there was one problem: Though being sentenced as "last" was not an unusual temporary punishment in convents, the fact that an obviously senior nun had been forever condemned would pique curiosity among the new, and the story would have to be retold. More immediately, Barbara feared that the others, including the confessor, would treat Margaret badly if she returned. This meant not only that Margaret would have no freedom in the confessional, thereby risking the old problems and possessions, but also made it possible that they might again lose their confessor.

If the sisters really had their way, then there would be no need for penance because there would be no return. As in 1616, almost all were fiercely opposed. Of twenty sisters who voted in August (Catharina was still away with Margaret), only Mater Barbara was in favor, and only Aleidis Doelmans expressed willingness to do as the archbishop pleased. Most were still prepared, despite complaints about already inadequate resources, to support Margaret at an as-yet unspecified place outside the convent. As in 1616, they would "rather suffer poverty than have her back," "eat dry bread," fast one day more per week, give up part of their daily portion, do almost anything to keep her out.

Dean Lucius dutifully sent along to Boonen the opinions of the sisters on both counts, appending commentary of his own, including that many sisters still suspected Margaret of sinister things and that the current confessor promised to quit if she came back. He also revealed the first evidence of a rift between the confessor and part of the convent on one side, and Mater and one or two nuns on the other. One sister told Lucius that what the confessor most enjoyed was to hear complaints about Mater Barbara, no doubt because Mater was less enthusiastic than some about having the Franciscans as superiors. Finally Lucius confirmed that the promises of the friars to fix things had indeed had an effect: Most sisters, he said, favored switching due to dissatisfaction with the handling of Margaret by Mater and the archbishop, not because of any merit in the Franciscan method of governance.

To ensure that their opinions were clear, sixteen of the twenty sisters went beyond the interviews with Dean Lucius and sent another petition to the archbishop, just as in January. This time the names of Mater Barbara and three others who could have signed were missing, reflecting again growing division in the house. All were "very disturbed" about the possibility of Margaret's return, as they considered the "great unrest that we have had with her, day and night." The tension, the strange events and fears, had all been "stilled" since her departure. We "pray for the love of God that you'll keep this person from us," they wrote. "We are prepared to give all that is possible to give, for we would rather live in poverty and want, serving God in peace, than to end our lives in such unrest."

These weren't the only opinions that Boonen received on the topic. Though Margaret had been out of Bethlehem for months, she also spoke out through her new and sympathetic patron in Scherpenheuvel. Bouckaert wrote to Boonen at the end of September and stated that Barbara Beli's charges against Margaret seemed untrue and unfounded. He also believed that the general accusations about Margaret's connection to sorcery were spurious, for the acts of which she was accused required more active powers—implying, like Evangelista before him, that Margaret was not a witch. On both counts, Bouckaert insisted that charges should either be made specific and proved, or they should be dropped. Bouckaert was also so bold as to advance some specific "reforms" that needed to be made at Bethlehem, suggesting that not all of the convent's problems originated with Margaret. These included reducing the size of the grille through which sisters spoke to outsiders, bolting the door to the confessional with locks on both sides (perhaps spurred by Margaret's tales of Henri Joos), more alert watch over the main door of the convent, and a halt to the occasional outbreaks of worldly dancing. Bouckaert had undoubtedly gathered the information needed to make these recommendations from Margaret herself, since he had not yet seen the place.

The fate of these suggestions we don't know. Nonetheless, they introduce to us two patterns that, over the following decades, would prove to be tremendously important in shaping the conditions and perceptions of the house. First, in answering charges brought against her by the other sisters, Margaret not only denied being an ally of the devil but went on the counterattack, commenting on the shortcomings of her sisters. Second, it became evident that Bouckaert's vision of conditions in Bethlehem was ever influenced by his special relationship with Margaret and his certainty that she was falsely charged. Unlike Evangelista months before, Bouckaert was not merely passing along information to Boonen in Margaret's behalf; he shared her basic convictions.

We also do not know precisely how Boonen reacted between late August and early November, whether he sympathized with the sisters at Bethlehem or with Margaret and Bouckaert. We know only that Sister Catharina, her companion cured, returned from Scherpenheuvel in early September, and that Barbara Beli was merrily telling awful tales of the absent Margaret. But at this point no one was making any real moves about Margaret's status. So, feeling whole and concluding that some action was better than none, Margaret decided to take matters into her own hands.

9. NO BALM IN BETHLEHEM

*She weepeth sore in the night and her tears are on her cheeks: among all
her lovers she hath none to comfort her: all her friends . . . are become
her enemies.* —LAMENTATIONS 1:2

TOWARD LEUVEN, NOVEMBER 4, 1624. The old road from Diest,
like every other road of the day awaiting satisfaction of the ancient
promise that crooked ways would be made straight and rough places
smooth, was a sometimes dusty, usually muddy, and always narrow path
that wound through half a dozen villages and encountered half a dozen
other such paths (which the inexperienced traveler might follow in the
vain hope of finding steadier going), until twenty miles later it finally
ran up, pocked and scarred, to the northeast walls of Leuven.

Anyone who saw the coach that rumbled through the gates of Diest
would have wondered what a veiled nun, sworn to observe *clausura,*
was doing on this road at all. This was a question of which Margaret
was painfully aware as she left the city behind. But of greater import
and depth as she bumped along was the need to clear her heart of the
rancor remaining from her first return to Bethlehem some six years
before. It was on this road, as they meandered past bleak, stubbled fields
and hills less dramatic than the cliffs in a Bruegel landscape but steep
enough to discourage a plow or pilgrim, that she again told herself she
was cured, for a few days before she had felt such "sweetness" within
that her heart seemed ready to melt. It was on this road, in the midst of
the usual November chill and mist, that she hoped her sisters would see
the change, her new determination to live the rest of her days in peace
with them and in submission to her superiors; but this hope alternated
with fear of rejection, for they might not forget the past or might react
badly upon learning that she, like a daring artist who acted on her own
in the hope that her patrons would be pleasantly surprised, had quit
Diest without permission.

She was to have remained in the city until Archbishop Boonen, Pastor
Bouckaert, and the sisters in Bethlehem all consented to her return. But
because she was cured, Margaret again told herself, because waiting for
the others to act might take forever—to the salvation of no one—and
because her intent was "pure and sincere," as she later put it to Boonen,
she had felt justified in making arrangements of her own to leave. No

82

doubt Margaret assumed that if the nuns of Bethlehem merely heard about her renewed determination to live peacefully and well, they would refuse to believe it. But if they could only see her in action, her willingness "to subject myself with a genuine humility to live the rest of my days as the least in our convent and do their will, doing nothing, refraining from nothing, except as they pleased," the chances of convincing them would improve. This "and much more" was her heartfelt purpose.

In the midst of such emotions, the coach continued to bounce closer to Leuven, past the Holy Trinity hill and the Jesuit-owned woods nearby, past a split in the road where the driver had taken the path most likely to be least muddy, and then gradually downhill until the city drew into view. The glimmers of light left in the day created a stark silhouette of the city's towers. Closer still and Margaret could hear the bells of those towers sounding the hour, at which she automatically made the sign of the cross and fortified herself with either Veni Creator Spiritus to the renewal of her spirit or Ave Maria in memory of the hour when God became flesh, just as when she heard the names Jesus, Maria, or Francis, or mention of the holy sacrament or sacred blood she always made a slight bow. She arrived just before the closing of the thick-stoned, oaken-doored Diest-gate, finer than similar gates around the city because it had been built by fastidious Josse Metsys, brother of the famous painter Quentin. A few streets more, a few turns, and Bethlehem was before her.

Margaret descended from the carriage and tugged on the bell that hung outside the main entry to the convent. The portress, given the hour, swung open the heavy door with caution. Aleidis Doelmans was sixty-five years old, or thereabouts. Like many houses, Bethlehem entrusted its gatekeeping to elder sisters; the eighty-one-year-old portress of the Black Sisters of Pamele in Flanders made Sister Aleidis seem an adolescent. Though not a fierce enemy of Margaret like the others, Aleidis must have turned pale at the sight; she sent immediately for Mater before allowing Margaret entry. There was an uproar as the whole convent heard the news, but it was Mater and her close helpers who came to handle the crisis.

Because they were suspicious or needed time to consider strategies, the delegation asked whether Margaret had brought official documents confirming that she had returned with permission. Shattered in only the first few seconds of this exchange, she desperately blurted the lie that Bouckaert would bring them one day soon from Diest. The delegation, skeptical, pointed her to the guest house—outside the cloister, outside the common dormitory—until the truth was known. At this point Margaret broke, hoping that the truth might soften them; she admitted that she had come on her own, without permission or knowledge of her confessor, and probably added that she did so because she was sure of her recovery. This only made the sisters more resolved to keep Margaret out, and they pointed again to the guest house.

With Margaret put away, Mater made preparations to dispatch two lay sisters in the morning to visit with Pastor Bouckaert and get a fuller account of things. Following the customary three bells after Compline to remind her of the eternal virgin the Mother of God, Margaret must have passed a lonely, bitter night.

BETHLEHEM, NOVEMBER 5, 1624, TO JANUARY 25, 1625. Margaret's unexpected arrival opened all the old wounds, plus a few more. As if her presence itself did not smart enough, it converged in near-cosmic fashion with the convent's other problems: Barbara Beli, the disappearing confessors, and diminishing respect for Mater Barbara.

Margaret was of course the most immediate concern. In a sense her current situation was even more gloomy than the dark events of the preceding January, for now there was no pilgrimage to look forward to, no relief in sight, but only dreaded, relentless sameness. Joost Bouckaert broke news of the escape to Boonen on November 6. The return had been "unknown to all," revealing either that Margaret had acted on impulse or that she had successfully kept her plans a secret. It was true that Margaret had been pressing Bouckaert about returning, quite in contrast to the sentiment growing within Catharina and Mater Barbara that Margaret might best remain forever in Diest; yet the very day before Margaret left, Bouckaert thought he had convinced her to remain. Her resolve was greater than he had sensed, he lamely conceded. Whether that resolve was born of God or of Margaret he dared not speculate, but since she contradicted the advice of her superiors he had at least a hunch. Who would help her now to avoid her old infirmities, since she and the house confessor would not speak? He pitied them all—the nuns who needed Boonen's "singular paternal help" and Margaret, who needed to stay free from "malignant corporal infestations."

News also came soon to Boonen from Bethlehem, in the form of two other lay sisters sent by Mater Barbara to Mechelen and a note from Catharina Rijckeboer. The details of the visit by the lay sisters were never recorded, but from Catharina we get a dismal picture. She condemned Margaret for having been so ungrateful to Boonen, who had labored so long and at such personal expense in her behalf. Yet Catharina urged him not to desert Margaret, lest she again become desperate. Since she got along with no one, Catharina wrote, the old troubles might begin anew—reminding us of the role of one's emotional state in possession. "The devil is not far from her; she fled her shepherd and guide

Another scene in the city of Leuven,
from a book of sixteenth-century watercolors.
ROYAL LIBRARY BRUSSELS.

too soon." Catharina realized that Margaret meant no harm, that "it was a temptation she followed through her own fantasy," but because of such rashness there would now be much sinning on all sides.

After a brief recovery, Margaret finally wrote to Boonen as well, pleading once more with the archbishop to forgive her "for the love of God, for I regret it bitterly." Though adamant that her intentions were noble, she was deeply ashamed of her decision. "I hope I'll never do anything again, with God's help, without counsel. I've deceived myself very badly." Margaret proposed that she remain in her guest room through the rest of the winter, perhaps forever, or that the sisters build her a small house in the garden where she would cost very little and live as a recluse. Obviously she had no hopes for leaving: "If I see things clearly, it seems it will be no easy task to find a convent that will take me; besides it would cost much money, and everyone will say, 'why doesn't she stay in the convent where she professed?' If they don't want

85

me here, how much less will another?" She needed time to prove herself. "I am not willing to leave with that name and such suspicions, for they'll never cease gossiping about me and passing it on to whoever comes and goes, and if I were somewhere else it might reach the ears [of those in her new house] and then I'd be suspected and by chance fall into error once more."

Margaret feared that even Bouckaert had lost patience, for one condition of his care, she recognized, had been that she remain away from Bethlehem. And then the two lay sisters recently assigned by Mater to visit Bouckaert had upon returning told Margaret that "by no means would he bear me any longer." She continued worriedly to Boonen, "I've written to him, but I think I'll never find comfort there again, I don't know what else to do, it's finished and must remain finished. I wouldn't for my life dare come to him again. I pray you most earnestly for the love of God, don't abandon me, and watch over me. If possible, let me remain here, I'll bear as much as possible, for wherever I come I'll have to suffer. I have such a horror of that suffering that I think death itself is approaching." Had she known the extent to which she would suffer, she "wouldn't have left the convent to begin with, for my life."

By early December Boonen sent Dean Lucius to Bethlehem to question Mater and Catharina about whether Margaret should stay put or leave for good; he also had the dean invite each woman to write letters that expressed their views in more detail. Significantly, Boonen addressed himself in both cases not only to Mater but to Catharina as well, revealing his esteem of the latter, who as yet held no office in the convent.

Catharina willingly responded. She asserted in her own letter to Boonen that the best solution was to return Margaret to Diest, where she could live in a hospital or convent near Bouckaert. Margaret certainly should not live as a recluse. Alone she would "have even more opportunity to yield to her fantasies and temptations, for she is little experienced in spiritual exercises and hardly knows how to get God to help her." The solitary life was best suited to a white-haired spiritual woman, someone who had already won great victories over Satan in her cell, who had a gift for prayer and could stand the rigor of being alone. As for Margaret's remaining in a guest room, it was still too close for the liking of the other sisters, especially after the stories told by Barbara Beli. "They are so estranged from her, that they quake at the thought of her someday taking up her old place." Catharina was not ready to believe Beli, as were the others, but this did not mean that Margaret should remain: "If Sister Margaret keeps doing as she sees fit and holds to her desire to stay in the convent, then I think her (though unawares) deceived by the whisperings of that crafty serpent from Hell who has long tried to trick her." The "sweetness" that inspired Margaret to return was one such trick; Margaret was too unseasoned to realize that "the evil spirit often transforms himself into an angel of light." In fact, as soon as Margaret returned all sweetness disappeared, she "was overrun by a multitude of temptations" and was once again on the verge of doing that "which in the eternities she would have regretted"—a clear allusion to suicide.

Besides the whisperings of the devil, continued Catharina, Margaret was determined to stay because of the shame that attended any nun who left her convent. But Catharina wanted her to endure that shame, for it would be brief, and with the help of her shepherd in Diest she could learn "better than she has in our convent to conquer her own passions and will." On this last point, Catharina had observed that Margaret's troubles were always preceded by a desire to express some angry feeling to the other sisters, "so that I've always had to struggle to get her to keep things to herself." This tendency, specified here for the first time by Catharina (though alluded to earlier back in 1616), would never die within Margaret, as will become ever more evident. It also again ties plunges in Margaret's emotions to an increasing likelihood of possession.

Mater echoed Catharina in several letters of her own. She lamented that Margaret was "so impatient and complains so much," demanding to reenter with such stridency "that it eats away at those who must hear it." She hardly seemed any different from the time "before she went to the hill." Margaret sat there daily "without comfort from God or sisters or confessor or Holy Sacrament." The plan to remain in the guest house so that she might have easier access to a confessor was a bad idea, wrote Mater, since the house confessor would not visit her, since Bouckaert was distant and estranged, and since a Jesuit who had been arranged for her proved unsympathetic he wanted her to tell her story "as he had already understood and heard it" from Barbara Beli, no less! Barbara, said Mater, had told not only other sisters but several Jesuits, "and what one knows, all know." Undeniably, Mater's patience with Margaret had run out. "I do my best to maintain peace and rest; I speak with [Margaret] sometimes daily or every other day or every third day, but I wish that she were so far from here that I would never have to speak to her again as long as I live, it would be a great comfort to me, for I now sit in great sorrow, may God improve it." The nuns were no more forgiving, reported Mater. "They say that they would rather walk out the door of the convent, that they won't live with her, and I can't blame them, for if she reenters then our convent will be ruined, that is certain."

Perhaps because he heard of the tumult, perhaps because Boonen asked him to go, Joost Bouckaert came by the convent unannounced one mid-December's day, to the delight of those who hoped he would take Margaret away and to the astonishment of Margaret herself. He informed Boonen that though she eventually confessed to him, something she had not done since her return, the visit began miserably. Margaret had to be led almost forcibly from her upstairs room in the guest house. During their conversation she not only suffered the "usual quaking, movements, and other agitations of the body," which he considered "of external cause," but also exhibited a horrible visage that he had never seen before, so horrible that she seemed to be threatened and embraced, and had to fight furiously to resist and escape the enemy. During "rebuking," no doubt a reference to further exorcisms, she displayed a complete resignation to God and her superiors and opened her heart, but the lasting effects of this were impossible for Bouckaert to measure. Certainly she needed a spiritual director immediately, and over the long run a place outside Bethlehem—though Bouckaert knew for a fact that the obvious choice, the hospital in Diest, had no more room and too many impressionable novices.

Though Margaret gave Bouckaert little evidence of improvement and told Boonen that she was "wounded in the depths of her heart" that her old confessor had seen her in such a state, she was thankful for his renewed attention and soon afterward felt "restored." But this feeling alternated with a heavier one: "I am poor and miserable, in soul and body, most wretched," she wrote the archbishop. She lamented her "great lack of wisdom that I cast him away so carelessly. . . . For I see and experience how the devil uses all his deceit and lies to separate me from him," and worked on her "in some things clearly" and in others more subtly. "I still have very much to bear, especially since I spoke with my lord the pastor and opened my heart as I used to do with him, for now I'm more aware of the signs that occur in his presence and then afterward, much more than before, I believe not without suspicion from various causes"—one of the more wonderfully vague sentences that she left us. "Seeing all this, and determined not to be deceived or tempted in choosing this or that in whatever shape it may come, so am I resolved to give myself over, soul and body, to the will of God, and the will and good opinion of your reverence, do with me what you please." And if his reverence cared for her soul, then would he be sure "to care for the rest" as well—or in other words, the temporal. Outside the community she was cut off from her regular portion and of course could not afford on her own to move elsewhere. She reminded him that "want of temporal things might bring me into error very easily once again." Boonen at some point responded positively, for later documents mention his long financial support of Margaret.

In other letters to Bouckaert and Boonen Margaret vacillated more than once in the next weeks about leaving—"As I think about it my heart buries me as if I were about to die; oh, if God would only take me from this world"; "I can't go forward or backward, I can't write it all, but I can say that I'm not as well as I'd hoped"—but finally she yielded to the advice of those closest to her and agreed to leave Bethlehem if the archbishop commanded it. She decided to be "away from here . . . for I suffer unspeakable persecution and confusion at night, so that every day as evening falls I feel death itself approaching." Whether she suffered there or elsewhere, "I know I've earned it, and much more, but the afflictions are great and I'm not yet very strong." By late December Margaret was sure that Boonen would come through: She refused to speak to any confessor of Bethlehem because "I expect any day to receive the command to leave." She felt that if she could only "be situated in a place where I can serve God according to my state, then I will with God's grace be so submissive and obedient that your worthiness will not regret the labor spent." On one letter full of such pleas and promises, she added for the courier, "quickly, quickly."

Margaret is our biggest concern in all this tumult, but Bethlehem was racked by other related troubles as well. According to Catharina and the dean of Leuven, the chief problem in Bethlehem after Margaret was the status of Barbara Beli. By late October Mater clearly wanted Beli out of the convent. Using as justification a certain "accident" from which Beli suffered—based on the context in which the word is repeatedly used, this was probably a recurring illness rather than a sudden injury—Mater and a majority of sisters voted in early November to expel the unwell novice. A more likely explanation than the "accident" for this expulsion, one Mater Barbara had foretold months before when Beli started telling her frightful tales, was that the sisters decided to throw out the messenger with her message. But neither Beli nor her patron, a beguine from Brussels named Barbara van Herssen who rode immediately to Bethlehem on hearing the news, would go down without a fight. Thus began the War of the Three Barbaras.

We need not know all the details, but three developments stand out for our story. First, Beli continued to reside within the cloister while her case was being debated and appealed. In an offhand statement to Archbishop Boonen, Mater Barbara noted that she would have put Beli in the guest house right after the voting, in order to keep her from stoking up the others, except that Margaret, who had arrived in the middle of all this, was there already. Mater feared "that they would have torn into each other, for Sister Margaret resents that Beli has said so much evil of her, that she still with tears in her eyes swears by her salvation that it never even entered her mind to do what the novice accused her of doing." Someone—we imagine Sister Catharina—had obviously informed Margaret about Beli's recent storytelling. Perhaps this was done in an effort to explain to Margaret why the sisters, nervous already about her, were more upset than usual when she returned from Scherpenheuvel. Whatever the source or reason, this piece of intelligence alone must have swept away most of Margaret's hard-won resolve to deal peaceably.

Second, there occurred between Mater Barbara and the just-arrived Barbara van Herssen a heated but vaguely reported exchange in which it was revealed that some nuns, especially Mater, suspected Beli of "dealing with the devil." This confirms the readiness we've already seen in this age—and this convent—to point fingers at the devil and his helpers when trying to explain perplexing events. According to Van Herssen, who now sought Boonen's intervention, the "accident" given as justification for Beli's expulsion was a sham. She recognized, like everyone else, that serious physical illness or emotional instability were common obstacles to profession, for a nun needed her health—but this "accident" was trivial. Indeed, the doctor who treated Beli had laughed in ridicule when asked by Van Herssen whether this condition would be a hindrance to professing. Suspicious, Van Herssen then pressed Mater for the real reason, at which point the nefarious charge of "devil-dealing" finally came out. Van Herssen's response was simple: her protégée was incapable of such evil, but if she had in fact become infected then the archbishop should note well that it had occurred within a convent run by Barbara Noosen.

Mater Barbara, having gotten wind of Van Herssen's appeal to Boonen, wrote the archbishop as well, in self-defense. She denied having ever said that Beli was linked with the devil—persecuted by, perhaps, but never was there a claim that Beli had engaged in "relations" with him. The mysterious rods on her bed or the upsetting of things in her room, suspected Mater, were probably not of the devil at all but more likely the work of Barbara Beli herself. She was unstable enough to have done so, for even Van Herssen admitted that Beli had stolen some things from her when they lived together. Then the key line: "We have so much to do to help one get out, why would we want to risk receiving another?"

The third and final notable detail in these events is that the vote against Beli was not as simple as it seemed. Many sisters, upset at the long delays in solving this issue and others, began to transform the question of Barbara Beli into a question of confidence in Mater Barbara. Momentum gathered soon after Van Herssen arrived in town, for she not only demanded from Mater an explanation for Beli's expulsion but insisted upon a revote among the nuns—this time on whether Beli should be given another six weeks in the convent, in order to see whether the old "accident" might reappear. Mater refused, but, encouraged by several of the nuns, Van Herssen went over Mater's head to the house confessor and a local canon named Paludanus. According to Catharina Rijckeboer, who condemned the act, the two men came as requested and sat at the grille hearing votes like a couple of merchants eager to sell their wares. The very fact of the revote was an obvious political defeat for Mater, whatever the outcome. And when the outcome was disputed, temperatures in the convent rose higher still. Catharina alleged that the totals were divided and uncertain, while Barbara van Herssen claimed that a majority favored allowing Beli the six weeks and that Mater Barbara had risen up against the confessor "like a scrubwife," saying that the affair didn't concern him anyway. Dean Lucius reconciles the two positions for us and in the process drops a heavy hint about the politics behind the whole controversy. Yes, a majority of votes favored Beli's staying, he reported to Boonen; but a procedural error had been made in that the six lay sisters had been allowed to vote on her admission. Since Beli aspired to be a veiled nun rather than a lay sister, the votes of the latter group should have been disallowed. With these subtracted, the majority of nuns were opposed.

After all the raging, Barbara Beli appeared on her way out. But by now her status was almost incidental, subordinate to the internal politics of Bethlehem. In the end, as Catharina Rijckeboer wrote to Boonen, it was evident to all that Beli would never become a nun in this house. Not even the strong minority who had favored the six-week probation would have allowed her to stay for good; these women had supported such a probation only in order to embarrass Mater Barbara. Dean Lucius added still more evidence that politics, not spiritual qualifications, were at the heart of the matter. He told Boonen that the vote was less close than it seemed—not only because of the procedural error, but because the number of those in favor had swollen through the lobbying of the house confessor, who once more had suggested that here was a chance to get the convent under complete Franciscan control. In other words, a vote for Beli was a vote for Franciscan jurisdiction and, by implication, a vote to solve the house's problems. Finally, Mater Barbara offered the clearest piece of proof yet about the real root of division over Beli. It wasn't merely the house confessor who schemed against her, she told Boonen, but the "hangers-on of Henri Joos," the first record we have of a person in Bethlehem revealing to the episcopal hierarchy the existence of factions within—factions organized around an outsider! She didn't name names, but the group included at least most of the lay sisters, who had voted in favor of Beli, and a nun singled out by Catharina: "Even the youngest professed dares to rebuke and talk back to her." The youngest, we know, was Anna Vignarola. The identities of other supporters would emerge over the years, but already it was apparent that Joos was not forgotten—indeed that he was still at the center of Bethlehem's struggles.

The conclusion to the affair of Barbara Beli finally came and was quite anticlimactic. Within days of the hotly disputed revote her status was decided once and for all by forces out of everyone's control: The old "accident" reappeared. Barbara van Herssen had been ready to continue to fight, even after the revote, but now all hope was lost. She claimed that Mater reacted in a most uncharitable fashion on hearing news of the affliction: "Praise God that something has happened to her," Mater supposedly said. "Now she'll be gone." Though Mater denied feeling any joy at the relapse, she did admit calling it a possible sign from God. However the accident should be understood, it's certain that by Christmas of 1624 Beli had gone to live with her patron, Barbara van Herssen, in Brussels. What many in Bethlehem remembered best was not their rather uncharitable treatment of Beli but their dissatisfaction with Mater Barbara's leadership. Half the sisters of the convent even took action into their own hands. Sometime in late December they sent another one of their petitions to Boonen, this time going so far as to ask that Mater Barbara be removed and someone else installed.

It wasn't unusual for Maters to resign or be dismissed from office as a result of conflicts, but it was always stressful—even when, as in this case, Mater herself supported the move. Wallowing in her troubles, and continually distressed by the sister mentioned before who was "tearing her eyes out" and wanted to go on pilgrimage, Mater pleaded with Boonen to be let go. "The unrest and tempest here are so great, the *fick-fackerie* so great, so many involved in it, that it's scandalous," she wrote to Boonen. The supporters of Henri Joos "can't bear that I'm in charge, and are so rebellious against me that I pray you for the love of God and in all humility to release me from my office; your reverence will do me a great favor." Some insinuated that she ruled by sorcery herself, that she was to blame in a direct way for Margaret's problems. "What greater misery is there than to be chained by the devil, and also to hear that I rule through the devil myself?" After pleading again for release, she further suggested the role of unnamed outsiders in the fray within Bethlehem: "My greatest desire is that the grille be completely destroyed, that no one will eat or drink or sleep there anymore, myself included."

But while Mater hinted that outsiders wounded her authority, through stirring up divisions inside the convent, Margaret argued that Mater herself was to blame for allowing them to besiege the grille in the guest house—a theme that will ring ever more clearly as we go. "It's very seldom," Margaret wrote, "that there aren't any worldly or clerical guests here, from inside the city and out, so that day and night I hide myself, in greater restriction than ever." Dean Lucius confirmed that the sisters, including Mater, wore out the tiles between the dormitory and the grille. He suggested that Boonen visit Bethlehem and personally amend the situation.

Even Catharina, Mater's strongest supporter, joined the chorus. The convent was in decline not just because of Margaret but also due to the continued attention to lay friends. "In house we scrimp and save," Catharina observed, but for guests nothing was too good. "In the three months since I've been back from Scherpenheuvel, and others tell me since Easter, the guest room has never been without laypeople as long as a week."* Catharina went beyond problems with this point of discipline to explain Mater's troubles more broadly: There were no bonds of affection between Mater and the community. "She is very blunt and rustic in speech, most unmannered in things outward, uses little discretion, and can't keep a secret; she has little ability to rule, she doesn't understand the art of keeping sisters in peace or of going forward with a good example." Further, she "doesn't honor her convent when in their absence she speaks so freely of them, and refers to them among outsiders as 'the mob' and 'the faction,' and so on." It didn't help that Mater often spoke "scandalously" as well of the confessor; this occurred "more out of simpleness than evil intent," but the friars often reacted badly to such ingratitude for their service. In return for Mater's backstabbing, "many of the sisters, in her absence, poke fun and laugh about her with lay visitors. . . . Even this very Wednesday past the friends gathered [at the grille] were entertained by stories of our contentions." Catharina longed for improvement, even a new election, for "reformation and better adherence to our statutes, which in truth are in decline and ruin."

The archbishop was not indifferent to this ever-growing stack of pleas and intelligence from Bethlehem, but as ever he was deliberate. In early January 1625 he finally gave instruction to Dean Lucius on all the house's problems. First, the dean was to inform the sisters that Boonen was now earnestly searching for a place outside Bethlehem where Margaret could be put and hinting at an allowance of 100 florins per year. This news brought elation to Bethlehem. Margaret herself seemed improved, now going to hear Mass on Sundays and feast days and regu-

*The sisters referred to the visitors' area in a number of ways: "guest room," "parlor," and so on, often using terms interchangeably. Both these visiting areas and the room where Margaret resided were in the same building, it seems, but Margaret's "guest room" (upstairs) was one of the old rooms to lodge visitors, while the "guest room" where visitors came to talk was more properly speaking a parlor (downstairs). For convenience's sake, I simply use the word "guest house" to refer to the whole complex.

larly allowing pastoral visits by an "Augustinian confessor." Catharina was "overjoyed to see Margaret in such spirits."

In regard to Beli, Boonen decided to leave things as they had ended, though he was displeased by the actions of the house confessor. Not surprisingly, he also spurned the sisters' petition. But criticism of upstart sisters and the confessor was not approval of Mater Barbara. He promised the dean that he would issue a set of ordinances soon, which he hoped would bring about greater discipline. More specifically, it seemed to him that Mater was "deficient in many things" and weary of her duties. Perhaps it was time to set her free from office, but if so, then steps should be taken secretly to that end, possibly by bringing into stricter adherence an often-ignored requirement about election every three years. This would allow change as necessary, and without the indignity and embarrassment that came up when a mater who expected to rule for life was "demoted" to a common sister. Dean Lucius reported soon after that he went to speak with Mater about her duties generally and that she had hinted during the course of conversation that she would not be "shamed" if her superiors decided to replace her with someone else.

Then suddenly, within days, Mater's soul became an even more pressing problem than her shaky authority. By January 25, one year to the day since Margaret's miraculous recovery, Barbara Noosen lay dying, of causes unknown. Her last written wish, composed a few days before, varied little from the goals that had consumed her for so long: to find Margaret a house and the convent a permanent confessor. Ironically (given her dislike of Henri Joos), she pushed for the services of the new and nearby pastor of St. Gertrude's, for "the friars have abandoned us; they won't serve us, nor set one foot in our convent." What if a sister should fall ill? She herself had faded within two days of posing that scenario. Joost Bouckaert happened to be there at the time and went in to attend her. He spent "a small hour" trying to lift her spirits. Thankfully, she enjoyed some moments of clarity and light. To make her last hours as comfortable as possible, he said nothing about any developments in Margaret's situation, but later he convened the convent's council sisters and personally repeated to them Boonen's decision to send Margaret away, "which resounded joyously" in their ears.

Mater Barbara lay oblivious to them all. Her days had been hard. She remained unsure of when the house would get its confessor, and she must have worried about who would succeed her, given the likely candidates. But with Beli gone, with Margaret almost gone, and now nearly gone herself, she had cause to imagine that this troubled community was on its way to being healed. And though the sisters had failed to show as much kindness to her in life as in death, she might have entertained the charitable thought that if her own rest could bring a modicum of peace to the place, then she would drink the bitter cup and literally give her life for Bethlehem.

BOOK II

HOW MARGARET SOUGHT HER
REVENGE AND BECAME THE
WATCHDOG OF REFORM ALL AT
ONCE, AND HOW SOME OF THE
OTHER SISTERS ALSO BECAME
ADROIT QUILL-PUSHERS

10. THE BURDEN OF BETHLEHEM, WHICH MARGARET DID SEE

I have long time holden my peace; I have been still, and refrained myself:
now will I cry like a travailing woman. —ISAIAH 42:14

BACK IN THE GUEST ROOM AT BETHLEHEM, MAY AND JUNE 1628. The nun continued as she had begun: confessing freely, in ink, the sins of her sisters. For days and weeks in that late spring of 1628 she shifted from her sewing to the small writing table and back— remembering the old, observing the new, jotting down, then to work again. And between prayers and choir and forgettable meals and discussions at the grille with Catharina, she watched and wrote still more, all in anticipation of the promised visitation from the episcopal palace. Her first two entries were busiest, even furious, but the rest carried emotion as well, and the fervent hope that something would come of her labors. At the same time, she worried that the visitors might not believe her.

If we could enter hearts completely, we could say with certainty how the events and feelings of the previous two decades figured into Margaret's decision to become such an ardent revelator of wrongs in Bethlehem. But we must instead be content to speak with mere confidence: These distant events and feelings—of which we have just learned in relatively little time, but which to her occurred over an eternity— festered at unburiable depths within her, and found some expression and relief as she reflected and wrote away. To the pile of old aggravations we can quickly add a few more recent ones, which must have moved her as well.

First, contrary to everyone's expectations and despite the moving and shaking in her behalf, Margaret did not leave Bethlehem or its suffocating guest room—not in 1625, 1626, or long after. Since even the well-connected Boonen had failed in his quest to find a place for her elsewhere, frustration and humiliation mounted. Unmovable, unreconciled with her sisters, unable to return to the cloister, she would have had a better future in Purgatory.

Second, the election of a replacement for Barbara Noosen in early 1625 turned out the way Margaret feared it would. As often occurred at even the highest levels of the church, power swung to the chief opponents of the last administration. The winner was Adriana Truis, the perpetual thorn in the side of Mater Barbara, Catharina, and Margaret, and loyalist of old Mater Judoca and Henri Joos. Catharina became Bethlehem's first vicaress, an office that only months before she had suggested should be instituted in the convent—and it was no small token, since it made Catharina, not yet thirty years of age, second only to Mater in authority. But to Margaret this was empty, for as Mater and as bursaress (a position Adriana had occupied since 1613), Adriana wielded all real spiritual and temporal power. Worse, Adriana had appointed to every other important office three allies, who together muffled Catharina and who, like Adriana, were all close to Henri Joos: Henri's sister Maria, now portress; her cousin Lesken Joos, a lay sister, now infirmarian and the woman for whom Maria most often opened the convent's door; and most repugnant of all to Margaret, the pretentious Anna Vignarola, now sacristan (or caretaker) of the choir. This was a rapid climb for Anna, who had professed only four years earlier. For Margaret, though, it was another disheartening blow; like Mater, Maria Joos, and Lesken Joos, Anna held her in conspicuous contempt.

A third disappointment occurred soon after. The convent's most regular contact at the episcopal palace, Vicar-General Van der Wiel, brushed off Margaret's complaints about Bethlehem's new leaders, rejected her insistence on the need for reform in the place, and dashed her hopes for her own restoration to the community of nuns. It was not that Van der Wiel opposed reform, but in his eyes the troublemaking Margaret was hardly the person to act as advocate; let her solve her personal troubles first before she condemned others. To Van der Wiel it must have seemed that Margaret acted more out of hostile, rather than pure, motives and that she urged reform to cast aspersions on her foes rather than to correct others out of sisterly love for their ultimate benefit. As for Margaret's exclusion in the guest room, he felt it perfectly justified: Since some were separated on grounds of physical sickness, then why not on spiritual as well? Even without the appearance of any new ailments in Margaret, it was enough for him to know that she had long plagued the community and thus threatened its salvation. Besides, they were convalescing well without her.

But a few small triumphs had made this flurry of defeats less onerous to her. To Margaret's delight, and notwithstanding the coolness of Van der Wiel, Bouckaert and the archbishop together began to push for the kind of reforms she had long put forward. Boonen visited Bethlehem in July 1625, Margaret knew with unmistakable satisfaction, to put an end to abuses at the grille—abuses not begun under Adriana, but not solved by her either. In the spring of 1626 came the dean, and then in June Boonen again, with the intent to bring about reform in Bethlehem from top to bottom. It was on this blissful day that he not only called upon

Mater, as expected, but visited Margaret in her guest room as well. Did he explain at this time that a move to another house was unlikely? We cannot say. But if Margaret held any resentment toward Boonen for faltering on this point, it never surfaced. Indeed, within months of this visit she became the strongest supporter of Boonen's intent to usher in reform. There are no explicit statements from Margaret to suggest how it happened, but recall hints from earlier years that Margaret was always keen to notice faults—this was mentioned in the 1616 interviews and in letters of Catharina Rijckeboer, and was implicit in the reforms that Margaret and Bouckaert had urged jointly from Scherpenheuvel in 1624. Perhaps Margaret and the archbishop simply and coincidentally shared the same vision, or perhaps her energy for reform was simply a way to get back at her enemies. More likely both figured in. However the dynamic worked, and however aware Margaret was of her possible motivations, her concern for her own plight and her zeal for reform became virtually one. Any criticism of the status quo not only satisfied Margaret's desire for reform but soothed her scorched ego and improved her chances of returning to the community.

The word "reform" had many meanings in Margaret's Catholic world. Thanks to the seemingly all-encompassing Council of Trent this became a general age of reform, but Trent was only one banner Margaret had in mind, since its basic requirements for female religious—especially the renewed enforcement of strict cloister—had long been accepted by the women of Bethlehem. She and her sisters could look as well to a venerable tradition of reforms within monasticism itself: reform in the sense of stricter adherence to an existing rule (Cluny in the tenth century or "Observant" reforms of the fourteenth), in the emergence of brand-new monastic families (Franciscans and Dominicans in the thirteenth century, Jesuits in the sixteenth), or in the branching off of an existing order (the Capuchins of the sixteenth century). There were more specific reforms as well: reform of a single house, of behavior at a grille or door, of communal property, of finances, and so on.

Clearly reform meant (and still means) different things. Generally speaking, we might say that the most common tendencies included a desire to return to something pristine and undiluted, a stricter observation of existing standards, or the establishment of something new and creative. Catholicism in this age was long known for the first two, essentially conservative kinds of reforms. Nevertheless, in retrospect the creative side has become ever more clear—partly in the zealous system-building evident in doctrine and programs, partly in the flexible, varied approaches permitted to different places and institutions. Both the conservative and the creative elements were present in Bethlehem. There was the stricter discipline promoted by Boonen and the nuns who supported him most enthusiastically, and, just as important, there was the de facto flexibility in the debate that broke out in the convent after his efforts began. Some standards, such as chastity and cloister, were simply closed to debate, even if the latter was periodically challenged. But the spirit and practice of particulars, even regarding the vows, were often "to be determined later." In Bethlehem we see reform being worked out by real people of contrary opinions, people with different priorities and differing interpretations of the proper religious life. And just as in most human endeavors, personal relationships—along with other ingredients that will emerge as we go—would affect the final outcome as much as the virtues of this abstract idea or that. It was a process that must have occurred, in different mixtures, in a thousand other communities as well.

For now we must know only that Margaret soon became one of the leading debaters on the issue of reform. Though before 1628 her opinions were expressed quite briefly, it was already apparent that to her reform meant more conscientious observation of the order's rule and especially of the new set of long-promised, long-awaited statutes issued by Boonen in August 1626, compiled soon after his fact-finding mission in June of the same year. There, in unilluminated but glorious manuscript, were twenty-two chapters on Worship, the Grille, Punishments, the Office of Mater, Profession, and on down the usual ladder of topics in conventual life. As significant to Margaret as the changes evident between these and past statutes was the fact that Boonen had sent a message of renewal and warning: If Mater held the keys of the convent, she also bore the responsibility for its problems.

Besides some satisfaction in the area of reform, Margaret felt increased hope about her own condition—despite the disappointment of having to stay in Bethlehem. Catharina wrote in 1626 that Margaret gave no further cause for resentment and in 1627 mentioned her "delight" with Margaret's "reasonable contentment." Even Mater Adriana, in March 1628, spoke hopefully: "Margaret Smulders has been quiet; if it lasts long it will work to our salvation." Margaret had to admit that things had improved but were still far from perfect. Her Augustinian confessor lasted a couple of years. Archbishop Boonen's attempts to reenlist Evangelista as her spiritual director never worked out. (Evangelista was busy helping to establish a new convent in Teruuren, toward Brussels.) A recent Jesuit had embarrassed Margaret by rarely showing up to confess her. Then in February 1628 she wrote to her protector, Bouckaert, pathetically stating that forgiveness was not for her and hinting that her troubles at night threatened to reappear. At this time she also asked for, as consolation, a painting of St. Joseph. Perhaps such a request was of no special significance, given Joseph's wide popularity;

but if she was thinking of his most famous gifts of patience and especially sexual continence, then there was larger meaning and evidence of dejection.

Still, Catharina and Mater Adriana were quite correct: Margaret was doing better. At some time after that miserable period in early January 1625, and despite her worries in early 1628, Margaret ceased to be afflicted by demons. She also ceased worrying to the point of incapacitation about the old events with Henri Joos. Was recovery due to further counseling with Bouckaert? New, willful, hard-earned resolve? Increased attention from Boonen? Although we can't know the definitive answer, it may well have been tightly connected to her zest for reform. This new cause may have preoccupied her, taken her mind off her old troubles—even offered a way to solve them. Or, since she was now healed, she had time to pay attention to an old favorite matter. Whichever represented chicken or egg, this time around Margaret was not debilitated or rendered desperate by bouts of discouragement; now she could put her full energies into reform.

Especially since the issuance of the new statutes, Margaret had come to disagree mightily with how the sisters of Bethlehem, especially the leading faction, were interpreting both the general reforms of 1626 and more narrow, subsequent reforms (such as those issued in November 1627 to improve behavior at the grille). There were no gross violations of basic monastic standards, but by early 1628 she saw more transgression, in letter and spirit, "than ever before." Her first observations to the archbishop, made in February, seemed almost reluctant. Margaret feared that by saying too much she would anger Mater, who would inevitably turn her wrath on Catharina or anyone else suspected of telling secrets to ecclesiastical superiors. "I see that anyone who tries to bring in something good is [Mater's] enemy, and she speaks harshly about how she'll teach her subjects as she sees fit." But Margaret grew more courageous as the prospect of yet another episcopal visitation was added to her expanding opportunity, longstanding motive, and enhanced clarity. Such visitation by the archbishop or his men always meant safety, at least in theory—for all sisters were involved in the telling, all were obliged to speak truly, and Mater was forbidden to punish or threaten anyone for what was revealed. Mater usually suspected the identity of the freest speakers anyway, but a visitation was relatively more secure and also offered real hope of change.

Perhaps because of Margaret's short letter of February 1628, which sketched the convent's problems (but which asked that no action be taken for the moment), or for other unknown reasons, the machinery at the episcopal palace started up within a few months, leading toward just what she and several others had requested: full-scale visitation. This is

The Black Sisters of Mons Receive Their Statutes,
1543 miniature.

when Margaret decided to begin her incomparable account and to tell almost all.

After making as many as forty-three different entries during that period of composition in May and June, Margaret abruptly finished her letter for the visitation, as if she had decided to write until the moment that the visitor showed up and called "stop." At some point as she worked or sipped her soup, or as she finished and realized for the first time the immensity of her creation, she might have broken her usual somberness to chuckle at the irony that on first arriving in the convent she had been unable to write at all.

11. FAVORITES

Diminish not a word.
—JEREMIAH 26:2

"MOST REVEREND LORD, if we had a Mater who was a lover of true religious life, observing and enforcing the praiseworthy statutes and wise ordinances of your reverence, given through the Holy Spirit, then there would be no need for any of us to trouble and burden your reverence with all these silly problems, for it's certainly within her powers to improve things if she pleased to do so." Thus the opening, characteristically prolonged salvo of Margaret's onslaught. It was one she fired with some variation, much repetition, and excessive passion throughout.

We won't read Margaret's letter straight through, for it was never intended to be a model of classical structure. "I fear that on some matters I've repeated myself," she readily admitted. Yet if we arrange or summarize it as the archbishop and his aides soon would, into a neatly organized, passionless laundry list of subjects, we obscure her different moods and emphases—her sin of repetition becomes a virtue when it reveals the intensity of her feeling. So we order Margaret's peregrinations a bit, by identifying three broad themes in her forty-three sessions, or entries: (1) Mater Adriana worried more about her power within the convent (2) and pleasing those without (3) than she did about monastic discipline—and her example in each area moved many to imitation. But as we go along imposing this order we must keep in mind the context of a given entry, something we can attain in part simply by noting its place in the letter as a whole.

We should also remember that the topics reviewed by Margaret were hardly new in monastic life. Even many of her most specific revelations sprinkle the documents of hundreds of other convents. What she did better than anyone else, however, was to leave us a work without seams. Put another way, she conveyed the texture and detail of monastic living within a cohesive picture, a picture more compelling and lifelike than one constructed from disparate pieces of evidence to illustrate "general trends." Instead of composite scenarios and personalities and motivations, drawn from dozens of convents, instead of treating issues in monasticism as if they had a separate existence from the people who experienced them, Margaret offered a complete cast of full-bodied

106

First page of the visitation letter of Margaret Smulders, 1628.
The underlining is probably the work of Archdeacon Van der Wiel,
to whom Margaret handed her letter at the visitation, and who eventually
made a summary of the whole.

characters—including herself—who mixed together their personal biases with lofty spiritual ideals as easily and half-consciously as one mixes a drink.

Finally, let us note that Margaret addressed this letter specifically to Archbishop Boonen—and not merely because Boonen was the ultimate superior of Bethlehem. Most sisters didn't bother to address their letters at all, but wrote them generally, for the eyes of whichever ecclesiastical official happened to be assigned to visit. That Margaret chose Boonen as her audience was due in part to her having begun the letter so soon before the visitation, so that it wasn't yet clear just exactly who would head the delegation to Bethlehem, and in part to her hope that Boonen would visit in person rather than send a representative. She was fully aware, however, that Boonen's overflowing schedule made it impossible for him to handle every visitation himself; since he had already come to Bethlehem recently, in 1625 and 1626, the odds of his coming this time around dwindled further. If, as was likely, Boonen decided to send a representative, then Margaret knew very well that the latter would read her letter first. But during this entire process she clearly pinned her hopes directly on the archbishop.

THE PRIDE OF ADRIANA TRUIS

However Margaret's comments are organized or approached, what always rings through is that Adriana was to blame for the convent's troubles. In theory, any Mater was ultimately responsible for what went on. But Margaret went beyond indirect liability, alleging that Adriana consciously and pugnaciously ruled by her own passion rather than out of respect for law, custom, ecclesiastical authority, and the Holy Spirit. "If something does not suit her then it's in vain to decree at all, if it's against her taste, as we see now in many points not observed." It was a will that developed long ago and would not easily bend, wrote Margaret, for Adriana rose to office "when just a child" (2)* and never learned the art of vanquishing personal desire. Even when bursaress alone, she "lorded it over the Maters. It's no wonder that she now does whatever she wants; previous Maters were always dancing to her tune, and couldn't have the smallest thing without being treated like little children. I can't begin to count how many tears I saw those women shed because of her; she was a princess in the convent before most of us were here" (1).

With these claims Margaret implied that the sisters fulfilled the obedience and reverence they owed to Mater. This would assume that when passing before Adriana the sisters all bowed, and when she entered a

*Parenthetical numbers indicate from which letter-writing session the quotations come.

room they stood or bowed; that when Adriana commanded or punished them, they humbly inclined and thanked God for his gift; that they regarded the house as Noah's ark, having but one helmsman and one door; and that they told their bodies "you shall be as a mule, for the mule goes where it's led, and carries heavy burdens, bearing the blows that are given it, and against all these pains it is silent." We are to assume as well that "each, whoever she may be," carried herself "with all reverence toward Mater, in her presence with respectful words, with silence as she speaks or as she desires to speak . . . and with reverential speaking of her when she's not present." Adriana would have scoffed at the notion that such deference existed in Bethlehem, but her turn to accuse will come later. For now, what matters is that in Margaret's eyes, Mater did as she pleased and ignored all counsel. There was thus no hope for redress of Adriana's misdeeds except through the archbishop himself.

One of the most damaging consequences of Adriana's egocentric rule was her natural tendency to play favorites—and, therefore, nonfavorites. "It would be well if [Mater] truly had a common, motherly love for each," observed Margaret, "otherwise there's alienation through murmuring, factionalism, resentment, gossip, little respect, much evil speaking" (1). Here Margaret tapped into a precept of monastic life that had deep roots and wide branches: Special friendships in a convent hindered a common charity. Though an old idea, such charity was forever hard to achieve. Teresa had only recently worried about favorites in her new convent in Spain. And while pregnancies and other occasional scandals in the convents of Lille (in the southwest Spanish Netherlands) were damaging enough, the most frequent and serious crime here as in other places was partisanship. In the archdiocese of Mechelen there is evidence that, though not the most frequent topic in visitation decrees, favoritism was one of the most detested. Van der Wiel and Boonen denounced in a 1632 visit the "plague against sisterly love," while the fresh 1626 statutes of Bethlehem required Mater to eschew partiality, to rule "more through love than fear," to admonish sharply and strictly as the transgression required, regardless of person. Sisters were warned, interestingly enough in the section on silence, not only to "avoid gossip as a shameful sin" but also that special friendships "are the source of much unrest, ill feeling, gossip, and such faults." Each was to "seek to bear and love her sisters equally," and when two nuns met each was to bow slightly, with one saying "Jesus" and the other "Maria."

Despite these exhortations and other small rituals designed to promote sisterhood, special friendships developed—and Maters were often at the center of them, wittingly or not. A Mater might deliberately lead a faction, or (as we saw with Mater Barbara Noosen) an opposing faction might use Mater as a target of all their complaints. The opponents often took another willing or unwilling player as leader, with the most obvious and natural rival of any Mater being her chief helper, the vicaress. Sometimes division was simply one generation against another, or women of one social rank against others—but again, Mater was often in the middle. As Professor Judith Brown has noted, when nuns entered the convent they brought with them preconceptions—about rank, loyalty, and economic position—that did not mesh easily with "institutional rules of obedience and humility." Add to these individual preferences for this style or that personality, and the dreaded monastic disease of factionalism was often the result.

THE UNFAVORED

In Bethlehem, according to Margaret, factionalism began with Adriana. She was no passive observer, no reluctant leader, no helpless target of attacks. The person Adriana happened to dislike most was Margaret's friend Catharina, who as vicaress should have been Mater's closest advisor. When Vicaress tried mildly to exhort Mater or pass on complaints from other sisters, the latter "gives Vicaress an answer that's scandalous for a superior." Margaret would have known that in some other third-order houses the vicaress was even given the name "co-mother," or "Mother Martha," and that everywhere in Mater's absence Vicaress was to be obeyed as Mater herself—a status that only confirmed the seriousness of Adriana's lack of respect. Margaret informed the archbishop that most of the time, "In order to maintain peace, Vicaress is compelled to silence and to allow Mater her own way, just as we have been compelled to silence; and so are we compelled to seek refuge in your reverence, and pray humbly that you will see fit to mark our situation well and improve it as you are directed by the Holy Spirit" (1).

By using "we" Margaret suggested that she spoke for many unhappy sisters, but clearly she was most concerned about Catharina herself. Mater "is so proud that she listens to no one and asks advice of no one, but she says only that Vicaress pays heed to marvelous gossip." According to Margaret, Vicaress, and for that matter the entire community, had lived through many disasters with Adriana, which is why they now all hoped for "that which Mater fears most greatly: namely, visitation. Mater even says that Vicaress won't be content until she's Mater herself, then she may rule as she pleases," an assertion that Margaret strongly denied. "Vicaress has a very great desire to be set free from her office; I'd certainly grant her the rest, and [such a request] doesn't surprise me, speaking both of rest for her soul and body, for Mater can't bear her." Indeed, continued Margaret, Catharina not only possessed no taste for

power, but was restricted whenever she tried to rightly exercise her
office. "It was vain to name a vicaress here, for she may not do the
smallest thing, but instead she must endure much from Mater, even
behind her back, in ridicule. She isn't regarded well by the community,
and that's Mater's fault; she overrules her without cause in front of all;
whoever wants the friendship of Mater won't dare speak first to Vicaress
nor be seen with her too much; instead [Mater] seeks to alienate all, even
the novices, in fact from the first day that the young ones come to live
here" (1). If true, this situation could only have further humiliated Catharina, since as vicaress she was also automatically novice mistress.

Margaret cared about this situation with the novices because it not
only diminished Catharina's authority, but reflected Mater's constant
efforts to win the hearts of certain sisters from the moment of entry. If
Mater was successful, Margaret reasoned, she could keep doing things
her way, and the convent would continue to be based on politics rather
than impartial monastic discipline. Except for Mater and the novice mistress, the sisters of Bethlehem were not allowed to speak alone with
novices, nor to admonish them in their faults, so that their training
would be singular and they would be unrecruitable. However, this ex-
clusivity also made Mater and Vicaress the most likely potential objects
of the loyalty of the new nuns—and here again Margaret denounced
Adriana's political motives. "[Mater] often speaks two hours long with
the novices, and if Vicaress commands or forbids them something,
Mater will tell them the opposite." Adriana worked to win the young
ones not only directly, but through her creatures as well. She appointed
Anna Vignarola "to teach the young ones" how to sing the Office, thus
diminishing Catharina's authority, and yet, Margaret complained,
"[Anna] is the most unsuitable of all, and was appointed for no other
reason than to pull the young ones to her." Mater told Catharina that
Anna would perform this task for two weeks only, but it had persisted
for eighteen months (1). Now, Margaret wrote, "Vignarola is much
freer in calling and commanding the novices than Vicaress, thanks to
the great blind love that Mater bears for her. She thinks that there is no
one more able with the novices than Vignarola, though she is certainly
the most unlearned and the most coarse of manner and as cliquish as
it's possible to be in the convent." What a disgrace, thought Margaret,
that Vicaress should be "snapped at by the youngest professed," or that
behind Vicaress's back Anna "dares to say that Vicaress is but a marvelous fishhead. And she has no reason to speak thus, for [Vicaress] speaks
ill of no one and does no one no evil" (2).

Another means Mater used to win over the "children," or the young
postulants and novices, contended Margaret, was to spoil them. Mater
allowed the young ones, as well as the professed nuns, to "do even more

than she would like so that they'll complain about her less" (2). Catharina engaged in no such pandering. "If Vicaress could exercise and teach them as she desires, we'd make some pretty fair religious out of them in time. But she breaks her head in vain" (39).

Margaret continued on and on with her defense of Catharina, but we'll note only the final blows. "Mater and Vicaress are of such contrary humor that it pains me. I don't know how we'll live in this situation, to leave Mater and Vicaress in their current positions. It has no great virtue." What Mater truly sought, in Margaret's worst dream, was the removal of Catharina as Vicaress and the appointment of Anna Vignarola—but if that occurred "it will become a sorry convent indeed" (2).

The second object of Adriana's displeasure was Maria Coninxloo, whom Adriana thought to be in league with the disdained vicaress. Indeed, it was these two whom Adriana suspected as the archbishop's chief sources of negative information about the convent. Before the whole community Mater heaped scorn and barbs upon both women, "and thus they are now hated by many others as well. Mater is so full of ill-will that when she sees two or more sisters talking together who are not of her people, she suspects that they are conspiring with one another over what to say in the next visitation. . . . She says straight out, 'what council is held here?' when the others had no such ill intent. . . . It's hard to express how worried she gets about Sister Maria and still others" (1).

Several sessions later Margaret explained one of the most visible ways by which Mater expressed her particular dislike of Maria. Instead of seating the women in choir according to seniority of profession or age, as was customary everywhere, "she has Sister Maria Coninxloo sitting on the same side of the choir with the young ones, and yet there are five younger than she. After much complaining, [Mater] finally placed someone beneath [Maria], namely the youngest novice!" It appeared to Margaret that Mater had tried "to stifle Maria's passions"—a basic goal of monastic life—"in one fell swoop," yet "Mater is greatly influenced by her own passions, and she raises up those she likes best; in a word, she's full of herself. She can't stand Sister Maria, for no other reason, as far as I can see, except that [Maria] is curious and observes everything, and that she occasionally writes it all to your reverence." Adriana knew that Maria was writing the archbishop, explained Margaret, because those who carried the convent's letters—usually the lay sisters—often whispered the fact to Mater. There was also the time that Sister Anna Vignarola overheard Maria uttering a few indiscreet words, which were immediately told forward to Adriana and remained "stuck in Mater's head." The result, according to Margaret, was that Adriana now warned all to "beware of Sister Maria as of a serpent, that she passes everything along to the superiors. . . . She fears that Maria will be heard, and not without reason" (4).

Margaret offered some indirect advice to Maria on the latter's unfortunate situation. "I myself find no better rest than keeping quiet and observing unobserved and then speaking when it's time." This statement sounds odd in light of Margaret's lengthy and severe complaints. Yet in Margaret's own eyes, there was certainly no contradiction, for she complained to few in the convent itself. She preferred to save up her big observations for letters like this, since "otherwise, one injures oneself and others." Perhaps Margaret exaggerated. Perhaps she refrained from criticizing in person because she rarely had the chance to speak with anyone from within the convent; Catharina was her only regular caller. But whether Margaret followed her own advice as strictly as she claimed, it's clear that her energy to accuse on paper never waned. On this question of the out-of-favor in Bethlehem, let us conclude with two final thrusts. "Mater is as double-hearted as anyone I've ever seen walk the face of the earth" (4). Or, "I say that there's no religious in this convent who is a greater respecter of persons, no one who is more full of passion" (2). Like the old medieval knights, Adriana was a scourge to her enemies and fiercely loyal to her friends.

CONFIDANTES

If Margaret expressed deep concern about the fate of Mater's supposed adversaries, she spent even more energy railing against her favorites. "All [Mater's] little friends are in office," protested Margaret in the first session. "Through her great cunning she knows how to twist and shape that which alone she can't do." At the next session Margaret sounded the theme once more, claiming that Mater and friends were "together always, early and late, during Silence, confiding in each other; the smallest word can't be said in private but that Sisters Maria Joos, Vignarola, and Lesken Joos run right to Mater and repeat it, especially if it's something that displeases them, and the opinion of those three is immediately the opinion of Mater as well." This kind of favoritism was repugnant enough, but it almost compelled Mater to allow these sisters great freedom. "They've become so bold that they lord it over everyone, and all that they don't dare say they get across with their smirks." If Mater knew something confidential about a sister either through the confessor or by other means, "we know it straightaway by the countenance of those to whom Mater has passed it on." Mater could smirk herself, for she had "a very ugly practice of casting silly ridicule and barbs into the wounds of those who cause her most trouble. . . . Her heart is so full of bitterness toward some that it often spills out. It's all a want of love" (2).

Most offensive of all to Margaret was Anna Vignarola, who, like Adriana, had professed at a young age and soon afterward assumed important office in the convent. Margaret discussed Anna repeatedly. Even when she began by berating Mater's entire coterie, Margaret always seemed to come back to Anna. "Mater is so crazy [for Anna] that in my whole life I have never seen such great love between two alike people [i.e., of the same gender]. They're like love-struck suitors who can't bear to be apart; usually one party loves more than the other, but in this case they are both blind with love, so bowled over. It's no simple favoritism, if you ask me, and it goes beyond them to all they favor; who Vignarola attacks, Mater has by the neck, and so it goes with all the cronies" (1). Though Adriana as Mater was most to blame for this familiarity, the feelings were clearly mutual, asserted Margaret. Anna had claimed publicly that there was "no more able Mater than ours," in regard to promoting a common love, reconciling foes, and in loving even her enemies.

Among Anna's other privileges, if we can believe Margaret, was her freedom to visit the sick in the infirmary, even outside the appointed hours to do so. Here was a place, presided over by another of Mater's creatures, Lesken Joos, where Mater and friends not only enjoyed excessive freedoms but where they also reinforced their already solid bonds. When Adriana lay ill in the infirmary, "then Vignarola must be there too or the scene is incomplete. And when they're not sick, they still aren't much outside the infirmary, at all times, early and late. Oh excessive foolish love! If someone else had ever done things which we must now witness and tolerate, the convent would have stood on end" (2). Halfway through her letter Margaret virtually repeated this charge and then embellished it, claiming that Anna would visit the sick Adriana at least seven times a day, just before or right after each hour of the Divine Office. The same was true if Maria Joos or Lesken Joos or "someone else from her brood" lay ill. And if Vignarola herself was ailing, "then Mater is there with her, like the most anxious mother in the world with her most dear child, as if Mater and the infirmarian had nothing else in the world to do." Yet Mater's great compassion, Margaret quickly pointed out, did not extend to all the sick, just as it did not extend to all the healthy. "Mater says regularly that she'll do for each what she does for one, but God forgive her that we see a different story with our eyes. If Maria Coninxloo or many other sisters I could name were sick, you wouldn't see Mater running to and from the infirmary, and the infirmarian [Lesken Joos] doesn't do much for these others anyway. Even when no one has told me who is sick, I can guess just by how many trips Mater makes to the infirmary; if it's someone she likes, then it's to the doctor, the druggist, the barber, seven maids for one sister sent immediately to the infirmary, however small her affliction, the whole time; others must almost sneak in their medicines and cures" (24).

In the same session Margaret synthesized her feelings about Anna's special relationship with Adriana. "Anyone who wants to test Mater's feelings for Anna need merely say something good about Anna, and Mater will agree with you immediately; she'll transform herself into a loving soul, happiness evident in all her expressions; but say something ill and at once she transforms again, baring her teeth, the face marvelously angry, the words spiteful. . . . She's so angry that it's impossible to write it down." To improve this situation, Margaret thought it a good idea that the two should have less to do with each other. "It's certainly possible to like one person better than another, but too much is forbidden. [Mater] indulges her too much; in a manner of speaking, she has her own little heaven here. I don't think that [Anna] could dream anything up that she doesn't already have."

If Margaret resented Anna because she was privileged and young and able, Margaret disliked Lesken Joos because she was favored, a lay sister, and a relative of Henri Joos. Mater enjoyed the support of almost all lay sisters, but Lesken occupied a special place, partly because of her family and partly because she was Adriana's best link with the outside world. Margaret's spite is evident during her first two sessions of writing: "It's of no need for us to have a lay sister as infirmarian; that should be done by a nun." Next Margaret alleged that "we feed her laziness in [giving her] this [position]; it's a person who doesn't particularly look for work. If there's something to be fetched, some medicine for the sick or something else, she must have a maid do it for her, unless of course it's for Mater, Sister Maria Joos, or Vignarola, then someone else cannot be trusted."

All of Margaret's complaints about Lesken were again grounded in the problem of favorites. So bad was it, and so ungifted was Lesken as infirmarian, that Margaret came back to the subject often and almost demanded that Lesken be removed. Like Mater and Anna Vignarola, Lesken was partial. "She is a respectress of persons," charged Margaret, using as she—and many other contemporaries—often did the feminine form of a noun to refer to a woman. Lesken paid little attention to the unfavored, beyond their barest needs. To compound her sins in Margaret's eyes, "She's also a terrible gossip, painting things as darkly as possible, and announcing in the convent all that the sick do or say. Those not in her good graces she hardly cares for or does little to help them relieve their sickness. Also, if anyone suffers from an embarrassing illness then she does little else but ridicule that person." Margaret condemned the convent as a whole in this regard. "There's a nasty tradition in this convent of poking fun at each other and taunting when there are any

115

secret or embarrassing accidents. Mater tolerates this and even laughs along. I'm ashamed that I've had to listen to some of this talk, and if I were so afflicted I'd rather die than admit it." Finally Margaret turned back to the deficiencies of Lesken alone. "Sister Lesken has a great loathing of carrying or cleaning anything; that which needs doing falls on the shoulders of those for whom she has little affection, and she even complains about them. Everything stinks to her and makes her feel faint, and this causes still more telling of embarrassing details" (22).

Margaret made plenty of complaints about the lay sisters as a group, even closing her letter with a long entry on the topic of their most-favored status. "Mater allows the lay sisters to have the upper hand over the veiled nuns. They concern themselves with even the smallest things. . . . Their chirping, murmuring, and ranting have no end, and they dare reprove the nuns even in the presence of Mater, who actually encourages them and backs them up before the whole community." Vicaress, as might be expected given what Margaret suggested about the loyalty of the lay sisters to Mater, was a favorite target. "In front of everyone they rise up against the vicaress like snarling dogs, as if they'd tear her to pieces." But whoever their target, the lay sisters dared "to say that which the veiled nuns don't dare say—they dare much. I suppose that there's not a convent in the world where the nuns are so snapped at as here."

That nuns should have been rebuked by their ecclesiastical and usu-ally social inferiors was bad enough to Margaret, but just as bad was the lack of respect the lay sisters showed in carrying out their assigned tasks. For instance, if the nuns asked them to run an errand outside the con-vent, "they growl at us so that we wish we'd never asked them to begin with; and when they return home with less than we'd asked, we keep quiet, or they say to us 'go get it yourself,' " which for a veiled nun was of course out of the question. "They're such costly traders that it's amaz-ing; we'd do as well if we sent children. If they buy for you and don't like you, they're not choosy at all, no matter how bad the item." Another sign of disrespect offered by Margaret was how the lay sisters irrever-ently poked fun at the contemplative regime of the nuns. "They make fun of things pertaining to choir and the Office. . . . Many of them impudently say that the nuns are but ladies, that they do nothing except hold a book in their hands." Such freedom to ridicule was possible only because of the close connection between the lay sisters and Mater. "Even if you commanded Mater to admonish them, she wouldn't do it. And if she did do it, out of obedience, she would do it only once and the next day they'd be back at it again." To Margaret, the archbishop's personal intervention seemed the only way to cure their impertinence. He should "reprove these lay sisters personally, in the presence of Mater and the vicaress, warning them not to chastise, harp, or otherwise, and not to trouble themselves with matters pertaining to the nuns alone." He should urge them to return to their appointed duties and to carry them out faithfully, rather than tolerate their small-hearted service. "They shouldn't go sit in some . . . place all together and make a gossip-house."

HAVES AND HAVE NOTS

As consequential in Margaret's eyes as the emotional and political favoritism fostered by Adriana were the tangible consequences: unequal distribution of the convent's precious goods. If all sisters were decently cared for, argued Margaret in her opening session of writing, then they would not complain; "We don't carry anything with us anyway [when we die]." But care was wanting, and the justifiable complaining that ensued was as much about favoritism as material needs and wants. Margaret began to show that for some in the convent to prosper, others must suffer. "All that we need we must get ourselves. For clothing, the convent gives us nothing, but those who've brought annuities with them have hose and shoes and even sometimes nice clothing, especially those who stand in the good graces."

Here Margaret reveals that as in most other houses of the time, a practical distinction existed in the temporal treatment of the nuns. The challenges of temporal existence will be reviewed in detail in the next chapter, but for now it's important to note how those challenges could be influenced by partiality. Most houses tried to support their members by a combination of endowments from friends, income from work, and annuities brought by the nuns at entry. In the ideal monastic environment, interest and income were to have been pooled in order to provide support to all the nuns in a given convent. But these sources were chronically insufficient and unequal. It became common practice, at this period and others—despite prohibitions by Trent, the zeal of many idealistic houses full of the communal spirit, and threats that anyone holding private property would be buried in unconsecrated ground with only dead animals as company—for individual sisters to support themselves with private annuities. To observe the letter of the vow of poverty, it was necessary to have these funds administered by Mater, but they were still largely for the individual sister's use. Lesken Nijns had brought a 50-florin annuity with her back in 1606; it was said that Anna Vignarola brought the same amount in 1624; and in 1628 the parents of Susanna Haechts also offered the magic sum of 50 florins a year, plus a one-time gift of 300 florins. (That the 50 florins pops up again and again suggests that this was the bare minimum for entry by the 1620s.) This kind of system, which to women like Margaret at best hindered the communal spirit and at worst constituted a breach of the vow of poverty, served to promote two different levels of material culture.

In this context, and in a series of strong accusations early in the letter, Margaret accused Mater of seeing to the wants of her own, while denying the wants and needs of others: "Mater knows well how to provide for those in her fold. . . . Part of the convent flourishes, the other has to look like simpletons." Most offensively, Margaret revealed, "when someone's about to die, then they start to haggle over what's left behind. . . . Mater can hardly wait until the soul has left the body to start handing out the goods, in the same way that lay people treat death so as to get the goods. The infirmarian [Lesken Joos] doesn't wait until they're dead, but starts going through everything; she can't do wrong." Besides such dramatic breaches of charity, Mater provided for her supporters in more routine ways. "[Lesken Joos] and Sister Vignarola are the only ones entrusted with the keys to Mater's room," Margaret wrote, "but we won't put up with this any longer. All the convent's possessions are in Mater's hands, and no one else is entrusted with them except Sister Lesken Joos, a lay sister, and Vignarola, the youngest professed." Or, recounted Margaret, "During Lent, when there is a great crowd at Collation and at other [meal] times, [Mater] would rather, so to speak, burst than give [Vicaress] the smallest thing, though she sits next to her; and that goes for other sisters too." Between Easter and Pentecost of 1628, Margaret maintained "that three or four days a week we had nothing for our [common] portion at noon except potage and an egg, and at night some milk. During the summer there were many days when we had nothing but some salad and potage at noon, and then again some milk at night."

According to Margaret, those who most needed the convent's provisions, the sick, got no more than the "common portion, unless each buys what she wishes to eat. In eating and drinking, we may not have so much as some white bread or a pint of good beer, even when it's on hand, unless we buy it ourselves." But Margaret observed that Mater herself had never experienced such want. "She has carried the purse for so long she gets what her heart desires. Her cronies don't know poverty either. But in all the years I've lived here, I don't think that I've ever seen the crust of a white loaf of bread, in sickness or health, nor have they ever sewn for me in the convent as much as a handkerchief, but that I've had to pay for it."

As we might expect by now, what especially rankled Margaret was the fine living of Anna Vignarola, in sickness or in health. "She has all her heart desires, piles of things, in secret and in public. And Mater says that she loves all of us the same, and that what she does for one she would do for another. Mater is blind. She sees through windows and doors of foolish love, so it should be forgiven her. Otherwise, I'd say with cause that she tells lies, hurtful lies." The two women shared not only emotions but goods, on a largely exclusive basis. "All that Mater has is Vignarola's too, so free are they." Margaret anticipated Adriana's response to such a charge: As Mater she controlled all the goods in the convent, and it was her charge to administer them. Margaret also guessed that Adriana would use as explanation for seemingly arbitrary treatment of the nuns another viable justification: that as Mater it was her duty to provide temporal necessities, but also to kill desire for temporal excesses. Thus Adriana giveth, and Adriana taketh away. But such reasoning was a cover, contended Margaret. For in killing the desires of others, Adriana fed her own, and those of her confidantes. "It's a fine art she has" is how Margaret summed it up (2).

Another practice that drove the emotional and temporal divisions in the convent especially deep, since they were not routine but by invitation only, was the new custom of private parties. Ostensibly intended as work parties, these get-togethers soon turned into purely exuberant affairs. "The sacristan of the choir, Sister Anna Vignarola, one Monday after Nones enlisted four religious to clean the choir. The next day there were six people to clean, the whole day; and the whole day with whooping, yelling, and ringing that you'd have to hear or see to believe. In the evening, some dishes were prepared for when they finished, an idea of Maria Joos, and then they can all respectably carouse." Margaret described all this with obvious sarcasm, perhaps while running through her mind the customary monastic rules that when talking was allowed it should be reverent and to the point, and that nuns should eat no meals outside the times prescribed, for reasons of self-discipline and community spirit. "And I've noticed that each year the party gets bigger, each wants to show great liberality and good feeling, and through this the group of little friends, or better said the dear ones, increase in number, for with honor they've earned the right to carouse. There were six dishes, by the way; it sorrows me to name them all. There was no want of noise either. They sat there long and very late, like drunks on the beer-bench, and were so giddy that you'd hardly think them religious." As if such parties were not bothersome enough to those within the convent, Margaret informed the archbishop that outsiders heard the noise also, disturbing their peace as well as their good opinion of the nuns (7).

Rather than stopping such occasions, Adriana actually promoted them; again, favoritism in any convent began or ended with the Mater. "These things are brought in more and more everyday, for Mater comes alive with all this, she's always at the party too. Tuesday it was in the choir; then Wednesday five reveling in the refectory, without as many dishes as last time, but with no less noise." Such precise information about the dishes prepared makes us suspect that Margaret got her information from Joanna Schoensetters, the lay-sister cook, with whom she sometimes chatted, and the lone lay sister of the convent's six to be out of favor with Adriana. "Thursday it was the workroom, and there they named one a lady and caroused some more; there were five for a job that took only three. The noise and clamor were as before, in eating and drinking, wholly unsuited. Then Friday, when Mater ought to give her community a good example in not breaking the fast without need, she took four sisters to clean her room, and in the evening she sponsored another get-together for them all, where the manners were as fine as at the others. What they've eaten that night I can't say . . . but they were so tipsy that one of the sisters had to be helped out of the refectory, for she couldn't stand on her own." Margaret's disapproval stemmed from her sense that interior cleaning (a good monastic and regional custom) was made an excuse for fun and games, offered a lucky few the chance to eat a relatively extravagant meal rather than the common portion, and became an opportunity not only to reward those in the good graces of Mater but to recruit other supporters as well.

Indeed, what perturbed Margaret further was that "to all these parties are invited postulants and novices, when we have them. They see and enjoy all this. It's a great scandal, if they leave the convent; having seen and heard such rudeness it must seem that in the convent women do nothing but clean and holler; when they're in the workroom it seems they may do all they please, and show all possible coarseness, from morn until eve, shouting, yelling, gossiping, clamoring, eating, and drinking." The revelers only occasionally came to eat with the others, Margaret went on, and even had the gall to wait until the common meal served in the refectory was complete before barging in themselves "so that they may do as their little wills please." Margaret predicted Adriana's response: These occasions cost the convent nothing, since the participants paid for them out of their own pockets, with permission from Mater. Such a practice was technically legal, allowed Margaret, but it wounded the spirit of monastic living. "Aren't these ugly customs for people in monasteries, that no common work can be done except with carousing? When we share as one, eating together, hushed, that is praiseworthy, but God help those who wish for such nowadays." Bethlehem's unfortunate fate was to be burdened with a mater who "loves to hold frequent small tavern-parties," an offensive practice in Margaret's vision of monasticism. "I hold dear the common life. But I think there are few here who desire such a life. They're much too accustomed to buying all they want, needed or not; they would suppose that someone who denied their request would simply be hardheaded" (7).

Such sentiments as Margaret's help us to understand why in the convent of Bethanie in 1590, the nuns complained that a Sister Lysken received "a large pan of sausage" and "all her bread, beer, and much fish, a special thimble, and a ring" from the prior of the abbey of Affligem. It wasn't merely concern about the spirit of cloister or Sister Lysken's vow of chastity that kindled murmuring. Rather, it was also jealousy that someone in the convent fared better than another. Margaret's complaints also make more clear why in 1592 Archbishop Hovius established in the convent of Thabor laws designed to erase economic distinctions. He outlawed entry fees, and decreed that if anyone received food from outside it should be immediately divided among all, cut into as many small pieces as necessary. These rules were crucial to poor women such as Margaret Smulders. Then again, perhaps Margaret desired the common life due to a genuine spiritual preference and truly wanted to think of food as medicine rather than as spice, as urged by many devotional writers, or believed with still others that there was no higher abstinence than controlling one's stomach at a table full of good food and drink. The problem was, she didn't have a chance to exercise such control because she had no choice—there was no virtue won through externally forced privation. Perhaps she truly wanted to abandon the all-too-human desire for worldly goods. But Margaret and other women of Bethlehem appear to have been no great fans of extreme destitution as a way to greater piety, nor should we expect them to have been. Except for the most ascetic, or those dominated for the moment by worldly excess, most monastic families emphasized moderation, rather than near starvation or gourmandism. Most nuns were not the elite medieval mystics who, as demonstrated by Professors Rudolph Bell and Caroline Bynum, sought every possible way to avoid food. They would not have been imitators—though they were admirers—of such persons as the Franciscan Alcantara, who was said for forty years to have eaten once every three days (herbs mixed with ashes, warm water, and a bit of bread), to have slept one and one-half hours a day, sitting up no less, and to have lived in a cell four and one-half feet long. Nor, on the other hand, were these wealthy nuns in Bethlehem, who required sumptuous fare or pampering. The Grey Sisters were generally of a middling status, and they found no contradiction between a decently stocked larder and good monastic discipline, as long as eating and comfort were not their chief priorities. But the blatant inequality of near-perpetual deprivation for some and plenty for others fell short of even that modest ideal, at least in the judgment of Margaret.

A final manifestation of Mater's less than full heart was her toleration of old stories. Such storytelling was not an uncommon cause of ill-will and division in convents. In 1590, for instance, a Sister Elizabeth of Bethanie, in Brussels, was said to have roused the younger nuns by repeating to them the past misdeeds of the elders; and when the elder nuns chastized the younger, Elizabeth instructed the latter to respond, "You did it, why shouldn't we?" Margaret was not immune from re-hashing ancient events involving others, but in this context she no doubt was complaining about stories that others repeated about her. The only one Margaret mentioned specifically was the affair of "Sister Lesken Nijns, who is now in another convent," an affair that of course touched Margaret as well. "Sometimes," she continued, "they start talking of things which of themselves are neither good nor bad, but then they continue and nothing is kept back; I say that this is the cause of many sins, even if they don't always realize it. Mater herself is often the cause of such talk, and it would be more honest and salvational for her to keep silent, especially since she knows that some things can be said about her [in these matters] as well." Hinting further that Adriana had a shady past of her own, Margaret noted that "others say about her secretly, 'though she's now Mater, she's not the holier for it.' " As part of her program for reform, Margaret asked that all such storytelling be sharply prohibited (40).

Thus it emerges that one of the greatest crosses of the monastic life, as well as one of its highest aims, was to live harmoniously within an area of a few thousand square feet with a few dozen other people, in the realization that such an arrangement could last forever. It was difficult, but as with the attainment of any virtue, it was the difficulty itself that helped to purify. One of the purposes of communal life, besides greater efficiency in providing for temporal necessities, was to serve as a fire in which virtue was forged. In these close quarters, the chances for anger, envy, or indifference were great and the refining fire of sisterly love hottest. Some made it through, some we see struggling along, and some hardly entered the fire at all. We don't see any killings or threats to kill in Bethlehem, or any stabbing with scissors, or the candelabra-swinging of St. Gertrude's, or certainly not the excesses of some medieval male monasteries. We do see love—but not necessarily among or for all. Thus there was rancor enough in Bethlehem, and always the threat of escala-tion. The experienced religious must have recognized that truly com-mon love was to be learned anew with each generation of nuns, indeed with each new individual. Yet in Margaret's eyes, some had little desire to learn, and they would not change unless compelled.

12. ALMSGETTING

IN ADDITION TO ATTACKING ALL FORMS of favoritism within the house, Margaret was deeply concerned about Adriana's displays of favoritism without. Specifically, Margaret revealed in her letter that she preferred to provide for the convent's material needs through the old-fashioned monastic methods of penny-pinching, belt-tightening, and honest, straightforward, spontaneously given alms from pious patrons. But Adriana sought temporal well-being through means that we might label as more modern, or at least more aggressive. She was a believer in vigorous public relations, which consisted mainly of pampering existing and potential benefactors with food, drink, and other privileges in the hopes of stimulating not only generous but relatively predictable alms. It wasn't that Margaret opposed the old monastic custom of hospitality to guests, but that Adriana's program went too far; it cheated the nuns of time for devotion or work, and it plundered the convent's meager goods. Even without the problems this created for discipline, Margaret considered the policy an economic failure, for it was her decided impression that it ended up costing more than it brought in.

We can find solid justification for both Adriana's approach and Margaret's. Each knew that temporal health was the sine qua non of monastic life, an ironic foundation given the vow of poverty. But in most orders by this time—with such notable exceptions as the strictest Franciscans—the vow implied individual, canonical poverty, not corporate, genuine poverty. The convent could therefore hold as much property as it wished, making those in wealthy houses wealthy together, while those in poor houses were poor to the bone. Moreover, even the most ascetic needed some sustenance. The trick was to avoid worrying about the temporal, thereby remaining focused on the most important activity in the monastery, prayer. To do so, one could either ignore physical needs or work to achieve a measure of security.

The last option was the overwhelming favorite in convents, including Bethlehem. The main footing was usually an initial endowment meant to support a certain number of nuns, and to that were added gifts offered by sisters and their families at profession or donations bequeathed by new friends. In return for such generosity the nuns were required to say prayers or perform other devotions. Although this seemed simple enough, serious problems existed from the start. First, nuns could not say Mass, the service most heavily funded and desired by testators. In addition, female convents then had to hire priests to perform Mass, something male monasteries did not necessarily have to do. Moreover, since nuns were forbidden to leave the cloister, they could not walk in processions and increase their visibility to potential donors—a practice in which monks often engaged. All this meant that nunneries tended to be less well off than male establishments, despite the fact that monks did not even bring along a dowry when they entered the religious life. In 1650, for instance, Bethlehem paid 200 florins a year, about 5 percent of the convent's annual income, just for priests to say Mass. But such an amount hardly made a dent in the wealthier, neighboring, male house of St. Gertrude's, which in 1607 included on its roster of employees not only numerous nonreligious servants for individual canons, but bakers, smiths, porters, gardeners, barbers, and apothecaries, two doctors on retainer (since one always seemed to be busy), and steep expenses for horses and carriages, plus the relatively inconsequential salary for the abbot's vicar. The Grey Sisters of Isegem boasted a total annual income of 1,002 florins by the mid-seventeenth century, but this was hardly more than the amount paid at St. Gertrude's for servants alone: 640 florins per annum. It's true that other female convents would fare better in a comparison with St. Gertrude's, and that some male orders were also notoriously poor. But in general it's safe to conclude, as various scholars have for the medieval period, that wealth among female houses was both comparatively and absolutely rare. In fact, though we might also safely conclude that conventual indigence was overall less severe than the temporal hardships in the outside world, many convents existed in a state of perpetual distress or even outright poverty—beyond the canonical version called for.

Natural disasters of war, ruin, and bad management also affected a convent's financial health. Before 1610 the Grey Sisters in Nevele celebrated Mass sometimes in the rain and wind, because soldiers had pillaged their church. Marauding soldiers threatened the sisters of Rosendaal that nothing would be left of their convent save a few beams from which to hang nuns. And the nuns' dormitory in the Cistercian convent of Aarschot collapsed on Christmas day of 1596, thanks in part to weakening by plunderers. Similar hardships were evident in Bethlehem, in the nuns' moving from Mechelen to Leuven, in the convent's continued pleas to the Privy Council for help in its "extreme poverty," in the remarkably frequent and necessary liquidation of capital endowments, or in the incessant complaints among ecclesiastical visitors to Bethlehem about poor record keeping. (At Our Lady-Ter-Rivieren in Bree, in the northeast, the sisters threw a confessor out the door after he chastised them for slipshod accounting.)

Whatever the root of difficulty, it was clear that a convent's endowment alone was usually inadequate and that other sources of income had to be generated. One such source has already been discussed: the individual annuities brought by new sisters. Besides this, a popular and traditional means to raise more funds was the common work, part of a long monastic custom which said that physical labor was good for the soul as well as the body. In spite of decrees that "handmaidens of the lord should avoid very heavy toil," this labor could take many forms, according to what the sisters thought would best engender spirituality and cash. Active orders engaged in care of the sick and aged, hostelry, education, washing, the renting of funeral palls and ornamentation, and of course sewing and handicrafts. Cloistered sisters were nearly as busy, especially with sewing but even with hostelry, child care, washing, and the production and sale of wine, beer, and spirits, thus ignoring recurrent edicts against such undignified moneymakers. The nuns themselves often complained about certain nontraditional tasks, suggesting that they took them on more for money than for the discipline of work. During the 1590s, for instance, the convent of Thabor housed a difficult canon, who, the sisters testified, struck his servant numerous times and once threatened to run him through with a knife, to the "great unrest of the convent." The women were "very glad" when he left, "even if he paid 1,000 florins a year." Boarders could also physically damage the convent, as when some inattentive guests at the Grey Sisters' convent of Velzeke burned the place down. And the White Ladies of Leuven barely stifled their protests against baby-sitting two children of supposedly well-to-do Irish parents. Such arrangements were precisely the reason why certain activities were long regarded as obstacles to the real business of cloistered nuns—praying. But in light of their chronic insufficiency of funds, and despite the ideals of Trent, even the most unpleasant activities continued. In Mechelen, the sisters of Bethlehem took in at least one old woman to help support themselves; and though in Leuven the quest for funds centered on the traditional activities of sewing and craft-making, other less agreeable tasks crept in as well.

On the debit side, convents might help themselves by tightening up and adopting more efficient practices of management, remedies of which Margaret was especially fond. One common technique, though never resorted to in Bethlehem during this time, was to reduce the number of nuns in proportion to the decline in the common endowment or rise in expenses. Convents might also require an even longer list of things a prospective nun must bring with her when she entered the convent, something that was indeed done in Bethlehem.

From all these—common endowment, common work, separate patrimonies, and attention to efficiency—a convent like Bethlehem hoped to get by. Scattered records from the 1640s and 1650s suggest that the house was essentially breaking even at those times, but they do not make clear how many capital funds were depleted in order to maintain this balance, or how much of the income came from emergency gifts and loans. Precisely because convents drained their endowments regularly or never had sufficient funds to begin with, there was always a demand for new alms to fill the gap: big alms that might enlarge the endowment, or one-time gifts in cash or property to be used right away. The most direct way of getting such alms was to go out and ask, as many old begging orders had long done, including the Franciscans. Yet partly because it was considered scandalous for female religious to be out on the streets begging, and partly because the method was too uncertain for the tastes of some, women like Adriana promoted the alternative method that Margaret so despised, the method based on Isaiah's concise dictum "Every one loveth gifts" (1:23). Adriana not only liked and wanted gifts for the convent, but also presumed that to get she had first to give. The fruits of such a policy could be obvious and immediate. Between 1636 and 1639 the Hospital of Vilvoorde was the beneficiary of twenty good deeds rendered by friends on its behalf—from cutting wood and hauling it at no charge, to hauling apples from Antwerp, to the receipt of fish, wine, and materials and labor for a rebuilt barn. Certainly Bethlehem and many other convents hoped for and relied upon such favors; and Margaret knew it, even if she disagreed strongly with how Adriana went about getting them.

THE SERIOUS BUSINESS OF THE GRILLE

Margaret didn't complain about the convent's paltry endowment. She said little about deficiencies in the common work. She protested more vigorously Adriana's unwillingness to share temporal administration. But what troubled Margaret's sensibilities most was a perception that Adriana directly and indirectly solicited alms by catering excessively to outsiders. Most of the subtle soliciting occurred at that small part of the convent so often the object of controversy in convents—the grille through which sisters and visitors spoke to each other in the guest room, or parlor. Many of the best fireworks in Bethlehem about this area had gone off even before the tumultuous visitation of 1628.

Between 1618 and 1624 it was decreed that with few exceptions outsiders were no longer allowed to lodge in Bethlehem's guest rooms; the 1626 statutes stopped once and for all the practice of serving food and drink to outsiders at the grille in the parlor; and to make sure that the sisters knew he was earnest, Boonen in November 1627 issued a special decree reiterating these and other points. Margaret, Catharina, and

Maria Coninxloo were overjoyed, praising the archbishop's decree with the usual argument that serving guests not only encouraged worldliness but also incurred expense. Significantly, Maria went on to reveal the participants in the matter: Opposition to the prohibition came not merely from many of the nuns, but from outsiders who wanted to continue enjoying their visits. Perhaps in Leuven, as in Teresa's Ávila, the lay women expected nuns to act as confidantes in return for moral and financial support. The nuns of Bethlehem, likewise sensing expectations of their own friends, wished not to displease. Thus most "stoked up Mater" to change the archbishop's mind.

Margaret offered in her letter of 1628 even more details about the reaction to Boonen's decrees than had Maria Coninxloo, alleging that many sisters became almost violent. The lay sisters were "as usual . . . ranting and raving like they were out of their senses. Even some of the nuns were ugly about it, with Sister Maria Joos the captain of all; she spoke without reason as if the community had been dealt the most unfair blow humanly possible. She went after the vicaress like a snarling dog intent on the kill," wrote Margaret, repeating as she did in several other places one of her favorite similes. According to Margaret, Maria Joos also said to Mater, " 'If I were you, I'd throw the keys at the bishop's feet and say to him, do it yourself, I can't do it this way; and I'd let him decree and command all day long, but I'd do as I saw fit and throw all his edicts in a pile, and let him pronounce and proclaim to his heart's content, but we will not do it; we'd rather rise up against him, rather leave the convent, than be ruled this way.' " If Margaret was exaggerating, the visitor didn't notice, for he made a big and rare "Note" in the margin.

Such adamance about the grille, that small point of contact between the world and outsiders, was hardly unheard of. When a medieval bishop of Lincoln commanded strict cloister and restricted conversation, nuns of one convent chased him to the gate and threw the official bull at his head. But unique or not, Maria's reaction was intolerable to Margaret. "God grant that the others weren't affected by such a display of disrespect for her superiors," Margaret prayed, "for many thought that she spoke under the influence of the spirit of God, because she appears to be more pious than the others, and she speaks so smoothly that no one is her equal." Margaret admitted that Maria had a good mind, but "her excessive liberality is known well enough. . . . [In times past] when her friends came, even great strangers, then we might as well have hung out a sign and called ourselves the 'Do Drop In' "—a name borne, incidentally, by an establishment right around the corner from Bethlehem—"with all the people who were eating, drinking, and sleeping; she simply can't let go of this, that we can't do as we used to; her complaining knows no end. She gives food and drink to everyone, from high to low, whenever she may or can; she says that the bishop supports us in this and will leave us in peace" (18).

The house confessor, who was sympathetic to the resisters, confirmed at least the essence of Margaret's letter. To all other points the sisters would submit, the confessor informed the archbishop, but beer for their friends they would have. Many asserted that no convent in the world had such a restrictive decree, that in any event they had never abused the practice, and that there should certainly be no penalties attached. Most telling, however, was their reasoning: The nuns wanted their freedom at the grille not for the sake of recreation, but because they were paupers and had better reason than "fat abbeys" to seek alms. Here explicitly was the assumption that in order to receive alms, one had to treat almsgivers with proper respect. Some friends who came bearing alms were "rustics," obviously thirsty after a long journey, and many nuns believed that the convent could not afford to offend them. The prevalence of such a belief among nuns also appears in a note by Bishop Triest about the convent Syon, in Oudenaarde. According to Triest, the convent's confessor was given to drink—not by nature, but because the nuns knew no better way to please their friends and patrons than to fill them with wine. And clearly assumptions within the convent were not the only force at work. Outsiders had expectations too, and expressed them so strongly that even Catharina would eventually urge Boonen to rescind the decree, if only for the sake of peace.

At the time of the 1628 visitation, the decree was still formally in place. Most said nothing about it, as if the nuns had finally been reconciled, and Adriana passed it off by noting that only the occasional glass of beer was given to an unmistakably thirsty outsider. Margaret saw things much differently. In her view, Maria Joos, Mater Adriana, and Anna Vignarola continued to wait upon the convent's friends as actively as ever, despite warnings to leave them dry.

THREE SPECIAL FRIENDS

Of all the visitors who came to Bethlehem at this time, probably the most important was Henri Joos. Even by 1628, according to Margaret's epistle, we see that Joos, though living now in distant Mol, was still a major figure in Bethlehem, not only because of his alms and his affability at the grille, but as the still-strong cornerstone of factionalism.

Though all Mater's friends were devoted to Henri Joos, Anna Vignarola stood out. Just after saying that Anna thought Mater the wisest woman on earth, Margaret described Anna's equally strong opinion of Joos. As Margaret told it, Anna felt "that there is nowhere to be found an equal to the pastor of Mol, nor will there ever be, in holiness, wisdom, discretion, love, mercy, and all virtues, that in our lives we have never enjoyed such an exceptional confessor and preacher as he, nor will we ever enjoy, and that we were the luckiest persons ever born when he served us." Further, said Margaret in her vivid prose, Anna believed that those who had said otherwise "deserve to have a red-hot iron through their tongues, and merit punishment now and hereafter." Anna was even so brazen as to wonder "what judgment those now dead have earned, the bishop [Hovius] as well as others who were involved."

While on the topic of Joos, Margaret explained her own feelings for the still-visiting ex-confessor, the first time she had done so since the unpleasant occurrences of years past. (Incidentally she referred to Joos always by his title only, the pastor of Mol.) Margaret admitted that he was not devoid of goodness, "for he in fact shows much virtue and mercy, and his countenance and deeds are good; especially the last time (not the very last) that he was here, was I surprisingly edified." This probably referred to a sermon that Joos had delivered, for we can ill imagine that Margaret would have held a private conversation with him. "But in regard to his past holiness, only they know who experienced it as it actually was, and they're not all dead who know what happened, though they can well remain silent and praise him so highly so as to play the game and keep the peace." This tantalizing but vague sentence is followed by another, which probably referred to Vignarola: "She would do much better to keep quiet; if she had lived here during that time, then she'd have some right to speak." Margaret explained that Anna was still years away from entering Bethlehem at the time Joos was confessor, and yet Anna now felt qualified to praise him and lament that he was wronged. "Sister Anna Vignarola speaks alone with him regularly; it seems she can't miss him, whenever he comes. She sends him frills yearly; and in gratitude, and because she's the special one of Mater, he sends her money, and in this she also pleases Mater. Who wants to be friends with Mater speaks and gives to him; the more it is, the more she likes it, and not only to him but all his friends" (1).

Here we see more explicitly the linking of inside friendships to outside friendships, and the often related hope for alms. It was still said in Bethlehem, relayed Margaret, that Maria Joos's "dear brother . . . served us for nothing, and that he gave 100 florins a year for his meals; but it would be to our ruin to have such a one again, [for] even if he gave 200 florins a year, he wouldn't be able to cover all that was consumed. In the first place, he used all the linen of the guest room, sheets, napkins, towels, beds, and all such things." With this and similar references to distant events, Margaret revealed the great depths of her resentment, since the visitation letter was supposed to discuss recent happenings only. "Rarely," she continued, "was he without guests of his own, people from his quarter on business, who stayed here for months and the convent had to provide their board. His friends were always here, one or the other. The nuns in his fold were invited to dine with him twice every week, and stayed there the whole day banqueting, singing, and making noise." Joos's guests stayed well into the night, and if any of the nuns complained about it, those most attached to him "ran right to him in disbelief, mouth gaping, and repeated it, for he made them gossips. And then he also spoke very nastily about those not in his grace, which after all was very ugly for a confessor, for it brought great oppression of conscience. And people complain that we lost so much." To Margaret, it was no loss at all to be rid of a man with whom it was required "to play and frolic," or who was so free in the convent that he was familiar with the nuns' cells and refectory, areas off-limits to outsiders. "Though he often gives us gifts, he still owes us. Even if he gave us half his goods, it wouldn't be repayment enough, in soul and body, he knows that well!" (18).

After Joos the house's most important friend, and thus another receiver of gifts, was someone Margaret identified as the "Woman In Den Luypaert," or In the Leopard, the name of a house around the corner from the convent, which may well have been a tavern or a brewery. This woman happened to be (probably not coincidentally) friends with certain nuns of Bethlehem and with Henri Joos. Margaret never mentioned this connection explicitly, but Joos's will names a person from the house "In den Luypaert" in Leuven; we wonder which outside party was first in contact with Bethlehem and who did the introducing of the other.

Margaret complained about this woman and her family nearly as much as she did about Henri Joos. "[Mater] is more concerned for the people In the Leopard than for her own convent and religious. Every day the [lay] sisters go there, sometimes two or three in a day, not only when she's in childbed," a time according to Margaret when the woman's appetite was especially keen, "but year out year in, never too early or late, whatever high feast day it may be or whatever we have to do ourselves." Margaret admitted, and Mater would respond, that the woman "sometimes gives us portions of beer and meat and other things. But we do as much kindness for her as possible, and have never really had any extraordinary gift from her, small or large," suggesting again that Mater's temporal policy was a failure. "She's very well cared for, and all that Mater and others can imagine or dream up, they make for her, whether something fancy to eat or some frill, all that they can invent to give her children. Nothing is too much for Mater if it's for that house. It's not possible for me to write everything I know on the subject, but everything Mater can do in secret she does, as quietly as possible, which we know only because outsiders are amazed, saying that we're not so poor after all if Mater can give such gifts to the children." Margaret went on to repeat more than once her worries about such giving, showing that she too was concerned about public relations, but in a way different from Adriana. If people thought them rich, then how many fewer alms would be given? But Adriana, according to Margaret, cared most about the perceptions and comfort of a group of select friends on whom she relied for a steady, regular source of alms rather than the judgment of the less predictable general public.

And so Adriana gave and gave. Margaret concluded that, despite Mater's bragging about all the kindnesses received from the Woman in the Leopard, "if it were all piled together they'd be more bound to us than we are to them." Margaret wondered what other convents did with overindulged patrons. "One or two or three times is fine, but always cooking and smuggling for her, now some pork, then a tart, cottage cheese, flan made in the dish, an apple spiced with wine and sugar, and so many other things that I don't know how to write it all. I see it all prepared, more than the others. Mater would say that the woman provides the goods, but it's like the old saying, 'Who sets the table has the greatest expense.'" Besides the temporal inconvenience, Margaret emphasized that the woman exerted a bad spiritual influence as well. "It's a woman who's full of gossip and complaining, and brings in much back-stabbing concerning one's name and honor, in regard to her maids as otherwise" (5).

The third major patron-guest was the house steward. Most convents had a layperson who represented them in worldly affairs, "diligently promoting and defending and overseeing, as a good faithful steward is obliged and ought to do." Such a person usually oversaw the collection of commonly held rents and annuities and the running of the convent's lands and farms, and was to make an accounting of all this to the convent and the archbishop's representative, usually the dean. For these services he naturally received a fee. Given his powers, and potential value as a long- or short-term benefactor, it was important to get on with the steward. Certainly he could be let go if the sisters were dissatisfied, but such a process could be long and costly. Moreover, if offended, an unscrupulous steward could cause damage, even when released.

The steward of Bethlehem was, in Margaret's eyes, more a consumer of the convent's goods than a defender. "I'll tell you this," she wrote, "I wouldn't let him eat here any more than anyone else, for this reason: [The sisters] all say, 'he's the convent's friend, we are the convent's children, thus our friends are the convent's friends, and they may eat a bit here as well.' But the steward is an expensive steward." Besides his high fees, explained Margaret, the man had a ravenous appetite. "When he comes he announces it well in advance, and the preparations commence as if he were a prince. To begin, he has the heel of a ham, a piece of spiced meat, seasoned mutton, all as costly as possible, a bit of *Hutsepot* [a kind of stew with good beef], and anything else they can dream up or lay their hands on. He devours it all, and is so ill-mannered about it that they don't dare serve anyone else before him. He usually stays long, five, six, eight days before leaving, and is so unspeakably delicious that nothing can be made for him that is too fine. He'd probably have to plead poverty if not for his acquaintance with us. But even if he served us for nothing, I wouldn't want him. When the meat's on the table, he won't eat it unless it's been cut into very tiny pieces, and cooked and recooked at great expense." Moreover, the man never ate alone and had only recently married—which meant even larger parties to come.

If it were up to Margaret, the house steward would board elsewhere when in Leuven, and they would pay him the usual fees and eliminate the extravagance. Until such arrangements were made, he would continue to visit three or four times a year, eating and drinking himself to sleep, "and if he's drunk, as he often is, then he can't be put into bed at all. There's not a worse sight than seeing a religious up so late with a drunkard" (15). Such a spectacle played out at more than one convent. Hovius's journal is full of complaints about his own steward or others. And in the very year of the 1628 visitation to Bethlehem, many sisters in the convent of Jericho near Brussels told stories of other sisters exiting the steward's room at 4 A.M. When the man was dismissed some time later by the archbishop, one satisfied nun concluded that all the troubles of the convent could be traced to him. But just as most sisters of Bethlehem still felt sympathy for Henri Joos, many of the nuns in Jericho thought it a disaster that their slandered steward had been removed. Interestingly, one of the tactics used by those opposed to the steward's dismissal was to question the jurisdiction of the archbishop. This was exactly the tactic used already in Bethlehem, and to be used again in the future, by those who always remained loyal in their hearts to Pastor Joos.

OTHER FRIENDS AND NEW RECRUITS

Clearly the kind of giving described so far by Margaret went well beyond the monastic tradition of hospitality, or even the practice in which wealthier monasteries could engage, the bestowal of pure alms on outside poor. Giving in Bethlehem was nothing short of recklessness, and it extended to others besides the big three.

Anna Vignarola was more heavily involved than anyone but Mater in charming friends old and new. Besides her deference to Joos, the Woman in the Leopard, and the steward, she had a special relationship with a chaplain. This was worrisome for a variety of reasons, but in one passage on the matter Margaret highlighted the potential for internal divisiveness. Anna told house secrets to the man, said Margaret, in order to win his favor. She "complains to him about certain sisters she doesn't like, and he agrees with her and gives her still more reason to complain. If those sisters knew about it, there'd be an ugly uproar. She ought to stop, and he ought to stop listening. . . . He knows many of the things which she does better than we who live here" (18). The chaplain was hardly the only friend Anna sought to enlist, Margaret continued. "Mater has no greater pleasure than providing the convent's guests with the company of such an agreeable religious. . . . She's an expert talker and could easily tempt someone. It's too bad she's so spoiled; she could have been a most able religious had she been well trained and exercised from the beginning, and made more respectable. Now there's nothing to be done about it, she has so much license." Male or female, whoever came, Anna was right alongside. "She is too familiar with young men, in fact with all sorts of people. Sometimes she visits with fourthhand acquaintances, visiting not only those who come to see her but when she goes to the grille to accompany a sister called there, she visits with [that sister's] guests as well, especially when they are men. It's her ruin" (19).

Was this jealousy on Margaret's part? After all, Margaret seemed to have no visitors herself, with the exception of Pastor Bouckaert, her friend by default. Was it envy of Anna's control of resources? Disinterested preference for more passive outside relations? Although the answer must remain unclear, Margaret at least recognized Anna's talents, much as she condemned their improper use.

Mater Adriana was no less adept at recruiting than Anna, with economic issues once again a major concern. For instance, financial standing played a big role in Adriana's attitudes toward prospective nuns, charged Margaret. Acceptance to the novitiate and profession was decided by a vote of the vowed sisters, but Mater and her "Discretes," or the council of three to six elder sisters, carried much weight and handled negotiations with the family. In Margaret's opinion, they went too far in worrying about economic rather than spiritual consequences. "They are all content to accept anyone, even if crippled, half-blind, and dull-witted, all are welcome, though Mater doesn't stop to think whether the person is able. If Vicaress suggests that they ought to consider health and ability, she gets no thanks; she is a true devotee of monastic principles, but Mater on the contrary is a spacious dish" (38). Not only were the candidates to be in good health, not only faithful Catholics, absent any prospects of marriage, and so on, cited Margaret from the statutes, but they should be inclined to the religious life. Yet Mater paid little attention to anything but a woman's florins, said Margaret. If she was right, it's again understandable, given the chronic shortages in Bethlehem and similar houses. But even if Adriana sincerely considered her approach prudent rather than completely worldly, there was still more room for consideration of spiritual gifts, Margaret groused.

As proof of her point, Margaret related the case of a woman whom Adriana had recently welcomed for reasons of personal friendship and a promising income. Yet the woman's curious medical history should have made her ineligible. She had "an imperfection in one of her eyes, for when young she fell into the fire. As a result, to keep her sight, it's necessary for her to wear golden earrings [probably a reference to eyeglasses]. If she doesn't wear them, she doesn't see well. Moreover, the eye also moves around, so that she can hardly bear the presence of light or fire." As if these physical afflictions weren't enough, Margaret added that there was a "blow from nature, for she must beware of eating various foods because of her bleeding, and it's not convenient at all to treat her so. Often when she comes into the choir, or workroom, or refectory, or whatever she's doing, blood suddenly starts streaming from her nose and soils all around her." The woman's temperament, continued Margaret, was also unsuited to the monastic life: She complained about the work, she chattered, was strong-willed, and spoke abruptly and rudely. Finally, this woman was expensive, illustrating that Margaret was as capable as Adriana of paying due respect to economic realities. Margaret wrote that she "will have lived here two years come October, and for each year she's had 50 florins in expenses, but we haven't had a single stiver from her father to cover them." She doubted whether the convent would ever receive anything at all. In fact, such had been the situation at the entry of Anna Vignarola: "She seemed such a wealthy maiden, until she was in for good." Despite this plenitude of impediments, Adriana welcomed this woman into Bethlehem because she and Anna Vignarola were "crazy" about her, and because the price was right (39).

This was still not the end of the list of intimate friends whom Anna and Adriana sought continually to please. Margaret told also about the son of Adriana's sister, who "got his meals from us almost every day for two years, and he's a very demanding fellow, eating more food than two of our religious. Before that, we had another who studied, and besides him she has a niece at the Grand Beguinage, another child of her sister, who often comes to eat and to fetch this or that." Margaret admitted that Adriana's sister had given the convent some grain, but she questioned whether it covered the cost of supporting these youths. Then, the sister "often comes here herself, four or five times [a year]; every noon we have to worry about making something for the children" (33). This kind of regular, lengthy contact with outsiders was looked down upon at the episcopal palaces in Mechelen or Brussels, Margaret knew. Yet despite decrees over the past five or six years against giving food and drink to guests, the practice died hard, in Bethlehem as elsewhere; this was partly because of good Belgian manners and partly because it was not always known how a good deed to one person might result in a gift from someone else. Thus the gatherings continued.

"It's as if the friends haven't been unless they've been seen into the guest room," wrote Margaret from her humiliating but well-positioned vantage point. "However late they come they are let in; it's a great marvel to me that friends come and stay so many days. . . . But we have the reputation and also the deed of being open and letting in, at whatever time." Margaret now sounded discouraged: "If it keeps up this way, I won't be so resolved to stay in this situation. . . . I often feel that I'm in a tavern, as they sit there and banquet, drinking beer and wine and eating different dishes, from noon until night, young beguines from outside and young religious from inside the city."

Such resentment was grounded not only in a sense of the virtue of frugality, but in the emotional pain that resulted in the stomachs of the have nots from the spectacle of fine fare being set before outsiders. "The meals are secretly cooked here, one after the next. Male and female sit and carry on so that by the evening they're so drunk they can't remember how to get back to their convents," telling us that many of the visitors were probably other religious. Margaret knew what Mater would say: "No one eats here." But, volunteered Margaret, that was only true "as long as no one comes." Mater might imagine that these deeds went unseen, but Margaret assured the archbishop that "nothing can happen in the guest room, however secretly it's done, but that I see or hear. They certainly employ much finesse and deception, but unless I'm in the Divine Office, it's all in vain." Based on such eyewitness testimony, and for reasons of thriftiness and respect for the poorer nuns, Margaret hoped that Boonen would caution Mater about her largess. The serving of precious food and drink to obviously parched outsiders did not necessarily offend Margaret, but the situation in Bethlehem was far beyond that. "To drink once for their thirst is one thing, but two people putting down two or three mugs of beer is not for the thirst," and thus a better measure of discretion should be employed. "It's also not for the thirst when a young religious comes from her convent and with her friend here drinks a whole pot of wine, such as happened here very recently. Wine's never been more expensive, but I've never seen a time in this convent when it was given more freely. There are several religious who do this now. I don't know if they're only trying to follow

Vignarola, for I'm not sure that most of them realize just how lavish she is with it." For such entertainments there was money enough, complained Margaret, and it went on right before the eyes of tattered religious who just moments before had been told that the convent lacked money to buy a few scraps of linen with which they might have mended their clothes (14). Indeed, "If [Mater] must give something away in house, it's as if she's giving up part of her soul," so stingy was Adriana with her flock (2).

To illustrate even more memorably the superior care of outsiders, Margaret showed that the nuns of Bethlehem not only lavished patrons with refreshment at the grille, but also went out of their way to home-deliver a still-famous Belgian specialty: waffles. "There is here annually a very ugly and harmful custom," Margaret wrote. "Every year on Shrove Tuesday Mater insists on baking a great pile of waffles, from convent funds, to be taken to very many places. Two sisters need an entire day to bake enough, one after the other. Three, sometimes four sisters then do nothing but carry waffles to every corner. Mater would certainly answer, 'I didn't start this custom, it's been around since before my time,' and that's true, but never was it done to such excess." A waffle here and there for the convent's good friends, such as the Franciscans or the dean of Leuven, Margaret was willing to concede. But the nuns filled up even those from whom nothing had been received nor could anything be expected. The labor was so offensive to the less solvent nuns, and wood for the stoves "so scandalously expensive. . . . I couldn't keep it in my heart any longer." At the most recent Shrove Tuesday "it lasted fourteen days long, that baking and taking, one to her mother, to cousins, nieces, nephews, others their sister or brother. That's not so bad, but then some send off to a crony, another to a cleric, young theologian, an Augustinian, another young male or female religious, and here to the needy or to pigs! In sum, if this goes on there won't be anyone left who hasn't tasted a waffle baked by the Grey Sisters." Not surprisingly, a whole chestful of waffles was sent to Mol—Margaret didn't even bother to mention the recipient, as if it was obviously Henri Joos. But more hurtful still to Margaret was that she was denied such delightful treats herself. "I was present when the waffles were being baked for the gift to Mol, but civility there wasn't great enough to allow me to taste even the smallest crumb. In fact, I was sick at the time and right before my eyes I had to see the convent's goods given away." Once again Adriana justified it by claiming that it was a custom with a purpose, but Margaret countered that for every ten who received from the convent, perhaps one gave back in return. Margaret's anger was now obvious. "If she's so devoted to baking waffles perhaps she should open a stall on the market and bake them on the spot for sale by the piece" (23).

Since it cost so much to care for the twenty-six nuns who lived in Bethlehem, Margaret couldn't imagine how the convent could serve up so many meals, run a delivery service for waffles, and still survive. Yet she held out little hope for change. "It would be well if [Mater] could stop that giving away without need; but it's her inclination, like a thief is inclined to steal" (2).

BEYOND FOOD AND DRINK

Although much of Margaret's criticism focused on victuals, Adriana's giving involved other items as well. "I see her often during the year," Margaret wrote, "spending three or four florins at a time, buying small images, and that's the least of it. There is one sister who for how many years I don't know has done nothing but make Agnus Deis and Gospel-books [perhaps book covers], all to be given away. . . . During the Winter there is also a lay sister who makes Gospel-books, and this isn't to mention all the flowers, bouquets, [carved] little animals, decorated flower branches, tree branches, embroidered dresses for Our Lady, and further a multitude of things I could describe if need be. I know that often one must give, but that must be with prudence, according to ability and as the situation demands." Mater always claimed that "she doesn't give without knowing where she's giving," but Margaret countered that most of the time the convent's efforts to get something in return were fruitless (2).

Anna, as usual, was the most guilty in Margaret's eyes of not only feeding and recruiting but at handing out other goods. "Vignarola is an expensive creature," Margaret began. "Mater says that if [Anna] gives a bit away, it doesn't hurt the convent," and besides, other sisters also presented gifts to outsiders. But Margaret responded, "I daresay that [Anna] alone gives away 100 times more than the whole community." This was only possible, presumed Margaret, because Anna got more from the common fund than the rest. And "if someone [outside] gives something to her, then she insists on giving something in return. She is the sacristan of the choir, and she makes a multitude of flowers and frills without need—wasted money. I say it's a sin that so much rubbish, which isn't any more necessary than it is for me to jump into the water, finds its way to the choir. Further, she damages as many things as is possible for someone in a convent." Margaret finished by revealing here, as elsewhere, a certain amount of envy for Anna's privileges. "It would be interesting to see whether she could do all she does now if Mater didn't have her hands on the convent's purse" (1).

A favorite practice of Adriana and Anna both, one we might look upon in connection to worldliness or lax discipline but that Margaret linked to the winning of alms, was the old custom, observed on certain feast days, of dressing small children as nuns and beguines. The "world upside down," a common theme in various celebrations at the time, will be discussed in detail later; for now it's important to know what this long tradition had to do with pleasing friends. "There is at no time to be any nun-making or beguine-making [of children] on St. Gregory's or St. Gertrude's day or otherwise, nor during any weddings"—all festive occasions. "It might seem a small thing but it causes a great deal of distraction." There was of course the time involved, for two or three religious had to neglect the Divine Office in order to attend the children. There was the threat of violating cloister, since much of the costuming of these children occurred before an open door in the guest house. Finally, and most relevant here, the crowds of children were growing since even strangers brought their children to frolic for the day, strangers "from whom we receive nothing, and from whom we can expect nothing but idle hopes; just as in everything else we do this in the hope of getting something back." When all was said and done, the convent's godly reward from most consisted of nothing but "dirty linen, and running after this, that, and the other." But Mater thought the practice good for public relations, and therefore sent especially Anna Vignarola to make friends with the parents of the children (37).

Another old practice possibly related to nun-making, though Margaret gives no explicit clue, was that of allowing small children inside the cloister. Perhaps there were sociopsychological reasons for nuns to dote over children, or perhaps since children did not present the same threat as adults they were let in for a change of face and pace. It could even have been grounded in the Franciscan tradition of meditating upon the childhood of Christ, thus giving the Grey Sisters a special affinity for children. Most likely, it was again tied to the desire for alms—to fuss over the children of potential and current benefactors. But as Margaret recognized (and as she claimed Mater ignored), this was not a practice the church condoned. "Once again it's necessary expressly to prohibit Mater from allowing children to come inside or be carried inside, however many there are, old or young, daughter or servant; it was once again done, very recently, despite the last decree against it" (27).

Mater also catered to outsiders by storing their goods, including wine. This was not only an inconvenient practice, but it raised legal issues as well, since monasteries were exempt from taxation and were not to extend that privilege to others. "Mater should not store in the convent any goods or materials from other people," Margaret cautioned, "due to the problems this brings. In the first place, it brings no thanks from the debtor who seeks to hide his things here while he pretends to be bankrupt; it also brings no thanks from those who leave their things and then come back some time later and say, 'there was more than this,' or, 'this wasn't spoiled when I left it here,' and so on. We can't keep the rust off iron goods, we aren't responsible to clean them! Further, by doing the dirty work of others we place our convent in peril, for example when we keep various animals, or when we make ourselves night and day the slaves of outside people, without need or profit to soul or body, or without any reward or thanks but only ingratitude, as I've seen too often" (31).

Finally, there was the even more burdensome habit of lending the convent's goods. "Mater has even lent grain from the attic to strangers, once a whole *mudde* [three U.S. bushels], which we got back only three years later with much ingratitude and shock that it had to be repaid, and then when they pay us back we feed them; she's also loaned a ½ *mudde* of grain to someone else. It's now four years since that happened, and we can't get it back; it was to a stranger who's never done a thing for us. And afterward you can well imagine that we had to buy more grain, at the highest possible price" (34). Mater also lent other goods, quite against the letter of the statutes, to the extent that the house had become a kind of rent-all in Margaret's eyes. "Beds, sheets, woolen blankets, pillows, tablecloths, napkins, tins, dishes, pots, pans, even by the dozen, chairs, benches, tables, even the beds and pillows of the infirmary! In short, all that we have is soiled or damaged by those people who borrow it, even lost, and we don't even know sometimes who's borrowed. If some people are having a big dinner, or are in childbed, or it's kermis [the famous Flemish fair], then they all come to borrow these things, kitchen utensils and otherwise, and . . . then bring them back looking like no utensils I've ever seen. We're forced to be the maids of strangers. . . . If we could expect any kindnesses from these people, it would be different; we are poor, and we want to be called poor, but by lending so we don't act poor. The richest abbeys would never be able to do this" (35). Even Maria Joos would later complain that the convent's furnishings, such as stools, linens, and beds, needed to be occasionally changed. All this suggested that, as with food, outsiders often fared better than many sisters.

Margaret offered an unwitting summary of her two main objections to giving. First, "Mater is rich enough to give outside, but inside she has nothing at all to give, for she doesn't have the will to. If she'd never in her life gotten her hand into the temporal pie, then we'd have what's coming to us. . . . No one else may do anything, for she holds every office, though not well; she is Mater, vicaress, bursaress, cellaress, novice-mistress, in short everything" (2). And second, to Mater's arguments that " 'we need to make friends and keep them,' " or " 'who wishes benevolence or favors from people must do favors themselves,' " Margaret responded, "I wish Mater could prove that we've ever gained one stiver or any friendship by our lending. . . . It burns my conscience deeply"—or even better, "How many mugs of beer has she given in vain" (2, 7)! Mater was not bound to maintain friendships at the expense of the temporal or spiritual salvation of her convent. "What good are the things of the world, if they're obtained by damaging the soul, as I believe we run the risk of doing with so much attention to worldly people?" As is always important to remember, Margaret did not address these questions to the wind. She had serious reforms in mind, for whatever reason, and tried to appeal to the sentiments of the archbishop himself. "If your reverence only knew as much about these things as I'm forced to observe, with great heaviness of heart. And I'm ashamed for the young novices. Your Reverence should speak to me about it all, my heart is full. It's too much for me to see and hear" (7).

Overflowing with memorable detail, Margaret's gloomy assessment speaks well, if incidentally, to the place of the convent in larger society. As the modern-day historian Roger Devos has concluded in *Vie Religieuse Féminine et Société,* a justly acclaimed study of nuns in seventeenth-century Annecy, France, "In a sense a monastery can be considered a 'practical utopia,' an 'other' society, dominated by values at odds with the society around it: . . . but this 'anti-world' was situated squarely in the world. The endeavor to live separately and distinctly was very quickly limited."

13. WORLDLY WAYS

LIVING "SEPARATELY AND DISTINCTLY" was a problem not only in the convent's day-to-day life, but in its spiritual affairs as well. This was evident in the last of Margaret's three major volleys: the growing worldliness of Bethlehem. Even more threatening than the sisters' dependency on the money and resources of outsiders, contended Margaret, were the emotional bonds that many nuns had maintained or developed, quite in contrast to the monastic ideal of being both literally and figuratively separate from the world. Whereas temporal dependency on the world upset good monastic discipline, emotional attachments presented immediate dangers to the soul.

THE TRADITION OF CLOISTER

As we saw in chapter 2, cloister was one of the most distinguishing characteristics of female monasticism. Cloister among male religious was not as heavily demanded or practiced, in the Middle Ages or afterward, while for nuns it was considered necessary for social and spiritual reasons. One early motivation to raise up walls around female religious was the need felt by many in church and society to physically protect these women from a brutal world. But it became ever more clear over the centuries that the walls were also there to protect society's notions of what a religious woman should be. A devout, roaming woman was long an oxymoron in European minds. Secular authorities in fifteenth-century Florence were not alone in expressing anxiety about ill-observed cloister, nor in their fear that want of cloister put nuns in peril of losing their virginity. Indeed, lack of strict *clausura* in a nunnery was often regarded around Catholic Europe as a sure sign of unchastity among the loosely bridled occupants. Finally there was the related notion that a woman by nature needed protection against herself, an idea articulated by Idung of Prüfening, a twelfth-century Cistercian monk. Since even vowed women were more susceptible to worldly delights than were men, he argued, it was in the eternal interest of female religious to remain shut up. He therefore advocated cloister to curb the "natural fickleness" of women and "also because of outside temptations which womanly weakness is not strong enough to resist." Let us note that Idung did not invent this idea, nor did it die with him; though it's hard

141

to say just exactly how pervasive such a view was by our period, it was certainly in various forms and degrees still alive and well.

More positive reasons for cloister were also rooted in ideas about purity. The Franciscan devotional author Ferraria agreed with Augustine that the conquest of all fleshly desires, implicit in the second monastic vow, was the severest battle any Christian, male or female, must fight. Still, Ferraria promised, three special weapons could help: cloister, spiritual exercises, and physical labor. The idea of cloister as an aid to especially maidenly chastity was heavily stressed by the Council of Trent. Trent viewed lax observation of the ancient law of *clausura* (along with the involuntary profession of young women) as the chief root of troubles in nunneries. It therefore decreed in strong language that violations of cloister by sisters or visitors would result in excommunication and that routinely given exemptions from cloister should cease.

Despite these standards, *clausura* was long a problematic issue, for practical and spiritual reasons. We've already seen how much energy Bethlehem and other cloistered houses expended in the outside world to support themselves temporally. In the spiritual realm, there were the obvious—though who can say how typical—scandals that resulted from lack, or violation, of cloister. When in 1609 a sister of the Hospital at Berchem was suspected of having given birth, and in 1596 the mother superior of the uncloistered Grey Sisters of Velzeke became a "natural mother," "scandalizing the people," the old societal prejudice about the need for *clausura* among women was only confirmed. Probably more common than such troubles, however, were fierce debates over imposition of cloister where none had existed before, such as at Groot Bijgaarden near Brussels, where between 1610 and 1630 the nuns raised the dander of everyone in the diocesan hierarchy through their refusal to accept cloister and their continuing to allow inside the convent their rumored-to-be-unchaste confessor. Just as problematic, because cloister contradicted notions of the autonomy and trust owed to the many elite women who populated convents, were casual violations of already existing cloister. At some well-heeled German Cistercian nunneries, vowed sisters left the cloister, took companions of their choice along with them on trips, and often lodged with laypeople. In a convent of Zichem, near Scherpenheuvel, we find in 1618 a Sister Gertrude ratting on a Mater who liked the occasional late-night glass of wine with visiting priests, while the convent of Bethanie in Brussels allowed in 1592 two monks from nearby monasteries to enter the convent's workroom, off-limits to outsiders.

Yet another quandary was enforcement, which might suffer due either to limitations of communication or a lack of willpower. More specifically, overworked midlevel bureaucrats could easily develop a sense of futility in dealing with one determined community after the next. At a dinner party given by a local noble family, a dean in the diocese of Gent complained to his well-born hosts that the bishop expected too much of him in the way of overseeing cloister in nunneries. When the daughter of the hosting couple rebuked the dean for criticizing his bishop, her "pained" mother "immediately boxed [the daughter's] ear." But even unpleasant moments such as this probably failed to change the dean's mind. Then, political reasons, such as resistance to the foreign leadership of a given monastic order, might make enforcement of cloister a difficult task. In 1669 the government in Brussels supported a local convent of Cistercian nuns in its attempts to resist imposition of cloister, not out of opposition to cloister per se but because those trying to impose it were French.

Yet it would be wrong to view the history of *clausura* as merely one of troubles, resistance, and sporadic enforcement. We must not lose sight of the power of the ideal. Since *clausura* was heroic, even other-worldly—perceived as a step above the natural human yearning for society—and since it had been around so long as the standard, it still possessed a forceful attraction. This remained especially true among nuns who sought the greater prestige of a cloistered house and among nuns who genuinely found spiritual fulfillment through the old and tried method. It must be admitted that the number of convents which had cloister forced upon them after Trent was high, but it's as important to note that the number of houses which took the initiative and demanded *clausura* may have been just as high. The fledgling Theatine nuns of Pescia were not the only house or order to do such things as refrain from telling outsiders about the convent's troubles, fearing that scandal would hurt their efforts to gain cloister and would scare "away from the convent the parents of prospective entrants as well as potential donors." And right in the archiepiscopal city, we find the nuns of Blijdenberg pleading with Archbishop Hovius in 1616 for the "privilege of cloister." Indeed, Belgian nuns were generally said to have a special affinity for cloister, argued several professors at the Universities of Leuven and Douai (in the southwestern Low Countries). With classic seventeenth-century medical logic, they maintained that while warm-blooded nuns in Spain or Italy required walls forty feet high in order to observe cloister, nuns in Belgium, where temperatures and bodily desires were cooler, required no such drastic measures—indeed they doubted that strict cloister was even necessary, but suggested walls of "only" fifteen feet anyway. "Cloister is here better protected by a single grille," they explained, "with three, four or five inch square grating, than over there with double grills of two inch square grating surmounted by protruding spikes a foot long." In fact, we can read of various houses besides Blijdenberg asking bishops to come and shut them up, though who can measure the role of bodily humors and the weather in such requests?

Although the history of cloister was not a calm one, its enduring prestige must be kept in mind when trying to understand female religious life after Trent. Many debates in convents during this time were not over the acceptance of formal cloister, or even over whether cloister should continue to be the ideal, for in most traditional orders—such as Margaret's—it already was. Rather, debate often was waged over the spirit of cloister, which usually meant the extent of contact with outsiders at the convent's points of potential vulnerability: grilles and doors. Margaret made a few complaints about actual threats to cloister in Bethlehem, such as unwatched doors, but overwhelmingly, as we'll soon see, she condemned what she regarded as violation of its spirit. Her emphasis reflects that while the basic guidelines—walls and grilles up, visitors out and nuns in—were almost assumed, it was unclear how dead to the world these nuns should be in practice, even if legally they already were. For Margaret, her cosisters were much too alive.

And the place they were most alive was, again, at the grille, that twelfth century invention of which we've already gotten a glimpse. Bethlehem apparently possessed four: two in the guest house (recall that the rooms with the grilles were variously referred to as "parlor" or "guest room"), so that more than one group of visitors at a time could be accommodated, and two in the church. Those in the guest quarters were used most heavily, but those in the church presented problems as well, especially since built into them were windows that could be opened (in theory only for liturgical reasons, at the time of communion). All grilles were potential hot spots—visitors and nuns were indeed allowed to meet and talk there, but under what circumstances and for how long and on what subjects and with what feeling? Strictest interpretation said that such visits were allowed as a necessary evil and should be avoided when possible. The 1627 decrees reforming various grilles in Bethlehem had even called for reducing the size of the holes in the grilles of the guest rooms while doubling the amount of iron—quite in contrast to what the defenders of Belgian nuns had maintained was necessary for women of cooler, northerly passions. Well aware of the old and new ideals, Margaret revealed to the archbishop the multitude of ways in which she thought it possible for a nun to sin against grilles, doors, and the spirit of chastity.

THE PRICK OF THE FLESH

Here as in all else it was Adriana who, in Margaret's view, was most to blame. "She comes alive when she can be around laypeople," Margaret wrote. "It would be the joy of her life to always have workmen, meals, and banquets; oh blessed statutes, what rest do we have now?" We already know that the biggest star in Mater's supposed galaxy of friends was Henri Joos. But Margaret went beyond her complaints about the heaping of food and drink for the man, and suggested that he was not only a threat to the convent's pantry but its purity. "That glow, and the unspeakable happiness shown by Mater at his arrival, and that frequent speaking alone doesn't edify some of the sisters. It can certainly happen without any evil . . . but it would be better if she avoided this" (1).

Margaret returned to the topic when, at a later date in her letter-writing, a new event demanded reporting. This event illustrated not only the lengths to which Adriana went to make Joos happy but the spiritual dangers that could result. It occurred, Margaret began, on the Monday before Pentecost: "After he had been here visiting for four hours with Mater and his sister [Maria] and Vignarola, Mater had four lay sisters accompany him so that they could all carouse on his way to Mechelen." Among them was one unnamed lay sister who had previously been "hit" by Joos, an idiom that an episcopal official would later render in his Latin summary of Margaret's letter as "suspicion of incontinence"—a common way of referring to sexual misconduct. Whether this sin occurred when Joos was confessor or afterward is unclear. In any case, the situation caused Margaret "to wonder greatly at Mater's lack of judgment; that she allows such is to be lamented, for the same sister is most uncomfortable in his presence but doesn't dare contradict Mater; and as often as he comes to Leuven, and returns in the evening to his lodgings, Mater always sends that same sister with him." Margaret went on to mention a conversation between herself and the unfortunate sister. "She once spoke of it with me, but if your reverence were to try to tell Mater that it would be better to be less familiar with [Joos], there would be such commotion that I don't know which would be worse, and the sister would resent me greatly for saying anything, which is natural, for she doesn't know the whole story."

We can rightfully wonder whether this "hit" sister was Joanna Schoensetters, the sole lay sister with whom Margaret was halfway friendly—and the sole lay sister to dislike Adriana and Anna—and who might therefore have possessed enough trust to approach Margaret. We also can ask ourselves whether this sister had spoken with Margaret coincidentally or because she had heard about Margaret's old allegations. In any case, Margaret continued, writing more heatedly now about Joos than she had earlier, "I wish that he never would come to Leuven again as long as he lives, but it's to be feared that it will happen often, at least two or three times a year, and then he always comes to our church and reads the Mass and preaches; God knows how pleasant that is for me and still others." The sarcasm is plain enough, but it is overshadowed by Margaret's attempt to extend Joos's crimes beyond herself—she was not the only one affected, or perhaps even violated, by the man, she implied. "Yet there are others who get such unspeakable joy from this that they think themselves ready to be taken up to heaven."

When Henri Joos was absent, Mater's attentions then turned to workmen. It wasn't that Adriana expected great alms from these workers, wrote Margaret, nor was she there to encourage them to do the best work possible. Rather, she simply seemed to enjoy their company. Here was yet another weakness Margaret asked the archbishop to reprove. As with her other friends, Mater saw personally to the generous provision of food and drink for the men. "The joiner, carpenter, engraver, wood-cutter, five masons at once, the plaster-carriers [kalkbrengers]" not only put away piles of food but "seem to have barrels for hands. What they call drinking! I think that when a man drinks 7 mugs in a day it's too much." But such complaints by Margaret we've seen before and will see again. What distinguished these was that they were not merely about food but unsuitable associations. Mater's generosity reflected sentiments beyond seeing her hired hands well fed; in Margaret's eyes Adriana was overly devoted to the men emotionally. And her example of fraternity emboldened other nuns, who went "to stand by the workmen and chat with them, and through all the chatter they don't work for hours. And in the evening at dusk the religious stay to prattle with the engraver alone, and the next day with someone else. This has no great grace for religious, to hear all the stories and news going on, and also to make others wise to many things that go on here" (11). And this was but one of several charges, all virtually identical, that Margaret shot off on the subject.

Just as serious to Margaret as the alarming popularity of Joos or the excessive attention to workmen was the private conversations held between Anna Vignarola and the convent's chaplains. These occurred most often at the two grilles in the church, which, because they could be opened, presented real dangers, at least according to Margaret. Because we lack any kind of sketch of Bethlehem, in whole or part, these grilles deserve some general description. An example of an imposing and not uncommon type of grille could be found in the church of the Grey Sisters of Comines, who to receive communion had to open a great window of wood and pull back a screen of linen that covered a trellis of iron. Within this trellis was another large window, also of iron, locked with a key and to be opened only by the mother superior accompanied by one of the council sisters. The arrangement and strength imitated the grille prescribed by Urban VIII in 1236: a wooden door with iron bars, the window within opened only during Divine Office or Mass. But some sisters got around these rules. At the noble Benedictine convent of Vorst near Brussels, the infirmarian told a troubling story about a Sister Barbara who not only received gifts of food and drink from a male admirer but often spoke with him at the open communion window within the choir grille, thanks to a third sister who snuck her the key. A fourth sister testified of witnessing similar meetings, with Barbara always looking around to be sure no one saw her. In the diocese of Gent, Bishop Triest noted a case in which a (hired) male church sacristan and a Black Sister were suspected of familiar conversation—although he didn't specify where contact occurred, the likely venue was, again, the grille at the choir.

We can infer from Margaret's letter that in Bethlehem the grille "above" divided the nuns' choir from the main part of the church, which was intended for the public and which included the altar where priests said Mass. This fit the usual pattern. Also fairly common was the grille "below," which was built into the wall of the church at the infirmary and which opened into the church so that sick sisters could observe Mass or receive communion. Both of these places, and certain doors within the church, were favorite spots of Anna, contended Margaret. As choir sacristan, Anna obviously had to prepare for services in the church, but Margaret argued that the woman abused her position by lingering too long around the sacristy, in order to chat with the attending priest. Though Anna's responsibilities required her to have some contact with priests—passing along information on the day's services and so forth—Margaret believed that Anna had turned this contact into near intimacy. "Anna Vignarola, the youngest nun . . . descends every day from the choir to go speak with the gentlemen" at the upper church grille. "She's also spoken for a long time at the open door of the sacristy."

What bothered Margaret here was not merely that Anna enjoyed speaking with outsiders, a topic with which we're familiar enough, but that Anna liked men, and especially these chaplains. Margaret had heard or noticed that Anna "speaks with the chaplain as often as she pleases at the window [in the grille] from the infirmary." (Let us not forget that Anna's friend Lesken Joos was infirmarian and, according to Margaret, would have winked at, or even engaged in, such conversations.) There stood Anna, "with the window open, leaning on it with her elbows and sticking her head into the church. . . . Sundays and Holy days she often neglects singing her hours with the community, even on the Holy day of Easter, as has happened." Anna also entertained the chaplain at other grilles as well, "whether in the guest room or the [upper-church] grille, talking an hour or two at a time, and even singing." A last sign of familiarity between the two was how Anna hailed the man to look through the guest-room grilles or doors whenever the

147

nuns engaged in recreation. Margaret had "nothing but praise for this gentleman's honor and virtue, for how he edifies us in all things," and for being "as accommodating as anyone we've ever had or could have. But I say it's perilous. She is much too attached to him and has many worldly ways about her, and she can gossip marvelously well. Thus it's better to put a stop to it now. We've seen higher mountains fall, which were better grounded and more wise than she."

Margaret again blamed Mater for Anna's freedom. "Mater trusts her too much, which amazes me, since she had a bad experience this way herself." Margaret's hint about a "bad experience" we've seen before, but this reference does nothing to clear it up. Was she suggesting that Adriana was compromised by a chaplain or confessor? We get no further clues until 1637, when similar allusions again arise. For now let us note that Margaret persisted in indirectly accusing Adriana. "If it's true [that it happened], then [Mater] ought to be careful that it doesn't happen [to Anna]. If she was deceived, as she claims, then why doesn't she show any concern that [Anna] not be deceived? . . . Mater would say, 'who is evil thinks evil.' Nevertheless, it's plain to see that Vignarola runs to the gentleman too often without need. I've never seen such running in my life. . . . She's crazy about that chaplain. If anyone shows any displeasure with him or suggests that she speaks with him too much, I don't know who'd be able to make peace after that. She'd grumble and pout for a week, and Mater would say as usual 'Vignarola is done with all that' " (19).

FURTHER VISITS AT GRILLES AND DOORS

The problem of attachment to outsiders went beyond Mater and Anna to other sisters as well. The trouble spots, however, remained the same: the grilles in the guest house and church and the convent's various doors. In this context, Margaret was again disapproving not so much of the campaigning for alms but of the unabashed joy of worldly contact. The grille became not only a place to carry out the critical business of placating gift-bearing friends but, to someone of Margaret's tastes, a veritable tavern where the worldly proclivities of the nuns became painfully manifest. "It happened only recently that the sister of Anna Coninxloo was here eleven days, coming all the time, and this is a yearly event; if it's no longer than this, then we're lucky. There are others who do this too; the mother of Vignarola also comes annually; Sister Anna Marcelis hosts every one of her relatives as well. It's most necessary to put an end to it with one blow, or I'll promise you that it will keep on" (14).

Much to Margaret's dismay, such visits in the guest rooms were all too lengthy. "What good is it for people to come here in the evening?" Margaret lamented. "Those who come from outside [the city], if they stay a few nights in town, come each evening to prattle for an hour, two, or three, with three or four nuns neglecting Compline" (1), the last service of the day. Margaret contended that eager nuns also spoke at the guest-room grilles during meals, and on confession and communion days, in blatant violation of house statutes. "It's very harmful to soul and body, that long and superfluous gossip at the grille for two or three hours, even a whole half day. What profit comes from this? Much distraction, much prattle, loss of time, little work, absence from refectory or the Office, and it results in much murmuring, for some are allowed more than others. Some sisters have their friends who come from Brussels and other distant places, and that's fine if it occurs over just one or two days," but there were too many who "come here eight, even ten days in a row," from "eight in the morning until night . . . chattering straight through with two or three religious." Such visits, we learn from a long string of examples offered by Margaret, involved more than one or two sisters, had once gone on "eighteen days in a row" (12), and were, again, not merely to please friends, but for the enjoyment of the nuns.

Besides Mater and Anna Vignarola, perhaps the nun most guilty of grille-sitting was no less than the portress, Maria Joos. To Margaret, Maria was hardly the model portress, a sentry who, according to the ideal, would watch the convent's doors and grilles "as if she were guarding the tomb of Christ." One of the most unflattering examples Margaret cited was later noted with alarm by the archbishop's visitor to Bethlehem. "[Maria] says that though it's forbidden for guests to sleep overnight, it's not forbidden to allow someone to sleep on a bed in the guest room during the day. Thanks to this reasoning she let one of the religious bring in some strangers, soldiers no less, who were completely drunk, to lie on the beds. Another sister let in her brother and his friends, who were so drunk that they didn't know what they were doing, until about nine that night. I well imagine that there are no female convents in all the world which would tolerate such things." Few people had trouble finding the entrance to Bethlehem, complained Margaret, but it was worse still when such undesirables arrived. Outsiders saw all this and might have charitably concluded that the soldier had a sister in the convent. But when those outsiders saw three or four other soldiers going in and then coming out drunk, "lying in the barley-plain," they would certainly pass on news of the unedifying scene to others, feared Margaret. Such "would never be allowed in other convents."

As for the grilles in the church, Margaret suggested that nuns besides

Anna were too easily tempted there. The communion window in each grille was "greatly in need of modification," insisted Margaret, "namely that they be made smaller and locked, and that they never be opened again except to commune. The one below is very dangerous; given the notion, a secret conversation could easily take place there, which in fact often happens while the rest of the sisters are in the choir, and things can be given away or received without anyone knowing it." Here was opportunity to violate one's vow of poverty as well as the spirit of the vow of chastity. "You can even fit a child through the window, which is often done," Margaret claimed, reminding us of her earlier assertion that the women of Bethlehem indulged children and often thought nothing of bringing such innocents into the cloister. Also troubling at the window below was that those who spoke there "are often left unobserved, even when the religious are in their devotions and don't realize that the true reason for a sister's leaving [choir] is so that she won't be seen. Also at other times, while the religious are in the refectory or have other concerns, there occurs much familiarity with men and women, in which there is much peril." To Margaret, it is clear that "the peril" lay not always in the actual violation of the vow of chastity, but in the promotion of a worldly heart. Yet this is not to say that more serious perils escaped her attention, for to such she has already made allusions enough. Indeed, a final point disturbing to Margaret about the window in the upper grille was that it was easily possible for a religious so inclined to climb through it from the choir and walk "right into the church," which was of course outside the cloister, off-limits to nuns, and open to the public. "It's a more dangerous matter than some would suppose. I pray you, allow it no longer. . . . It's not just the salvation of one or two, but shows the license that exists here generally" (36).

If the communion window in the grille at the choir was the larger of the two in the church, then the window in the grille that opened from the infirmary was again the most popular, and, at times, even the most public. Some sisters, advised Margaret, would try to tell the archbishop that they used this window solely to witness the elevation of the Host, the most significant, dramatic part of the Mass. But beware, she warned, for "that's not really the reason nor is such necessary. They gather there like it's a gossip school, so that it's a scandal in the presence of God." If the sisters were well enough to crowd around the infirmary window, then they were well enough to take up their places in the choir, Margaret reasoned. "If the [infirmary] grille remains as is the gossiping will never cease, nor will the gaping. Not one person comes into the church without the sisters peering through that window and looking in and reporting to their friends who is there, and what they're wearing, and what they're doing, even during the Benediction they chatter with each other: 'She is there, she's doing this, has that,' and laugh and make noise. It's like an egg market. Often eight or nine or ten people gather round, making such noise that I'm ashamed, for the chaplain can hear it all from the altar." It wasn't enough for these sisters to look through the bars of the grille, but they insisted on opening the whole window and spilling out arms, elbows, and chins. If they didn't feel like hearing Mass from choir, or if they simply wanted a better view, then they stayed in the infirmary and watched from there. Whenever weddings or other special occasion were celebrated in the church, "there is such running to the [infirmary] window and gaping that they trample one another. If the women In the Leopard come to church then it's talking for an hour; the chaplain also talks with them, without need. I pray you to cast all these stones away. . . . Oh unholy windows! If they had been closed many years ago, what problems could have been avoided!"

Various doors in the guest rooms and church caused further distress to Margaret, not so much because of actual incursions but because such could so easily occur, given the general indifference to strict cloister in Bethlehem. The door in the guest room affected her most directly, for when guests came eating and drinking, Margaret was only yards away. Then Maria Joos often propped open the door between the guests and the cloister with an iron bar, "so that the people if they wanted to could easily come inside [the cloister] and be out again without anyone having noticed" (16).

At least for the guest rooms there existed a requirement that a nun be present to admit any visitor. But this was not the case with the doors inside the church, which were often open to the public. According to Margaret, the "cloister door" between the nun's choir and the church was as unguarded and unlocked as the communion window nearby. Recall that Anna Vignarola was the sacristan of the nuns' choir, but the sacristan of the church was a lay sister, who of course was allowed outside the cloister. This church sacristan often left "the key right in the [cloister] door when inside the church, also during the Mass. If any of the chaplains or someone else really wanted to, they could easily come inside the convent and with the sisters in the choir who would notice? As a remedy to this problem and for the sake of *clausura*," insisted Margaret, this sacristan "should always carry her keys with her, and never leave them in the door, neither in the sacristy" (17). It didn't help matters that this sacristan chattered away with outsiders in the church while the nuns were in choir, or that she delighted in walking through the neighborhoods surrounding the convent to tell all the world what went on inside (20).

EXCURSIONS

There were at least two other violations of the spirit of cloister, according to Margaret, and these had little to do with the grilles or doors. First was the practice of allowing novices to make one last trip outside the convent before profession. Perhaps this was part of the one-last-fling syndrome, or was intended to please the novice's generous family, or was granted to allow the novice a chance to arrange affairs (though this should have been done before she entered). Whatever the reason, Margaret believed that these final journeys made for bad discipline in the convent: Admittedly the novices had not yet taken their vows and were not yet bound by the demands of cloister, but such a practice once again violated its spirit. "Their playing they can do before and not after, but this is not followed." Margaret believed that a woman who intended to be a nun should come to the convent once only, for if they left they might "grow wild" (*verwilderen*), and "that which they learned outside they might not forget." Then there was always the risk that once outside, they might "reenter the world which they have left and bid adieu."

To Margaret, it was "a very harmful and a very ugly practice." Certain novices had actually protested against leaving on this trip, she asserted, but Mater had forced them to go anyway, " 'because it's the custom.' " Once outside, they're deluged with invitations, "eating, drinking, nothing in moderation; moreover, they then have more opportunity to tell what goes on in the convent; this shames me deeply that there's no firmness or care about this." Some novices were sent with a "play companion," which might have allayed the temptation to reveal details of life within Bethlehem, but if any went alone there was no holding them back, lamented Margaret. They "tell everything that's happened in the past many years since they've been inside, things of great importance"—such as Henri Joos, Lesken Nijns, and Margaret Smulders, no doubt (39). Outsiders then as now were curious about life within these establishments, and it's likely that Margaret's name—or at least the basic outline of her past—was known in many households beyond the convent of Bethlehem. Recall the remarks made by other sisters during the 1616 visitation—that outsiders were very much aware of the rumors surrounding Margaret and threatened not to visit Bethlehem if she returned from her exile.

The other violation of the spirit of cloister was committed by the lay sisters, and especially by Lesken Joos. Admittedly, these women were by definition supposed to have more contacts with outsiders than were nuns. Yet they abused that responsibility, declared Margaret, by being too interested in worldly affairs rather than viewing their excursions as necessary evils. "The lay sisters have their beaks in the street too much, without need. In an hour's time, five or six lay sisters often leave the house, one before, the other after, one here, another there, each as she pleases, though not without permission." Here Margaret reminded the archbishop that Adriana at least tacitly consented to all this. "Two sisters could do it, but they are too tied in with their worldly friends and pass their time unprofitably with them." Then, rather than send out the lay sisters in pairs, as decreed by statute, Adriana sent them out individually. This, explained Margaret, was due to Adriana's claim that if every sister went out in pairs then all the work could not be accomplished (2). But Margaret was offended by this breach of tradition, which insisted that women go two by two—for the sake of appearances and no doubt for a measure of protection.

Besides their irreverent manner while outside, the lay sisters brought back to Bethlehem news of their often unseemly visits. Margaret wanted Mater "to forbid the bringing home or recounting of all unprofitable news and tidings. I don't think there's anything that happens in the world, of engagements, weddings, how and what, and also what happens in other convents, in other cities as well as here," that the whole of Bethlehem did not know. "Sister Lesken Joos is the ringleader, the one who brings home news in abundance and chews on it. . . . It's happened that no one has lain ill in the infirmary for more than six months, so that she spends at least half of her time in idle gossip or the whole day in the street learning all the news and wonders and stories . . . and how they rebel in other convents." But Lesken was not the only offender in Margaret's eyes, of course, for final blame rested with Adriana, who encouraged such tales and who "listens to all this like it were one of the Gospels, as do many others; sometimes they sit at the table for two hours to listen to all this." Indeed, trumpeted Margaret, "Often you hear nothing but everyone sitting around and gossiping, telling much, passing judgment and sentence, each according to her taste and affection for the person under consideration" (5, 22).

The lay sisters assembled most of this news while attending women in childbed—not only at the time of birth, thus, but weeks and months before. Margaret realized that certain orders of religious women regularly engaged in midwifery and sick care; such was obviously not the task of cloistered religious who had chosen "the better part" of life, but neither was it the task of lay sisters who served cloistered religious, she argued. "How harmful that is, and how much trouble that brings to cloistered people can't be shouted too loudly." Yet Adriana defended the practice, said Margaret, alleging that "those who object are disturbed in the head and sanctimonious, and she is so amazed at others who disapprove that she doesn't know what name to give them." In Margaret's "humble opinion, I judge this to be very damaging to the convent, in soul and body. It doesn't concern us" (5). She concluded this topic with another emotional appeal to the high ideals of *clausura*. "God knows how harmful such things are for cloistered religious, and what thoughts they conjure up. Many would never have imagined such matters their whole life long save for these discussions. I pray you for the love of God that the brides of Christ ought not be familiar with such things. . . . What have we to do with such affairs? We've left the world to serve God; these things don't concern our vocation. There's so much to learn about God and matters divine, so that our hearts can be moved to love and gratitude; with other things we ought not be concerned" (22).

14. MORE WORLDLY WAYS

ACCORDING TO MARGARET, the world was allowed into Bethlehem not only directly, through grilles, cloister doors, or the stories of the lay sisters, but indirectly, in the distraction such activities caused from the pure religious life. More specifically, by clinging so tenaciously to the world, many sisters inevitably came to imitate its ways. The most obvious symptoms of this malady, from Margaret's perspective, were the wastefulness and irreverence of the nuns.

SQUANDERING

In chapter 12 we saw how the women of Bethlehem spent resources on visitors in the hopes of receiving alms in return. Although Margaret found this practice wrongheaded and offensive and that certain well-fed guests represented dubious investments, at least there was a discernible purpose in the giving. More disturbing still, therefore, was when the nuns wantonly threw away time and goods on outsiders from whom it was obvious that no alms could ever be expected, or when they engaged in activities that even the most simpleminded sister would have recognized as absolutely profitless. To Margaret, such profligacy could be explained only by the common worldly desire, still rooted deeply in too many nuns, for popularity, friends, and praise.

Margaret pointed first of all to the dilatory lay sisters, who should have been busiest inside as well as outside the convent. Yet they often ignored the common work, thus robbing the convent of potential goods and income. Lesken Joos "sits in her cell sometimes four, five, six days long, and pooh-poohs the common work. She's the young woman who puts out her hand at no time except for herself, or for a bit of sewing for Vignarola. . . . She does nothing all day long." Unfortunately, as Margaret noted, the cloistered nuns themselves failed to provide a good example to the lay sisters. "Vignarola must have the best in everything," Margaret exclaimed, "and all her things rather done by seven maids than one. I doubt that she's ever had a needle in her hands; everything's done for her" (2).

One of the main reasons so little work was accomplished Margaret has already explained: Nuns and lay sisters alike preferred to entertain their friends instead. But she went beyond the issues of public relations

BOOK II

or emotional ties and hammered on the problem of unmitigated, intentional waste. With some guests, of course, it was hard to draw a line between pleasure and business, but what could the convent hope to achieve by entertaining non-gift-bearing nuns? "When the sisters from St. Elizabeth's in Brussels come, and other sisters from Aalst, . . . then there's so much activity that it's scandalous," exclaimed Margaret. "I say it's a crime that we suffer and put up with it. If Mater were warned on this point, she would say it's not true, as she's done before, and say that it's done to slander [Anna]; but . . . God knows what St. Elizabeth's and other convents have cost us" (1). As part of the game, the nuns of Bethlehem also gave away gifts to other convents. "When they go to Flanders, they go expressly to stay in Aalst several days, for love of Vignarola, since she has a friend there whom they visit, and carrying whole packages and boxes of frills, as if we fished it all out of the water" (2). The pointless liberality was so great, Margaret argued later, that "if a filly off the street came to the convent, she'd be let into the guest room, and given bread and butter. It's as if they've been given a commandment to set bread and butter before everyone, or to threaten them with violence if they don't eat" (12).

Wasting money on frills—not just on items meant to be given away as part of the policy of public relations, but on items that served no common beneficial purpose—was another sign of the convent's lax discipline. "It also isn't appropriate," continued Margaret, "that Mater lets the nuns wear socks and shoes, each according to her taste, one white, the other black and white. . . . Who knows what they'll wear next? It's as if whatever the sisters dream about at night, they get the next day from Mater; it's all wasted money. I like to see the religious all the same in all things; I'd bet that if someone made some paper shoes that they'd want those as well" (6). There was even uncalled-for ornamentation in the workroom. "There's no special grace in Mater's using a silver thimble, nor any of the religious. She ought to set the example for her religious, in humility and simplicity without any curiosity, as befitting the children of St. Francis. We've never had a Mater who used a silver thimble, but they were an example to us of simplicity in all things" (28). If Margaret's observations were correct, then they reflect a variety of issues discussed earlier—especially that nuns brought with them from their past lives deep assumptions about rank and its symbols, and that they held a variety of views on how one achieved or measured true separation from the world. Many were comfortable with a looser interpretation than Margaret yet undoubtedly considered themselves equally devout.

Finally, there was the great spilling of funds on the ailments and discomforts of those nuns who were too easily sick and on whom still other nuns intently honed their medical powers. This kind of dabbling in curatives or medications was common in convents, and many sisters outside Bethlehem also showed interest and claimed expertise. For menstrual cramps a Spanish nun heartily recommended sticking plasters, bleeding, and cupping, a treatment with which she was clearly familiar in every detail. The nuns of Bethlehem favored plasters as well, or medicinal pastes placed directly on the body—though Margaret never specified for what purpose. Bleeding, more likely left to the professional surgeons and doctors of the time, was a common medical technique designed to balance the body's humors by draining off part of one's blood. Cupping was simpler and may have been practiced in Bethlehem, though Margaret again made no specific mention: It involved the placing of glass or wooden cups (the Spanish nun recommended oak) on fatty parts of the body to create a vacuum—the idea being that bodily impurities would be sucked out into the cup.

In any case, Margaret disapproved of all such amateurish, costly enthusiasm. The religious "waste the resources of the convent through their insistence on making potions, pills . . . and plasters which they just can't be without; they make themselves unable to do anything, and they do this all without advice of the physician but as they dream it up, and in fact it's often contrary to his advice. There are some who would quit all that plaster and medicine, and in fact the doctor often expressly warns them of the ill effects, but Mater then allows them to go on anyway, some because they've got their herbs all ready, and others whom she urges on without need, all money thrown in the water, knowingly and wantonly." Margaret would not have turned away any doctor when there was a need, but the nuns were so often sick that it raised her suspicion. The supposedly ill said, " 'I'm melancholic, I've got no appetite, I've got this or that in my head, or I don't feel like getting out of bed, or to follow the community like everyone else,' and other excuses I don't wish to write" (30). But it was melancholy only, insisted Margaret, who knew the condition firsthand and who clearly felt that it could be overcome in less elaborate, costly ways.

A CHOIRFUL OF POSIES

One of the most striking examples of waste in Margaret's letter was overdecoration of the nun's choir. We don't know to what extent the choir was visible to the public—this would have depended on the size and design of the grille and the layout of the church as a whole. It was certainly at least partially visible, especially when the communion window was opened during Mass, for the nuns knew very well that the sight and sound of their choir were the two main attractions of a monastic church. Decoration of the choir was therefore at least partly designed to please patrons, and could be treated as part of almsgetting. But since Margaret made only one explicit connection between decoration and patrons, while in all other cases where she perceived an attempt to satisfy friends she was unmistakably clear, it is likely that to her this topic was primarily a question of lavish, worldly waste, with no possible return involved.

In whatever context it ought to be understood, extravagance ate away at her. She first raised this when she expressed a desire for a halt to the "ugly practice" in which sisters annually made a donation for the adornment of the choir. Whenever a nun celebrated a birthday or feast day, Anna brought out the *peys* (or pax)—the object the nuns kissed instead of each other during the kiss of peace—and handed it to Mater Adriana. Mater then "goes around the choir with the *peys* and a plate to gather money," and "then one must give. . . . It's a sight to behold, and it's all wasted money, lost money, the reason there's so much rubbish made for the choir." To Margaret it was mere "puppetry" rather than worship. Not that she was annoyed by a well-adorned image of a saint, "for that pleases me in the extreme." But the overabundance offended and even embarrassed her: Among other consequences, who would think the nuns poor after seeing such excess? This was no mere game to Margaret. It was important that outsiders see the convent as poor because it *was* poor, at least in her experience. Misguided attempts to arouse beneficence served only to squelch it, as Margaret saw it. What was the public to make of "all those small shrines, little altars, and little animals all covered with silken flowers, extravagantly made so as to be lifelike. First it was plain flowers . . . , after that it was fancier colored flowers, made of fine linen, but now recently it's changed again to silk, with gillyflowers, roses, *alemonien,* and other flowers. By the time they're finished they'll cover the whole wall. The great case with Our Lady at the head of the Choir is covered from top to bottom with flowers, and on each occasion there's something new" (7).

These little altars or shrines, so utterly condemned by Margaret, were among the most stylish items in Catholic devotion of the time. Developed in the fifteenth century, and perfected by nuns and beguines who worked in tandem with lay painters and woodcarvers, such shrines came to the Low Countries by way of Brugge around 1500 and spread from there. A few of these little altars, crafted in Mechelen during the early sixteenth century, remain to this day. They are in the form of a triptych, as most altarpieces, but are much smaller, perhaps 39 inches high by 50 inches wide. The wings, usually painted by professionals, portray saints or benefactors of the house and order. The central portion, which was the crucial and distinguishing part and usually fash-

A sixteenth-century "Hortus Conclusus."
In the middle section, this one highlights Saints Ursula,
Elizabeth, and Catherine.
OLVROUW ZIEKENHUIS, MECHELEN.

ioned by the nuns, consists of a fairly shallow case full of meticulously carved figures—saints, angels, biblical characters, and so on—and adorned with a wagonful of carefully crafted artificial flowers, usually made of silk or parchment or even metal. This central scene, because it was always situated behind a small fence that stood amid imitation grass, represented the *"hortus conclusus,"* or enclosed garden, which was not only the usual symbol of Mary's virginity but also the place where the inspiring characters portrayed—and by implication the chaste viewer as well—could best work out salvation. One modern-day art critic has praised the painstaking detail and lifelike precision of these "eternally green and blossoming paradises."

Beyond the artistic significance of the works, we might also wonder whether this and the other elaborate decorations about which Margaret complained were reflective of a distinctively female way of expressing religious feeling or artistic prowess in early modern Europe—distinctive at least among the female religious, since cloistered women inevitably restricted worship to their home convent, while the better-traveled male religious might worship in a multitude of places during his life and possess less motive or opportunity for the careful embellishment of his own house. A comparison of decoration in male and female convents, or for that matter between female convents and parish churches, is certainly called for. Although this is not the place to conduct such a comparison, it may lead to the detection of genuinely different attitudes between the genders about form and manner of worship—just as Professors Bell and Bynum detected in the Middle Ages differences between men and women in attitudes toward food. For now we can say at least this: There is not yet any evidence that the male religious of the region also created such objects. In any case, despite acclaim for this absorbing kind of art by contemporaries and subsequent generations, despite undeniable beauty, despite the recommendation of St. Teresa that the production of religious art was an ideal means to combat monastic melancholy, and despite the fact that construction of shrines was a common way for convents to please themselves and patrons, it was to Margaret yet another disgrace in Bethlehem.

She went on for long about the subject in that original session, and as was her wont with most everything else, she came back to it with a fury later on, now adding to earlier comments her sentiments about genuine flowers and other finery as well. "Earlier I gave examples of certain things, and I feel I should give still more." Margaret focused her attack on one of her favorite targets, Anna Vignarola. "Every Saturday [Anna] spends the entire day in the choir. She begins in the morning with picking flowers in the garden; she then spends the whole day plucking and making bouquets. There's another who helps her with the bouquets, and then there's yet another who spends the whole time from noon until evening sweeping the choir and polishing the candelabra. That's three people for one poor, smoky choir. Sister Anna Vignarola goes neither to Vespers nor Compline nor to refectory, and this is every Saturday. In the evening until long after eight o'clock she's running from one side to the other like an unbound calf, calling out and chattering as if it were the middle of the day, and the same thing in the morning when she first arrives in the garden, oblivious to the time."

Margaret blamed Maria Joos for initiating the practice, but Anna had grown worse on her own. Instead of an occasional bouquet in the choir, there were now "every day, winter and summer, . . . 12 pair of bouquets, whether of flowers or something else." Such required extensive—or according to Margaret, excessive—planning and maintenance. "Every high day, whether Easter, Pentecost, or any other, she works three days straight in advance, one day to clean thoroughly, another to redo things, and the third to decorate, and don't forget all her little helpers, and not to mention all the special little shrines that each decorates for herself. Is it not a great scandal for people who wish to present themselves as poor, when each feast day and high day they spend so much on putting up and pulling down in the choir?" Margaret again showed her awareness of the need for public relations, but of a certain sort. She concluded the session with another denunciation of the little altars. "These shrines are made up in gold and silver linen, and satin, all finely embroidered, and each day they make an inventory of what needs to be made new for the choir. If I wrote down all the waste you wouldn't believe it. All the Our Ladies and other Saints have so many different robes that you'd think the sisters were clothing real people." Margaret not only liked her images to be few, but big and visible; she placed no value on the patience and dexterity required in miniaturism. All this effort "on shrines that are so tiny—what a waste of money" (9).

Sometime after writing this, Margaret cited a new example of Anna's immoderate tastes. Just as Anna told chaplains about things in the convent, so did at least one chaplain purposely or inadvertently reveal some intelligence about Anna to the nuns. They had learned "that Anna has fashioned from the most expensive silk flowers, made to look real of course, a large arrangement intended as a gift for her Godfather." When the chaplain saw a few of the petals already made, he wondered how such a costly gift from such supposedly humble nuns could be explained to the godfather. Margaret explained that Anna intended to use this gift to extract a quid pro quo: She hoped that the godfather would in return finance the painting of the large shrine to Our Lady in the choir. "I've heard that for the one shrine alone it will be 60 florins," an amount, knew Margaret, greater than what it cost to support a nun for an entire year. And what if the godfather didn't reciprocate? "Oh he'll promise her, and she'll assume that he'll come through, but when reckoning day comes it will be holy garden-water, and who will pay for it all then? Probably Mater from the convent's funds. . . . If it keeps going like the last two years and as it's going each day now more and more, we'll be ruined" (18).

Even as Margaret wrote, the decoration changed. For weeks, early in the morning and late at night, with the infirmary as their secret working place, revealed Margaret, Mater and Anna sewed "a skirt for Our Lady, from excellent satin and very lavishly embroidered." The same women, with the help of Maria Joos, had only weeks before that embroidered the same skirt with another decoration, to replace the pattern that had existed before, and so on. "If it's all Vignarola's money, where does she get it all? And assuming it is, I say it's a great sin [that it's thus spent]." There was money enough "to buy velvet in Brussels for still more little altars, and there must be gold fringes, and Our Lady must have yet another robe of gold linen, even though she already has two satin robes, two or three of *armesijn* [a kind of silk], and a few others of still other material. But that's still not enough to satisfy them, because they still don't have one of red velvet, and they lament it. There are still other images of Our Lady in the choir, and I couldn't begin to describe all their clothes." Margaret pointed out that not only she but especially Catharina was against such ostentation, partly because the convent had not yet even finished constructing one of the cloister walls. Catharina's quiet but constant vigilance helps to explain why Adriana and kind carried out much of the sewing in private, and why Margaret knew so many of the details about the provenance of the decorations.

NOT-SO-DIVINE OFFICE AND OTHER DEVOTIONS

Besides being wasteful and less pleasing to God than the sisters imagined, the excessive decoration of the choir was downright unhealthy, wrote Margaret near her letter's end. Here she referred to what she regarded as excessive candle-burning around the shrines and images so lovingly created by the sisters. Candles were common in churches, of course, in part for light, in part as a symbol of Christ the Light of the World, and also as a symbol of personal devotion to a particular saint. They no doubt made the highly detailed shrines more attractive as well. All these reasons combined to motivate the nuns of Bethlehem to burn candles in abundance.

To Margaret, a better word would have been exorbitance. "I think it's too much. Unless it's halted, they'll soon burn a candle before each image; I could speak all day about this. It used to be that only one was burned, sometimes two; but now it's around and in front of every shrine." In the refectory, where "no more than two skinny candles" burned, the nuns could barely see their food. Resources were spent on frilly decoration instead, and so the choir overflowed. "The choir is very small and one can hardly bear the stink from all the candles. Because it's so small, one must kneel right beneath many of these candles and their smoke is then overwhelming. Sometimes during the service the novices or other sisters must make four or five trips to care for the candles. It causes much distraction and one can hardly hear the Mass. As for me, when it's dark in the Winter I ruin all my clothes from accidentally kneeling in the grease [left by] the candles. . . . It seems a small matter, but it's most inconvenient." Perhaps what irked Margaret was not only the robbing of the common purse, but that she was reminded of her economic inferiority, since most candles used to garnish and illuminate shrines were purchased by individual sisters. After all, she did ask the archbishop to prohibit the individual purchase and burning of candles and to command that all offerings be made in the name of the convent as a whole.

Or perhaps we should take her at her word and simply accept that the smoke overwhelmed her. "The choir must often be whitewashed because of all that burning. One sister spends the whole Saturday cleaning all the candelabra, another makes it her special task to preserve all the private[ly purchased] candles. The young ones spend a lot of their time occupied with those candles." This part of the letter is torn, but we can make out that there were often nine candles before the shrines and images, according to the devotion of each sister involved. "I'll let you judge how healthy that can be in such a small place. There are several displeased by it, but no one dares show it because it's Mater's will. . . . The humidity that rises from one's head is like steamed cooking." Such burning was almost daily, if we can believe Margaret. "If someone wishes to scrub and wants good weather, then they burn the candles for a changing wind. . . . If one of the sister's patrons or patronesses visits, then it's light all day. If someone has a special devotion to a certain saint, then it's eight days of burning" (42).

Related to these distractions of overdecoration and smoke was the general irreverence in choir. Margaret was dismayed that attention to outward matters distracted the nuns from the inner adornments of spirituality and prayer. "I'm greatly saddened that there is never any stillness in the choir, but always chattering and railing; long discourses are spoken and much visiting occurs there. And that which needs saying is said with so much noise and abundance of words that the whole choir is disturbed by it, and this includes Mater as well as others. Almost all the religious tramp and stamp across the choir as if they were shodden horses, so impious is it; it's a scandal that it's all heard in the church too. And when Mass or the Divine Office is done, they walk out of the choir talking so loudly that [those who remain] can hardly read or pray in the choir. Mater hears and sees all these things, but says nothing, even if someone talks right in the choir. However inappropriate someone might be, I don't think she's ever said a thing, but keeps a happy face" (10).

More than merely showing little respect in the area of the choir, the nuns neglected their duty to perform the Office with reverence, with careful attention and movement. Visitation reports from the time regularly included minor or major criticisms of the performance of the Office. Perhaps Margaret wished that Bethlehem had a requirement, as did the convent of Thabor, that those who didn't sing well would make a place in the choir for those who could. Or perhaps Margaret sought something similar to a later precept that if a nun disturbed the simplicity of the Office she should be silenced with a sign by Mater and be forced to read in silence. Whatever the case, Margaret was hardly alone in her reproofs. The sisters of Blijdenberg also complained that the vicaress there sang too fast and distracted others. Such notable concern for choir reflected the central place in monasteries of prayer and singing to God. This was especially true in regard to the seven daily "hours" of the Divine Office (which in fact took closer to three or four hours to perform). Related to these were regular confession and communion, attendance at daily Mass and regular public sermons, and meditation, prayer, and self-discipline. All these activities began, ended, and filled the nun's day, and helped to distinguish her from lay women, most of whom could not afford the luxury of so much devotion.

Again, though, the Office was central—for the laity, active religious orders, and especially contemplative nuns. Unlike busy laypeople who scratched for time to say the "small" Office, or active orders who were sometimes too tired or busy to perform all their prayers, contemplatives ordered their lives around it. They represented the "best part" of the Holy Church, according to the Franciscan author De Soto, the Marys over the Marthas, precisely because thoughts of the other, better world were to occupy their minds and hearts the whole day through.

The women of Bethlehem, similar to other nuns, were to arise promptly at 4 A.M. (except on feast days, when they rose at 3) and proceed to their humble church for Matins and Lauds together, the first service. Then from morning until eve they were recalled six times more by a signal, given by the youngest sisters, for Prime, Terce, Sext, Nones, Vespers, and Compline, each different from the others in the arrangement and selection of prayers, readings (usually from the Church Fathers), and hymns (usually from the Psalms), and also different according to the time of the liturgical year. Entering the choir, they sprinkled themselves with holy water and fell on their knees to honor the Eucharist, then moved to their seat, according to seniority, in the rows of stalls that faced each other across an aisle. During the Office, the sisters continued to face one another as they either read aloud or sang, according to the day and the singing ability of the convent. (The Black Sisters of Leuven didn't even read aloud; though they sat together in choir, each nun read quietly to herself.) In cloistered houses, group singing or reading was ideally from the "Great Office," or in other words the Latin full version rather than the vernacular abbreviated version used by most laypeople and unlettered or less-lettered female monasteries. The women of Bethlehem, though apparently not all literate by 1628 (eleven out of fifteen veiled sisters signed their names in a 1624 interview, two out of five lay sisters), seem to have been among the many nuns and even laypeople who recited or sang the Great Office but who probably did not understand it fully—many of Bethlehem's statutes on prayer use the familiar Latin titles and phrases. The original rule of the order even distinguished among those religious who could read the Office, presumably in Latin, and those who could not, who were simply to recite Pater Nosters and Gloria Patri at each service. This provides more evidence that even if un-Latined, one could make its "completely religious sounds," which only enhanced the sense of mystery and power.

The sisters also attended Mass at least once per day, sitting again in their choir seats. Almost every day meant a prayer during the Office or Mass for a different benefactor or saint or deceased sister, or a feast that required more elaborate services than usual, or general prayers for the success of Catholic or national armies or the conversion of sinners and heretics. The nuns of Bethlehem could not perform the Mass, but they could help sing or simply listen to it, as some benefactors requested. They didn't have the 27 high Masses or 2,600 low Masses per year of a St. Germain des Prés in France, but the convent church was home to hundreds of Masses per year, in most of which the nuns probably participated. Their biggest days of celebration, like other houses of Grey Sisters, were the Four High Seasons, Our Lady's Ascension, the Circumcision of Christ (New Year's), Three Kings, the Ascension of Our Lord, Holy Trinity Day, St. Francis's, St. Elizabeth's, and the feast of the dedication of their church (the Sunday after St. Francis's day, October 4). And there was of course St. Renildis' day, the special patroness of the convent of Bethlehem, on July 16.

Because the Office—on ordinary or high days—was the longest and most public aspect of devotion in Bethlehem, it was logically here that Margaret centered her attention as she gauged the spirituality of her sisters. "In regard to doing the Divine Office properly and with pauses, with all reverence and respect, as is proper and as called for by the statutes, this is not observed in the least. . . . Sister Anna Marcelis stamps like a wharf-horse if the pace isn't fast enough. Sister Maria Joos and Sister Anna Vignarola chatter away as if that's why they were there. Many words and phrases fall away. One wants to do it properly, someone else another way, so that there's rarely agreement. Also in singing it's like a contest. Mater adds to her fame by boasting that her people can be done so quickly with the hours and other services. After writing this, I must say that they've begun to do the services more properly, but if it will remain so I can't say. God grant that they would be so hasty in speaking at the grille or in their chattering and carrying-on at the table" (21).

Through this and other letters, Margaret gave at least a clue that other forms of private devotion were carried out in Bethlehem as well. This is evident when she referred to the "discipline" of Barbara Beli, or when she mentioned the use of hair shirts. But did the sisters who participated in these devotions chastise themselves regularly, to the point of real pain? On special occasions, did they endure self-castigation with a "discipline" "until it bled," as prescribed for a penitent sister in the diocese of Brugge? "Make it bleed, but don't cut off the neck," wrote the famous Franciscan De Soto, who urged authentic anguish but at the same time warned against overdiscipline. And Pinelli, another devotional author for religious, reminded that "if you don't mortify your flesh, it will be unchecked and become wild."

As De Soto suggested, there were also plenty of admonitions in the monastic tradition regarding moderation and much insistence that excessive mortification was to be engaged in only with permission. The less extreme, acceptable measures of devotion and self-denial were numerous enough. Were the sisters silent from Compline until 7 A.M., and on Sunday and holy days until noon? When sitting around the fire, did they really contemplate the faithful souls and think of the Psalms De Profundis or Pater Noster? Did they really have much time for private prayer in their three half-hour periods per day? When retiring at night did they lie in the manner they imagined they would look in the grave, and if they awoke from sleep because of "the enemy" did they run to a crucifix and pray to the sweet, mortified, wounded Lord, as recommended by the regionally famous reformer of the Grey Sisters, Peter Marchant? Could it be said of the sisters of Bethlehem, as it was of Francis, that his prayer was like thunder and his life like a bolt of lightning? Did they lard their souls with two kinds of spiritual fat, as suggested by the devotional author Guevera? When they worked, did they imagine that they helped the Lord to carry his cross, or when they ate that they were taking mouthfuls from the wounds of Jesus and drinking out of his heart, or when they suffered that they hung with their bridegroom on the cross, and when they slept that their pillow was the thorny crown of Jesus? Did they attend all the sermons of the friars in the convent's church, and did they imagine that they were with Mary Magdalene at the feet of Jesus? Did they hear preachers as colorful as the medieval master Jan Brugman, whose favorite allegory in speaking to female religious and others was heaven as a banquet with an abundance of Rhine wine? Did any of them pray like St. Angelina de Fouligny, whose tears burned her face and could only be put out with cold water, or like St. Mechline whose knees stuck in the ground for so long that they filled with worms? Did they confess humbly, never putting their head above the level of their confessor's, and take communion with the mouth reasonably wide open so that the priest wouldn't touch their teeth, but not too wide lest they be suspected of witchery, and then quickly swallow lest the host be disturbed by coughing, sneezing, wheezing, or otherwise? Did they think about the miracle of transubstantiation, but not too deeply, lest they become clouded, and merely ponder that if Christ could feed 5,000 with a few fishes and loaves and provide the Old Testament widow and her son with unending oil and meal, he could certainly be present in hundreds of different places at once? Margaret and the other nuns of Bethlehem had little to say about these topics, though a few admitted to brief lapses in silence around the fire. Perhaps there was much enthusiasm for spiritual exercise, but if so then how many sisters had time for such lofty thoughts, or did simpler themes of devotion prevail?

PLAY

A topic about which we know more concludes Margaret's discussion of the growing worldliness in Bethlehem: the overcelebration of recreation days.

Recreation in convents mirrored the two equal but opposite ways of observing feast days throughout Catholic Europe generally: by fasting and by merrymaking. Depending on the occasion, one mood or the other prevailed. Historians have written especially about the days of merrymaking, given their potential for protest, unrest, and overall excitement. Here an example from Mechelen will serve to illustrate one of the most common themes of such days: the world upside down. In that city, the widely popular "Feast of Fools" took place soon after Christmas with the usual parody. Several religious and laypeople of lower rank chose a person of low status to serve as their leader, and he was called Mule-pope, Mule-bishop, Fool-bishop, and other, more coarse names. This person clothed himself in an outrageous way, often wearing mule ears; then a mock Divine Office was performed in the church, sung off key and including readings with comic interludes and the splashing (rather than sprinkling) of unholy water on the audience. Depending on one's interpretation, this was all done to emphasize the proper order of things—through such blatant contrast with the ideal—or to allow venting of pent-up feelings, or a combination of both.

Though it was not unusual for convents to join the fun of such days—usually behind their own walls with private celebrations— Margaret believed that her sisters should have been more subdued. She would have granted that the inhabitants of Bethlehem should hardly have been expected—or encouraged—to attain the sophistication evident in the entertainments put on by various convents in Italy, where sisters composed complex plays based on the writings of Petrarch or the Song of Songs, occasionally dressed as men (in tights and short pants to look like soldiers), and often performed before outsiders. Although less refined than this, the Grey Sisters of Bethlehem were at least as enthusiastic in their celebrations, and therefore tempted, as Margaret and various experts on monastic life maintained, to speak an abundance of words, or to murmur against neighbors under the guise of recreation. As the widely published Franciscan author Guevera wrote, when the stomach was content, which it easily was on feast days, the mouth began to work in earnest. More than one letter from Maters and sisters around Europe showed that such warnings were not always heeded, and that sisters took their merrymaking so seriously that hardly anyone got a good night's sleep. Moreover, many of the songs they sang under the pretense of fun were so pointed and piercing and "poison" that love was greatly damaged. "Through laughter, people are wounded to the heart," said Guevera.

This was Margaret's chief complaint when she finally turned her attention to the subject. Merrymaking stung various unnamed sisters—perhaps herself among them—and it also contributed to lax standards in general. "The Mater plays so wildly on recreation days," began Margaret, "from start to finish, as if she were the youngest, and she compels one and all to play as well, without ceasing and without permission to quit until the end. And if anyone does happen to leave, she runs to get them or commands them to return, and gives a special command that everyone must play, and says that they'll earn more merit from playing than they would by going to do their devotions to God during that time." On such days there was no quiet, except perhaps during Mass, Margaret charged. But as soon as the Mass was over, "then it's back to yelling, lightmindedness, and ranting, which one can see or hear the whole day through, and which the worldly folk all stand around to hear." Here was another major point of offense to Margaret: Although the celebrations occurred behind walls, as they should have, the nuns through their racket essentially joined in with the wider celebrations of the community. More than once had Margaret found herself at the grille, speaking with "a distinguished man" (we imagine Bouckaert), when the noise caused her heart to "sink with shame." And it was Adriana who egged them on. "She never urges them to play in a proper conventual manner, but she who yells most Mater considers to be most virtuous. And she says that no one can dare call herself devout who doesn't play, and where pleasure in playing dies there dies devotion and love. That's a regrettable thing. Then where does that leave the Capuchins and other convents who never play? Playing itself doesn't bother me, but that hateful yelling and ranting! There isn't one item in statute or rule which they are so careful to observe and which is so strictly enforced as this one." Indeed, said Margaret, Adriana told the sisters that "by playing they earn more merit than from wearing a hair shirt," and she handed out penances more readily to those who failed to play up to her standards than for truly serious breaches of monastic protocol.

Some of those breaches occurred through play itself, Margaret continued, though Adriana ignored them. On recreation days, the nuns often sat at the refectory table late into the night, "howling and banging the table like drunkards sitting on a beer-bench. That makes so much noise, with all the dishes, pots, and utensils on the table that one isn't sure where one is. Those who don't like to see or hear all this are then spoilsports, hardheads" (29).

The biggest day of all in Bethlehem was Epiphany, or Three Kings Day (January 6), which in seventeenth-century society at large was an even bigger day than the Feast of Fools just described. Here was yet another chance to turn the world—and the convent—upside down. The nuns of Bethlehem did so with zest, according to Margaret. In fact, the merriment got out of hand, at least by her standards for women religious. "It would also be well that on Epiphany the religious who plays the fool not be dressed in fool's clothes. It's possible to play and be merry without engaging in such silliness. Even one day of it might not be so bad, but she wears these clothes for two days." It bothered Margaret profoundly that the nuns so looked forward to and prepared for this occasion, drawing lots more than a month before, during Advent, for the chance to play the fool. The "winner" was not at that time clothed in the silly costume, clarified Margaret, but during the week before Epiphany until the glorious day arrived the lucky one was called "*henneken*," which we might render as "little hen" or "mother hen." An upside-down queen was also chosen for the day—we imagine, based on patterns from similar celebrations, that she was selected from among the lay sisters or the younger nuns—"and she is called My Lady. That's observed at all places and times," though Margaret admitted that at least the dormitory was somewhat subdued.

The pages are torn at the part of the letter where Margaret describes the fool's costume, but we can still get enough of a sense of it to understand better why anticipation of the festivities was so great and why someone of Margaret's tastes might have objected. The fool wore a (blank) dress, embroidered in yellow and other colors uncharacteristic of nuns, a long white apron, a red (blank), a veil, a paternoster and all kinds of flourishes around the neck, a type of nightshirt with big needles stuck into it, a *craperuin* (probably a child's bonnet) on her head, all kinds of sticks with bells on them, a doll in her arms, a ham on her side (a sign of the excess food characteristic of such celebrations), and a large fool's fiddle. All of this, obviously, was in contrast to the dignity prescribed for nuns. "When it's time to eat, the sign is given to go and each must come ready to lead the woman to the refectory, singing and jumping along the way, the fool playing on her fiddle. Everyone in house runs to the woman and plays in front of her, hitting keys on their kettles, shovels, and further all that they can lay their hands on, thus they go noisily to the refectory. People hearing it all run to their attics, climb trees in their gardens to see." If there was good weather, then the nuns ran into the convent's garden, which was visible from a variety of vantage points around the neighborhood, to Margaret's chagrin. Margaret prayed the archbishop "in all humility to allow this great silliness no longer, neither that any religious should be dressed as the fool. Whoever is dressed as the fool supposes that she is free to do whatever she pleases, laughing at and ridiculing one and all, lay or religious, and spitting out anything that's been in her head. The fun turns into anger and unrest according to the disposition of those involved, so that it sometimes happens that someone gladly plays the fool so as to say anything she's ever dreamed up before. Some know how to make jokes out of little thorns, with which they greatly puncture many hearts. Though it's supposed to be said in jest and laughter, they're too prepared with their lines" (41). We wonder how many of those barbs injured Margaret herself, even if she was removed to a guest room. "It's a scandal," she decided.

A NEW REGIME?

The overall thrust of Margaret's complaints was that despite all the walls and the vows of being dead to the world, Bethlehem was not much better than the world around it. Throughout her letter, Margaret suggested specific emendations to the bishop. The most drastic reforms she sought, however, we may find at the end of her second, long session. They make a good way to end this review of her letter.

Margaret believed that there were two major steps the archbishop needed to take. First, he would have to strip Mater of her direct hold on temporal power and appoint a separate bursaress. "Though no one seems capable of being bursaress, try someone; if she doesn't work, then try another, until finally somebody catches on." This focus on temporal power resulted from more than just Margaret's annoyance with the giving away of worldly possessions. She also knew that the control of things temporal supported and fed Adriana's destructive tendency to play favorites within the convent.

Second, Margaret called on the archbishop to replace Adriana as Mater—or at least think about it. At one early point in her letter, Margaret stated that she wrote not to have Adriana removed, "but only that she'll be reproved and improve herself, both in regard to the great favoritism, and the eating and drinking as if we were a small café." Perhaps she meant this, recognizing that Adriana and friends in opposition would be even more insufferable than they were in power. Yet if Margaret was sincere about this, why did she then later proceed to use so much ink to lay out systematically the strengths and weaknesses of the most likely alternatives for Mater? It's not clear at all, unless her purpose was to confirm the utterly hopeless state of Bethlehem: Adriana was bad, but having no replacement was even worse.

"I doubt that there is a convent in the whole world where there is less capability," Margaret judged. To prove the point, she reviewed each potential officeholder. "As far as Sister Anna Marcelis goes, well, she wasn't capable some years back," at the 1619 or 1625 election, "and she's even less so now; I'd daresay that she's much worse in many things than she was then. She is a slacker of all good discipline; she's good only at pampering her body, doesn't come much to choir, sleeps late, never observes silence, is tied to too many worldly folk, too easily tells them everything that goes on; the other things I could mention I'll omit, but say only that once pants fit a certain way, they don't change." Margaret did suggest, however, letting Anna become bursaress, since everyone knew that she'd "wanted her whole life to be Mater, but I hope that God will preserve us from such a plague."

Her assessment of Maria Joos wasn't much better. Though a "very devout, pious nun," she was also "very quick-tempered and fickle." More troubling was that Maria would bring in an administration just like the present, with the same factions. Just as Adriana never governed without Maria's advice, so Maria would not govern without Adriana. "She would carry Mater through water and fire; it would be the same hangers-on, for she's also crazy about Vignarola, and Sister Lesken Joos—well, these all together are as one." Maria "certainly has good ability, but what the community would have a hard time enduring is that she's very righteous, and she speaks hard to all, however old, without discretion or tact. If she gets an idea in her head, then it must be carried out immediately, and she'll keep nagging until her will is done. But what I dislike most about her," Margaret wrote, saving the biggest punch for last, "is that she too much enjoys the company of young men, although she doesn't have as much chance as she would like. She should give herself more to God." Maria held fewer grudges than Adriana, but was inclined to engage in "*fickfackerie*" with outsiders, to allow plasters and medicines, to oppose reformation, to tolerate "curiosities and reveling, and thus in too many things will be like our current Mater."

Vicaress Catharina Rijckeboer was another obvious candidate, but despite Margaret's sympathy for her longtime friend, she couldn't see her as Mater. "I'm sure they would never choose her as Mater, even if she were the most able person ever to live here. First, if she were Mater, the community would fear that she would allow me back into the dormitory, but that's already been asked for and not allowed and she won't do it. They'd also suppose that she would be much stricter in all things than Mater, that the community would not enjoy as much freedom." It also didn't suit Catharina's temperament. "Knowing her as I do, there would be no greater burden for her in the world. It would bring her to the grave. . . . She wouldn't be able to bear their unbelievable deeds, for she is sincere, good-hearted, and has that great vice of always seeking to avoid the unpleasant, and without unpleasantness it will not be possible to put things here on a good foot. She who will be or remain Mater here must put on her harness, get a grip on courage, and hang on for dear life." Margaret also feared that Catharina had no knack for temporal matters, caring as she did for the things of the next world rather than this. "She wouldn't miss a step even if the front door of the convent were moved to the back." It would be "an eternal cross" to all concerned.

With these possible candidates ruled out, Margaret could only imagine one way to resolve the problems in Bethlehem. "The best thing to do would be to hear the voice of the community, to see whom they desire," she urged, sounding more and more in favor of Adriana's removal. But even this offered little promise. For beyond Anna Marcelis, Catharina, Maria Joos, or Adriana, "I know no one else in the whole convent who would be capable, though we could certainly do better" than Adriana. Margaret concluded on a less than optimistic note. "The more I observe the behavior and personalities of all these, the less I can say who would be qualified."

When the day of visitation finally arrived, and it was at last announced that Archbishop Boonen would be unable to come himself to Bethlehem, Margaret prepared to deliver her thick narration to the man appointed to the task, Vicar-General Van der Wiel, the archbishop's second-in-command. Long before had she become self-conscious of the letter's length and the tendency a reader of such an unusual document might have to think that she was exaggerating. Margaret also realized that the reader might wonder why she was more concerned about various conditions than the rest of the nuns, who after all were firmly inside the convent, or why they hadn't mentioned some of the same problems. She took care, in advance, to explain: Some of them were simply less troubled and more lax than she, and some had less opportunity to write. But despite her embarrassment at the letter's length, Margaret would submit it anyway "out of hope that something good might result from it. I trust that it won't sorrow your reverences too much to read it" (8), and "I say with the Holy Apostle Paul that I lie not" (24).

Before submitting the letter, Margaret made sure to show it to Catharina first, yet held back certain parts for "obvious" reasons. It's no surprise that Margaret and Catharina agreed on many points, though the letter Catharina wrote went into much less detail. We wonder how many other individuals or pairs similarly compared their notes for the visitor. As Margaret reminded him: "You'll hear plenty from others as well, and may God the Lord grant you knowledge of His pleasure and what will promote His glory and the salvation of us all, to the peace and rest of the whole community, to the observance of all good monastic discipline, and the edification of all people."

15. THE VISITOR

BETHLEHEM, JUNE 19, 1628. There was very little about conventual life that Peter van der Wiel, another in the growing cast of official visitors to Bethlehem, hadn't seen or heard before. Indeed, as a former teacher of philosophy at Leuven, as canon of the cathedral chapter since 1599, its archdeacon since 1602, longtime book censor of the archdiocese, former editor of provincial and diocesan decrees, and especially during the past decade as the archbishop's vicar-general, he was familiar with every kind of ecclesiastical institution. His tireless visitation of parishes and convents around the archdiocese brought him cheek-to-cheek with the leanest of the flock as well as the fattest.

Even before arriving at Bethlehem for the usual day or two of private, individual interviews, Archdeacon Van der Wiel knew from years of experience that today there would be the usual range of motives, of charges and countercharges, that some sisters acted out of pure desire for reform while others urged reform for the pleasure of watching a foe receive punishment or as a way of gaining control over rivals. He knew that though all sisters would swear with the utmost sincerity that they spoke the truth, some would see things as night and others day. Among some sisters there would also be amazing correlation of views—not that such was necessarily premeditated, for different people could without previous agreement see things quite the same, but planning was not unheard of. It was also not unheard of for even an entire convent to withhold incriminating information, precisely because as an outsider the visitor might not understand, or because sisters who might have been willing to speak of such things were intimidated into silence by other sisters. Was this operative, for instance, in a 1590 visitation to Bethanie in Brussels, when a report emerged that during the evening meal a Sister Lysken had yelled at Sister Grietken, "You're a public whore, you've had so many children," to which Grietken replied, "You've done the same with the prior of Affligem"? Though the nuns, when pressed by the visitor, admitted that the exchange had taken place, they quickly explained that it was all in jest, "a peasant game." Whatever the case there, Van der Wiel knew that in Bethlehem as elsewhere some sisters had pleaded for visitation, some had wished it into the North Sea, and still others had merely been indifferent, probably hoping that visitation would be neither too frequent (a sign of trouble to townspeople and benefactors) nor too rare (a sign that the place wasn't worth the trouble). He knew that they would likely be on their best behavior, unlike the German nuns who between 1440 and 1442 so disliked a visitor that once they tried to kill him and another time locked him in the cellar when he went to inspect it. He knew that some sisters, perhaps reluctant to speak to the rarely seen visitors, would have to be reminded that under the circumstances the passing of unflattering information about their cosisters was—if done in the proper spirit—by no means gossip or backbiting, while other nuns would launch in with great enthusiasm.

It must be remembered, after all, that the implicit purpose of visitation was not so much to commend but to improve, and the visitor's questions encouraged one in this direction. As enough historians of the subject have pointed out, the tendency to focus on shortcomings rather than virtues means that visitation records—of convents or other religious institutions—may often reflect a distorted picture of actual conditions. Just because a problem was mentioned did not mean that the house was wholly bad or constantly in turmoil. Yet it's equally true that even one serious scandal, or one chronic problem, could devastate a convent's morale or reputation, meaning that we should be just as careful to avoid treating problems as trivial or routine. Put another way, let us keep in mind that correction and improvement of shortcomings were part of the raison d'être of monastic life; faults should not be ignored, but neither should they be cynically regarded as proof of a continuing "*chronique scandaleuse.*" Suffice it to say that given this emphasis on finding problems, it's no wonder that visitation usually resulted in a diverse and bountiful harvest through which the experienced visitor would have to sift in order to construct what he saw as the truth.

With such a complex task before him, Van der Wiel must have been thankful for the experience of hundreds of visitations, and even more weekly meetings of the episcopal *Vicariaat*, which heard petitions from all of the 500 or so parishes, convents, hospitals, chapels, and other institutions within the bosom of the archdiocese. There was hardly a predicament that he would not already have encountered. From nuns alone there were reports of too little food, improper clothing, violations of *clausura*, of reverence, and of the monastic vows. Or there were difficult cases, neither black nor white: whether, for example, a confessor who had kissed a nun should be summarily dismissed. He would soon listen to the noble nuns of Groot Bijgaarden complain that one sister was "too familiar" with a man who visited her, that other sisters kept meal tables in their own rooms, and that Mater entertained the confessor in private. The beguines, who again were neither religious nor lay but lived together in community, caused him headaches on these counts and more. Those at Vilvoorde despised one of their mistresses because she was "*rustica*," or a bumpkin, with "no more understanding than an animal." Still others swore that they had seen beguines visiting with "diverse paters and monks, . . . kissing them dishonorably, sticking the tongue in the mouth." Angela Speyskens "at diverse meals" was said to have kissed numerous priests and other men, especially on feast days. One beguine had even observed her take a napkin, wipe her mouth and say, " 'I must get it clean to go kiss all these gentlemen,' which deed she fulfilled," and that her brother had come to kiss yet another beguine, "sticking his nose in my mouth, or mine in his, I couldn't really be sure through the confusion." Another man supposedly said: "how vigorously these beguines kiss; my wife won't kiss me so." Clearly it would take much to surprise Peter van der Wiel.

Arguably most remarkable about the man is that after four decades his notes, used to construct a report of his visits for the bishop, were consistently fresh and detailed. He faithfully recorded the common as well as the scandalous, the old as well as the new. Many others would have been worn down by the constant grind. The places might have begun to blur and look alike—from the Poor Clares and Black Sisters in Mechelen to the Augustinians of Kabbeeck in Tienen, from the Beguinage of Vilvoorde or the lofty noble canonesses of Groot Bijgaarden to the particularly poor Leprosy houses of Brussels or Mechelen. In addition to these, Van der Wiel maintained as well his small, neat list of those priests interviewed for worthiness to preach, hear confession, and care for parishes. And in the days before photocopiers, he never tired of writing out the same examination formula for convent after convent and sister after sister during interviews for profession.

Nor is there sign of discouragement or resentment that his otherwise impressive climb up the ecclesiastical ladder had stopped where it did. There is no hint that Van der Wiel simmered about being passed over for the archbishopric at the death of Hovius. He had been fifty-six at the time, had long served with distinction and diligence, and then had run the diocese with the episcopal throne vacant, a responsibility that not uncommonly led to the archbishopric itself. He had been present at Hovius's deathbed and probably was even traveling with him, until Boonen showed up to administer last rites and hear last requests. It was Van der Wiel who stood proxy at Boonen's installation in November 1621, since the latter was too busy to come himself. (Upon hearing that, many dignitaries stayed away as well and sent proxies of their own.) But there is no evidence that, as he regarded the long procession in the cathedral, bore the papal documents, heard the bells ring *maxima campana*, proceeded into the red-draped choir to near the high altar, where canons, dean, municipal leaders, and others paid him reverence, and then as he knelt to take the oath of loyalty and of the episcopal office and was finally enthroned, Van der Wiel ever let the tempting thought pass through his mind that the position should have been his.

With him for this visitation of Bethlehem was the dean of Leuven, the plodding but reliable Peter Lucius, even more devoted to record-keeping than Van der Wiel himself. While the latter kept records as a means to an end, Lucius delighted in the record for its own sake. His annual visitation reports were brutally consistent—in length, regularity of submission, even subject. Spotty on spiritual matters, they contained everything the bishop might want to know about altars, services, foundations, accounts, or decor. Lucius's greatest strength was his tolerance of tedium, for he reported these things annually, all as if a new and unusual discovery. Every year when he described his own church, St. Michael's, he wrote faithfully that its pastor was Peter Lucius. And every year from 1623 to his death in 1629, he noted the same problem in his parish (one-tenth of his 1,800 parishioners lived outside the walls of Leuven and he could not easily minister to them) and requested the same solution (a vicar). Among his other notes was news of a visit to St. Gertrude's monastery in 1621; the pastor (still Henri Joos) was absent on account of attending a profession feast across the street for a beguine. Lucius's superior wondered whether Pastor Joos had been told of the visitation in advance, and if so then why he had been absent. Lucius didn't respond, for he clearly wasn't any more forceful than he was imaginative. This is evident in his reluctance, unlike later and earlier deans, to visit the collegiate churches in Leuven of St. Peter's and St. James's, telling the bishop that the canons of each opposed it, yet knowing full well that his predecessors had pushed their way inside anyway.

If not the strongest or most interesting personality in the world, Lucius could be counted on by the bishop to do such things as assist with the interviews of the sisters of Bethlehem. Though less experienced than Van der Wiel, he had seen enough to make him unruffled, including a recent visit to the convent called Florival, where four sisters were accused of, among other things, engaging in sexual relations with men. Thus the learned, intelligent Van der Wiel and the trustworthy Lucius brought deep background to this current visitation in Bethlehem.

They knew this house about as well as any other. It was Van der Wiel who had visited in 1616, on one of his first assignments outside Mechelen, and since then he had been at least four or five other times—this in addition to mail received. He and Lucius saw that there had been six official visitations over the past sixteen years, which was short of the ideal of once yearly, but in a diocese with over four hundred parishes and fifty to one hundred other convents, about as good as it got. Unfortunately, of those visits only the last had resulted in any official written proclamation or *determinatio* at the end—a declaration to the sisters of what needed to be corrected—and so the visitors probably doubted that much change had come about. Despite lack of past reports, both were familiar enough with this place and with conventual visitations generally to predict the chief issues.

In the first place, Van der Wiel and Lucius knew about Margaret, about the incident with Barbara Beli, and about the eternal reluctance of the Franciscan confessors to serve the convent unless granted full jurisdiction. They also knew about the 1626 statutes that had ushered in a new era of reform in Bethlehem and the troubles that had resulted from the 1627 reforms of the convent's grilles. And last, they knew that Boonen had done as much as could be expected for this house, perhaps as much as he had done anywhere else. Besides a couple of personal visits, the archbishop had just last December—no doubt to soothe the wounds from the decree on receiving guests—sent the nuns an anointed ring and paid to have a copy made for each one of them, twenty-three rings in all. The rings were made by February, at which time the sisters offered thanks for his "fatherly affection" and invited him regularly to come and put the rings on their fingers. But Van der Wiel might have wondered why they did not show thanks through their behavior.

All this and other thoughts and experiences unknown to us were in the minds and souls of these men as they presented credentials to the sisters, probably in the church, and then retired to the parlor to speak with each sister at the grille. The entire process usually took a day or two. Van der Wiel would question and prompt, Lucius was there to employ his skills at recording. This ensured that there were at least three filters in the process: the sisters themselves, who had to choose from all the possibilities exactly what to tell the visitors; Dean Lucius, who decided what should be written down and what not (these could be extremely brief notes, or go on for greater length, but how accurately they reflected the comments of the sisters is impossible to say); and Van der Wiel, whose task it would be to pull everything together at the end, decide what should be addressed, and organize it all for presentation to the archbishop.

As customary, the two visitors interviewed the sisters in order of seniority of profession, though Mater and Vicaress might come at beginning or end. Today Mater Adriana was first. Before Van der Wiel could even begin with the giving of the customary oath, she solemnly requested to be removed from her office. As a sign of her seriousness she handed him the convent's keys. Even Van der Wiel must have been taken aback, and he undoubtedly eyed Adriana to decide whether this was bravado. Lucius diligently wrote it all down in his thick black letters and straight up-and-down hand. Van der Wiel calmly refused her request and began with the administering of the oath, which reminded her that she was bound to tell the truth so as to unburden her conscience and improve her convent. With Mater he wouldn't necessarily go down the list of questions prepared—a list similar to what he used in other cloistered houses—but he did touch upon all the major issues, asking her suggestions and opinions.

Tension in the house became even more evident in the second interview. Vicaress Catharina Rijckeboer enacted a scene similar to Adriana's, asking to be let go, complaining that Mater did not trust her enough. Again Van der Wiel refused and continued. After Catharina, and armed with new ideas for questioning the other sisters, the interviewers turned to the longest professed, eighty-one-year-old Anna van den Broek, and proceeded through to the most recent, twenty-four-year-old Anna Vignarola. This included fifteen veiled sisters in all. As for Margaret Smulders, she came last, given her status outside the community. Then it was on to the seven lay sisters, until all had been asked their opinion on the general state of the house and on the usual major points of *clausura,* outside friends, and other persistent or recent problems.

In Bethlehem, and probably elsewhere, there was more to the visitation than just interviews. Sisters who wished to bend the ear of the archbishop or Archdeacon Van der Wiel, or who suspected that visitors might neglect pet issues, brought along letters as well, which they swore were as valid as interviews. In fact, for the historian this witness is even more valid because it was unfiltered by a secretary, good as Lucius was. From interview summaries, one can only guess at the length of the conversation or what a sister thought most important. But letters by the sisters themselves, potentially of unlimited length (a potential most dramatically fulfilled by Margaret), allowed much greater freedom and offered a chance for fuller revelation. This is what makes them important—that while the nuns obviously still chose and excluded, they did so entirely on their own.

Five sisters presented such letters at their interviews: Mater, Maria Joos, Catharina, Maria Coninxloo, and of course Margaret. Anna Vignarola also handed over a letter, but only the next day, perhaps after learning that some of her rivals had done the same and after deciding to respond to what she reasonably guessed they had said. The way she learned about a rival's intent may not be such a mystery after all—for she talked with the visitors just before Margaret, and on her way out she could not have helped noticing Margaret's conspicuous deposition, which even ample religious habits would have been able to conceal with difficulty (assuming of course that Margaret tried to hide it at all). Originally Anna explained, "I said nothing about a few issues, thinking it unnecessary." Now, however, "recognizing that we must bear it upon our conscience if we know something and say nothing," she had more to tell. "My intent was to say nothing to anyone in the world," but "after investigation of my conscience I desire to reveal what I know and you and the archbishop may do your pleasure with it."

Most letters were about the length of Anna's, one to two sheets, usually written on both sides, and composed probably in an hour or so. Van der Wiel couldn't help but notice the eight-page letter of Maria Coninxloo, but even this anomaly was dwarfed by the incomparable pile left by Margaret Smulders—it was so large that making any notes of her interview was practically unnecessary. Even Van der Wiel had never seen anything like it. He knew that Margaret had written the bishop several times, but none of those letters had been extraordinarily long. This one was longer than the interview summaries and the other five letters put together (all of which added up to twenty-four pages). Whatever Van der Wiel or Boonen thought about Margaret's emotional stability or rambling style—and at least Van der Wiel did not regard them highly—they never ignored what she wrote.

Van der Wiel gathered up these letters and Lucius's notes and took them all with him back to Mechelen. Unlike us, he may have saved Margaret's unmissable treatise for last and begun with the shorter testimonies of the others.

16. OTHER VOICES

EVENTUALLY VAN DER WIEL would discover that on many points a good number of sisters agreed with Margaret, if in fewer words, while others saw things in a wholly different light. The more modest views are as important to the story as Margaret's panorama, not so much for testing whether she was "right" but simply for revealing the extent to which sisters concurred or dissented. We can thus, again, learn not merely about the state of reform (if such a thing can be assessed), but about how personal relationships helped to shape religious life and to influence one's view of its well-being.

Because of the prominent role that factionalism played in this shaping, the sisters' comments, whether drawn from letters or interviews, can best be organized as Margaret suggested: around those who praised Mater and those who did not. Six or seven neutral sisters alternately criticized and applauded Mater as well as her rivals, but most other nuns saw issues from the viewpoint of one of the two informal groups. This was especially true of the letter-writers, led willingly or not by Catharina and Maria Coninxloo as critics of conditions in the convent, with Mater, Anna Vignarola, and Maria Joos as the defense. Indeed, the vast majority of what each of these women wrote focused on only those nuns involved in the two factions, as if the remaining twenty sisters hardly mattered. It may be that some of these twenty were illiterate or too busy to write yet still played important roles in the day-to-day life of Bethlehem—Anna Coninxloo or Joanna Schoensetters come to mind as possibilities. But given the nearly exclusive focus of the letter-writers on each other, it's more likely that the struggle over the past, present, and future of Bethlehem was truly to be won or lost among these few.

One other preliminary point will help in examining the letters and interview summaries: Criticism of Mater Adriana was louder than support. Catharina's letter was four pages and Maria Coninxloo's eight, while Mater's was one page, Anna's two, and Maria Joos's a half page. But criticism also dominates the half- or quarter-page summary of each sister's interview. Such want of balance between praise and censure was not unusual in visitations, partly because of the habitual focus on problems and partly because if political motives were involved, then usually more effort was expended in showing that things were wrong than right. Those who favored the regime of Adriana summed up their praise quickly or implied their approval by saying nothing at all when the visitor asked about problems. Still, Adriana's friends were not without sharp teeth of their own.

LOVE SOME OF THY SISTERS AS THYSELF

It may be helpful to begin as Margaret did, with the issue of Adriana's general leadership and her favoritism. At least six nuns—several of them neutral—agreed with Margaret that Mater was too distant from the community, partly because she was consumed by temporal affairs (which she managed poorly anyway); partly because she favored Anna Vignarola, Maria Joos, and Lesken Joos; and partly because she was hard—"more to be feared than loved." One suggested Mater be replaced as bursaress by Maria Coninxloo, while another argued that Adriana should be left as bursaress and a new Mater elected instead, preferably Catharina.

Catharina and Maria Coninxloo themselves had more to say about the sentiments against Adriana. This they did by occasionally repeating Margaret, but often by producing fresh commentary of their own. Although the object of much support and sympathy in the convent, Catharina had no wish to be seen as head of a faction, especially one in rebellion against Mater. It was true, she admitted, that Adriana disliked her, yet she tried to downplay personal tensions and the existence of any cliques. "I think that there is no one among all the sisters who is more suited than [Adriana to that office]. If there are any complaints about her, she can improve herself through admonishment, for she has good understanding." Still, if favorites were played in the convent, Catharina was willing at least to hint that Mater was most to blame: "There is no one who, if she wishes, is better able to mold the sisters to her will than this Mater, for there are many who are very devoted to her, who to please her would do or refrain from much; if there are some, as happens, who would gladly have her removed and rather have another appointed as superior, then there would also be others who are devastated." Catharina pointed out that the very sisters who complained most about Adriana had shortcomings of their own. Such detachment by Catharina, though not perfect, is impressive. And if some griped that Mater "doesn't respect me or that we don't speak much with each other or the like," wrote the vicaress, "I pray most humbly that for my sake she not be reprimanded or admonished in this regard by your reverence. For though neither affection nor goodwill is very great between us, it may be that the blame lies more with me or in me. I believe it would be best simply to appoint another vicaress with whom Mater would see more eye to eye, therefore I pray most humbly to be removed."

In trying further to remove herself from any hint of sympathy for any faction, Catharina explained her sometimes uncomfortable association with Maria Coninxloo, a woman who quite openly criticized Adriana and rather embarrassingly cheered on the vicaress. Mater presumed that Maria was the source of any criticisms Catharina brought. Catharina didn't deny that she spoke often with Maria, but pointed out that it was Maria who came calling upon her, not the other way around. "It's certainly true that I have a marvelous Gabriel," a term Margaret once used as well in referring to Catharina's relationship with Maria, "who comes to announce all things to me, so that I must often exert great effort to remain calm as I listen to all the prattling and take pains to see that it not reach the ears of Mater." Certainly, though, Adriana constituted a bigger test of patience for Catharina than did Maria. "Everyone knows," the vicaress went on, "that I'm not held in much esteem by Mater. . . . It's well that it will last only for this life. . . . It injures and greatly wounds my heart that I'm now so alienated, and that necessity compels me to be silent and to observe only. I don't know why [Mater] regards me so badly; I have never denounced her to the superiors, neither to my illustrious reverence [the archbishop] nor to his vicar, much less anyone else. For in truth I know nothing that I could say about her which would contribute to the lessening of her good name or honor. If she's spoken ill of me, perhaps that occurred without fault, it doesn't really matter to me. Nevertheless, I must still work with her and will gladly do all I can to obey her will in all reasonable affairs as it's required." Catharina worked hard in this letter to pull punches, to hide resentment or bury her anger—yet at least her frustration was hard to conceal.

If Catharina hesitated to condemn Mater, Maria Coninxloo did not, as already hinted. Maria pointed out a wide variety of transgressions, including Adriana's failure to protect the precious papers of the convent in the customary well-locked chest. But more than anything else she denounced Mater's partiality against Catharina and herself, and in favor of Lesken Joos, Maria Joos, and Anna Vignarola. Besides a number of examples already trotted out by Margaret, Maria added that when Mater was to be absent from choir, she appointed, even on holy days, whomever she pleased to sing in her place. By rights, Maria reminded, "she ought to allow the vicaress" that place. Further, Mater had several years before arbitrarily appointed Maria Joos as portress, without counsel. Although this appointment had been made in the presence of the Discretes (or council of elder sisters), they complained quietly that they never had much say but were forced to be content with the desires of Mater, for "they fear her biting response." It pained Maria Coninxloo to hear Mater speak so curtly to these older sisters, some of whom had celebrated their fiftieth year as nuns. And of course there was the favorite whipping child, Anna Vignarola. Her appointment as novice teacher, according to Maria, "caused many in the community to be highly disturbed, partly because she was too young and still had much nasty passion and many unsuitable manners and also because she has told so many unbelievable things to the novices." As it did with Margaret, the matter of seniority pained Maria deeply. Maria wrote next of how Mater spoke "much too long" with her final friends, the lay sisters. "When they return from an errand, there is such laughing and whooping, as if it were a wedding, that it shames me to think that people outside hear it all, for her room is next to the street; the people look up, from behind and in front."

To Maria it seemed that Adriana backed all these friends relentlessly, "however small the matter," and acted not on principle but simply because she liked them. "Everything they suggest to her she does; if the community says a word, either in complaint or as suggestion, especially in any matter touching her office or her dear ones, she'll root it right out and make a scene about it. So that I may well say that it's no wonder the members are sick when the head is so sick itself, for I find more perfection in the community than in my superior, whose footsteps I am supposed to be able to follow." Such favoritism resulted not only in ill-feeling but, as others pointed out as well, profound material inequality and poor discipline. "In regard to transgression of the rule or statutes [Mater] takes little or no notice," and when she did punish it was arbitrary—now light, now severe. "In chapter, she's handed out punishments to the young sisters which didn't amount to much at all," punishments that "your reverence never even mentioned in our new statutes, nor which anyone here—even the eldest—has ever witnessed or heard of." Indeed, instead of admitting a fault and then accepting the penance stipulated by statute, some sisters simply invented a penance for themselves or made a general public confession "without accusing themselves of anything in particular." To Maria, part of good discipline was making faults public, rather than trying to sweep them under the rug. The young nuns, regrettably, would never learn the good old ways.

Maria summed up: "It seems as if we're all children. . . . [Mater] lets it be known that she is worthy of all honor, for she thinks ill of her flock; for as the community stands in the refectory to read Benediction and as she passes by and the community shows her honor [by a bow], she'll never return the bow until she comes to Vicaress, and even that's a sight to behold for it's as if she's got a kink in her neck. I'm ashamed that she admonishes others to this or that, but doesn't act herself."

Mater and friends saw the problem of favoritism much differently. This may have been for political reasons, but it may just as well have resulted from sincere difference of opinion—after all, there were ancient monastic edicts and warnings against idle talkers and complainers. Though they never mentioned it, Mater, Anna, and the Jooses could have justified their seeming indifference toward certain nuns through long-standing injunctions to flee from gossipers and complainers as if fleeing the plague. Francis had said that a gossip in a convent was worse than a murderer, for a murderer kills the body but a gossip kills with the sword of the tongue. Guevera wrote that there was nothing worse in a monastery than "to have a neighbor with an unbound tongue," for "if you have much communion with him then he'll teach you to murmur; and if you flee him, he'll defame you. . . . A long tongue will break the peace in a community. Superiors must have unending patience with faults, but they won't easily dismiss a long tongue." Where was the line between the competing ideals of common love and the shunning of nuns with loose tongues? Mater and friends may have genuinely and consciously chosen to give greater attention to the latter, while continuing to hope for the day when love would prevail.

What is explicit in the letters of these women is the contention that if the ugly sin of factionalism existed in Bethlehem, then it was the fault of Vicaress and Maria Coninxloo. Anna Vignarola here exhibited to good effect her reputation for refinement, especially when compared with the repetition and name-calling in the letter of Maria Coninxloo or Margaret. Even her stylish script revealed long experience in writing, while Maria and Margaret both learned their skill after entering the convent. Given constraints of time, Anna necessarily kept her letter short, but it would have been short regardless. She hit hard and fast, and deliberately gave the impression of having left much unsaid—thereby saying still more. Adriana, Maria Joos, Lesken Joos, four of the other five lay sisters, and Anna Vignarola all agreed that the community was well run and in good shape, except for the faults of a cranky few—all of them shamelessly open foes of Mater, none of them qualified to criticize.

Mater, the Jooses, and Vignarola expounded upon a fault in Catharina that was pointed out by several "neutral" sisters as well—her painfully obvious inability to instruct the precious novices to sing. This, wrote these women, was why Anna had been appointed to the task, not for reasons of partiality. Mater Adriana suggested that the root of the novice's inadequate training was in part want of diligence by Catharina, but all came right out and stated that it was largely a question of ability. While Maria Joos merely referred to Catharina's "various impediments," Anna Vignarola—who had the most at stake here—went into greater detail. Anna tactfully suggested in all calmness and dispassion that a special mistress be appointed permanently to teach the novices the most basic elements of singing the Office and reading "and all other things necessary until they profess," at which point they could then come under the sole guidance of the vicaress to complete their spiritual training. The stated reason: "The vicaress is unable to teach them to sing because she has such a poor voice," and though she never said so, Anna probably had a good one. Later, in her most reluctant tone, Anna wished that Catharina would cease her irritating habit of drawing out the last syllables in singing or reading the hours.

But according to Anna, lack of ability was just one of Catharina's faults. Catharina was "also too empty of heart to teach the young ones." For instance, the idea of temporarily appointing Anna to teach the novices to sing the Office originated with Catharina herself, claimed Anna. Anna also declared that she had hesitated to accept this assignment, "fearing the gossip that might proceed from Sister Maria [Coninxloo] and even more the gossip that would flow to her, but Vicaress had promised that she would heal that, and would even ask your reverence expressly to forbid such attacks, but they were all human promises. Before one of them was reprimanded for gossip the vicaress had changed her mind, and they burdened me with fanciful lies which are known to none except God and my confessor, whose counsel I sought, and which no one else will ever know if it pleases God." Inspired by the now-vengeful Catharina, the silent reproaches of the other nuns "almost killed me," lamented Anna. "My conscience couldn't bear the evil that resulted out of hate, because I was the youngest [professed] and was able to teach the young ones to sing." Anna contended skillfully that the others acted thus because they were "so eager for office, which is completely contrary to my condition, for there is no better rest than to have nothing extra to do so as better to serve God; that's the reason why I left the world in the first place."

Perhaps more grave to some than the vicaress's attitude toward the novices, or her chronic "tardiness" to the common workroom (Catharina was preoccupied with private devotions, said Mater), or her skipping of Divine Office to speak with Margaret at the grille, was that she was "factional." Adriana led the charge, "protesting out of sisterly love and for the peace of the rest of the community" that Vicaress favored Maria and Anna Coninxloo, "cranky persons who have not yet killed their passions"—a favorite phrase by parties on all sides. Catharina gave too much ear to their tales and "proceeds from that," so that she was now the "cause of much contention, murmuring and bad feelings." Catharina was also too quick to complain herself, "whether concerning confessor, superior, or cosister." Adriana believed that Catharina needed to pay more attention to "bearing a common love," entreating each who was in need rather than "passing her time with two or three persons only." Maria Joos followed, even stating that Catharina was despised precisely because she favored Maria Coninxloo. And Anna Vignarola was close behind, writing that Catharina was too indulgent of Maria Coninxloo: "not that she imitates her in her silliness, at least I hope not, for she is God-fearing, but she doesn't reprove Maria or tell her she's wrong or steer her to humble ground, as our holy Father Francis suggests. I have already experienced often that she says much but does little; I'll leave it at that." Such an abrupt end effectively aroused more doubt about Catharina than if, like Margaret, she had gone on ad infinitum.

As for the vicaress's chief "hanger-on," Maria Coninxloo, opinions grew still worse. Adriana wished that Maria would be more modest and "reverent toward her superiors." According to Mater, Maria had even tried to tamper with the novices, attempting to persuade one of them not to speak with Mater at all, besides committing other express violations of the statutes. The situation was so serious that Mater had been compelled to lead this novice through a kind of deprogramming session. Anna characterized Maria in a way that was sure to get the attention of any obedience-loving seventeenth-century cleric: "She is becoming so stubborn that I fear she will be almost unrulable, for she is not to be admonished; if the confessor admonishes her, then she calls everyone around to proclaim that he restricts her conscience; when our reverend Mater warns that she does more harm than good, Maria complains that she says it out of hate or that she doesn't like her; but in truth she isn't worthy of all the effort Mater makes to humble herself to show that she loves Maria." As for Maria's treatment of Anna herself, it was so despicable that Anna refused to comment further—again implying much by saying little. "It's as if Maria had made a vow at her profession to cause unrest," Anna speculated, for she would stir sisters up who had been assigned penance by telling them that Mater acted out of passion rather than judgment. "Let's hope that God won't reckon such behavior too heavily."

One of the most serious accusations which Mater and Anna leveled against both Catharina and Maria Coninxloo (and which Margaret had also implied against Mater and the lay sisters) was that they used ecclesiastical visitations not as instruments of loving correction but as weapons against other sisters. Such a claim could discredit Catharina and Maria in two ways. First, it emphasized the damage to common love that resulted from abusing the visitation. And second, it suggested that anyone who engaged in such was not to be fully believed in any of the statements she might make against others during a visitation. Mater wished that Catharina and Maria Coninxloo, along with cousin Anna Coninxloo, would refrain from telling the world about their contributions to the visitation. Proclaiming to others that a given decree was the result of their initiative could only have been a self-serving effort meant to prove that they had influence among the visitors while the other nuns did not. Similar behavior was frequently mentioned and condemned in visitations during the Age of Reform, and many visitors must have seen it as one of the unfortunate consequences of the latest burst of zeal.

Anna Vignarola had the longest tale of all this time around. "When the visitation decree is first read, or is read subsequently at the prescribed intervals, there are a few who sit and laugh proudly and make a ruckus, especially Sister Maria Coninxloo, who sits there counting on her fingers each decree which she supposes was made at her behest, showing by her manner and expressions that those persons who are wanting in any of these points are to know with certainty that it was she who sought or suggested it. But that isn't enough, for she stays long to loiter and chatter, bragging that she'd been heard in all her requests, so that everyone knows it." She spoke loudly enough for all to hear, continued Anna, and would claim that in the next visitation she'd certainly have a few more choice bits of information to pass along. Anna warned the visitor that Maria was adept at framing her words and requests in such a way that it was impossible for an outsider to realize that she was motivated by passion alone, not by love. "Love is certainly broken by all this, and many lies and sins result; she brings into the house great unrest in every way." Naturally, Anna had tried "all means, with goodness, to win her," to show that "I have compassion for her soul, but it does no good, so that I know not what to do but to pray and to have patience." Anna concluded her letter with yet another stroke of tact and moderation, which by way of contrast only accentuated the less refined nose-to-nose style of Maria Coninxloo: "Though I've written all this, I put it completely in the discretion of your reverence, and take it upon my conscience to declare that what I've written is true, for I'd not write one bit more than necessary; I've intended to unburden my conscience . . . for my heart wishes nothing but peace; we must bear one another's crankiness, that's why we live together." Hoping that the Holy Spirit would guide the visitor to a good decision, she signed "worms for lunch if God wills it."

Rather than refute their rivals on every point that was sure to be made, Mater, Anna, and the Jooses decided instead to target the reliability of their expected accusers. They made some direct accusations, but overall Mater and her supporters struck by showing their foes' penchant for passion and vengeful factionalism. Who could believe a person motivated by passion? They saw little need to say much about any other topic, implying that all else in Bethlehem was quite well.

MAMMON

The remaining comments, on the myriad of other subjects of conventual life, are therefore even more heavily weighted against Mater. Those belonging to Mater's faction were absolutely silent about almsgetting, waste, and devotion and had only a bit to say about cloister—to these women conditions in Bethlehem were obviously quite satisfactory.

But again, we don't have to look hard for critics, beginning with the popular subject of the convent's cuisine. Then came several protests of ill-guided economic policies, including the waffle-baking ("you can find more about this in Sister Margaret Smulders's Bull," using a term usually reserved for reference to papal documents), mass production of Agnus Deis or little flowers ("there is nothing but Anna must have it"), and the familiar catering to outsiders ("I've heard many sisters say that in seven years they have never laid teeth on such meat" as was prepared for outsiders, or "It didn't cause [Mater] any pangs of conscience to set before the community food that was fit for our cow" or bread "which seems as if it's still on the plow").

Maria Coninxloo even complained that Mater robbed from the community not only in what she gave away but in what she withheld. "When Mr. La Motrousen, our steward, gave a recreation here when he was married, he said at that time to Mater that he would give the community wine to fill their stomachs; when he asked how much wine they would like to have, he was amazed at how little; and then on that day I think that no more than two pots of wine were drunk. For she hadn't given the community more than that." And in general when the convent received a gift of food, "Mater must always have a double portion; if she's given something personally from her friends or the convent's friends, then she shares that with her pets." Maria was far from the only sister to bemoan the convent's spare table, but more than almost all the others was she willing to blame Mater's largess.

MONASTIC DISCIPLINE

In only a single area, that of cloister, do we find a bit more response from the party of Adriana. In fact, all sisters agreed on at least one small aspect of cloister: the peril of the two grilles in the church and the need to do something about it. That Mater, Anna Vignarola, and Maria Joos would have raised this problem when they knew quite well that they would have been the chief accused is a puzzle. Or perhaps not. This may have been a sincere wish, an act of humility, a confession of wrongdoing. Such were expected in visitations and in regular chapter meetings, and perhaps we are too eager to find political motivations behind all the recorded comments. On the other hand, as Margaret and Maria Coninxloo would have more cynically seen it, this may have been an attempt to preempt criticism. The violators may have wished to surprise the visitor, to throw him off balance, with their encouragement to reform the grilles. As with so many of these statements, though we know them in rare detail, how can we penetrate the heart behind them? Certainly Anna was often in the choir, certainly several sisters told Van der Wiel of her familiarity with the chaplains, and certainly Anna knew what Van der Wiel would hear. But whether this collective urging of a Margaret-like reform was a prearranged plan, we will never know.

If there was much agreement on the need to close the church grilles, there was so little on other points of *clausura* that we wonder whether certain women were speaking of the same convent. A number echoed Margaret. Catharina and Maria complained that the spirit of cloister in general was poor and noted Mater's failure to appoint two sisters to remain with workmen who labored inside the convent. The vicaress and Maria also mentioned the inconveniences and threats to cloister brought on by the nun-making, merrymaking, birth attending, weddings, and other worldly affairs. Maria added a public relations twist of her own: "I wish that Mater wouldn't let our sisters go to attend women in childbirth, for lay people are very observant of such things." Instead, "it would be better if [Mater] spent her time comforting her sister who is downcast," which may have been an allusion to Margaret or a few other unhappy sisters. Eighty-one-year-old Anna van den Broek contended that the conversations at the grille were lasting too long and that they occurred on communion and confession days and during "Divine Office" and meals.

But many sisters, even Anna Coninxloo, suggested that both the letter and spirit of cloister were well observed, especially among the veiled nuns. Maria Joos admitted that the occasional conversation occurred on feast days and wished that fewer lay sisters should be designated "outside" sisters, but otherwise conditions were strict. Adriana herself claimed that *clausura* was generally better obeyed since the last visitation. She recalled only one breach during the past year, when "a woman brought in firewood, unknown to me." Her one small recommendation was that certain veiled sisters be urged to stay away from the large gate when it was opened, since too many were curious to see what was going on. Yet the admission of these small lapses had a clear implication: They were unimportant exceptions in the ordinarily well-regulated array of doors, windows, and bars. That such an impression was in obvious contrast to Margaret's, Catharina's, and Maria Coninxloo's opinions must be ascribed to explanations mentioned before: The women had not seen the same events in the convent or, more likely and for whatever reasons, reflected different opinions and thresholds of what constituted noteworthy violations of the monastic standard—or even of what that standard may have been.

Greater criticism of the status quo came on the subject of waste. More than a few sisters joined with Margaret in saying that the convent was poorly administered. Many called not only for a new bursaress but also for a new cellaress (charged merely with giving the goods out, not managing and procuring them), a post currently held by Jacomyn de la Haye. Interestingly, Maria de Smet saw no one capable, except perhaps Catharina, but she had "a want of strength" and might not be up to it (our first sign that young Catharina wasn't in top physical health). The criticism reached down to more specific problems as well, the most prominent of which was the question of lavish decoration. Maria Coninxloo stated, among many other things on the subject, that "in all the time I've been here I've never seen so much time spent on the preparations for services since Anna Vignarola became sacristan."

It was Catharina especially who spoke out, no doubt after she and Margaret had long strengthened one another in their views. "It is most desirable that his reverence would prohibit henceforth so much wasteful expense for the decoration of the choir; the amount of money spent is too scandalous to repeat, since we are called—and in fact are—poor." She told a familiar story: Nothing was too costly for them, something new appeared daily, the silken flowers and little altars were so lifelike. She also anticipated Adriana's defense almost exactly as Margaret had done: "Now it's true that Mater will say, 'the decorations don't burden the convent's funds much at all, for the money comes from the private incomes of the sisters.' I don't deny this, but the sisters are the children of the convent, therefore I regard what they have as the property of the convent." Like Margaret, Catharina wished for a greater spirit of communal living, wished that money had been spent on finishing the cloister wall rather than "frills," and she condemned at some length the excessive burning of candles in the choir—for economic, spiritual, and medical reasons. All the smoke even caused Catharina "shortness of breath," a problem not experienced by Margaret herself, and another hint that the vicaress's constitution was delicate.

When it came to devotion per se, rather than its cost, critics of the current order were again easy to find. Joanna Schoensetters and Maria Coninxloo added some detail to Margaret's charges about worldly dress in the house: "It's not right that religious should wear secondhand shoes and slippers," contended Maria, "one wearing white, the other black according to taste, but we should all wear black; I hope that this will be brought into practice." It was not only unseemly to Maria Coninxloo, but "caused much gossip among laypeople, especially the white shoes, for such belongs to the world and not to religious." She wished they would all wear black, as had been the custom, for as the saying went, "like monks, like hoods"—or in other words, people expected to see religious of the same order dressed the same way. There also emerged several comments on the topic of devotion, which had little to do with current struggles in the house. For instance, Anna Coninxloo wanted a priest during the "wee hours," for the man appointed from the college of Regulars had not performed well. Maria Joos and others expressed the wish of many seventeenth-century nuns when they requested weekly communion (and thus confession), "for the promotion of our souls."

But more frequent than such requests were the potentially loaded criticisms. Personal tensions were quite apparent, for instance, in the subject of proper performance of the daily services. Anna and Mater had criticized Catharina for want of musical inclination. Instead of denying that she had a bad voice, Catharina countered by hitting Anna and Mater in areas where they were vulnerable, including failure to seat the sisters by seniority of profession. Maria also chimed in, since after all she was one of the nuns most injured by Adriana's humiliating seating arrangements: "Mater says that it's not necessary to observe this point strictly, which I take a very different view of, for if it were so then why do we need a rule or statutes at all?" If Maria and Catharina had lost standing and power in the convent, they hoped at least to preserve some measure of respect through an acknowledgement of their seniority and position. Maria was even more insistent about the lack of reverence during the Office, perhaps out of a true devotion for it, perhaps out of resentment toward Anna Vignarola's recognized expertise in the choir. She asked the visitor to command that "during the Office as well as during the sung Mass the sisters would not close their books before the services are done, for all the rustling is disturbing and distracting to the service of God." More adamant still was a denunciation of Mater's apathy: "It would also be fitting if there wasn't any sleeping in the choir after our [midday] meal, of which Mater is the most guilty, for she sleeps not only on Sundays and feast days, so that she won't sleep during the sermon, but it happens almost daily so that I've begun to think that she's made her bed in the choir, for she sometimes sleeps there during the entire service. It is a cause of dissension, and it is necessary to have greater reverence in the choir, and to sleep after rather than during the Divine Office." Maria went on that services and devotions were also lax on special days, marked by too "much strolling in the garden, for some are more inclined to go and pick lettuce on these days than on work days, and to play and sing and such things, which in my view probably is not practiced in any convent. . . . There have been friars who came to preach and then saw many of our sisters in the garden; when they went back home they said that they assumed it had been a recreation day."

On that topic of recreation, only three women bothered to comment, and all were strong critics of Mater. This implies that few sisters had any problems with past traditions of play in the house or in monastic culture generally. Catharina confirmed one of the problems pointed out by Margaret: that Mater was the ringleader of excess. But Catharina did so in a way to confirm once and for all that she and Margaret had bolstered each other regularly in their views. "She commands them in chapter and out that they must play, as if it were a matter touching upon the glory of God and the salvation of the soul, and says that she considers that sister most devout who most does her duty in playing. Perhaps in some cases this mixture can occur, but that no one can be devout except she who is most earnest at play? So is it most wondrous indeed then to consider all the devoted Carthusians and Capuchins who seldom or never indulge in recreation," reminding us of the precise example employed by Margaret. "I am not saying that play should be forbidden on recreation days, but only that the sisters not be so compelled to have fun."

As a postscript to this sampling of views, it should be noted that there was one remarkable omission: Though many sisters agreed with Margaret, almost no one bothered to mention her, as if she were out of their minds. Only old Anna van den Broek, around long enough to possess a deep well of charity, volunteered a single comment—namely, that Margaret be allowed her place in the refectory, choir, and workroom, though not the dormitory. To most others, Margaret Smulders was clearly not a part of the community. But as much as they wished to forget her, obviously she had not forgotten them.

17. DETERMINATIO?

If thou, Lord, shouldest mark iniquities, O Lord, who shall stand?
—PSALM 130:3, PART OF THE SIXTH PENITENTIAL PSALM

MECHELEN, THE ARCHIEPISCOPAL PALACE, LATE SUMMER 1628. What the episcopal officials thought and did about Bethlehem was another part of the ongoing process of shaping religious life inside the convent. Their opinions and decrees were not, at least in a practical sense, absolute and final—they didn't mark the end or "result" of reform, for the give-and-take with the sisters was only perpetuated by formal pronouncements. But, in theory and fact, they did matter to the women within.

It was Archdeacon Van der Wiel who as chief visitor had the primary task of drawing up the balance sheet and suggesting action to the archbishop. In addition to the documents taken from the visitation, he now had in hand very recent news from Catharina, dated July 3, a couple of weeks after his visit, which she wished him to consider before composing a final *determinatio*. It informed him that "certain sisters," especially Maria Coninxloo, eagerly awaited the official pronouncement. But Catharina's main purpose was to retract several accusations and reiterate others, both of which offer a closer look at the politics of reform within the convent. The retractions first: Since workmen were now accompanied by two nuns, there was no need to correct Mater on this point; as for the excessive bouquet-making, it wasn't that bad after all, and thus would his reverence please ignore that point as well. But Catharina remained adamant about reducing expenses for decoration, especially since these expenses showed no sign of abating—painting of the large shrine in the choir had begun the past week, and the artist was already threatening to quit unless he was paid immediately. To Catharina this was all waste and trouble, for the shrine was already built of finely crafted wood, hardly needed adornment, and on feast days was so covered with flowers that one could barely see the painted scenes anyway. Anna Vignarola insisted that she'd find the funds, but this only reminded Catharina of when the shrine was made in the first place: Mater had claimed that a gift from Henri Joos would cover expenses, but the convent had ended up paying for most.

Though Catharina insisted on change, she expressed the usual nervousness about how it should occur. Van der Wiel should return to

Bethlehem to "see for himself" this overdecoration as well as the two church grilles (or more accurately the communion windows), for he had only *heard* about these things at the visitation. The reason for this suggestion lay not in the need to convince him that complaints were true but in the politics of reform. As Catharina put it, she wanted the vicar-general to see personally "so that both Mater and the sisters can lay aside all suspicion about which sister might have complained. For in this manner they'll be more likely to endure a change, if they suppose it came straight from the superior." Another way to reduce resentment within the convent toward complaining sisters and to heap it upon superiors who were more likely to be obeyed, as well as a clue of Catharina's consciousness that favoritism influenced what the sisters said during their interviews with the visitors, is found in a final suggestion. Before pronouncing, Van der Wiel should speak with their longest-serving permanent confessor of recent years, Johan Martens, much-esteemed *Lector* in the convent of the Franciscans. "I don't write this to suggest that my illustrious lord the archbishop, or the reverend lord his vicar, lack wisdom. . . . But since I've considered that our depositions were undoubtedly spoken from various points of view, one no doubt promising this, another perchance complaining about that, I point to but one person who is probably right, and who speaks with a simple affection for God, without partiality of persons, and who's served us very peacefully and faithfully, and who's been seen this way by one and all."

That Van der Wiel followed these suggestions reaffirms the esteem in which Catharina was held at the episcopal palace, and, since there was now still other work to do, it also lets us know that he didn't begin working on his *determinatio* for Bethlehem right away. But at some point in the late summer, after receiving a general report from Pater Martens (which unfortunately was either not put to paper or did not survive) and with all other documents in hand, Van der Wiel turned to weighing claims.

Certainly the heaviness of the sisters' letters could mislead, in regard not only to the length of the interviews but to the everyday dynamics of the house as well. Margaret had no voice in the monastery yet had most to report; how seriously should she be taken? If a few suggested an almost complete overhaul of the house, while most were content with the status quo except for a few minor failings, then how vigorous should any action be? Even if warranted, how much real change *could* occur? And of course, what motivation lay behind contrasting views—partisanship or devotion? Margaret was not the only one who might have walked a shaky line between the two.

The best way to get a sense of who and what the archdeacon believed is to follow the four steps he took at this point. First, he made notes—

organized roughly by topic—based on Lucius's interview summaries, the sisters' letters, and his own marginal scratchings. Ordinarily he made one set of notes regarding the comments of all sisters in a house. But given Margaret's "prolixic" letter he decided, like Moses, to divide the sea in two: one set of notes for Margaret and one for everybody else. Leaving a large left-hand margin, he summarized faithfully the major complaints, thus revealing his sincere effort at impartiality. We know that he didn't think highly of Margaret, yet he distilled her treatise thoroughly and fairly. And though in one marginal note he reminded himself that Maria Joos "favored Mater," divulging his belief that factions indeed existed, it was with much dispassion that he considered claims from both sides as well as from relatively impartial sisters. In essence, Van der Wiel was detailed, accurate, comprehensive, and yet efficient, condensing into three pages nearly every claim that Margaret had made and into one and a half pages the claims of the others. If his notes on the criticisms of Mater were lengthier than those in support, this was only a reflection of the proportions evident in the interviews and letters. It did not necessarily mean that he believed everything said, despite the assumed sincerity of the nuns.

A better test of what Van der Wiel and other officials believed and what measures they considered most necessary is reflected in the second and third steps: composition of a memo (*memoriale*) listing potential points for the final *determinatio* and then submission of that memo (along with other documents requested) to the archbishop, who added his comments and instructions. This annotated memo, farther along in the process than the raw notes, reflected the vision not of the sisters but of Van der Wiel and Boonen—though the names of sisters relied upon for a given point are usually mentioned. (Most often named as a source is the trusted Catharina, despite Margaret's superior garrulousness.) Next to each point is a note to proceed "verbally" or otherwise. Whether the "verbally" indicated a public pronouncement to all, or merely a private discussion with Mater, is unclear. Some of the points are crossed out, but was that meant to indicate "carried out" or "abandoned"? There's no way of knowing, but by briefly examining the whole we can see at least in which direction superiors were leaning—in the end, the mysterious crossings-out mattered little anyway.

The long notes on factionalism should suffice as a detailed example of how the principal topics were treated: Two points implicitly favored Mater and two favored her critics. Van der Wiel and Boonen condemned the partiality cultivated by Mater, Maria Joos, Anna Vignarola, and Lesken Joos ("a lay sister," as if to say "no less") and criticized their going to the infirmary en masse. This was to be discussed with the confessor and "tactfully" with Mater herself. Here the visitors recognized the potential, which Margaret and Catharina had mentioned earlier, for visitation and reform to sow discord as easily as uproot it. But Van der Wiel found equal fault with the vicaress, especially for having failed to reach out enough to the novices, despite her being "otherwise peaceful and diligent." The instruction was simple: Warn Vicaress. The same warning was attached to the last criticism of Catharina, that she lacked discretion and too easily fielded and shared complaints. But right after this, seeking that ever-elusive balance, Van der Wiel noted that Anna van den Broek (age eighty-one, implying that she was to be believed), Joanna de Vorster (age sixty), as well as Maria de Smet and Anna Servranx (a younger sister, whose age was not mentioned) all praised Vicaress.

And so it went, though ever less in favor of Mater Adriana, while never completely justifying the vicaress. Brief marginal notes repeatedly indicated the action to be taken: Cut back the gift-giving, beware feeding the steward, eliminate the specter of private property, at least now and then use the gifts given to the convent in the infirmary and not merely among "the partial ones" (*partiales*), finish constructing the last segment of the cloister wall, and take seven other steps to improve cloister and behavior at the grille (making this the lengthiest section of the memo and also the heaviest criticism of Mater), allow a personal inspection of the decoration in the choir and of the communion windows in the church, seat by profession in choir, choose Vicaress to lead choir on days when Mater is absent, no more white shoes, find a compromise on play, and stop dressing up a nun as the fool on recreation days. Many of these measures were to be discussed with Mater in private, an unknown number were to be put onto paper for public pronouncement, some were to be pronounced verbally only, and some were to be handled in the presence of both Mater and Vicaress, a scenario that must have made both uncomfortable, especially in light of Catharina's expressed distaste for confrontation.

Reading through this document, however quickly, it is apparent that except for a couple of criticisms of Vicaress, a couple of general points regarding cloister, and a few other miscellaneous items (lock up the convent's papers securely, and yes, you may commune weekly), the conclusions were quite in line with those of Catharina, and by extension Maria Coninxloo and Margaret. Despite the possibility of partisan motives and his distrust of Margaret, Van der Wiel concluded that the problems were real enough. Certainly he did not act on all of Margaret's complaints; the most obvious omission is any specific mention of Henri Joos. But the overall thrust of criticism against Adriana, Van der Wiel seemed ready to believe. At the end was even a reminder to think about an "election of a Mater," and if so then the election of a new vicaress (which suggests that the visitors anticipated the elevation of Catharina to Mater) and the appointment of a separate bursaress. Neither action was a mere formality, for everyone knew that if Mater was doing well, the prospect of an election would never have been raised.

All that remained to seal the victory of Mater's critics (though some would not have wanted to regard it in such political terms) was the fourth step: composition, in Dutch, of the final *determinatio*. This document would normally have been put in Boonen's name, sent to the sisters, and read by them together in chapter four times a year along with the house statutes—and considered just as binding until further notice. The *determinatio* was usually put in general language, with the abundant names mentioned in memos and notes now removed, to avoid public embarrassment of offenders or accusers. Along with the *determinatio* there usually went a separate set of decrees directed at Mater only, delivered privately to protect her position and status. But here was the rub: The archbishop never sent *any* sort of concluding document to Bethlehem regarding the hard-fought visitation of June 1628.

THE FATE OF VISITATION TO 1632. Despite the labors of Van der Wiel, Dean Lucius, and certain sisters, the final, loose ends of the visitation were never tied up, at least not securely or quickly. In August 1628 Pastor Bouckaert wrote Boonen to warn that the door to the confessional in Bethlehem, for "good reasons" known to him, needed permanent shutting up, while in November he could report that Lucius had "heroically" sealed this and several other doors, "driving in the keys with his own hands." The dean also had commanded that the communion window in the choir be fortified with iron bars, so that passing through might be prevented. But besides this, no action based on intelligence gained during the visitation was taken, and the tensions in the convent remained unrelieved.

By 1629 the cries of impatience with the lack of episcopal resolve mounted. A *determinatio*, the sisters knew, usually followed the visitation by a couple of months or less. In some cases it was composed virtually on the spot. For Margaret and other critics the season to expect fruit from the visitation was slipping by. Probably not coincidentally, both she and Catharina Rijckeboer implored Boonen in February 1629 to "conclude" the visitation. Both insisted that completion of the cloister wall, ordered back in 1627 but still nowhere in sight, was especially imperative; as Catharina put it, nothing now prevented the sisters from easily violating cloister except a flimsy hedge and the "fear of God," which in her eyes were insufficient deterrents. Margaret illustrated her anxiety similarly, and added that the romping in the guest room showed no signs of diminishment. Unaware of Bouckaert's regular letters to

Boonen in behalf of her vision of reform, Margaret even questioned her sometime confessor's zeal. Had Bouckaert told the archbishop, she wondered, of her willingness to forgo her allowance from Boonen so that the archbishop might more easily finance the construction of the wall? As a postscript to her several other requests and comments, Margaret reminded Boonen that she didn't want her unkind words about Bouckaert, or knowledge of Boonen's allowance to her, to go any further, and so asked the archbishop to burn this letter. "No one of them knows what I receive annually from your reverence, except Vicaress, under whose obedience I stand. If they knew, then there'd be no peace or love; they wouldn't be able to bear the thought that your reverence does so much for me, otherwise I'd be glad to let them know about the charity your reverence bestows upon me; Vicaress also finds it unwise to tell, for it would hang from the steeple and be on every tongue." Margaret also requested a fragment of the holy cross, or some other "bit of holiness," to combat recent unidentified "troubles." If Boonen sent the relic, he obviously decided against burning the letter.

At the very time that Margaret and Catharina were pleading in early 1629, the vigilant Bouckaert was responding to a request from Boonen for advice on how to wind up the visitation in Bethlehem. Clearly the archbishop had not yet made up his mind, and clearly Bouckaert was now a major figure in the convent. Once again his opinions ran parallel to his charge's, and, like hers, they extended far beyond the issues Van der Wiel had intended for review. Bouckaert touched upon the familiar themes—the need for the new wall, invoking the rule about election of a new mater every three years, better watch over all the doors, and so on—but now Bouckaert claimed to have even more pressing and specific reason for this request: He knew for a fact that there was great peril to chastity in Bethlehem, because of easy ingress and egress. The dean of Leuven agreed with him on all these points and added that if Mater had been more frugal and abstained from "less necessary works," the wall could have been built by now. Bouckaert went still further, turning to problems that had been ignored during Van der Wiel's visitation. Please block and remove, Bouckaert beseeched the archbishop, "that filthy way" the sisters had "of warming themselves," which "is an instigator no doubt in many persons to movements of the flesh." Especially sick religious engaged in this activity, claiming it part of their treatment. But Bouckaert found it a want of modesty, in women generally and in nuns in particular. Though details are sketchy, the "warming" included conspicuous stripping of clothes around the common fire in such a way that, dare he say it, even "common whores" would not tolerate the indecency of it all. Then Bouckaert asked Boonen to bar from Bethlehem "that known person," no doubt Henri Joos, who continuously made his presence felt at the convent by writing, bringing gifts, and receiving presents in return from the nuns. "It may be that this fellow has changed his flesh and soul, may not have any evil intention, but nevertheless," Bouckaert wrote, "I am unconvinced." If Boonen did decide to forbid contact between Joos and the sisters, Bouckaert urged that all arguments and evidence used to do so be based not on notes from the visitation or other depositions but rather on documents put together under Archbishop Hovius. From these Boonen would be able to see Joos more clearly, and would realize that at an earlier time there were serious restrictions upon the former confessor. What Bouckaert left unsaid was that such a method would also shield Margaret, since the campaign against Joos would not be seen to have come from her. Indeed, Bouckaert's pleas and suggestions must have come by way of Margaret, for they also intimate that Boonen had not heard the whole story about Henri Joos. "I'm not sure whether I'm crossing my limits in saying this," Bouckaert tiptoed, "but his presence diverts me from the care of that one whom it has pleased [you] to commit to me."

Despite such urgent warnings, the waiting in Bethlehem dragged on. Nearly a year after the visitation, in April 1629, Maria Coninxloo grieved that the business remained unfinished. She had hoped to write to Boonen sooner about her sorrow, but the house confessor had forbidden it. Indeed, Maria now told the archbishop, he had ordered her to cease writing at all unless there was "great violation of the three monastic vows," saying that "the sins of our Mater were none of my business." "He thought he'd be able to get out of me how many times I'd written to your reverence," Maria reported proudly, "but through the promptings of Our Lord, I was able to leave him empty-handed. . . . I learned later that he took much trouble to discover whether I'd written or not . . . but now he won't know at all. Your reverence can well appreciate the difficulty of the restrictions under which one can live within four walls." In any case, disturbed by the fact that all the evidence offered at the visitation against Mater was being wasted, Maria encouraged Boonen to come and pronounce the final decrees himself. Knowledge that the archbishop had recently been to Leuven but had failed to come to Bethlehem moved many to "great sorrow" and caused the spilling of "many tears of sadness." For "the sins committed here are great, and Mater displays her passion daily, more and more, against the community and the community against her, though Mater is the cause of it all, for she badgers the community more than she exhorts it. . . . They're moved to show their passion as well, so much that my heart breaks to hear and see it all. It's not convent life here; we might as well live in the world." Maria urged an episcopal visit not only to ensure obedience, but for "the comfort of Vicaress, whom I trust will win her place in heaven from all she's had to bear from Mater, but it pains me deeply that she's becoming so thin. If it goes on like this, she might well soon die. She's forced to suffer much, and there's much bitterness against her."

In September 1629 it was Dean Lucius's turn to push for a conclusion and to comment upon the state of the house's doors. According to Lucius, even Catharina was against locking them up now, if only to impede murmuring. In a moment of resolve Lucius denounced such a view: "If concessions are to be made on account of murmuring, they will often murmur against reforms." Finally, in March 1630, there is evidence that Boonen responded, but only in several minor ways. He ordered the confessor of Bethlehem to admonish Mater about unseemly eating or drinking at the grilles—just as he had in 1627—but he made no decisions about the still-unfinished wall. This was all old history and a stopgap solution at best, much less comprehensive than the memo Van der Wiel had drawn up.

How do we explain the archbishop's reluctance to move, especially in light of his deserved reputation as a loyal, diligent shepherd? Did he and Van der Wiel fear issuing a *determinatio* that would have amounted—however carefully worded—to a severe public chastisement of the head of Bethlehem? That it might cause more trouble among the sisters than existed before? Were the two men content with a loud bark rather than strong bite, too zealous to ignore the ideals but too politically astute to enforce them strictly? Did they hesitate due to lack of any suitable replacement for Mater? Did they dread the intervention of outsiders in the convent, as had happened in Florence when the religious in favor of reform had run to the pope for aid while resisters turned to their friends, family, and civic authorities? Or was it merely that Boonen and Van der Wiel were preoccupied as usual? A look at Boonen's agenda between 1627 and 1633 reveals the usual hectic pace of the man. He rarely stayed more than two weeks in any location, and his concerns were crushing. In February 1629 he denounced to pastors and preachers the unfortunate habit of eating sausages and other such foods on unlawful days. He was soon asking for continuous prayers for the church and "this Netherland." There were the usual letters of recommendation to be written, such as one for Philip Antoine van Sestich, Sieur d'Oppem, whose greatest virtue was that he was married to Boonen's niece. In October 1629 Boonen worried about Masses for the soul of his sister, after which came the constant circulars from Isabella in Brussels, and then complaints against a priest whom parishioners mocked with the title "preacher à la mode" because of such extemporaneous sermons as his recent one on the fundamental nudity and fleshiness of humans, for which Boonen had the dean interview the man and warn him of the

hazard this imagery could cause in the weaker minds of the audience—
and on and on.

Was this constant pressure of matters large and small the cause of
Boonen's painfully slow response to Bethlehem? We cannot say for sure
what contributed to the delay. But some time between his warning of
March 1630 and the end of 1632—perhaps just after his cathedral followed the latest fashion by getting its brand-new Rubens altarpiece—
Boonen at long last went to Bethlehem and delivered an oral *determinatio*, of which we have no account at all. And what explanations were
there for this oral pronouncement rather than the standard written one?
Perhaps the officials at the episcopal palace truly had been too busy to
draw up a formal document. It is more likely, though, that the oral
determinatio allowed Boonen to avoid upsetting the political situation in
Bethlehem any more, while still showing that he was concerned with
conventual ideals. Many must have known the contemporary idiom,
"the spoken word flees, but the written remains." Lack of an official
document was therefore unfortunate in the eyes of Margaret, Maria
Coninxloo, and Catharina, and unfortunate as well for us. Though the
private thoughts of Van der Wiel and Boonen seem to have condemned
Adriana, we will never know exactly the extent to which these two men
were willing to agree publicly with those sisters who had so passionately
criticized her.

It would have been much easier, and much less revealing, had the
visitors been able to come to that rare simple conclusion arrived at by
Bishop Triest in a visit to a house of Black Sisters in Flanders at about
this same time: All things were in good order, tranquil, and exemplary.

18. MARGARET'S SECOND BURDEN

THOUGH A BIG ATTENTION-GRABBER and document-producer, it must be noted that visitation was not the only occasion for contact between episcopal officers and the convent. Since formal visitation came to Bethlehem fairly irregularly—thus far 1611, 1616, 1623, 1625, and 1628—we can be certain that informal contacts, and issues besides new reforms, were more common, albeit more poorly preserved.

One such issue has already been mentioned: the question of whether the convent should elect a separate bursaress. The holding of such an election was at last afoot by mid-1629, no doubt thanks to Boonen or Van der Wiel, and the coaxing of Adriana's critics. Adriana hoped to restrict the field to two hand-picked candidates, but Catharina and others opposed such an arbitrary limitation, preferring the customary monastic method of an "open" election. "God sometimes reveals his secrets to the small and weak," Catharina reminded Boonen in a letter of August. "The community is not so simple-minded that they wouldn't miss that something was brewing" if they were suddenly limited in choice. Moreover, Catharina shrewdly pointed out, the subsequent murmuring among the sisters "might come to rest upon your Illustrious Reverence, which I would not be able to bear easily, because they would think that your reverence found it unnecessary to respect their choice." It would be better to destroy the statutes than let the sisters cast "empty votes. . . . I think that Mater wants to hold an election, to have the goodwill of the community, but secretly she wants to be sure that her choice is secure and her pleasure done, which your reverence has undoubtedly been able to discern." In the end, Catharina's advice was heeded, for an open election was held under Lucius's direction on August 20, 1629, four days after Catharina posted her letter. The result was not as Margaret or Catharina had hoped. Maria Joos emerged victorious, with a plurality of votes (ten, including those from Anna Vignarola, Mater, and four of the lay sisters). The remaining thirteen votes were divided among five other sisters. Catharina was one of two sisters who voted for Maria Coninxloo, and Maria Coninxloo was one of two who voted for Catharina. Margaret was not allowed to vote. Thus the sisters had their freely elected, long-sought bursaress. But as some saw it, this hardly restrained Adriana at all.

A second issue was a request from Adriana in June 1630 that Boonen reduce the number of religious services performed by the sisters for friends and benefactors of the convent. This was interesting not so much for the request itself, which was quite routine when a convent felt over-burdened with services and poorly remunerated for them, but because the requested reduction had already been effected in 1617, with the un-official approval of Henri Joos. Besides this, there was Adriana's com-plaint that sisters ran too eagerly to the grille to confess to Jesuits, rather than use the house's permanent Franciscan confessors. She hoped that Boonen would impose order on "two or three restless heads who molest me," thought the house confessors "dignified," and believed that allow-ing different confessors in a house only promoted feuding.

An equally important and better-documented matter was the status of Margaret. In September 1630 Boonen sent a delegation to check on her physical and spiritual health. Did Margaret, annoyed at being ex-cluded from the recent election of the bursaress, ask to be returned to the convent? After all, it wasn't as if she had been excluded at the insis-tence of ecclesiastical superiors. Had Boonen wanted to imprison her, he possessed the will, for—like Hovius—he initiated the locking up of plenty of nuns in his day. But Margaret's situation had not required such action. Boonen probably had an eye on her eventual return, and thus ordered Bouckaert or the new dean of Leuven, Henri Paridanus, to carry out an inquest on Margaret's condition. Six points were estab-lished from this inquest, most of them in Margaret's favor:

1. She was for the time being to remain in her guest room, but only on condition that the guest room right below hers be kept free of outsiders—otherwise she would return to the dormitory.
2. When Margaret was sick Mater was to see that she had the same treatment and service as the other religious, but in her cell rather than the infirmary.
3. Margaret was not yet to be heard as a member of the community, nor to have a voice, except during visitation, as was already the case.
4. When the whole community came to greet an important guest, or when there was a general activity in the parlor, then Margaret was to be free to join in.
5. Sister Catharina was to look after Margaret's temporal needs, in clothing, fire, and light, as Mater looked after the other sisters. This arrangement formalized Catharina's special relationship with Margaret.
6. When there was any distribution of alms to the sisters, Margaret was to have her portion as if she were living in the community with the others.

Margaret must have been encouraged by all this; had her letters helped? Still, her privileges were only partial, and Mater may have done quite as she pleased after the delegation left.

After all this, it remains generally true that what tell us most about life in Bethlehem and other convents of the time are the documents so bounteously generated during visitations. We know quite little about the course and fate of the issues just discussed. But when the next official visitation got under way, the ink began to flow in torrents once again. Though the last visitation had ended with a whimper, it was past time for another—especially in the eyes, hearts, and souls of those whose genuine hope for improvement, or whose desire to see an adversary chastised, sprang almost eternal.

BETHLEHEM, OCTOBER 14–15, 1633. In the year that the old Arch-duchess Isabella died and Leuven was besieged by the Dutch, and the moneyed religious orders left town to wait out the warring season in their private refuges built for this very contingency, and a year after Jacob Boonen joined another diplomatic delegation to negotiate with the Dutch only to see that the cold-blooded Cardinal Richelieu intended to carve up the Spanish Netherlands between France and Holland, thus rendering such negotiations almost useless, the plain, housebound Grey Sisters of Bethlehem received another set of official visitors from the episcopal palace in Mechelen.

Many features of this 1633 visitation mirrored the visit of 1628. Once more the sisters produced a respectable stack of detailed documents. Once more it was Peter van der Wiel who led the visitation, though for reasons unknown he was now accompanied by a colleague from Meche-len rather than the dean of Leuven, and his interviews required two days instead of only one. Once more Van der Wiel called the sisters to the parlor in order of profession, though this time Margaret—the fifth most senior nun—was interviewed in proper sequence rather than last. Once more the interview summary, though composed now by Van der Wiel himself, was more concise than the accompanying letters. Once more six sisters wrote letters (Joanna de Vorster replaced Maria Joos), though now the supporters of Adriana, having divined the onslaught upon them in 1628—no doubt thanks to rumors or the keen perceptions of Anna Vignarola—were better prepared than before. Yet once more was Margaret the champion author, with sixteen pages, while the others wrote the usual one to four. For purposes not completely clear—perhaps to defend her slowly improving position in Bethlehem and to make it better still—Margaret had composed a second monumental document, one that was even more bold than her last.

Margaret's interview consisted of one topic only, if we can believe

Van der Wiel's notes. Though "because of bad times" the pastor of Mol, Henri Joos, now came less often to Bethlehem, Margaret wished that he would stay away completely—yet if Joos were banned she knew that an angry reaction would follow. And that was all Margaret had to say about the man. Clearly Joos's presence still troubled her, but she apparently spent no more effort on him during this interview and she made virtually no mention of him in her letter. Whatever lay behind this, the absence of Joos in her writing may alone explain why her 1633 letter was only half as long as the magnum opus of 1628.

Margaret's report of 1633 was not only shorter but also more organized than that of 1628—even almost pithy. Instead of extended stream-of-consciousness entries interspersed with choppy anecdotes, here were forty-two consistent, briskly delivered accusations, two or three paragraphs at most (save for a couple of one-page outbursts halfway through and a four-page barrage against Maria Joos near the end). In form, it resembled closely the concurrent visitation letter of Catharina, who of course was privy to Margaret's writing. We wonder whether Catharina had suggested this simpler pattern, and whether it reflects an effort to improve credibility with order-loving officials? Margaret also tried to promote reliability through the usual disclaimers: "I'd intended to say or write as little as possible about these subjects, especially since I can imagine that no one else will mention them and thus I'll appear all the less believable. But my conscience moved me to write it all and thus I've relieved my conscience. For there are many things about which they have no regret, because they do them all so gladly" (35).* At another point, Margaret expressed similar thoughts. "I hope that your reverence will excuse me for writing so much, but I protest that I haven't written anything but the truth, God knows that, neither is it possible to write everything. . . . But since we have no refuge in Mater, who ought to help us according to her ability—God improve it, it's far from there—I have taken my flight to you, who art our father" (41).

DIVIDE AND RULE

As in 1628 and as hinted in this last sentence, Margaret focused on Mater Adriana and the three major areas in which her leadership proved deficient. But this time Margaret called for more drastic measures, urging the replacement of Adriana as Mater rather than mere chastisement.

The root of all ills, according to Margaret, continued to be Mater's

---

*As in chapters 11 to 14, parenthetical numbers indicate from which of the forty-two letter-writing sessions the quotations come.

persistently arbitrary, noninspired, self-guided rule. Mater made many important decisions without first consulting her Discretes, contrary to the statutes. "She would say, 'I don't do the least thing without advice, for I don't gladly stand on my own.' I believe that's certainly true . . . but from whom does she seek advice? Sister Vignarola and Sister Maria Joos" (37, 19). A specific and new example of rule by the proud and few was the decision to take in the laundry of the Jesuits. "We've had to endure it two years and keep still, but who's been asked about it? Not one of the Discretes was consulted. Maria Joos and Mater simply decided it. They would say, 'it's good profit,' but if that's so then why didn't Sister Maria see that profit many years ago?" When the idea first came up in 1625, Margaret recalled, Maria had opposed it. " 'What will come through this wash but unrest,' she said. Someone reminded her of that, but she denied it; we know to the contrary that it's true. But her lord brother was no rector at that time" (36). With this last, vague comment Margaret insinuated that the convent took the wash in not only for the income but due to goading from Henri Joos, who was now nurturing some vaguely recorded relationship with the Jesuits of Leuven. Perhaps his efforts to get Bethlehem to take the wash represented a quid pro quo: After all, the Jesuits' support of Joos's candidacy for the pastorship of Mol back in 1624 had helped him to win the position. Or was it merely the latest mutual scratching of influential backs?

In any case, the primacy of favoritism in Bethlehem showed no sign of waning. Those who were out of favor not only remained stifled, but more than ever were in want of proper affection. Except for her coterie, Margaret alleged, "Mater bears no care nor love for her community; those she doesn't like she treats as if she doesn't even know them. . . . She exhibits neither sympathy nor compassion, as if she were a stone" (21). Day after day Adriana "prances with her neck in the air, so that one hardly knows whether she should dare address her." What kind of a mater was that? "Very bossy, hard, sarcastic, quickly agitated and so upset that she shakes and has death in her eye for the smallest word that contradicts her will" (32). Clearly Adriana's preference for power above love and discipline had endured, at least as Margaret saw it. "She's got some who come and inform her of everything, they bring in many lies which no one had ever dreamed of. They're quick to tattle on those whom they know don't stand in Mater's grace, and they please Mater in this. It's an evil that does much harm. Mater has told me herself," no doubt in the context of a threat, for we can hardly imagine Adriana and Margaret speaking casually, "that not one word is said but that it's repeated to her immediately" (22).

Adriana's continued intimidation of unfavored sisters was just as unsettling, and it grew sharper after every ecclesiastical visitation. Margaret wished that when the visitors left Mater wouldn't say " 'I know well whence this or that comes.' God knows," lamented Margaret, "all the things I've had to bear and suffer in this regard, in sighs and words," confirming that others did begrudge Margaret for what they guessed she had written. Adriana also allowed Maria Joos, Anna Vignarola, and even Lesken Joos to belittle other sisters and to threaten them with punishment or removal. "So and so will have to go to another convent, or live as a recluse, if she continues to be so difficult, and many other things; they've done this to Vicaress, and were on her like barking dogs in front of the full community, as if they intended to turn the convent upside down." Margaret admitted that she recycled this last piece of intelligence from the previous visitation, but however old the news she obviously thought it an eternally effective prod for authority-conscious clerics. "We wouldn't dare speak in such a manner, even if right" (36).

To her friends, on the contrary, Mater was the same old angel. Mater allowed Maria and Anna "to talk very impudently to her, and her other friends as well; she lets that go unnoticed and it doesn't bother her, but if it comes from someone else, then that must be paid with penance. Even if a word's been said against her in secret, she makes sure that it's paid for mightily in public" (32). As for Anna and Mater, they were closer than before. Wherever Mater went there went Anna merrily as she pleased (18), and whatever Anna wanted Anna got (20). Yet Margaret insisted that such freedom was dangerous for a religious who had not yet "killed" her passions—including her old grudges against Margaret. "Who doesn't like Vignarola won't find herself in the graces of Mater, God be praised I've had my portion of this, for Vignarola has scorned me from St. Anne's day until now, so that she's spoken but three words to me." Such mistreatment was due not only to resentment, implied Margaret, but to Anna's pride at being "fully in charge of teaching the music" (19). Margaret wrote that her relations with Anna had once been better; the two women had actually held conversations years before, "when I was more in her grace" (37). Now "Vignarola surpasses all the rest" in her loathing. "When she approaches me she looks as if she'd like to kick me far away" (42). Whether manifested in general or toward Margaret, Anna's haughtiness was in any case due to Adriana's indulgence. "[Anna's] entrusted with everything, and if the least word is said to her displeasure, then she's on the unlucky one's neck; it's unbelievable, you have to see it to believe it. And what's worse is that Mater and Sister Anna are both blessed in well speaking, and that they're good at denying the truth, as is Maria Joos, and in defending what they will." Then, in her most explicit charge of conspiracy against the three, Margaret wrote that "they know well how to get their way and come to agreements and to make things seem the opposite of what they are. I watch their game of deception in amazement, but the truth will one day be revealed . . . may God give [Mater] grace and us patience" (20).

In sum, Margaret found that "great favoritism" still caused "much murmuring, sorrow, backstabbing, and otherwise. It makes for little love and little reverence for the superior" (22). More specifically, "That familiarity among Mater, Vignarola, and others is so harmful that in my view they ruin each other's souls and as long as it continues then things won't be well here. And I say in good conscience, if there were someone capable of changing things, it would be salvational to change" (19).

THE MISERESS

While Margaret had focused overwhelmingly on Mater Adriana and Anna Vignarola in the letter of 1628, and though she certainly did not ignore them in this new letter, she now shifted her attentions to the sins of Maria Joos, who had become unbearable since her election as bursaress. Maria was merely an extension of Adriana—and just as arbitrary, partisan, and proud. She spoke with "self-righteousness to the other religious, as if she can do nothing wrong herself. She holds her sisters in low esteem, shames them and criticizes each. I fear that her office isn't salvational for her, at least she hasn't been made humble through it but to the contrary" (24). Arrogance made Maria unsuited to a job that required more than accounting skills, but fairness and compassion. She was "much too stingy to her community; when they're sick, she doesn't give them the least thing, except a poor egg," but as before expected the ill to procure things for themselves. "I know we're not rich," Margaret conceded, "and the convent can't pay for all our needs, but to have to go out and buy small things which are already in house is not right. If she had gone to school all her days to study miserliness she couldn't have mastered the craft better" (23).

Margaret explained these charges in more detail in her longest, last, and most impassioned entry. Among other things, she imagined a detailed, back-and-forth scenario. If the archbishop were to warn Maria about such behavior, then Maria would probably say, " 'I can't do it any more'; then you might say freely to her, 'We shall see whether another can do it then'; that might shake her up a bit, for she's very pretty in her office and imagines herself *the* one." As it was, Maria was proud and alienated from her sisters. "We are easily content and we know the means of the house as well as she, but she makes words over the smallest rag. The likes of her can't be found in any convent in the world, I'm sure of that. She has no more compassion nor emotion; whether one talks or is silent with her, she maintains her wooden face. If a portion is distributed and someone says, 'The community doesn't particularly like that,' she replies, 'That doesn't concern me; if I give the portions I've done my job, and if they don't want to eat what I give then let them fast.'" Margaret assessed such an attitude thus: "so impolite and doglike is she." Then further, Maria would "rattle and grumble" over "roasting a turnip or two, or an onion." "For she's a nasty rattler, she'll start in over a draft of beer . . . and if someone wants to buy a hundred pots of beer and they're a penny short, then she wouldn't give it; in her life she hasn't given away a drop of beer."

Another area in which Margaret suffered Maria's close-fistedness was the latter's reluctant redistribution of alms given to the convent—a distressing matter for the poorer sisters. The "Woman In the Leopard has said many times that if any one of us were sick, we may freely fetch a mug of beer for that person, and for anyone who pleases at least once a month." But when anyone tried, "Sister Maria has so many excuses, 'oh that was many years ago and isn't in her means anymore,'" or "'[the sister] isn't sick enough' or 'she can buy beer herself' or 'the month isn't over yet.'" (Note that beer and especially wine were commonly regarded as restoratives for the ill, besides being used to quench thirst, to accompany meals, or for recreation.) Similarly, if someone granted food and drink to the convent for an *extra* "recreation," then Maria gave it out only on scheduled recreation days, so that in the end there was no bounty at all. Though Maria was the "smallest nun in the house, she's the master of us all, God forgive her and grant her love in her soul for her community. . . . She does all that's in her power to yank food right out of our mouths. We have no one who'll speak for us, therefore I pray you for the love of God, give her no foot to stand on in being sharp, but in God's name admonish her."

Clearly Maria, like Adriana before her, had in Margaret's estimation become consumed by economic concerns. "In the summer she walks from morning—during Prime—in the garden, picking apples while the martyrology is being sung, out of fear that someone else might pick them first. It was so wet and misty that I wouldn't have gone into the garden for all the apples in it. . . . But it's the stinginess that does it to her. In the winter when she comes into the kitchen, and however cold it is, she puts three logs on the fire, with no pot hanging over it, and she warms herself, and when she's warm, she pulls the burning logs out of the fire [to extinguish them] right in front of the shoes of the others sitting there." It was such penuriousness that Margaret always returned to, with example after example. She even drove her friends the lay sisters too hard, Margaret decided, "like mules who may never rest, except her cousin [Lesken Joos], who is governess of them all and who helps Sister Maria to be so stinging."

Beyond these broader examples, Margaret could speak from personal experience. "In my life I've never gotten a drop [of beer] I haven't paid for," she protested, "no matter how sick I've been." When Margaret lay ill during the past summer and requested a bit of extra butter from Maria, the latter refused, offering instead only the usual half pound that was distributed on Saturdays. "She had to be so careful about that half pound," Margaret practically wept, "but would the convent have been made poor because of that, I ask you? I could tell a hundred such stories." Maria, on the other hand, lacked nothing, in sickness or health. "If she doesn't like the table [*Klein*] beer, she has the keys and she goes and drinks [the good beer] in the cellar." Margaret conceded that the convent's soup was very good, but on Friday and all meatless days Maria insisted on the strict interpretation that dairy products were off-limits as well and thus prohibited butter in the soup, a move that nearly provoked the sisters to violence. Then, "Last Friday our portion was beans; they tasted like they'd been cooked in muddy water. Saturday we had a spiced pear; when my portion was finished, which wasn't large, my hunger was more piqued than satisfied." In another recent meal the cook wanted to give the nuns more but Maria "ranted that it was enough." A simple " 'I wish I could do better,' " asserted Margaret, would be enough to at least show Maria's goodwill. But there was "no succor, no comfort."

Margaret's review of Maria's avarice ended with the sorry account of withering Catharina. Two years before, when the vicaress first became seriously ill, Maria surmised that she wouldn't live much longer. Thus, "[Maria] laid claim on a white petticoat [of Catharina's] and had many words about it with others; is that not a sign of her great stinginess?" Through the entire time that Catharina's illness lingered, Maria waited in heartless anticipation. "Last winter Vicaress was again very sick, and it seemed her soul would depart. Sister Maria had her eyes on the fire kettle of Vicaress, saying that her own was too small and shouldn't she and Vicaress trade for a time? Vicaress didn't dare speak against it." But Margaret, who was visiting Catharina in the infirmary, responded sharply, " 'Let her in God's name use her kettle as long as she lives, you'll have time enough to get it when she's dead, why isn't your kettle big enough, you've had it for years now.' " Maria chafed at Margaret's rebuke, responding in "all her authority and shamelessness" and then running to tell Adriana about the flare-up, but Margaret didn't care. "That poor [Catharina] needs her kettle." In general, and just as in 1628, when anyone dies "and any clothing is left behind, [Maria] pouts and frets if she can't have it, and if she has to buy it then she doesn't want it" (42).

CLUB BETHLEHEM?

As already mentioned, Margaret's 1633 letter was more belligerent than that of 1628. This was true as well of many of her old complaints about visitors. But the line between Adriana's weakness for outsiders and her shameless fund-raising was virtually blurred away, as if Margaret hardly needed to make such a distinction now—after all, either was wrong. Moreover, this time around, there was a new consideration: Mater flagrantly ignored the findings of the inquest of 1630, which required the sisters to keep quiet in at least a certain guest room. Since the guest house was still brimming with jovial guests and nuns, Margaret could make a case that she was entitled to reenter the convent's dormitory.

With the greater courtesy that was supposed to have been accorded her, Margaret hoped that her familiar descriptions of the seemingly unbreakable tradition of wining and dining outside friends would take on fresh significance. It was "impossible" to write about all the laypeople who ate there, said Margaret, yet "Mater says it's simply not true, and if Mater is so inclined then I have no hope of betterment." Just as before, even strangers stayed to visit "four, five, eight days, even ten, even more; they're here from morning till night." Mater even called her niece to the communion window in the church so that one of the nuns could teach the young girl the art of lace-making. Then five or six nuns sewed two weeks long for a cousin of Adriana (31).

But it was again at the grille, with its bustle and commotion, that the religious most clearly showed their worldly inclinations. Of all subjects in Margaret's 1633 letter, this was the biggest. At one point she even declared that it was her duty to write especially about two customs, both of which she knew the other sisters loved and would therefore not mention to any ecclesiastical visitor: going to the grille and feeding friends (35). They weren't merely pleasing their friends in this, but themselves, and forgetting the monastic ways. In addition to appearing at the grille without a wimple, "when the religious are in the workroom [and they are called to the grille], they simply throw on a coat over their dirty rags and look so unsuitable that it's scandalous. They look more like shepherd boys. It's most necessary simply to prohibit them at all from going to the grille from the workroom, for now it's too easily done. It often happens that they're fetched in the midst of washing or cleaning or otherwise, and then they stay there two or three hours without need, gossiping" (3). No one checked the length and frequency of conversations, complained Margaret, despite all the limitations and prohibitions from Mechelen. Some conversations didn't even begin until 9 P.M. and then the parties stayed up "prattling until midnight," even on communion eves (12).

The usual miscreants were not the only ones blamed. Margaret also implicated her ally-in-complaint, Maria Coninxloo, who sometimes spoke alone at the grille or violated the spirit of going there in pairs by taking her cousin Anna rather than an impartial nun (7, 34). Still, the familiar culprits continued to stand out. The lay sisters were as guilty as before in going alone to the grille, with "more privilege than the nuns" (11). Adriana herself had a new friend whom even Margaret was willing to concede might have been a creature in need of charity—convents after all had a tradition of giving alms as well as asking for them. But the two spoke "2 or 3 hours at a time," evenings included. "It's a rare day when during the meal or Divine Office Mater isn't before the grille, to the great amazement of the community. It's also a great difficulty for the cook and a great irregularity" (13). In other cases, however, Mater was clearly at the grille either to entertain or to amuse herself. "She'd probably answer, as she tries to convince us in-house, that there is nothing so heavy and burdensome to her as to be frequently at the grille. If that is so, she should show it by her actions, and speak there only when absolutely necessary, that she might be a good example to her religious. It wasn't long ago, a week ago Thursday, that Mater to my certain knowledge was at the grille from about one o'clock until evening," speaking successively with a beguine, the sister of a Franciscan (with children in tow), and the woman In the Leopard (who waited until the others had left), "another hog who often comes here to call"—as if Margaret had not already identified her well enough—and who not surprisingly happened to dislike the same sisters as Adriana. How, Margaret wondered, could Adriana desire to be under the jurisdiction of the friars? "If she were under them, she'd have to unlearn her usual ways real fast or she wouldn't rule for long, I daresay. For those are things that really make them boil, all that talking with worldly folk, and that free talk. That's the reason why [the friars have] tried to be rid of us before" (33).

As on the topic of favorites, we learn more about the foibles of Maria Joos than before. "Sister Maria is gladly with her friends, and she supposes that more is allowed to her than others. Once it's a student, for four or five days, then another time a cousin, then another cousin, her sister another time, her brother's children." During Carnival she had invited her most famous brother, Henri Joos, to visit, and recently there'd come often a niece who was a beguine. "In sum," decided Margaret, "I seldom have any rest, and all that noise sorrows me so, eating and drinking, singing and clinking, banqueting and merrymaking, whether I'm sick or whole, whether I want to hear it or not, it's nothing but a house full of whining children, including all those dreadful children from The Leopard. . . . I doubt that there's one chair or stool still whole. I think sometimes that my head will break." Margaret couldn't imagine why Mater walked around complaining that the convent was so restricted. "I don't know what more they could desire, unless it was to feed everyone and open a tavern. I often complain to God, and pray that he'll give her another disposition" (42).

Mater denied all this more than once, especially the assertion that the beguines had eaten in Bethlehem. "But," countered Margaret, "I see the food being cooked and carried in, I see the dishes that come; she says it was for a sandwich, and she said this to others too, but I know better. She wants to make a liar out of anyone who accuses her. I see once wine broth, then flan tarts, meat pies, almond cakes," Margaret listed, "and then a broth with small breads, cinnamon sugar and wine and butter, then rice, and further all that they can think up to bring people. And then they bring other friends because the fare is so good, as this past summer when they were here in such abundance; one group was barely gone when another would ride up, and even the young nuns are called to come and banquet with them." Margaret had once been brave enough, because of the agreement of 1630, to complain to Adriana "in a loving spirit" about this perpetual mirth. "She took it as badly as if I'd stabbed her, and with great vileness. She was disturbed, she shook and shuddered with anger. She threw up her arms and stuck her neck up high and made such gestures; the color and the consternation and all those painful wounds she gave me in return, and the amazement and alienation that I've since had to bear from her, and Vignarola, Maria and Lesken Joos, and others, I couldn't begin to describe" (42).

Other familiar themes that abided were the granting of gifts to outsiders (Anna "gives so much that it's impossible she could possibly have earned it all in her [free] time alone," and "she's so often at the grille that she appears not to be a religious at all" [18]), the storing of wine for special friends, to help them avoid taxes (the people from In the Leopard came secretly by night to carry pots and bottles of the stuff [38]), and the lending of beds ("If we have too many beds, let [Mater] sell them; we don't need to keep so many beds just to lend them out" [2]).

Margaret said much more about visitors, but she still couldn't exhaust the subject. She made her usual appeal to Boonen to change this situation, and suggested "If it pleases your reverence you might tell Mater that if she doesn't improve these things, she'll be removed; that will ruffle her up" (34).

THE SHADOW OF THE WORLD

Whether seen as a matter of giving in order to eventually get, or of indigent spirituality, such excessive generosity and special attachments were not becoming of nuns. As in 1628, Margaret argued that these only fostered worldly tendencies, so that the nuns were more like outsiders than insiders.

Lax discipline remained as much of a problem as before. Easy dispensation from the refectory ("for trifling matters that could be postponed"), wandering during the Divine Office, Mater's continued use of a silver thimble and now a Spanish chair ("unbecoming the children of St. Francis") agitated Margaret as much as before. So did a new situation: Maria Joos's failure to do her part of the convent's chores. "The others complain that [Maria] speaks so much about the common work, and yet doesn't come to the workroom; she simply doesn't want to come. She wanders around the house twittering and busybodying without ceasing, and what's worse she speaks for so long. She ought to give the sisters a good example of diligence; but she won't go one step out of her path for something that doesn't interest her" (30).

Routine violations of cloister, in spirit or fact, could still be found at the usual places. "No one is to be permitted to come inside," quoted Margaret chapter and verse, as she often did, from the house statutes, "whoever it may be, neither children nor great nor small; this isn't observed" (8). Also people wandered through the church, carrying wood, kindling, and sacks of apples, which represented a lack of respect as well as a potential problem of *clausura*. "Your reverence has forbidden it before, but it's not upheld. They think that if it can be done without anyone seeing it, then it's allowed" (1). Margaret mentioned next a violation that gives us new insight into the layout of the house: "No religious is to speak near the wagon gate, neither above from the attic, nor from the rooms with windows that open into the street. Mater herself stands at the wagon gate almost an hour long and chatters with people. Above in the attic there are some who stand gaping and then later chew on what they've seen with their friends about what happened, who went in and who out, and they even speak to the people below from the attic and from their cells." Often this occurred while the nuns were doing the laundry of the Jesuits—which was another unfortunate consequence of the hateful task (6). Another new and vulnerable place was the *rolle*, a round, lazy Susan–like contraption fixed in the wall or grille of the speaking areas of the guest rooms, in which the religious placed and took up written messages or objects, and which was currently large enough or ill-made enough that children could be brought through. Naturally, "we lack only the money" to make it right. In any event, "Sister Maria [Joos] is very spacious about *clausura* when it comes to letting children inside, and letting them in by the wagon gate as well" (5).

Besides the threat and reality of trespass, the lay sisters still wandered outside as they pleased, chattering among the neighbors or on their way to Brussels. "That isn't a good thing for religious to do, wandering the streets, especially outside Leuven" (10). And these were just some of their acts of poor judgment. "I wish that when anyone was out at some- one's house they would never use silver spoons nor silver cups; it hap- pened awhile ago that a few of our number dined with a notable person who gave them silver spoons with which to eat; the sisters were so en- amored of this that their hosts said, 'are you really religious of St. Fran- cis who use silver spoons? You aren't poor sisters at all' " (15). In addi- tion to still setting plasters and waiting at childbeds, which resulted in much unsavory news, lay sisters now engaged in nursing this person and giving that one "an enema." Joanna Schoensetters even wanted to attend people who had suffered burns, which Margaret admitted could be a charitable work but which "brought great unrest for a cloistered convent, for many reasons" (9, 14).

The common work had also remained worldly—not merely in the curiosities some nuns used, but in requiring unbefitting physical labor and in being more focused on the income than the spiritual reward. Here Margaret referred primarily to the new wash of the Jesuits, "and all other washing and folding, for this is no salvational wash; it is the ruin of all conventual order." This task, and the sewing that accompa- nied it, was "the root of unrest and discontent, great slavery and little profit. It would take too long to write all that could be said about this, but . . . we should wash for no one, neither friends, nor clergy, whoever it may be" (4, 31).

The penultimate item in the litany of troubling consequences of worldliness was choir, where sisters continued to indulge in the tempta- tion to be bored, irreverent, and extravagant. Some sisters attended choir without wimple, Anna and Mater held even more frequent private con- versations than before—Mater even laughed aloud during Mass—and Maria Joos had an "ugly custom" of giving out errands and even count- ing her money during Mass. "She is so irascible. She chases sisters around from Matins on, requiring immediately all that comes in her head, regardless of time or place" (29). Decoration, meanwhile, was as colorful and vigorous as before, despite personal inspection of the choir by the dean in 1628 and warnings against ornateness. "In the last visita- tion," Margaret began, "I wrote long and wide about all the candles in the choir, which is very small and close, especially in the summer. . . . I'll leave it to you to imagine how lovely it all smells. I take it your reverence at the time didn't say much about it, thus I fear that yet an- other long complaint from me will be in vain." More interesting than the repetition of Margaret's complaint is her temerity to imply that Boonen had wrongly ignored her previous alarms. "Imagine on the high days" all the large candles, not to mention "all the flowers lying on and sticking out of the little altars and benches. . . . When I first came to live here there were never more than two candles burned at once [in the choir]: one for Our Lady and the other for Our Lord. And there were but two candelabra, which is a far cry from how things stand now. . . . Every day it's light in Bethlehem" (39).

One new twist to the ostentation was the desire of some sisters to purchase a new instrument. In general, Margaret believed, attention in the convent to music was overdone—two or three hours of practice at a time was common—and more for the glory of certain sisters than for God. And as of late this enthusiasm had grown feverish enough to inspire a number of sisters, especially Maria Joos and Anna Vignarola, to advocate acquiring an organ. To that end "various alms have been socked away," Margaret knew, thanks to a slip of the tongue by Maria Joos. While the funds were being raised, these same sisters hoped in the meantime to purchase a harpsichord on which they could learn, but at the last minute, Margaret related, the harpsichord was sold from under their noses. To her usual argument that a poor convent such as Bethlehem should have spent its resources on more basic needs first—"think of the alms they'd rather save up for an organ than to take care of the community"—Margaret added a comment which reminds us that such matters as decoration and music were not merely about tastes in worship or deficit-spending but prestige and standing. Though rehearsals had become shorter, Margaret explained, she doubted that they would remain so, "for that great inequality they'll not soon forget." In other words, music and, for that matter, adornment of the choir or other kinds of art were two of the few visible means through which a nun inclined to stand out from the crowd could do so—there was no opportunity for them to preach, participate in processions, or perform Mass, and very little chance to become a famous devotional writer. We can interpret this as well from a less worldly viewpoint, perhaps the very viewpoint of the music boosters: Choir was one of the few ways an artistically gifted nun was allowed to worship God most fully, with all her heart and soul. But to Margaret, the attraction of these arts was too often the assumed rise in stature that they might bring to the practitioner.

Finally, Margaret told a familiar story. Adriana, her enthusiasm for play unabated, was still appointing the children of guests as mock mater, bursaress, vicaress, and culinaria. "That much I don't object to, it's in the name of recreation, but that to which I do object is that Mater [Adriana] then starts acting like a buffoon; from her mouth, during all that time, from morn until eve, comes not one wise word, but a stream of silly speech, like a bad child who insists on getting its way. And when she doesn't get her way immediately, then she rolls up her sleeves and grumbles and throws things, jumps around, hits and breaks, knocks and yells and keeps it up until she gets what she wants, at table and else-where, whatever comes into her head." Adriana was quite expert at impersonation, it seems, which Margaret admitted could be done in fun but which too often was done to injure. "You have to see and hear it to believe it, how she mimics others in their words and their mannerisms, it all comes bursting loose. And she moves others to do the same, she laughs and makes everyone laugh at the person in question, with those peasantlike, droll farces of hers. But to say it better, she spits out words of ridicule and shame. . . . God knows how she wounds hearts in this way" (32). And despite Van der Wiel's intent at the 1628 visitation to ban the practice, and its apparent prohibition in the oral *determinatio* of 1632, the nuns of Bethlehem were still playing the fool on Three Kings Day. At least, urged Margaret, let a lay sister dress as the fool, rather than nuns who ignored choir and called their "friends from all corners." May the Lord, on this and all else, "give your reverence his holy bene-diction to do all that pleases Him, and pray in God's name for me" (40).

FINALE

If the visitor doubted the seriousness of any of these matters, if he con-sidered them peripheral to the monastic life, Margaret assured him that they were issues "on which salvation hinged." Moreover, Margaret bra-zenly stated that the episcopal officials should avoid carrying out this visitation like the last one, at which much was heard but little accom-plished, "without improvement" (32).

To conclude we should end as Margaret did. "What more can I say?" she asked rhetorically. "I fear that I break my head in vain, for if Mater doesn't want something it's all a waste of time, whatever might be deter-mined at the visitation." Adriana could change things if she wished, "but it seems that she cares not at all once the visitors have left; she then goes her old ways. It's as if she'll never have to answer to God." Besides this, Margaret was "often amazed at how fiercely and readily Mater lies"—a point that the visitors would note firmly in the margin—"and holds up a lie for a truth that we've seen with our own eyes and heard with our own ears." In light of such obstinance and obvious defects, Margaret presented a more vigorous recommendation than she had in 1628: "Mater is worthy to be removed." Until she was, visitation would continue to be of little effect. Margaret urged the archbishop to send the dean right away and regularly, to see that every ordinance was being observed and enforced, but she feared that even the closest watch would

The Blessed Ida of Gorsleeuw
(long thought to have come from Zoutleeuw),
a medieval nun famous for her illuminations.

not deter Adriana. "Mater will go her old ways once more, in all things" (42).

These are the last sentiments Margaret left us in her own hand. It's fitting that she go out with a fiery trail of accusations burning behind her.

19. SIC ET NON

TURNING TO THE LETTERS and oral depositions that Margaret's cosisters produced at the visitation of 1633, we remember that Adriana and her supporters were much more on the offensive than before. Perhaps this was due to their near-certain knowledge that Margaret had written a massive document about them back in 1628; there must have been great suspicion that she would now compose another and a new sense of urgency to throw up the defenses. So even though Adriana's critics had hardly backed off, her closest followers made the accusations and apologies about even in this latest exchange. This alone is a good sign that the stress in Bethlehem had intensified since the previous visitation.

CONCORD

There were three issues on which virtually all agreed. One of them, which Margaret herself had hardly mentioned, was the ancient muddle of jurisdiction. All who commented on the subject in 1633 favored a switch from the archbishop to the friars. What is important to note here is not the now-tedious issue itself but rather the fact that it was the sisters who raised it. All previous polling on the subject had been initiated by the visitors and was systematically recorded, but at the interviews fourteen of twenty-one sisters suddenly volunteered that they preferred a change. Were the remaining seven against the switch? Or were they simply not privy to, or in agreement with, a plan to lobby the visitors? It was the lay sister Maria van Roy who divulged—purposely or not—that such a plan existed. She told the visitors that she was asking for the leadership of the friars because many other sisters had urged her to do so.

A second point of general agreement, indeed arguably the most urgent issue in the entire visitation, was repugnance at washing the "church-linens" of the Jesuits, already introduced to us by Margaret. The only clear supporter of the task was its mastermind, Maria Joos. Even Adriana remained silent on the issue, so that Maria alone was left to make the solid, commonsensical argument that through this commission the convent earned 60 florins a year and the expense was but 20 florins—more than the sisters involved with the wash could otherwise

221

have made. But to everyone else the awfulness of the task outweighed the indisputable need for income. Catharina contended that the wash took too much time and energy: four times a year, three weeks at a time. She prayed "in all humility that our community may be cut loose from the great slavery of washing for the Jesuits, or anyone else." The profit was meager and the sisters ruined their health and their clothes, an especially serious consequence since "the convent doesn't provide for the poor younger sisters. And the religious engaged in it are sometimes so worn out that they couldn't be any uglier and run-down if they were lying in the wilderness. Our provisions are too sober to slave this way, each time there's unrest about the whole thing, and all good conventual manners are shoved aside. Choir and workroom are neglected, and we can't even do our common prayers. I trust firmly that your reverence will remove this burden from us, in the name of a true religious life."

The others echoed Catharina, at varying levels of volume. The wash caused contention and took eight people from choir. Joanna de Vorster wrote that two "weak nuns" and six lay sisters did the wash, and then "often miss[ed] choir and refectory, and most of the community doesn't like it anyway through the great compassion that we have for those who've been charged with the task." Even Anna Vignarola urged a halt, though she assigned no blame. Maria Coninxloo seemed more burdened than anyone. For two long years she'd "had to endure the trial of the wash of the Jesuits. I pray your reverence for the love of God . . . to require Mater to release me from that task, for I can't work my salvation much at all with such a task, for it troubles my inward person, and I can't do the job as it ought to be done. I've enough to do with my struggle against the results of what I suffer. I'd rather choose rest in God than wellness in body. What's worse, we gain nothing anyway; our food's no more and no better, even much worse than when I first got here." If it continued, "there will be no peace here." Coninxloo urged quick action before a new contract with the Jesuits was signed in December.

A final point of accord was a general antipathy for Joanna Schoensetters and Margaret Smulders. More than merely reporting on a few faults, as was expected in visitations, the other nuns expressed profound aversion for these two sisters. To many, Joanna was opinionated, strong-willed, unpeaceful, an angel to outsiders and a devil within, hard, coarse-speaking, "in charge of everyone," "boss of everything," and so ill-tempered that even Mater didn't dare reprimand her. Lesken Joos blamed Catharina, who rattled on with her in the kitchen. Maria Coninxloo was likewise weary of Joanna: It was "a good community," save for her. "There isn't anyone without a burden to bear from her, for she treats us all alike: She wants to boss and rule us all, more than Mater herself, and she goes where her passions drive her. It would be better if she had nothing to do but spin her spinning wheel, rather than be our cook as well; then she wouldn't have so much occasion to harp on everyone. For anyone who needs fire can't avoid the kitchen, for fire is only kindled there, but who must enter there takes up her cross, believe you me. We've aired our complaints long enough to Mater, but we're not heard."

As for Margaret, it is worth remembering that in 1628 the others hardly mentioned her at all. That she was named often this time around is another sign of growing strain within the house, and of her increasing boldness. The threat of Margaret's return had moved her from the sisters' subconsciousness to their nerves. There was grumbling that Margaret made "great clamor" when someone came to talk beneath her room, though in light of the 1630 inquest we can imagine that Margaret was sticking up for what she thought were her rights. Others revealed that Margaret took some of her meals in the kitchen, and while there eagerly tabulated with Joanna Schoensetters the weaknesses of the other sisters. "Through this, if it happens that [Joanna] can't keep quiet, there arises much dissension." Maria de Smet was disturbed by the same scenario, putting the length of the conversations in the kitchen "from morn until eve" and noting how "they reinforce each other's opinions; thus they ought to be kept apart." Mater Adriana was more general: "I pray that Sister Margaret Smulders be warned not to be such a busybody in what happens in the convent, nor chastise each of the sisters with her unruly and impassioned words, to the great disquiet of the community." Though still excluded, Margaret was no longer content merely to save her criticisms for private letters to ecclesiastical officials.

DIVISION

Beyond these points, we see familiar divergence of opinion, with much fresh language and illustration. Those who in 1628 had seen Mater as the root of ill-discipline and at the head of factionalism restated their criticism. As usual, Catharina worked hard to be charitable but ultimately failed to hide her disapproval. Though admitting that the statutes were generally well observed, she added that the orally pronounced decrees which finally resulted from the previous visitation had not been edited into the statutes and were obviously taken less seriously than written proclamations. In regard to factions, there was no "notable" discord, stated Catharina, but she stopped short of denying the reality of discord altogether. Also subtle were her recommendation that Anna and Mater be separated in choir, since they tended to carry on, and her criticism of certain murmur-provoking private parties around Three Kings Day.

Most sisters who attributed division to Adriana were much more blunt than Catharina. Even if they thought conditions in the house generally good, several condemned Mater and her friends for fashioning "a small convent" of their own. One negative consequence of this was the crippling of discipline. Maria Joos and Anna were incorrigible precisely because of their favored standing. According to these dissatisfied sisters, Maria Joos was safe even when she disregarded penances handed down in chapter or wore her work apron to refectory or neglected to lower her veil, while Anna was so free that she "speaks boldly against Mater and your reverence." The latter phrase implicitly gave Boonen a bigger stake in the visitation, for it showed that familiarity had bred insolence as much as its notorious child of contempt. Still other sisters believed that favoritism hurt morale and wished that Mater were a bit more friendly ("Mater makes it her custom to stay out of the community, away from choir, away from refectory and workroom, and also to know everything"). She punished in chapter as if there were a "cabal" against her. "What more can I say except that favoritism is a devilish affair," wrote Joanna de Vorster. "There's too much familiarity between Mater and Vignarola, who has all that her heart desires, while others get only through much pleading."

The detested Joanna Schoensetters went as far as Margaret in presenting an unsightly picture of lax discipline. Fearlessly she attributed this, the "closing of hearts," and continued factionalism, to infrequent ecclesiastical visitation. She also condemned sisters "who intrigue" with Mater, and noted that nuns who tried to become favorites of the confessor only impeded the freedom of those who remained outside of his good graces. Maria Coninxloo backed up the otherwise disagreeable Joanna on this point: "Mater is also very wanting in that when anyone sends for a pater [confessor], she usually goes first and then chatters with him and takes his time so that there is little remaining for the person who sought him out; it doesn't look right, and it also robs the freedom of the subjects if the superior always goes before."

Maria Coninxloo had more to say on the topic of favoritism than anyone but Margaret. In addition to the regrettable but usual lack of "common love" in Maria Joos or Mater, and other repetitions of Margaret, Maria pointed out a new blatant symbol of favoritism: Mater's private "pomp" table, where the invited came to wine and dine. "It's a big obstacle to her ability to watch over her flock and it also inhibits freedom," argued Maria, "for people would more willingly come to her with requests if she were alone, but she's with her dear ones. I truly believe that by forbidding that table the factions would disappear, and

Mater would then, I hope, better care for her community, and better observe the first chapter of our statutes which concerns her office, to which I happen to think she pays hardly any heed." An event from the previous summer had reinforced Maria's opinions. She and Anna Servranx, who had been stretching out washed choir robes, descended from the attic to ask Mater for the irons. Outside Mater's room they met several sisters who had "fared well" there and who "showed us the spoons with which they'd eaten. We walked in without a second thought; but Mater came barking at us. I asked her with a laughing mouth whether she didn't have just one benediction more for us; she grew very perturbed and said 'No.' I didn't take it badly and took her in my arms and kissed her, but then she pushed me from the step with Sister Anna and we both almost went down, head over heels, after which she slammed her door very angrily. . . . I told our confessor, who heard this all very unhappily; still he maintained his affection for Mater."

Despite all this factional solidarity that Maria Coninxloo portrayed for the visitors, she also offered the first evidence that there was now some strain between Mater and Maria Joos. Here was familiarity's usual consequence. "I would well wish that Sister Maria Joos would improve her evil custom, when Mater is in a cranky mood against her, of being so careless in her words; that she wouldn't say 'What a marvelous Superior we have; we ought to remove her,' and other disrespectful things, to young and old sisters alike. . . . Others think to themselves, 'If bursaress, who is so favored by Mater, speaks this way, then I may certainly speak this way as well, who am not so well regarded by Mater and must suffer so.'" Maria Joos confirmed that something was amiss between herself and Adriana. She began rather innocuously in her interview, claiming that there were no notable transgressions in the house, except that Mater and Vicaress didn't get along. But instead of pinning all the blame on Vicaress, as before, she now argued that part of the reason for such discord was Mater's hard manner of speaking. Perhaps Maria Joos was distressed by what she saw as Adriana's inordinate attention to Anna Vignarola, a problem Sister Joos hinted at in stating that "Mater and Vignarola" sometimes spoke with each other after the others had left from the evening meal, to the disgruntlement of the excluded community.

In two final and sensitive areas of potential favoritism—care for the sick and distribution of goods—the sisters angry with Maria Joos stormed almost as fiercely as had Margaret, and seem just as unaware of any rifts in the convent's leadership. Maria Coninxloo argued that "to Sister Vignarola [Maria Joos] gives a double portion, and Mater also has a better portion; in fact when something is left over at the table of the guests, which normally should be for the sick, it's given to Mater, who is also not terribly friendly to the community." The increasingly feeble Catharina held back as usual, but not enough to conceal her disapproval. In sickness or in health, she said, some still had it better than others, in proportion to their place in Mater's or Maria's heart. No doubt about it, the common table was getting worse, and Maria Coninxloo didn't hesitate to name the greatest offender: "Sister Maria Joos is also very harsh against those sick sisters who, because of their weakness, must miss the Matins. She speaks to them very sharply, and asks when they plan on coming to choir again. These are matters for Mater, not the bursaress. She'd do better to see that the sick had better food, to be strong."

On the other side of the spectrum of opinions were the equally vocal supporters of Mater Adriana, who repeated and enlarged their conviction that the true driving force behind factionalism was Catharina Rijckeboer. Maria Joos, even if alienated a bit from Adriana, contended that the greatest affections in the convent existed among Vicaress, Maria Coninxloo, Anna Servranx, and Joanna Schoensetters, all of whom were inclined to murmur. Anna Vignarola's perfectly toned three-page letter (with concise indictments and brief, pointed examples) supplied more detail. According to Anna, Catharina continued to speak to others of Mater's faults and sympathized with anyone who did the same. "Mater for her part is of a contrary nature," Anna wrote, "in that she always speaks up for those not present, and never against; concerning the faults of Vicaress in this regard there is much more that could be written, but there's little hope of improvement, for she may not be reproved because of her illness."

As a result of Vicaress's inclination to nourish criticisms rather than root them out, Anna believed that there had grown up a greater willingness among various sisters to conspire against Mater. Here Anna showed more nervousness for Adriana's position than she had in 1628. "I say, on the witness of my conscience, that . . . they go and embellish lies and speak them as truth about Mater, among other things that she can't keep a secret, and for evidence they haul up some triviality that they've told her, and thus they feign offense and then go around gossiping such that they end up revealing their secret anyway. . . . And if the confessor urges them on and confirms their anger, then they really insist they're right and they must be told they're right or there's no peace. You'd never know that these women could keep a secret themselves." While Margaret had shown the confessor to support Adriana, here Anna presented just the opposite picture.

If Anna is to be believed, Catharina even tried to include the impressionable novices in these conspiracies. In 1628 Anna had focused on Catharina's inability to instruct or love the novices. This time around she portrayed Catharina as the recruiter—almost exactly opposite from Catharina's own account of the subject, or Margaret's. "When the novices enter," Anna began, "the first command given them is that they may not speak of their own accord with Mater, and many other marvelous things are they told. God knows that it doesn't do much for edification." Several unnamed friends of Catharina "watch out when the novices do chance to speak with Mater, and they then engage in a thorough questioning afterward to find out what was said, for since they know their prey, they are greatly concerned that their affairs not reach Mater's ears, and then they primp them with promises to do as they say and not to reveal a word of it to Mater. . . . And what's most damaging of all, and to tug their hearts still further from Mater, they try to tell them the affair or supposed events from our past involving the secular confessor [Henri Joos], and further all that they can dream up to adorn their gossip knows no end." We wonder again exactly how Joos was linked to Adriana, but as before we must be patient. For now, it's important to note that Anna offered more specific examples than ever before of how Catharina sought to undermine Adriana, including the tendency some had to run to the novices and young nuns and say that any punishments they received were unjust, the result of Mater's passions. But the stories about Henri Joos obviously disturbed Anna most. Besides the ill consequences for the atmosphere within the convent, Anna pointed out that those novices who chose to leave the religious life could then tell Bethlehem's internal affairs to outsiders. "If they do leave it's a big scandal for the community if they're not silent about what's gone on inside. That this will all be corrected, there is no hope, but at least there should be some fear or a second thought about such doings, in my opinion. For as I've said before, all that they care about is keeping Mater and Vignarola from knowing what they're doing, as if God himself didn't know their hearts or minds. I suppose that Mater knows things better than I, though through her discretion and expression, put on for the sake of peace, you would never know it." Quite in contrast to Margaret, who feared that stories about herself were the main kind that Bethlehem exported, Anna offered another slant to the problem.

Sounding a bit like Margaret and Maria rather than her usual dispassionate self, Anna expressed a desire for very specific measures to stop such maneuvering and ill-speaking. It ought to be decreed, she suggested, that "Mater, at least monthly, should question the novices about whether they've been told something harmful, or that tends against the religious life. I'm sure this will bring much profit, and then if they won't keep silent for the love of God, then at least fear will do the trick. And it should be specially expressed that the novices should freely enjoy the good counsel and conversation of Mater as well as their [novice] mistress, without the mistress's preventing them or displaying jealousy that they have shown more freedom to Mater than to her." The novice mistress of course was Vicaress Catharina.

Margaret Geraerts, the most newly professed nun in Bethlehem and thus most recently a novice, backed up this last claim of Anna, though much less eloquently. Geraerts told that as a novice she had never dared to seek counsel or comfort from Mater, for fear of Catharina. Jacomyn de la Haye confirmed Anna's charge that Catharina entertained complaints about Mater, though she added that Mater acted in much the same way when someone came griping about the vicaress. And all the lay sisters except Joanna Schoensetters supported Mater or criticized Catharina. "The community was united, without significant contention," one said. "The rule and statutes are well observed," stated another. "Vicaress needs to bend more to Mater," recommended a third. Lesken Joos did admit, however, that Vicaress agreed with *anyone*, whether they came to complain or to speak well of Mater. According to Lesken, Catharina didn't seek at all to be a mediator, a role that sisters must have expected from a vicaress, but rather preferred to be a confirmer of opinions. If Catharina did contribute to contention in the house, then a charitable interpretation of Lesken's statement would suggest that it was inadvertent; Catharina sought to avoid confrontation by agreeing with everyone in sight.

Adriana wrote and spoke so strongly on this topic in 1633 that she seemed prepared to wage the battle single-handedly. This time she defended her regime to the hilt and railed against Catharina, quite in contrast to the resignation and dramatic key-throwing of the last visitation. The tone of her vigorous letter is confident and accusatory. Like Anna, Adriana pounced upon Catharina for tolerating the criticism of superiors, and as in 1628 she noted the problem with Catharina's voice, urging again the appointment of a permanent mistress to teach the novices reading and singing. Adriana also worried more manifestly than ever about conspiracy, the undermining of her authority through old nasty stories—undoubtedly about Henri Joos—and Catharina's potential to stoke the fire of disloyalty within the novices. Due to this last fear, Adriana repeated Anna's suggestion of periodic interviews with the novices and stressed that sisters were not to hold private conversations with postulants and novices at all.

On the last issue related to factionalism, the division of goods within the house, several sisters kept silent and several were only mildly critical of Maria Joos. The usually dispassionate Jacomyn de la Haye believed that the sick were well cared and provided for, according to the means of the convent, and she thought exactly the same about the food in general. Her only complaint was that at table when people were allowed to speak, Maria Coninxloo had the ugly custom of making big scenes and lots of noise, just as she did at the gate. Maria Joos defended her office calmly, though she gave one hint of criticism in her wish that each religious should have the same amount of linen. While the convent's linens were evenly distributed, Maria observed that some sisters received more from friends or otherwise. We can only speculate whether this comment was directed at Anna Vignarola or merely the result of a broad fair-mindedness. Maria also criticized her cousin Lesken when she wished that the infirmarian was a sister who didn't go out, for while she was away the sick were poorly served. Lesken did not defend herself on this particular point, but made a mild criticism in return. Ill sisters who desired some good beer—a common prescription for the sick—had to pay the bursaress for it. However, Lesken then vindicated her cousin and contradicted others by alleging that if the sick had no money themselves, then the convent would foot the bill.

OUTSIDERS

The topic of favoritism and special friendships depleted more ink than any other among sisters, reaffirming the gravity of these sins in monastic life. But the question of contact with outsiders produced its share of interesting comments as well. As in Margaret's letter, rarely now did anyone specify whether this was an issue of worldliness or public relations and fund-raising; but clearly the sisters were still divided on how much outside contact was enough.

Some said not a word, some believed things were in good order. But several sisters resented the old custom of giving away and lending (manifested lately in alms to the house's indigent friends), for it only kept the nuns poor and took Adriana to the grille. Adriana undoubtedly considered her efforts among the needy to be good acts of charity, but even Maria Joos complained, adding that the presents Mater gave away were usually the very gifts that Anna Vignarola had just received from some other outside friend. Several pointed out minor breaches of the rule about allowing children inside or the need to accompany doctors, surgeons, and workmen who had to come inside the house. "This is never observed," said Maria Coninxloo, and Joanna Schoensetters told that once during the previous summer the "daughter from The Leopard brought some cabbage, and the religious led her around, to the infirmary, and to the choir, and in the cellar, and other places." When there was a recreation day or when visitors brought a gift, "they are also let in, under the pretext that they are helping to carry it."

But the most persistent trouble spot for some critics remained the grille, which in their opinion was about to cave in from overuse. According to Anna Coninxloo, the worst offender in talking at the grille too long and often was still the woman appointed to control such things: the bursaress and longtime portress, Maria Joos. It was like the local proverb about hiring a poacher to guard the forest. She "spent a lot of time at the gate chattering with strange persons," said Anna Coninxloo, "and alone no less." From Maria Coninxloo came the usual stream of details, with chapter and verse from the statutes. Maria Joos, claimed Coninxloo, was a respecter of persons within the convent but not outside, "for she'll talk to anyone, friends and strangers, alone or not." At least the old practice of outsiders sleeping in the guest room had been checked, save for the occasional Grey Sister who visited from beyond Leuven or the confessor come to console a sick nun. But the serving of food and drink to friends was as unbridled as ever. Maria de Smet complained of the attendant expense of such gifts and the desire of the lay sisters for news, while Joanna de Vorster regretted that the grille was so busy that two veiled sisters had to be posted there and thus were taken away from the choir—even more serious since those two possessed the "best voices."

Catharina concurred with most of these points and added particulars of her own that sounded much like Margaret's. The main grille in the guest room was still too large, despite having been reduced—it was "possible to give a hand to a worldly person, or secretly pass something through or receive if someone were so inclined." In addition, sisters were still placing silver spoons before guests when they set the table, "which has hardly edified some of the visitors." Finally, the "jawing at the grille" was still too long, in violation of statute, and whether by Mater or others. "It happened on October 2 that three young nuns sat with the same people for three hours, and again on October 5 another three hours."

Jacomyn de le Haye, usually neutral, made accusations that contradicted the charges of abuse at the grille and supported the view that violations were rare. While she did acknowledge many events just cited, she interpreted them as minor aberrations rather than signs of poor discipline. She admitted that food was sometimes given to friends, but only when absolutely unavoidable; she conceded that some conversations were too long, but only with people from outside the city. More positively, she argued that the pastor of Mol, Henri Joos, rarely came to the convent—no more than the two to three times per year suggested by monastic experts for outside friends and family—and when he did he ate with no one from inside. This was a question that Archdeacon Van der Wiel must have put to Jacomyn directly, perhaps after getting wind of the subject in a previous interview—for until coming to Jacomyn he had asked it of no one else (or had ignored the responses he received).

In any case, Jacomyn continued by disputing those who said that sisters ever spoke alone at the grille. Most damaging was her claim that if anyone was guilty of more than minor faults then it was probably Maria Coninxloo, who for hours sat with her mother, a sister, and a second sister from the Grand Beguinage. As for Mater Adriana at the grille, Jacomyn said little.

More than Jacomyn, Maria Joos put a favorable twist on the same set of potentially serious circumstances just described. She contended that expenses for entertaining guests amounted "merely to some butter and bread" and repeated her pride in the fact that no one stayed overnight in the guest room anymore (though she wished that beguines would be allowed to stay over, quasi-religious as they were). Cousin Lesken chimed in to support Maria on every count, down to her request to host beguines overnight, "just as we sisters traveling outside may stay at beguinages."

If there were problems at all regarding the grille or cloister more generally, then several sisters asserted again that these were not due to Maria Joos. We have already seen sister Jacomyn's views, but should add here her observation that Margaret Smulders violated at least the spirit of cloister by going frequently to the gate to give messages or to see who was coming and going. Anna Vignarola painted the scene even better. In her highest, most patronizing tone (and as a postscript rather than in the body of the letter, as if Margaret was hardly worth the trouble) she wrote that "though I realize that we must exercise patience with the wonderful manners and conversation of Sister Margaret Smulders, I nevertheless pray that she be warned, that when there are workmen or when the wagon gate goes open for other reasons, she not come and stand with her hands on her hips to see what's happening. . . . Through her behavior the workmen then ask what kind of a creature she is, and those standing nearby don't know what to say, for they must preserve the convent's honor." Here is another clue that Margaret was making her presence felt directly, more than she had in years.

BITS AND PIECES

On most other topics considered during the visitation, there was less volume and intensity than in 1628, confirming the primacy of internal and external relationships among all sisters and official visitors. There were some "neutral" comments on worship. Some said that the read Mass should occur before the high Mass; that there should be more time for private prayer, more consistency in attending the morning services, fewer memorial services, weekly communion, time to speak after the meals about what was read, and so on. The person in charge of setting up the church for services, Maria van Roy, complained that she had to see to all things needed in the church—wine, bread for Mass, communion bread, everything except the candles—and asked to be released from the costly office. And there were some new complaints about the old problem of irreverence. Anna Coninxloo complained that her cousin Maria Coninxloo brought forth "dissonance in singing with too high a tone, and this overwhelms, among others, the voice of Anna Marcelis." Others condemned, as had Margaret, the chatter between Mater and Vignarola in choir; the walking around in the dormitory above the church during Mass; Maria Joos's making assignments to lay sisters in choir and then directing and scolding everyone about the performance of the Office; the private speaking among Mater, Maria Joos, Anna Vignarola, and Margaret Geraerts after meals; the inconvenience caused by the new organ; and Mater's continued exuberance on recreation days, which caused the other sisters to act like "wharf children."

But all such complaints came from Maria Coninxloo, Catharina, and a few others. And except for a brief admission by Anna Vignarola that the services were wanting, Mater and her friends had nothing to say on these subjects of devotion or recreation. As with much else they simply did not consider these to be problems, or at worst they wished not to make such problems known.

20. WHEAT AND CHAFF

AN ECCLESIASTICAL RESIDENCE SOMEWHERE IN THE ARCH-
DIOCESE, OCTOBER 1633. From Peter van der Wiel's point of view
as a shepherd, five years between visitations was too long. But from our
point of view, which includes solid documentation for the visits of 1628
and 1633 only, five years may not be quite long enough to pursue very
profitably that favorite line of historical inquiry: the extent of "change"
or "constancy" over time. For what it's worth, the overwhelming impression that emerges from comparing the two visitations is one of constancy—save for some hardening of sentiments and the specific examples which the sisters used. This probably comes as no surprise. Given
merely the facts of a five-year interval between visits, the tendency of
visitors to ask about the same questions as before, and suppositions
about the steadfastness of human nature, we would have guessed that
constancy would win out.

More important to Van der Wiel, however, than the questions of
future historians or the generation of neat, consistent records for their
benefit, was to sort out the mass of detail in front of him and address
the foremost spiritual and temporal concerns expressed by the women
of Bethlehem during this most recent official visit. He brought his usual
dispassion to bear and followed his usual method, faithfully distilling
comments of the sisters on the right side of the page while placing
names to the left, though on this occasion he deemed no separate sheet
necessary for Margaret—he probably could have used it since the bulk
of his notes came from her letter. When finished, he put an "M" next to
some entries, indicating those to be handled in private with Mater.

A document for the next intermediate stage of the process—labeled
the *"memoriale"* at the 1628 visit—is missing for 1633, but in compensation we have something better, a piece absent the last time around: a
draft of the formal *determinatio* itself, which in more polished form was
delivered to Bethlehem shortly after the visitors left. Along with this
came a separate set of decrees for Mater, some to be handled in person
with her, some to be set in parchment. Of course either the general
pronouncements or those for Mater alone could have been modified by
the time they reached Bethlehem; because we have only the drafts of
these documents and not the final copies, we cannot say for sure, but we

can say that the drafts offer a better guide to Van der Wiel's purposes than did the rough memo five years before.

Many commands and platitudes in the *determinatio* were common in conventual decrees from this time, but our knowledge of the detailed complaints that sparked them lends more particular meaning and takes us beneath the surface of monastic formalities. The document began by commanding the sisters to "greatly prize silence" in the choir, for such was becoming to a house of the lord and made it easier to meditate and be one with God. No names of offenders were listed, but we know the accusations well. It then granted a request from the religious to commune every week, "for greater comfort of your inner selves," but attached was a quid pro quo: The religious were to shun the grille altogether on these communion days, while on other days they were to take with them to the grille a watchful companion sister and avoid long and private conversations. To this last stipulation there was one surprisingly lenient exception granted, even though no sister had requested it: A religious was allowed to speak to an outsider at the grille beyond the earshot of her companion sister, provided that the outsider was a close relative. Last in this opening section was a decree commanding more vigilance over cloister doors and the wagon gate, with not even women or children allowed to come through except as allowed by the Holy Council of Trent and the statutes. When anyone did enter, they were to be accompanied by two religious appointed by Mater, who would remain with the visitors until they left. Here was a triumph for Mater's critics, since the corrections of 1628, reported upon by Catharina at that time, apparently had become lax once more.

The document turned to the charges of favoritism that had come from both sides. The holy fathers of the church, explained the decree, always considered as cancerous factionalism, special friendships, hangers-on, and alliances that formed between two or three religious. They instead encouraged common and impartial love among all, without respecting of persons. Mater was therefore solemnly to root out familiarity, surely and discreetly, and to halt all private gatherings of a few religious. Those who refused to quit were threatened with "remarkable" punishments and prohibition from speaking to each other for an indefinite period. The decrees continued with the topic of recreation days. On all such, including Three Kings and Christmas, activities that detracted from religious respectability or edification were to be eschewed—and certainly no outsiders should witness the merrymaking. Here again was satisfaction for Catharina, Margaret, and Maria Coninxloo.

After a minor point on providing an adequate supply of linen to each sister, to avoid all appearance and inclination to private property, Van der Wiel returned suddenly to the problem of cloister by warning against the lodging and feeding of outsiders. Again this matched criticisms by Margaret and Catharina. Then he struck a couple of blows against the lay sisters: no more busying themselves with plasters and enemas, no more attending weddings, no more going to taverns and the market and then coming back to tell all. By now Van der Wiel was writing in short statements, probably reflecting his desire merely to get the main topics down—he could embellish the phrasing later, perhaps even rearrange if he thought some kind of priority or topical progression necessary. He hastily prohibited irreverence in chapter or rebellion against punishments, something that Mater and friends had complained about. On the topic of worship he added a requirement to meditate for half an hour after Primes, as suggested by Maria Joos. To finish, Van der Wiel ordered a halt to private discussions with postulants or novices, as requested by Mater, and an admonition—directed at Maria and Lesken Joos though no name is mentioned—to better provide for the sick.

Taken as a whole, this general document had a bit of something for everyone. It contained decrees that women on either side could have seen as aimed at the other, decrees that all knew were meant for a particular camp or individual, and decrees that the charitable or dispassionate could have viewed as simply part of the process of continuing monastic discipline. Still, the majority of the decrees at least implicitly condemned Mater. The specific instructions to Mater were even sharper, suggesting that Van der Wiel took seriously the heavy criticism against her. Whereas the public *determinatio* was projected to contain sixteen points, the document for Mater would consist of ten to be handled orally and about seventeen to be given in writing.

Most of Margaret's criticisms, and those of many others, came through clearly in these instructions for Adriana. Van der Wiel intended privately to exhort Mater to use more discretion in organizing the burdensome wash of the Jesuits. In her favor he would grant her permission to appoint a novice mistress, if she really thought it necessary. But his next points censured strongly. Be less withdrawn from the community and urge "certain religious" to come more frequently to refectory. Do away with the silver thimble, as well as the silver spoons for pudding, for such went against the vow of poverty. Punish faults with more softness and be somewhat "sweeter." Show less attachment to poor friends, despite good intentions to help them. And allow no talking "behind the streets" during Compline. Van der Wiel also gave Adriana what would be the delicate task of exhorting Maria Joos to be more generous and kind, but as if to balance this out, he asked her as well to warn Joanna Schoensetters about being so hard-headed.

The sloppily composed written instructions included commands for Mater to treat Anna Vignarola less partially, concern herself less with the "pomp" table, strive for greater accord with Vicaress, halt the lending of beds to others and the carrying of wood through the church, place a lay sister at the gate, warn the infirmarian to remain with her patients, and suspend the music school. Every one of these orders reflected criticisms made either by Margaret or Maria Coninxloo. But there were some concessions to Mater as well. She was to warn Vicaress to pay less heed to criticism of Mater from Coninxloo, Servranx, or Schoensetters and to order Sister Margaret to mind her own affairs, whether at the wagon gate or in the kitchen.

In many ways Van der Wiel must have felt that he was repeating his conclusions from 1628. But we should avoid being necessarily cynical about this. He and the sisters were used to this, since everyone knew that it was healthy monastic exercise to review one's faults regularly, to try to correct them, and to accept punishment. Problems and imperfection were assumed, even in Mater, and the conquest of sin was the most idealistic reason for being there. What impresses again is how seriously Van der Wiel took each charge.

Still, if that's all there was to it, then the process would have ended for now and efforts at improvement would have begun. There would be little need to write this story had the process been casual and routine. It did not end here, and it involved much more than the quest for perfection. Some opinions expressed were not simply about the need for penance and abnegation in oneself or in others but about one-upsmanship. Correction was in part about politics, terrestrial though it sounds. Desire for a certain kind of monastic discipline was mixed together often, even if in unsure quantities, with personal antagonisms or friendships and the desire to see a rival embarrassed or humbled. Thus, even as he hoped for deeply spiritual correction, Van der Wiel was careful not to promote factions by giving either side an absolute victory. The voices of the critics of Mater had been loudest, and they resounded loudest in his notes and his instructions for Mater.

Besides the composition of an actual *determinatio*—which occurred but the document did not survive—there was one other important difference from the last visitation, and that was the speed with which the sisters received word of the visitors' decisions. In 1628 the visitors had left after a day and reported back only months or even years later, but Van der Wiel had actually composed a draft of decrees on the second day of the 1633 visitation. And five days after that the sisters had their polished *determinatio*, their "conclusion" to the whole business. We know this because immediately the house's three leading officers asked not for mitigation but tightening of one crucial point.

On October 21 the officers of the house, consisting of the uneasy combination of Adriana, Catharina, and Maria Joos, sent a letter in

Catharina's hand to Van der Wiel. The topic was one on which all these leading members could agree—namely, that the sisters should never be allowed to speak alone at the grille, not even when close relatives came to call. "We note one point which we fear will not be profitable (for we know the nature and condition of some of our religious). . . . We certainly assume that your reverence did not intend this to result in license, but some will certainly understand this as they please, for they are very inclined to speak with their friends alone or secretly, so that it's to be feared that there won't be much in this convent that remains secret, as we've sometimes experienced." Here we see that private speaking was an issue not only of monastic protocol but of ever-present public relations, of the need to control the escape of information beyond the convent's walls. "Thus we pray with all humility that your reverence may please to remove this point in the charter [or *determinatio*] of the visitation, which we send back to you. For we understand that among one another they're already busy talking about it and letting themselves imagine that Mater would never have any right to refuse such a request"—making us wonder how the sisters had learned the news—"and yet in fact if this is necessary Mater has always been willing to grant a bit of time alone, which she will continue to do as necessary. If it pleases your reverence, we beg you to excuse us, and remember our request comes from the freeness of our hearts and in good spirit, and pray again your reverence for the love of God." At the bottom they prayed that when returning the *determinatio*, Van der Wiel seal it up so that the sisters delivering it might not know its contents, making it thus easier to control the other sisters' expectations.

This request is significant for several reasons. First, it reveals the desire of the house's leaders for a more stringent requirement than the one allowed by ecclesiastical superiors. It was a desire not at all unusual in this age, and surprising only to those who imagine that deep down every monastic community wanted a rule of the most lax observance. Second, since the visitor had not come himself to read the *determinatio* aloud, as often occurred and which made it easier to impose, it is striking that the sisters had enough nerve to refuse to accept the mailed rendition until revised. Last and most remarkable, from later documents we learn that when the sisters sent back the *determinatio* to Mechelen for revision, they never received it again. Perhaps the document was lost along the way or at the episcopal palace, or perhaps no one at headquarters had time to revise it—we do not know because the document didn't survive. It is even possible that the visitors sought to repay the temerity of the revision-insisting nuns of Bethlehem by refusing to conclude what was begun and thus leave them hanging. Whatever the reason and however the *determinatio* came to be destroyed, here was yet another visitation in which the official decrees were of short duration.

BOOK III

HOW MARGARET'S HARD-WON TRIUMPHS ONLY PARTLY FIZZLED OUT

21. THE RETURN OF SISTER MARGARET

[The] burden shall be taken away from off thy shoulder, and [the] yoke from off thy neck.   —ISAIAH 10:27

BETHLEHEM, ST. VALENTINE'S 1635 TO MID-1636. In the year after the plague that followed the siege of Leuven, and while some nuns of the city were still burning pitch to purify their convents, heartening developments unseen by most of the brooding world occurred in the life of Sister Margaret Smulders.

Not that things had begun so well. As if disease and war had not brought enough distress, Margaret also lost her only friend, Catharina Rijckeboer, who died in late 1634 or early 1635. She may have succumbed to the "illness" long mentioned but never named, or perhaps to the recent plague. Either way, she died young, less than forty years of age.

A new vicaress would have to be elected, an event that took place on St. Valentine's Day. To Margaret, the results meant further disappointment. The vote revealed that most sisters failed to share her unfavorable opinion of thirty-one-year-old Anna Vignarola. Of twenty sisters who cast their votes before the bishop's men, ten voted for Anna (four nuns, six lay sisters), six for Jacomyn de la Haye (five nuns, plus the last lay sister), while the remaining votes were scattered among three others. Mater told the visitors that Anna possessed "good understanding, is pious, and peaceable." Jacomyn nobly supported Anna (rather than voting for someone she knew could not win in order to pull votes away from Anna), because Anna could read and write well, was peaceable, discreet, and most important of all she got on well with Mater, "as it ought to be." Others asserted that Anna had already taught the novices "more than the previous vicaress, and . . . she's lived a true religious life from her profession until now," or that Anna was able, virtuous, "one with Mater, and strict about observing the rule and statutes, and can read and write well," and was "for the convent." The lay sisters also judged that Anna was "for the convent," a capable novice mistress, virtuous, and of good understanding. Anna's abilities, her close relationships with Mater and most lay sisters, and her advocacy of the convent (against external authorities, it seems) all served her well in this business.

Those who voted for Anna's competitors offered some equally interesting explanations. Margaret Smulders, who by now had somehow earned the right to vote on such matters, took a characteristically pessimistic approach, supporting Jacomyn because she was the "least unable" in the convent. Margaret was also one of the few to gratuitously offer a reason why she did *not* vote for someone else. "Sister Vignarola and Bursaress [Maria Joos]," said Margaret, anticipating the likely choices, "are too hard-headed and want to rule everyone." Anna Marcelis preferred Jacomyn because of her devotion to the Divine Office, Anna Coninxloo chose Jacomyn because she wasn't factional and was "well edified" in God, while Maria Coninxloo thought Jacomyn "good in God" and devoid of hangers-on. Joanna van Outhagen voted for Anna Marcelis because she was the next eldest and peaceable. Most surprisingly, Maria Joos voted for Margaret Geraerts because "she's pious and simple in her obedience." Was this a backhanded slap at Anna Vignarola, who was not simple at all? Anna herself, in customary fashion, voted for someone besides herself. She chose Maria de Smet, a young nun, because, as she said, "she is good-hearted, and would get along well with Mater." It is also possible that Anna knew that Maria de Smet didn't have a chance of winning, unlike Jacomyn.

The visitors were pleased with the result and decided to confirm the sisters' choice, even though Jacomyn received more votes from the veiled nuns than did Anna. Did the visitors settle on Anna in part because Jacomyn could not write, a fact they noted? More likely it was because of Anna's total votes and because they truly thought her best. One of the men, Dean Paridanus of Leuven, reported to Boonen the day after the election that he and the Guardian of the Franciscans, who knew Bethlehem well, agreed that Anna was clearly the most able of all and the most suited to the office. The visitors also considered the position of Vicaress to be good preparation and trial for Anna in the event of election for a new mater, a possibility that was more real than they knew. But since even Anna might falter, they suggested an initial probationary period of two or three years, a condition that Paridanus now revealed had been placed upon Mater in her first assumption to office but that had never been observed. This warm official endorsement of Anna and the fact that Anna received the support of half the convent make us pause and consider what our picture of her would be like if we had Margaret's evidence alone—or our picture of Margaret if we had only Anna's. In any case, Catharina was dead. Long live Anna.

Though these events surely did nothing for Margaret's spirits, her situation nonetheless began to improve. Even before the election there had been rumors about her return to the convent, rumors that were no doubt solidified by her very participation in the voting. Soon afterward determined steps were taken, culminating with her reinstatement in the spring or summer of 1636. Driven perhaps by memory of the broken promises of 1630, or perhaps feeling that with Catharina gone her plight outside the house would become even worse than if within, it was Margaret herself who accelerated the process by lobbying several old friends, including Bouckaert. And through yet another new dean of Leuven, named Mannarts, she sent a message to Boonen: Might His Most Illustrious Grace condescend to consider her petition regarding her reinstatement among the nuns of the convent, for she had long been separated from the other sisters and in her old age (having recently turned fifty) she would like to enjoy the fruits of community?

The local Franciscan Guardian also entered the fray, enlisting the prominent bishop and diplomatic envoy Joseph Bergaigne in his cause. Both vehemently opposed the return of an unnamed "separated sister" who had been removed "by the voice of all." The matter was "by all means" grave, they declared in their letters of April 1636 to Boonen, such that Mater should "fear and lament and the whole community protest the restoration of that person." The men believed that if she returned then the problems that already existed in Bethlehem would only be magnified, and the Guardian couldn't say with any confidence that anyone in the Franciscan house of Leuven would be willing to offer spiritual comfort to "that one." They eagerly awaited word from Boonen and indeed would be happy to appear personally to speak in more detail. For the moment they would simply say that if "that one" returned the effects would be clear "within an hour."

By now the sisters had become genuinely alarmed themselves, for they pleaded with all their souls, to anyone who would listen, that Margaret should remain in the guest house. Van der Wiel informed Boonen of "mournful" letters he had received from Bethlehem and foretold a "cloud of great dissension" ready to burst open over the community if Margaret returned. He also confirmed that Bouckaert was the driving force behind the action, "propped up by the authority of Your Most Illustrious Grace." Dean Paridanus had once predicted that Margaret's reentry would ruin the convent and Van der Wiel agreed. Despite his dispassionate summation of Margaret's letters at past visitations, Van der Wiel's opinions of the woman were clear: "The knowledge I have of the person of Sister Margaret gathered over many years" did not suggest that her reinstatement would be for the best. Van der Wiel by no means wished to impugn the archbishop's authority, but he thought it his duty to make clear his support of Adriana's proposal to delay Margaret's return until the matter had been more fully considered.

Despite these somber warnings, Boonen pushed ahead. At his request Bouckaert drew up the principles of Margaret's return in two documents, one in Latin for episcopal officials, one in Dutch for Adriana. The similar drafts contained four points:

1. The Latin insisted that Margaret was to have a choice of vacant cells, while the Dutch softened the blow by stating simply that Margaret could no longer be barred from the nuns' dormitory.
2. Both documents decreed that Margaret could not be expelled again, except for cause, and then only with the permission of the archbishop.
3. Both urged Mater to persuade the friars to minister to Margaret, so that she had a confessor.
4. So that Margaret may be kept in good spirits and feel accepted, both demanded that her infirmities were to be dealt with lovingly and secretly (unless she committed public faults that absolutely required public punishment), and Mater was to encourage the other sisters to bear Margaret's weaknesses.

While this would do for Mater, Margaret's return had to be explained as well to the sisters themselves. Boonen therefore had Bouckaert prepare another, longer draft, in Dutch only. "Jacob by the Grace of God and the See of Rome, archbishop of Mechelen," and so on, had deliberated "ripely" upon the "long" pleas heard in the past and still daily, "with more and more urgency," from Sister Margaret Smulders, to re-enter the community, from which she had been forcibly separated for about ten years and denied her place in the chapter, the choir, the common work, the refectory, and the dormitory. She had agreed to this separation at the time, it explained, "not for any cause but by her own free, uncompelled will, and at our request," for the "sake of the peace of the convent." Boonen and Bouckaert must have known that most sisters would hardly share this interpretation of the events of 1624 and 1625. The two men did not deny the reality of Margaret's problem, but they implied that this was a "bodily" ailment, which therefore mitigated Margaret's responsibility. Moreover, even if troubled "for some time," they stated that Margaret had been freed thanks to various "spiritual remedies." Though no one could ever be sure (modified later to "absolutely" sure) in these matters, "we willingly believe her," especially since they had seen that her resolve to stay free was "constant."

Therefore, in the absence of any "legal obstacle," Boonen declared his intention to grant Margaret's request to return. After a "long trial" of ten years, without any evidence of "supernatural troubles in her body, we must be content that she is redeemed, unburdened, and free of them, and consequently the community will have nothing to suffer from her in this regard."

The biggest question of course is whether these instructions and decrees were ever put into effect and whether Margaret actually was restored. But in all likelihood she was. First, it's unlikely that Bouckaert would have composed these documents on his own initiative. Moreover, they were drawn up after complaints about the possibility of return had come in to Boonen from sisters and their intermediaries, not before, implying that Boonen made his decision while conscious of mighty opposition. He must have felt absolutely determined—perhaps Margaret's pleas and her lengthy revelations had swayed him to act at least in regard to her person, however reluctant he was to attempt her version of reform for the convent. Further, as yet unbothered in these years by the consuming headaches of the Jansenist controversy, the theological dispute over grace and works that embroiled Catholicism during the seventeenth century, Boonen more than anyone else in the world would have been able to see Margaret's return to its completion.

The best clue of all that Margaret returned was the designation of Bouckaert to lead the next full-scale visitation to Bethlehem, in 1637. Though long an official visitor to the place, Bouckaert's tasks to this point had been specific, to follow up on this problem or that. It could be that he went because Van der Wiel was too busy with other things; or he may well have been chosen for the 1637 visit to defend the interests and the position of the freshly returned, especially vulnerable Margaret.

The final clue of her presence within the community is the flurry of old, controversial issues raised at this new visitation. Though largely muffled in its details, the debate was certainly heated, and the remaining documents suggest that Margaret was in her familiar position at the center of it all. Indeed, we should probably regard the visitation of 1637 as the culmination of all Margaret's emotions and struggles in the convent. Here was her moment in the sun: She was fresh from the triumph of return to the cloister; as a bona fide member of the house she could insist more respectably than ever upon her predictably long list of necessary reforms; and with her own patron assigned as official visitor she had good reason to expect substantial and pleasing results. Margaret could also use her reclaimed equality to work on salvaging her long-lost reputation. Though restoration *implied* a clearing of her name, she was not one to leave things to chance—especially since few sisters would have readily forgotten the ancient rumors that surrounded her. She therefore decided to make semi-public herself, for the first time in years, the details of painful old events that she kept locked in her heart. If her shame was to be removed, then the circumstances that brought it on would have to be retold and explained.

22. JUSTIFICATION

BETHLEHEM, LENT 1637. The later visitations that the sisters of Bethlehem continued to receive from the representatives of the archbishop have come down to us in much thinner detail than the visits of 1628 or 1633 and add little to our burgeoning picture of life among the nuns themselves. But on this score we can hardly complain, since the Grey Sisters have already taught us uncommonly much. Moreover, the later visitations, scrutinized in this chapter and the next, are important in other ways. They make more transparent than ever the role of inside-outside politics, and the limits of enforcement, in conventual reform. They also produced a final twist to the drama of Pastor Joos.

The visit of 1637, which came in late February or early March, stood out from the previous episodes in two ways. First was the vigor, firmness, and perseverance of Joost Bouckaert, who brought things to a rapid, clear end, in contrast to past delays and indecisiveness. Second, no letters from the sisters have survived, nor has any summary of the interviews conducted—they were too sensitive, no doubt. This time we have only the decrees in final form and some letters written after the fact by ecclesiastical officials. We must therefore be content with parts of the story, but they are intriguing parts nonetheless.

From the final *determinatio* and knowledge of past visitations we can reasonably infer that the interviews with the sisters and any accompanying letters were, as usual, wide-ranging. But what caused greatest consternation was something which from the *determinatio* alone we never would have been able to guess was even discussed: the raising of the "old, sordid tales" about Henri Joos. The earliest clue lies with a request by Dean Mannarts, who accompanied Bouckaert to Bethlehem in 1637. Mannarts asked Van der Wiel for any documents in the episcopal archives that would shed light on various difficult issues raised during the recent visitation to the convent. Needed most of all, Mannarts specified, were documents on the removal of Joos as confessor in 1618. Obviously the visitors had heard some things during the visitation that they now wanted to clarify. Then on March 9 Boonen, reminding us very much of Archbishop Hovius two decades before, suddenly prohibited Joos from hearing confessions or preaching in the entire archdiocese, on pain of suspension and other arbitrary penalties. Would these tales and this man never go away? Twenty years after his fall Joos, or at least memories of him, still played a leading role within the convent.

A confessor who served seventeen years at the convent of Our Lady Ter-Rivieren in Bree long acted as a wedge to split the sisters of that house in two, especially in his refusal to grant absolution to sisters of the "party in opposition" to himself and Mater. This example of factional dynamics we have already seen in Bethlehem, and such existed in many other houses. But Henri Joos had ceased to serve as confessor two decades before! That the case should arise again in 1637 illustrates how long such relationships could persist and exert influence. Admittedly, it's possible that only a few thought Joos's influence real, or excessive. Margaret was, after all, virtually alone in even mentioning the man during the visitations of 1628 and 1633. Was he, to most, just another of Bethlehem's many callers? Or did the sisters' silence in years past belie the frequency with which Joos was discussed among themselves? Anna Vignarola still argued passionately in 1672 that Joos had been wronged, suggesting that the topic had never been far from her influential heart and mind. Or was silence merely the usual reluctance to discuss unpleasant events with most outsiders, including episcopal officials? Indeed, it's likely that few in the episcopal hierarchy were aware of the details from 1618. Even Margaret had failed to state explicitly in past visitation letters just exactly what her troubles with Joos had been—she merely cast a few vague aspersions on his "past holiness." Recall as well that most of the papers Mannarts sought from the episcopal archives in 1637 had probably been burned by Hovius two decades before, and thus there was almost nothing for Van der Wiel to look up and send. The latter admitted to Boonen that he too knew very little of the matter—and he probably wanted to keep it that way. Hovius, explained Van der Wiel further, had spoken about the event in very general terms only, "thus preserving the honor of the place." This general sense of events was probably all that Boonen had come to possess as well.

Whatever the answer to these mysteries, and whether the ex-confessor deserved to be or not, it's clear that Joos was again at the center of attention in 1637. Part of the explanation must have been Margaret's formal return to the community, where she now had the chance to speak with more sisters, especially the young, and offer them her own interpretation of Bethlehem's checkered past. Another part was Bouckaert's willingness to pursue an old issue on which he felt his client had long been wronged. A final reason for the urgency was probably that, more than ever before, Mater Adriana was linked directly to the old scandals.

It's Van der Wiel who offers most of these clues. When he heard in early March that the old stories about Joos had been repeated during the visitation and that Bouckaert had vigorously questioned a number of sisters about them, he immediately lamented it. The older sisters had heard them all before, of course, but now all the younger sisters and every new visitor to Bethlehem would have to be briefed on old family secrets. Most significantly, he suggested that because of the stories Mater Adriana was "now greatly disgraced" (*valde infamata*). It's not clear whether Van der Wiel believed the content of the rumors or not. He did note that at the time of the old events Adriana was bursaress but "was not removed"—as if to say "she might have been." It also must be remembered that Margaret had previously made vague references to Adriana's past difficulties. Thus it would not be surprising if Margaret, determined to clear her name, was repeating those claims now—even encouraging others to tell what they knew—or if Bouckaert, already in the know given his relationship with Margaret, was pursuing every last clue.

In any case, Van der Wiel and most sisters blamed Bouckaert—and by extension Margaret—for resurrecting the stories. Van der Wiel was also flabbergasted that Bouckaert was agitating for Adriana's dismissal as Mater, since the events in dispute were so far away and memories had faded. Opposing Adriana, continued Van der Wiel, may have been Bouckaert's way of trying to defend the position of Sister Margaret, who had for many years been the cause of so much trouble in the place "and will continue to be, even if by a vote of the sisters a new Mater is appointed." Here was another clue from Van der Wiel that Margaret was the chief tale-bearer in 1637, as she had been before. Van der Wiel further lamented that Catharina was no longer among them and bemoaned the fact that several in the house were now "campaigning" for the office of Mater. Clearly Bouckaert's plans for a new election were already circulating.

If Van der Wiel regretted the raising of the rumors, it did not mean that he would fail to act. In fact, the rumors compelled action. Though he was critical of Bouckaert, he shared the man's conclusion about Joos: The former confessor should be kept out of Bethlehem to preclude evil suspicion and gossip. Van der Wiel soon informed Mater Adriana of that opinion. But then came more distressing news. Adriana wrote back to say that Joos was already invited to a novice-clothing on the "22 of this month" (probably March) and wished to know from Van der Wiel whether they should now uninvite him, or ask him to restrict his presence to the grille and keep out of the church. Although she sounded acquiescent, Adriana knew that this put Van der Wiel in an extremely difficult position. Banning Joos after everyone knew he had been invited would only induce questioning and explanation. Van der Wiel still favored the complete banishment of Joos from the convent, but he left the final decision on the situation to Boonen. Putting a lid on this dispute was crucial, for the community was doing quite well, he believed—save for an obstinate lay sister who had impertinently suggested to Van der Wiel during a recent informal visit to Bethlehem that she would ignore any decrees he might leave behind, for she preferred to wait instead for the decrees that would soon emerge from Bouckaert's equally recent and formal visitation! This, by the way, was Joanna Schoensetters, who also, we remember, had possible cause against Joos.

To the list of those who had a stake in the outcome of that visitation of 1637 and who were busy writing Boonen during the middle weeks of March in order to influence the shape of the *determinatio*, we must of course add Adriana. Like Van der Wiel, she blamed Bouckaert for the recent disaster, though rather than say so directly she simply tried to discredit the man generally. Significantly, she was careful—here and elsewhere—to avoid naming Joos specifically. Her first request was only tenuously related to Bouckaert's visit: Would Boonen please command the sisters to be content with a modest feast when there was a novice-clothing, for many had shamed one novice whose mother spent "only" 70 florins for a three-day feast and were warning the next novice-to-be that their bellies had better be full. This led Mater to her second point: that she had intended to pass on this request through Bouckaert, since he had promised to come by the convent again before compiling a *determinatio*, but on his last trip through the city he had failed to show. Last, Adriana predicted that Bouckaert would say to Boonen that the sisters were neglecting to read the 1633 *determinatio* every quarter, as decreed. When Bouckaert had asked her about this at the visitation, Adriana explained that she was flustered, but now she remembered that the convent had returned the decrees to the episcopal palace for emendation and had never received a final *determinatio* back; they had the 1626 statutes only, which were read. Thus this was not neglect caused by disrespect or irreverence, but by want of a written copy.

Bouckaert finally wrote to Boonen to offer his own version of what had occurred during the visitation of 1637. He was late in reporting and forced to write rather than come in person because of another recent bout of ill health. He stressed that the raising of the "sordid old disgraces" was initiated neither by himself nor Mannarts. The notion that he, Bouckaert, was responsible for reviving the stories came from certain sisters at the convent who "do not cease" writing to Archdeacon Van der Wiel. As for the archdeacon, continued Bouckaert, he "has not ceased, it appears, to believe them." If Bouckaert was right, then clearly the sisters had grasped an old lesson about bureaucracies: If one official will not listen, another of roughly equal power might. More specifically, since Bouckaert seemed against them, most sisters put their hopes in Van der Wiel. The minority who distrusted Van der Wiel, on the other hand, turned to Bouckaert—as illustrated by the anonymous lay sister mentioned earlier who told Van der Wiel that she eagerly awaited Bouckaert's *determinatio* and who indicated that she would obey this rather than Van der Wiel himself. In the end, Bouckaert did not deny discussing the old tales, but he insisted that he did not initiate them and that Van der Wiel be told so.

Also troubling to Bouckaert was that sisters who had given depositions about Joos were now accused of having done so in vengeance. Bouckaert refused to acknowledge to Mater Adriana that such was the case, or even that depositions had been made at all on the subject. If he did acknowledge even the fact of the depositions, Bouckaert realized, then Mater was "so crafty and cunning" that those who had testified about the old stories would come into her knowledge and reap their unpleasant reward. Bouckaert guessed that Joos himself had made the claim about malicious depositions, or that Adriana, not knowing exactly what was said during the interviews, hoped that by corresponding with Van der Wiel she would incidentally learn the identity of the culprits. So sensitive was Bouckaert to these accusations that he was even prepared to return to Bethlehem and inquire more carefully into the sisters' motives. But he had just learned that "it is not possible that she could have deposed in revenge regarding that most scandalous act and other things," or that "she" could have revealed them to others. The use of the singular feminine in this sentence, rather than the plural as everywhere else, makes us wonder whether Bouckaert didn't slip a bit to reveal that there was one main accuser, and that her name was probably Margaret.

This is the end of the evidence that Joos was a major topic of the visitation, a fittingly inconclusive way to complete the vicious and uncertain circle that began back in 1618. But it was not the end of the visitation as a whole, nor the efforts of Bouckaert to achieve reform. Whether Margaret was the chief accuser in the stories about Joos and whether she told these stories as part of her long-standing effort to discredit Adriana, we do not know for sure. We do know with certainty, however, that the decrees being planned by Bouckaert fit like a glove over Margaret's vision of monastic life and reform. Moreover, even absent any measures against Joos, Bouckaert's conclusions would have given Margaret satisfaction in her small war with Adriana.

In early April Bouckaert sent a "concept" of his *determinatio* to Boonen. None of the decrees was new, he pointed out; virtually all could be found in the house statutes. Yet because the community "regularly and notoriously" sinned against the statutes, repetition was in order. He swore to Boonen that both he and Mannarts had composed the ordinances with goodwill, that they had "carried out the commission by the grace of God" without any concession "to passion or vicious inclination, but in diligence and good faith." They therefore hoped that their decrees, at least in essence if not in form, would be pronounced and enforced. On the question of an election for Mater, Bouckaert judged that though Adriana was unsuited, she ought to be put up with for the time being.

If Bouckaert reluctantly gave up hope for immediate election of a new Mater, it was due to political realities. All knew, since Adriana had been in office so long, that to call an election now would only deepen wounds and bitterness. In houses where it was routine to elect every three years, then a change of Maters was not so obviously a slap in the face. Of course in cases of manifest scandal, genuine "Maters unworthy" (as every Mater routinely signed herself) were often removed. This could be true even when the scandal was distant in time. At Kabbeek in the city of Tienen, a sister Helwigem Clerx was elected Mater in November 1588, but the next day the visitors convened the sisters again after hearing rumors that Clerx had been involved long ago in a scandal with a certain Victor from Tongeren. Sister Helwigem came forward and resigned after a day in office. The crucial difference in Bethlehem was that Adriana had already been Mater for a dozen years by the time the rumors surfaced. Given the lack of regular elections in the convent, the lack of obvious cause, and the length of Adriana's tenure, even Bouckaert decided it best to postpone the election and concentrate for now on drawing up good ordinances. In concluding, he hoped that when Boonen formed a judgment about the suggested decrees, he would remember Bouckaert's efforts and goodwill, and not merely the suppositions of Van der Wiel.

We don't have Bouckaert's draft of the *determinatio*, but we do have a letter of his urging Boonen in mid-April to approve it and conclude the visitation quickly, "while fruit is to be hoped for." And we do have the final *determinatio*, issued in Boonen's name on May 20, 1637. As Margaret and at least one lay sister hoped, and as we might have expected from Margaret's protector, it was nothing less than excoriation of Adriana, much harsher than even Van der Wiel's private memos after the visitations of 1628 and 1633. Here finally was the document so ardently hoped for by certain members of the convent—not lost or misplaced, not flabby, not words in the wind, not to be forgotten. The thirty points of the *determinatio* (more than before) covered familiar ground but put the blame squarely—rather than implicitly—on Adriana. This public humiliation was so severe that one can only wonder what Bouckaert's private instructions to her, which were not put into writing, might have included.

Particular chastisement was obvious from the beginning. The *determinatio* seriously charged Mater to fill her office well, especially to apply herself and adhere to all things required of her office in the statutes. She was, "for good reasons," to increase the number of council sisters by two—namely Joanna van Outhagen and Maria de Smet, neither one of whom was partisan to Adriana. The reason for this addition was implied in point three: All temporal and spiritual affairs of any weight, all changing of officers or ordinances however small, all building or major repairs, and so on, shall "henceforth" be done with the advice of the council sisters and the approval of the dean.

"Henceforth," the *determinatio* continued, Mater will very carefully attend to and assure from the common income of the convent that all the religious, especially the sick and the weak, are provided with all bodily needs and comforts, in food, drink, medicines, clothing, and necessities of the cell, choir, and so on. This was to be done with common love and without any respecting of persons, and so well and fairly that no one will be compelled to seek any necessities for herself from without. To this end and to more easily achieve decent provision, the *determinatio* commanded that she observe and see to the observance of the last article of the sixteenth chapter of the statutes (on outsiders lodging and eating at the grille, a point that at first glance hardly seems related, but given our background about the cost of such entertaining makes sense). Another blow came with the decree to close and nail shut the doors to the guest room and the confessional in the church and the door to the sacristy, "as they were before" (in 1628). They were always to remain shut, on pain that Mater would be removed from her office if she neglected this or acted to the contrary.

Numerous decrees in the middle of the document indirectly reflected on Adriana. There was to be no more carrying wood through the church, no chattering with laypeople at the doors or windows of the church, stricter observation of *clausura*, no staying alone by workmen at any time or place, no workmen on recreation days even if it meant a project would be ruined, no recreational activities near the grilles or elsewhere where outsiders could see the nuns, no meals with outsiders on profession or clothing days, no conversations at the grille after Compline and none on communion days, no more speaking by Mater or Vicaress with confessors until all the religious have been able to confess first (to preempt the priming of the confessor). After several points of general improvement for all, there were more for Adriana alone. She was ordered to cease letting novices leave the convent one last time before profession, to remind the dean annually that he should come to visit, and to stop the convent's giving away to friends more than 18 florins' worth of items per year. Almost all of these topics reflect the decade-old concerns of Margaret and thus must be seen as a victory for her and as a reflection of the trust that Bouckaert had in her words.

The *determinatio*'s final points were also reserved for Mater. It was never intended that a mater should rule for life, but for a certain time. Thus the council sisters were to remind Boonen every three years that time was up and he should preside over a new election, appoint a new mater, or allow the current one to continue in her place. The same thing was to occur with the vicaress. And since the current mater had already ruled a "notable time," and the vicaress had served already for two years, this reminder was to be given at the next Lent, in 1628. Elsewhere, Mater was ordered to cease neglecting the proper punishment of faults, as called for by the statutes, on pain of being disciplined herself. Further, Mater now had to make an accounting of the monies collected to help (re)build the convent and of other ordinary and extraordinary alms. Last, Mater was to see that these decrees were obeyed and not only read quarterly in chapter, as customary, but even "put . . . into the hands" of the sisters. This meant that each sister would have her own copy of the decrees—not at all a common arrangement from my reading of visitations.

Unlike Van der Wiel, who over the years clearly tried to maintain some balance and harmony in public declarations, Bouckaert fashioned for Boonen and Bethlehem a document so one-sided that we wonder how, if the decrees were well observed, Adriana could have maintained any dignity and respect at all. The very first audible reading would by itself have been enough to humiliate any Mater. That it was to be repeated and then actually put into print for each sister would have only prolonged the agony. Even if Boonen still thought highly of Van der Wiel, as there is every reason to believe he did, clearly Bouckaert's hard line had won this time around.

And Margaret's too, for the whole document, and the arrangement for its regular proclamation, could just as easily have come from her mind and hand. We can imagine that for at least a fleeting moment, or during the initial reading of the *determinatio*, she was more content than she could ever remember having been in Bethlehem.

We cannot say the same for Adriana. The new decrees stung sharply enough, but add to them the probability that it was she who broke the distressing news to Henri Joos of his latest and everlasting exclusion from Bethlehem. A likely occasion for this scene was the novice-clothing of March, as he rode up expecting merriment. Or did she wait until after the ceremony? What emotions ran through hearts? They may well have always regarded each other merely as kindly benefactor and pious nun. Or were they linked more intimately by a faraway event? Any astute witness to the farewell might have found a clue in the demeanor of each. Did Joos ride off in a real or concealing huff? Was that anger on Adriana's face because the convent unjustly lost a valued patron, or were her eyes swelling? All in all, it was a very bad year for Adriana Truis.

23. CAPITULATION

LENT 1638 TO EARLY 1640. Neither Margaret's contentment nor the precariousness of Adriana's position as Mater lasted long. Many chronic problems combined to undo Margaret's triumph and help Adriana abide the political crisis. Among these familiar but now unusually clear problems were the bishop's reach exceeding his grasp; an escalation of ecclesiastical politics among Bouckaert, Van der Wiel, and Boonen; and whether the jurisdiction of the house should go, perhaps once and for all, to the Franciscans. The harsh, seemingly unbreachable decrees of 1637 were destined to become just as vulnerable and unimportant as those of 1628 and 1633—not because Adriana knocked them down, but because she would simply go around them.

When it came to enforcement, it was impossible and probably undesirable for any outside superior to check in with the nuns of Bethlehem daily or weekly to see that all were obeying the latest decrees. Compulsion was not supposed to have been paramount in monastic life, since voluntary submission was a sign of piety and was implied in the vow of obedience. But it's hard to imagine that decrees such as those authored by Bouckaert were, under the circumstances, willingly accepted in Bethlehem. Certainly Adriana took her duty to obey her superiors and their decrees seriously, but ultimately she did this in the way she saw fit. The standard of a good solid religious was shaped as much by Adriana and the other nuns as by outsiders; if the rules imposed upon the house were unsatisfactory, nonconforming sisters might still find justification in the thought that they were living up to their original vows as they understood them. Not even the vow of obedience was clear-cut in its details and practical consequences. If a superior wanted to ensure that reform went in a certain way, he would have to do more than merely issue decrees.

The local dean was the most likely candidate for securing compliance, but Mannarts does not seem to have possessed a strong personality. In his accompaniment of Bouckaert in 1637, or of Van der Wiel in a coming visitation of 1638, Mannarts passively went along with the nearly opposite decisions of each. As for the Franciscan confessors, though they were serious about discipline, they were not about to play the bishop's policemen and insist on the sisters' conforming to episcopal decrees with the dispute over jurisdiction still lingering. And direct enforcement by

Bouckaert, Van der Wiel, or especially Boonen was out of the question. Given differences in zeal, expertise, sizes of a diocese, and external conditions such as war, how many bishops at all could make the required annual or biennial visits to convents and parishes, much less compel strict conformity to their version of religious devotion? Bishop Malderus of Antwerp could report to Rome in 1615 that a third-order monastery in his diocese called Sion had been visited every year, as had other houses subjected to him—but Antwerp had 150 parishes, plus convents, while Mechelen had over 400 parishes alone. More common was the situation described by the Country Priest of Bernanos only decades ago in France: "We can barely manage our ordinary parochial round, the kind of thing which—when it is strictly carried out—makes a superior exclaim: 'There's a nice well-kept parish!' "

Even the energetic Boonen was hardly perfect. He expressed surprise in 1625 that the Grey Sisters of Diest had no special statutes of their own, a surprise made greater since the house had long asked for its own set of statutes and since Boonen knew the zeal of his predecessor and of himself. Moreover, he sent only five Ad Limina reports to Rome (the quadrennial report on the state of his diocese) when he should have sent nine, and like most everyone he always sent a representative rather than travel to the eternal and distant city himself. We have already seen from the 1628 and 1633 visitations to Bethlehem how difficult it was just to get the visitation decrees onto paper. Further, in October 1630 twenty-four sisters from Groot Bijgaarden wrote to Boonen and asked him to hurry and put an end to their recent visitation, primarily so that they would no longer be held in suspense about the status of their confessor—a question that had been in dispute for over a decade. Examples of infrequent visitation and irregular enforcement outside the Low Countries are similar or worse. Bishop Jean d'Aranthon, installed in 1661, presided over 550 mountainous parishes, most in Switzerland, 90 in France. He managed to make the rounds three times, often on foot and through precarious terrain, and then died on the fourth—but his exceptional vigor is precisely what earned him attention. Recent studies of English politics and religion have shown that arguments which "imply that the Tudor State had a formidable coercive capability" are greatly exaggerated, for neither at the "center nor in the localities" was there sufficient force to guarantee conformity. If that was true of England, one of the more centralized states in Europe at the time, we might hypothesize that problems were at least as difficult in hierarchies elsewhere, including in the dioceses of the Spanish Netherlands.

Besides the physical limits of what the bureaucracy *could* do, perhaps there was also a limit to what the visitors *would* do. We have seen this with Van der Wiel in Bethlehem in 1628 and could bolster it with dozens of examples. In 1640 Abbot Benedictus Van Haeften of Affligem showed another part of the reasoning behind what seems at first glimpse to be inaction. In dealing with a difficult nunnery, he decided that it didn't need new statutes, more visits, and mountains of decrees, for there were plenty, but rather just a few laws and more observation. "An abundance of laws is anyway often disadvantageous." Moreover, Van Haeften felt that these women, "by their nature," were not easy to reason with, and an abundance of laws only compounded what he regarded as their inherent stubbornness. Bouckaert never expressed this exact attitude toward female religious, even if he probably would have agreed with it, but based on other evidence it's not unlikely that such a view was hovering about in many diocesanal hierarchies. No wonder church officials sometimes exerted themselves to a certain point only, enough to make clear the ideals and punish obvious violations of major rules.

Closely related to what visitors could or would do were questions of rivalry and personality, of which we've had samples already. Ideally, of course, neither of these factors was supposed to have mattered; the bishop should have been able to send any visitor at any time and get back a dispassionate, reliable account of the conditions in a given establishment. But in practice, temperament and other earthly considerations did matter and led different visitors to different conclusions and actions. We saw political considerations at work in 1628 and 1633 when Van der Wiel withheld certain criticisms of Adriana, not because he was shy about reform but for fear that it would only make conditions worse in Bethlehem. And then in 1637, when Bouckaert let loose his stinging decrees, it was partly because of his personal grudge against Adriana. More blatant examples of these dynamics would arise in the forthcoming visit of 1638, along with some new twists—especially between the visitors themselves.

In accordance with the 1637 decree, Boonen sent a visitor to Bethlehem during Lent of 1638. This time it was Archdeacon Van der Wiel, accompanied by the same man who had assisted Bouckaert the year before, Dean Mannarts. Boonen may have sent Van der Wiel because Bouckaert was otherwise engaged this time, but it's also possible that he sent him to deny—despite the archbishop's respect for both men—an absolute victory for either faction within the convent. Boonen hoped to maintain, no doubt, some kind of balance through using both these visitors, for he knew that they would not respond in the same way to the situation. Bouckaert worried about protecting Margaret, while Van der Wiel feared that to concede practically everything to her would spoil Mater's authority and the state of the house. Boonen saw the merit of both views.

The different approaches of Bouckaert and Van der Wiel became apparent enough in the visitation of 1638. Based on the decrees of the year before, Van der Wiel's tasks should have been to make the usual assessment of conditions in the house and also to oversee the mandated elections of a mater and vicaress. As was customary in a formal visitation, the archdeacon in fact interviewed every sister. But, based on his other actions, it seems unlikely that Van der Wiel actually intended to produce any new decrees, or to strictly enforce the decrees of 1637, or to hold an election.

As in 1637 there are no surviving letters by the sisters or interview summaries that would reveal the nuns' points of view. But more striking than this is the lack of any hint that the visitors intended to come to a firm conclusion. At least in 1628 Van der Wiel had drafted a memo on possible decrees, while in 1633 and 1637 an actual *determinatio* had resulted. Now there was only a string of informal reports on what had occurred, though some of these are invaluable in revealing the theme of ecclesiastical politics. "I see not a little dissension among them," lamented Van der Wiel in a letter to Boonen. But the problem was not with Mater, he believed. Rather, it was with three or four veiled sisters and one lay sister who "conspired" against her. The lay sister, none other than Joanna Schoensetters, was particularly defiant, railing in her interview, "with much repetition," that neither Mater nor Vicaress was suitable for office. Van der Wiel warned her to cease being so suspicious and to be wary of her accusations, for he had not yet heard from Mater herself. When Mater arrived for her interview, she complained that only two days before, when the house was to be scoured for the solemnities of Pentecost, Joanna had refused to join the others in cleaning. Van der Wiel called Joanna again and commanded her to obey Mater and improve her ways, lest more serious remedies be taken. But this had little effect, reported Van der Wiel, and Joanna refused to confess to the house confessor as the feast day approached. Instead, Joanna insisted—as she had so resolutely in 1637—on waiting to confess until she could speak with Joost Bouckaert, whom she also intended to inform about Van der Wiel's "thoughtless judgments." All this offended Van der Wiel, but it offended the house confessor even more. The latter told Van der Wiel that Bouckaert's presence in Bethlehem was "not particularly healthy." Important here is not Joanna's defiance, which is hardly new to us (besides, two days later she recanted and begged forgiveness). Rather, what matters is the not-uncommon appeal to the visitor of one's choice.

Another point on which Van der Wiel disagreed with Bouckaert was the touchy issue of a new election for Mater. Van der Wiel was very much aware that this new election had been ordered for 1638, but since "from diverse sisters" he sensed "that no one or scarcely anyone ought to be preferred to the current Mater," he decided that to hold an election would be useless and even harmful. As for the accompanying election of a vicaress, "I do not think that there will be much difficulty, unless perhaps someone is elected displeasing to Mater or who dislikes Mater." Though this sentence is vague, it suggests that an election for vicaress was held, but the election for a mater was not. Whether any election was held or not, however, it's certain that Adriana continued as Mater and Anna Vignarola as Vicaress.

The third example of conflict between the men also involves the prestige of Adriana. Several of the sisters requested during their interviews that various parts of the common, public decree given by Bouckaert in 1637 be transferred to a private document, for Mater's eyes alone, thus mitigating some of the public humiliation inflicted upon her. The nuns' explanation for this was that "penalties noted there seem to impede Mater's authority." Van der Wiel was sympathetic to the request, and though he couldn't change the 1637 decrees without permission, he did send a copy of them along to Boonen with a recommendation to revise.

To tie up this review of ecclesiastical politics, let us note that if we examined the decrees—final or intended—of 1628, 1633, and 1637 alone, we might conclude that the situation in Bethlehem worsened considerably over time, especially between the last two visitations. But then we would also have to conclude that, given Van der Wiel's mild actions in this new visitation of 1638, the situation in Bethlehem suddenly reversed itself and became manageable and routine once more. A better explanation is that official perceptions and action depended largely on the eyes of the beholder. Van der Wiel would never have denied the place's problems, but when it came to the degree of seriousness and to public action he differed mightily from Bouckaert. To their credit, both men appear to have been more zealous than jealous and tried to carry out their tasks in good faith.

Since for more than a year we hear no more about the tension between the competing visitors, or between those who looked to either for support, we don't know the outcome of the 1638 visitation—if it may be called that. But it's clear from later evidence that tensions had not subsided and that nothing had been decided. This evidence also reflects brilliantly the last important component in the shaping of religious life: namely, the stubbornness of the sisters, a characteristic we have already seen on numerous occasions in Bethlehem (and that we could multiply times one hundred with examples from other houses), and that was illustrated more conclusively now than at any other time.

In early August of 1639 Adriana informed the archbishop that Bouckaert and Dean Mannarts (who constantly must have felt like the man in the middle) had recently and suddenly arrived at Bethlehem to demand the *determinatio* which they had delivered personally to the convent after the visitation of 1637. Adriana responded that it had been carried away by Van der Wiel during his visit of 1638. Once again, as in 1633, the *determinatio* had gone missing. Adriana informed Boonen that Bouckaert was planning to return to the convent still one more time, in the very near future, so that he could (re)conclude his 1637 visitation. Adriana found this strange, since the 1637 visit had already been concluded. Clearly, she opined, this showed his intent to exercise his own brand of control over the house; he obviously planned to disregard whatever Van der Wiel might have decided in the visit of 1638. We also wonder whether Bouckaert wasn't trying to ensure that the 1637 decrees would have more force than the kinder, gentler decisions which Van der Wiel was likely to introduce.

Bouckaert quickly learned of Adriana's story and immediately dismissed it, writing to Boonen that her interpretation was false and even an outright lie. He explained that he had simply happened to be in Leuven, seeking advice from doctors there whether he ought to continue drinking the waters of Spa, since their benefits for his health had so far been dubious. While in town, he continued, he decided to drop in on the sisters of Bethlehem. His treatment of Adriana on arriving was, therefore, hardly the rude conspiracy that she made it out to be. On the more important question of the whereabouts of the *determinatio*, he believed that "under the shrubbery are plenty of falsehoods." Van der Wiel himself had told Bouckaert that during the 1638 visitation he had made and taken a *copy* of the 1637 visitation decrees—not the original. Therefore, feared Bouckaert, Adriana had perhaps "mutilated" if not "destroyed" the original. This helps to explain Adriana's claim that Bouckaert intended to reconclude the visitation of 1637; if the *determinatio* had been "lost," he would bring a new one of equal force. Certainly Anna Vignarola possessed, he surmised, a "raging enough soul" that she could have done such a thing and "conniving enough language to have persuaded Mater to the same." But Bouckaert would not excuse Adriana, even if this was Anna's doing. Bouckaert therefore urged Boonen himself to request the decrees from the women and to beware of any meek demeanor they might display in their response, for there was no question in his own mind that they wished to "throw off the yoke" of good discipline.

This was far from the first or even the hundredth time that a vigorous man such as Boonen, who often overcame the diverse physical hurdles to make his visits and who possessed a genuine religious fervor, was faced with the problem that he could not control all. In many instances he had to be content with exhortations only. For example, after visiting the beguinage of Tienen he wrote: "We've observed, not without sorrowness of heart . . . that the statutes of our predecessors . . . are grossly or wholly neglected . . . and have understood as well that love among you has been broken, and respect for authority trampled underfoot, the simpleness of clothing and furnishing replaced by novelty, high-minded-ness, and wasteful excess." And this sad assessment came in December 1654, after Boonen had invested thirty-five years of exemplary labor and inspiring leadership.

How the 1637 decrees for Bethlehem came to disappear will never be solved, but the ruling sisters were not about to exert any efforts to get them back. Another manifestation of their stubbornness was their en-gaging in an old but finally successful maneuver: appealing to the friars to come and take them away from the archbishop. Obviously certain members of Bethlehem had possessed such a desire for years, and vari-ous friars had long been cheering them on. But as a consequence of Bouckaert's visit of 1637, the energies of some sisters became more vig-orous than ever. By the time Bouckaert came calling in August 1639 to demand his old decrees, a secret deal had already been struck between the archbishop and the friars. It was a deal that would have infuriated or at least embarrassed Bouckaert, for it served to render his decrees, and his authority in Bethlehem, null and void.

By 1638 Boonen had already exchanged letters with Franciscan head-quarters in Rome in support of the switch, while the women of Bethle-hem had sent some long-distance petitions of their own. In an undated plea, they fell to the pope's feet complaining that, notwithstanding nu-merous bulls which had placed third-order houses under the friars, their particular house had long been separated from the Franciscan family and they wished to return. Let us note that such an argument, suppos-edly based on principle, was in fact a convenience, for it had never been employed or needed in the days of the secular confessor Henri Joos. By February 17, 1639, enough details had been ironed out that papal docu-ments ratifying and proclaiming the transfer had been dispatched. The document explained, "Having seen the request of the convent of Bethle-hem to be placed under the jurisdiction of the friars," especially since those friars had enjoyed for many years "license from [the archbishop of] Mechelen to hear confessions" and had been greatly concerned for the souls of the sisters, and so on, Urban VIII was willing to grant jurisdiction to the Franciscans.

But the deal was far from done. In April 1639 Boonen told Adriana to keep the decision to herself until he had discussed the matter with the members of his cathedral chapter. "For if they're against it you will have great difficulties," Boonen warned. We have already seen the truth of such a statement back in 1619, when Hovius was ready to relinquish the place but the chapter prevented him from doing so. Boonen promised that he would see to the switch "as soon as possible; if the mob doesn't allow me to write any more, then I pray God for you all and the convent His highest welfare, and commend myself to your prayers."

Was Boonen using the notoriously stingy chapter as a scapegoat for his own reluctance to approve the change? Perhaps, but he seems to have been genuinely eager to be rid of Bethlehem. In a similarly messy situation that occurred in 1637, Boonen tried to solve the problems of a house of English Benedictine nuns by handing them over to the jurisdiction of nearby English Benedictine monks. In any event, Adriana followed Boonen's admonitions to secrecy, so that when Bouckaert came calling in August for his decrees, she refrained from breaking the news of the jurisdictional switch. Adriana focused instead on the misplacement of the 1637 *determinatio*: "I didn't want to give him the slightest hint, nor anyone else," she explained to the archbishop, "thus I fall before the feet of your eminence, praying for the love of God that you'll put an end to our problem." While Adriana's discomfort in putting off Bouckaert must have been real, it lasted only a moment and was eased by the knowledge that a switch to the friars would keep out Bouckaert and his decrees forever.

As Boonen predicted, the cathedral chapter did not go down without a fight. In June 1640, in order to avoid impingement of their perceived rights, they appointed two canons to take their case to a secular tribunal in Brabant, where it was hoped that a decision against the papal decree to return Bethlehem to the Franciscans would result. Here was a favorite trick of lawyers in this time, as the authority of the secular national state was ever increasing vis-à-vis the international church. The chapter also spoke with the papal representative in Brussels, who for unknown reasons and motivations decided to write to Rome in support of the chapter's request for revocation. The various documents composed along the way called upon arguments that served their cause: The convent had been subjected to ordinary jurisdiction since time immemorial; there was lack of consent within Bethlehem to the switch (probably an exaggeration); visitations had taken place nearly every other year (another exaggeration, unless informal visits and letters counted too); the friars were infamous for their excessive strictness, and "inquietude and turbation" would result from the friars' refusals to allow sisters to hear other confessors.

To avoid becoming mired in the bottomless bog of lawsuits by and among chapters full of canon lawyers, let us simply note that the importance of this suit for our story is that it further complicated—and indeed almost pushed to the background—what seemed in 1637 to have been a prominent, cut-and-dried series of reforms in Bethlehem. The sisters didn't immediately leave the bishop's jurisdiction in 1639 (because of interminable legal action), and many sisters would later seek a return to the bishop because the friars would indeed prove unpopular. Nonetheless, the argument over jurisdiction served to enhance the confusion about the 1637 decrees from Bouckaert and sent them almost to oblivion.

We must not forget about Margaret in this continuing debate, for she obviously played a large role. In August 1639 Bouckaert lamented the nuns' bullying of the "innocent Sister M," for which he now believed himself partly to blame. Bouckaert first learned about this bullying from a scathing letter—about Margaret—sent by Anna Vignarola to the dean of Leuven, who had in turn confidentially alerted Bouckaert to this sisterly ill-will. Bouckaert wanted to discuss personally with Boonen Anna's unkind remarks, since they "ought not to be written," but in the meantime Bouckaert had persuaded "the afflicted Ma., (the name I delete)," to greater and more frequent exercise of faith, for "there did not seem to me a more commodious and stronger means to conquer infirmities, temptations, and so forth." He also urged her to recite frequently the (translated) profession of faith by Pius V, and by this and other means he hoped that she would attach her mind to obedience and faith, the foundation of all salvation. At first, continued Bouckaert, Margaret responded that by no means would she do it. However, "with the benevolence of God," she changed her mind, "with exorcism having first been dispatched. I write all this to the consolation of Your Illustrious Grace."

Whereas Margaret might have originally expected to gain some satisfaction from the decrees of Bouckaert, now she was the one suffering most for them and undoubtedly for her perceived role in the expulsion of Henri Joos as well. The mention of exorcism also makes us wonder whether her old troubles might have returned temporarily. Bouckaert was pained to no end and thought it unjust that the sisters blamed her for the *determinatio* of 1637 "as if she were the cause of it all."

We don't know what went on in the convent between 1639 and the remaining nine years of Margaret's life. We can imagine that her situation had changed little from what it was before 1624 or even during the years of exile in the guest house. True, her fortitude and resolve and experience had swelled, she was back inside, and it was no small thing that Henri Joos was gone. But did she again require regular exorcising? And even if she didn't, and succeeded in remaining relatively healthy, she was faced daily with the hard fact that Adriana remained Mater until the end, with Anna Vignarola her loyal, eternal vicaress—despite all the turmoil that surrounded them during the 1620s and 1630s. That Mater and Anna endured the storms is not to say that they or the other sisters no longer took monastic discipline seriously. Rather, there were other matters to consider, such as jurisdiction, the reality of sincerely different opinions on what truly mattered in monastic life, personal tastes in relationships, and ecclesiastical and conventual politics. One might argue that under the circumstances, even with the closer, surer presence of the ready-to-write Margaret, the leading sisters were freer than ever to shape religious life and reform quite as they pleased.

24. FINIS

THE INFIRMARY OF BETHLEHEM, DECEMBER 17, 1648. The year 1648 is remembered best in European history for the Treaty of Westphalia, an accord so important that it not only ended long hostilities around Europe, but from then on became a stopping and starting point of innumerable courses and books. In our story, however, 1648 is monumental for a different reason: the demise of a woman who for decades had toiled—in her idiosyncratic, often irascible way—to carve out a niche for herself within the world of Catholic monasticism.

The illness that preceded the death of Margaret Smulders was "long," according to the only brief account of it, which could have meant weeks or months or even years, since the last word we have about her before this account came in 1639. If her care went according to statute, then Mater Adriana should have visited her daily in the infirmary, provided for her needs from the common resources of the house, and especially exhorted her to penance, reminding her of the inevitability of death and the strictness of divine judgments. In Mater's absence, the infirmarian Lesken Joos, in the spirit of loving God and not herself, was to serve the patient faithfully, all the while keeping the infirmary spotless. Like Mater, she should have urged the sufferer to bear her illness with courage, speaking softly and briefly, while encouraging visitors in the place to do the same. Perhaps this all happened. Perhaps the sick one was finally conceded, at no cost, the fresh butter, white bread, and nice draft of beer or glass of wine she had so long desired. Or perhaps her nightmare of loneliness and absolute poverty came to pass.

If the patient heeded all the exhortations, which we know she was conscious enough to have done, for the dean of Leuven wrote that her mind and spirit were sound to the end, she would certainly have taken care to confess her sins, which she knew were many. Unlikely was she as heroic as the third-order Saint Elisabeth of Hungary, who kicked everyone out of her room three days before death to refresh her memory for confession and to contemplate the terrible judgment that awaited her, who sang like a swan with the angels around her, who fought off the devil's last-ditch attempt to grab her soul, and who died with words about the birth of Jesus on her lips. Though probably less dramatic, Margaret's last hours were undoubtedly just as anxious. Fortunately she could take advantage of the recent proliferation of books that offered tips for dying well. A Franciscan named Leutbrewer prepared a convenient handbook (that ran to thirteen editions soon after its first publication in 1646) on the *Golden Art of How to Prepare in Less Than Two Hours for a General Confession of One's Whole Life, with the Guarantee That No Deadly Sins Will Be Forgotten.* A basic general principle to remember was to confess regularly during one's life, something that at least by monastic standards this sister had not always done. Another goal was to ensure that confession was complete, for too often people were sloppy about confessing, especially at the end. In considering one's whole life, one should include a list of all the people known and possible sins against them, a list of all possible sins against the Ten Commandments, a list of sins common to one's station—whether merchant, married, lawyer, notary, soldier, ruler, child, tavernkeeper, workman, peasant, or of course religious. For each of these lists the author generously provided a string of the typical sins to jar the reader's memory for that last dreadful hour.

Besides Leutbrewer, there was also Van Gorcum's *Comfort of the Sick.* In addition to offering specific techniques to prepare for one's last breath, Van Gorcum explained such abstract points as why the devil was especially concerned and present at the time of death, a crucial topic given the history of this nun. The reason was that even someone who had served the devil for twenty or thirty years might abruptly decide to leave his employ, while those who had led exemplary lives might now be tempted to give up the fight and go over to the other side. In short, though the devil had worked on all souls for long, this was the moment when the final decision was made. Therefore, Van Gorcum exhorted, struggle, call on God and the saints that holy angels may come, just as Satan's demons were sure to come. Use the crucifix for a comfort, just as Moses raised the serpent. See the Lamb of God, think that the cross drives Satan away, that it's the tree of life. Let the sick hold a candle, reminding who is the light of the world.

Who knows what last thoughts, or temptations, or scenes from her past, or snatches of joy flashed in and out of Margaret's mind as she pondered her life and death? And what did those standing around her feel? Were they relieved? Did they feel at least a moment of pity, even Anna Vignarola, who in the long run would forever hold a grudge against Margaret? We don't know, but we do know that all sisters were supposed to be present when the infirmarian gave the sign that the sick one was about to expire. They read the Pater Noster, Credo, seven psalms with Litanies and prayers, and one sister read aloud the Passion of Our Lord. These were some of the most fundamental statements in the Christian tradition and were chosen as if to reemphasize what it was that they all believed about life and death, and what united them even

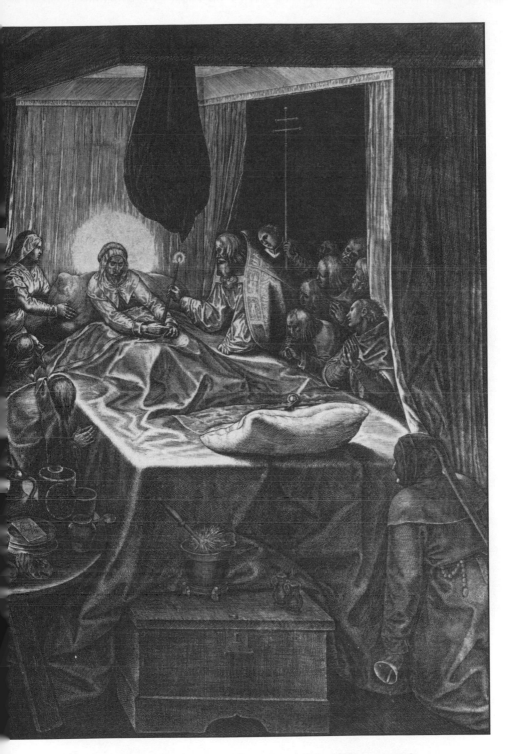

The Death of the Holy Virgin, Pieter Bruegel the Elder, sixteenth century. Margaret's room may not have been as full as the Virgin's at death, but this scene suggests the busy-ness of the event, physically and spiritually.

as much else might divide. In the meantime, the confessor (or one of the sisters) sat near the dying Margaret and urged her to give no quarter to the enemy. This may have included mention of the plenary, or absolute, indulgence granted to all third-order religious who at the hour of death called out with their mouth or heart the most holy name of Jesus. Given Margaret's poverty, few sisters were likely to have been thinking of how they would divide up her meager goods, a practice she had always found so tasteless.

When death was near, two nuns left to recite the long Commendations, outlined in the breviary. When death finally came, the other sisters all disciplined themselves with a rod, to remind them of their sins and that death would befall them as well. Soon after these came the Vigils with nine readings and the funeral Mass, and the body was placed in the ground "according to custom." The memorial services would continue for weeks. In the midst of them, Mater Adriana was to ensure that the death was announced in all other convents of Leuven and the archdiocese, so that the deceased's soul might be faithfully prayed for, out of love. Mater didn't announce Margaret's death herself to Boonen, but she did tell the dean, who in turn wrote to a canon at the episcopal palace. At the bottom of a letter full of other monastic business, the dean asked whether the canon wouldn't mind going to the trouble of informing the archbishop that on December 17, in the Monastery of the Grey Sisters of Leuven, "Sister Margaret Smulders, known well enough to him, had passed from this life, after a grave and lengthy illness, but with optimum disposition of spirit and full senses until the end."

If the dean was right about her good spirits and sound mind, then here at last was an undeniable victory.

268

AFTERWORD

WE WONDER WHETHER MARGARET, around sixty-five at the time of her death, died of new and recent physical ailments or of old familiar ones. We wonder how Boonen responded, since more than any other piece of evidence, the very existence of the letter by the dean reflects the archbishop's long concern for Margaret. Not one other such letter for any nun of Bethlehem is filed among the papers of the house, though no doubt many were written. Boonen would not have denied that Margaret had caused him frustration, but given his recent troubles with the Jesuits that would erupt into the shattering debate over Jansenism, this news must have taken him back to what now seemed simpler days. It is probably thanks to Boonen that Margaret's unusual papers have been preserved. He did so perhaps with no clear sense of future purpose, but for the same reason that many people save: because it's hard to part even with seemingly trivial things that remind us of our past, even the unhappy past.

Whatever the case, since Margaret died within the bosom of the church and her calling, the best theology of the day would have concluded that her life was scarcely in vain. But we can speak only in the less exalted sphere of historical worth. Here we can conclude more forcefully and confidently that, troubled as it was, Margaret's life was worth much. It is through her that we've gained a rich and multilayered image of an important part of the religious scene.

This is not to say that the animating details of Margaret's story and her house were universal. It's true that provocative evidence of other individual sisters—or confessors—who could embroil an entire convent, exists. A Sister Maria of the Black Sisters in Leuven told Van der Wiel that there was peace in the house, save for the "difficulties caused by Sister Barbara, who isn't well in her senses." A sister in Bethanie of Brussels was accused in 1590 of stealing two hats, of committing "crimes" against two cats that she owned, of throwing a key (a serious act in a day of large keys) at the head of one of the other sisters, of stating one day in choir "please read a Pater Noster and an Ave for our Mater, lest she lose her soul in how she treats me," of yelling at the confessor when admonished for this, and then screaming at Mater "You're my enemy to the death, I'd rather see the devil than you." Bishop Triest noted that there were "two rebellious sisters" among the

Black Sisters of Pamele, that new sisters Anna and Jacoba were insolent libertines, that Sister Anna in the hospital of Hulst was "greatly rebellious, turbulent, and irreverent," that Mater was too "morose and choleric" and indiscreet in chastisement, and that Sister Coleta among the Brigittines of Dendermonde was "greatly rebellious." Even in the later decades of the history of Bethlehem, Anna Vignarola was burdened by a certain Sister Regina, who made reports to the archbishop about the convent that Anna termed "utter fantasy." Similar instances, plus a mass of examples about other features and trials of conventual life, are easy enough to cite. How many of the sisters involved built a paper trail as long as Margaret's, only for it to be destroyed and their stories lost?

As is often the case in history, we can't answer these questions. But we can say that Margaret's story has further illuminated religious life in the Age of Reform. Through her we see better that Reformation involved more than expunging and proclaiming, that personal relationships must be accounted for in the drive for reform and the shaping of religious life, and that the complexity of reform was rendered more intricate still by the limits of outside enforcement. She and others have shown us that the Grey Sisters of Bethlehem, though unquestionably influenced by the official style of reform, had the last word in fashioning religious ideals and myths. And this, I suspect, was how most people of the time lived their religion.

Of course on this last general point we can speak with certainty only about the members of our own cast. Since they have served us so well on the matter, we should end by at least taking the trouble to trace their fates.

Henri Joos in 1624 had been replaced as Vicar of St. Gertrude's by a certain Gaspar Schillemans, whom the canons called an "idiot." Joos's successor at the Three Kings altar in Gertrude's was a theology student named Carolus de Blehen, who in 1628 went mad and was locked up among the cell-brothers, which explained to the dean why the prescribed Masses went unsaid. As Pastor of Mol, Joos made wonderfully neat accounts, including a volume that listed endowed anniversary Masses and the major benefactors of the church. And of course he still took time to travel to Leuven and visit his devoted admirers.

After the controversy stirred by the visitation of 1637, Joos would live but one more year. With many others he fled Mol in 1638 because of war. He took refuge with one of his sisters, who lived at the beguinage of Diest, and died there in exile on September 14, 1638. His burial marker next to the ironstoned church there contained an epitaph that in 1900 was still partly legible but said nothing significant. Most of the symbols and words had by that time worn smooth, probably because the marker lay under the corner of the roof and for centuries was constantly pelted by all the water that ran off, as if Margaret herself were trying to erase his memory. The tombstone no longer exists today, apparently destroyed during the world wars.

From what we can tell, Joos remained to the end a champion of well-ordered documents and ecclesiastical tithes. But perhaps he was not a bad pastor either, for the magistrates of Mol, on announcing Joos's death, noted their hope that "God would be merciful to his soul, for he had served the community well and faithfully." They hoped further, though they couldn't have appreciated the irony, that one of the pastors of Bouckaert's oratory of Scherpenheuvel might come to take his place. In his will Joos left gifts to various people and institutions but gave no direct clue that he had ever even known the nuns of Bethlehem. Was he wounded by the second expulsion of 1637, or did the nuns never mean quite as much to him as he did to some of them—or as much as Margaret said he did?

Because of old age, Peter van der Wiel concluded his long days as vicar-general in 1641, a few years after his last visitation to Bethlehem. He asked that when the end came he might be buried before a "privileged altar" or at least a "suitable place" in the choir of the cathedral, called St. Rombout's, preferably near the stall where he had sat for so many years. And he saw to it that alms would descend upon a wide range of people and institutions, especially male and female religious houses, even outside Mechelen. But he did not think the Grey Sisters of Leuven merited or needed his aid, for they were not to be found among the many names listed in his will. Nor was there anything else to suggest that he had ever been anxious about the convent. He died in January 1643 and was buried as he requested, with his grave marked by a stone that noted his strenuous labor for God. The grave was demolished on May 21, 1810, probably after being damaged during the Napoleonic wars. As late as the twentieth century, the anniversary of his death was still sung every June 18.

Joost Bouckaert, soon after his hassles with Mater Adriana in 1639, was nominated to the see of Ieper (in the western Spanish Netherlands), left vacant by the 1638 death of the now-notorious theologian-bishop Cornelius Jansenius. Thus Bouckaert departed his dear Scherpenheuvel, where he had been pastor thirty-two years, dean twenty-two years, and prior of the oratory eighteen years. Did he ever see Margaret again? We would have to guess that he did, but there is no record of such. He died in 1646 on All Souls Day, age sixty-three—not bad for a body wracked by so much affliction. His tombstone praised him as a true pastor of his flock, who desired neither filthy money nor honors, but only to love God and his neighbors.

Archbishop Jacob Boonen remained as busy and generous as ever, donating 10,000 florins to the local Mont de Piété over the years, 8,000 to the "Repentants," 30,000 for "expenses to introduce reform," and so on. The expense sheet for 1636 alone totaled 43,277 florins, including numerous gifts to individuals and convents—but there was not a word here or in his will about his dependent Margaret or the Grey Sisters. He also continued to promote a strict style of religious living. In August 1644 he issued a proclamation calling for a general renewal and rededication in the archdiocese, wondering how God would hear people's prayers to stop wars and plagues as long as they continued to wear "shameless clothes" and engage in drunkenness. It was precisely such strictness that got Boonen involved in the support of Jansenism and that, ironically, probably helped to erode his good reputation in Rome during the 1640s. Ruin finally came in 1652, when the pope suspended Boonen and Bishop Triest of Gent from office for refusing to oppose Jansenism vigorously enough and therefore placed them under the hell of the interdict. Boonen had to endure the humiliation of seeing the notice of dismissal posted on the door of his own cathedral and the collegiate church of St. Gudule in Brussels. On August 1, 1653, Boonen acquiesced, throwing himself "at the feet of his Holiness, and asking of him, in the manner of a submissive son, what I should do to perform satisfaction." By October he was restored, the ceremony taking place at the palace of the papal internuncio in Brussels. In 1654 the Congregation of the Council of Trent in Rome even wrote to commend him for all his hard work regarding the seminary, the visitation of his diocese, and the creation of new canonical prebends. Yet the last years of Boonen's life were sad ones, as he was forced to proclaim and enforce measures that he neither believed in nor liked. Some in Brussels, Madrid, and Rome labored to pay him a final indignity by removing him from the archiepiscopal seat. But before they could do so, he died in June 1655, age eighty-three. In the eyes of most he long remained suspicious, and his name, which may someday be great, has always been muffled by the taint of disobedience.

Finally, what became of the women of Bethlehem themselves? To subsequent generations it may well have remained just another obscure, plain monastery, if all that remained about it were such statements as those by the Franciscan historian Carolo van Coudenhove, who in 1680 wrote that "little was known of this house," since none of the great Franciscan historians had mentioned it or even knew its date of foundation. A loose document from around 1670 asserted that the sisters in Leuven had "persevered under episcopal discipline, and in good order, both spiritually and temporally, until the death of Boonen," but nothing more. In 1659 a visitor noted the "abundant praise of great unity there," that it was a good community, and "full of sweetness," and left it at that. A Guardian in Leuven named Steenbergh also glibly commented in 1646 that "the monastery is well regarded (as I think) among the people of Leuven, God be praised." Even if these assessments are true, they still don't tell us much. Most obviously they fail to mention how people like Adriana and Anna had worked so hard to maintain such a favorable reputation, and how women like Margaret and Joanna Schoensetters had tried equally energetically to improve that reputation as they saw necessary.

Fortunately we do know more, thanks to information not available, or not interesting, to these major Franciscan historians. We certainly do not know about all. We wonder what happened to Lesken Nijns, who with her cosisters was in 1629 run out of Den Bosch by the Dutch? We wonder how long Barbara Beli lived and whether she didn't spend many of her days in the beguinage of Brussels spinning her tale, just as the sisters of Bethlehem feared she would? We don't know when Maria Joos (still alive in 1659) or Lesken Joos or most of the others died, but they certainly were gone by 1669, when Maria Coninxloo now prevailed as the eldest sister in the house. We do know that in her old age some of Coninxloo's zeal had flagged, for during a 1669 visitation the recently jubileed nun had "nothing to say," except that she did what she was able to in the house and that Mater too rarely came into the community.

We know best of all that the period after 1639 was the heyday of Adriana Truis and Anna Vignarola. All the foundation-laying they had done to control Bethlehem was finally secure, and it resulted in an unbreakable structure and friendship that lasted three more decades. Adriana continued as Mater to her death around 1668, the year of the elevation of Anna Vignarola, who presumably had the experience which the visitors of 1635 had hoped she would accrue.

These women concerned themselves much as they saw fit with the usual challenges of the place: general discipline, ever-pressing temporal shortages, and the unending problem of jurisdiction. And they still did not solve them to the satisfaction of all, within or without. A visitor of 1663 summarized his impressions of Bethlehem: The statutes of 1626 were ignored on many points, not least in regard to the excessive authority wielded by Mater Adriana, but also in *clausura*, the grille, silence, and proud lay sisters; moreover, Anna Vignarola was distracted by too many offices, for she was vicaress, bursaress, and novice mistress all at once. A visitation in 1669, with Anna now as Mater, yielded some praise. The statutes were completely adhered to, said one sister, while another stated that silence, the statutes, poverty, *clausura*, and the Divine Office were all well observed. But most of the nuns continued to criticize. Several disliked their new fund-raiser, the school for girls. Others said that Mater Anna was too familiar with certain sisters and thus lost respect. Old Joanna Schoensetters believed that "Mater does as she pleases," and commented that the statutes were badly observed. A Sister Margaret Fredericx noted two points: She didn't have a stiver to her name, and the choir services were awful. Among other complaints: The Discretes were hardly consulted, Mater dispatched a lay sister to attend a certain lady friend of the convent, and the lay sisters were as incorrigible as ever. In the most damning comment of all, Anna's new enemy Sister Regina noted that Anna hadn't been to Matins in three months and that the noon meal sometimes lasted from ten to three. Sister Els Caussmans testified that not only was the Divine Office sloppily performed, but that Mater [Anna] seldom attended. Even when present, revealed Els, Anna "sometimes counts money in the choir." And there were more such charges in 1671.

During these troubles, Anna and Adriana vacillated on the age-old problem of the Franciscan confessors. Their loyalty to the friars proved to be no stronger than their wavering loyalty to Boonen had been. They seemed to prefer whoever was most convenient—vigilant on some points, relaxed on others—at the time. Jurisdiction went to the Franciscans after 1655, then back to another aggressive bishop. Anna tried on occasion to achieve a happy solution; indeed just before the end of her long life she composed in 1672, for the benefit of the current archbishop trying to conclude the matter, a brief history of the convent's confessors. The account reserved particular praise for one Henri Joos, who had served in Bethlehem more than half a century before: it also explained his unfortunate removal, and expressed resentment so deep at his "unfair" treatment that it was as if the event had happened only weeks before. The troubles over confessors and jurisdiction were not solved by the time of Adriana's or Anna's death. In 1691 and 1693, because the house had suffered from want of new novices and new dowries over the preceding ten years, the old-fashioned Grey Sisters "reformed" themselves into third-order Franciscan Penitents, a group that absolutely required the jurisdiction of the friars. By promising to speak less with outsiders, to live in true poverty, to worship more devoutly, fast even more, confess and commune more frequently, and engage in many other pious and mortifying exercises, they hoped to attract fresh faces.

For our purposes it's not crucial to know the effects of this switch, economically or spiritually. We need merely to know that the convent survived the onslaughts of Emperor Joseph II in the eighteenth century (who generally insisted that only "useful" orders be allowed to continue) but did not survive the ravages of Napoleon. In 1796 French soldiers came twice to Bethlehem, first to demand the convent's bulky tax and property records (Mater Maria Theresa refused to hand some of them over), and then in November to expel the sisters and destroy the convent. Like many other displaced nuns of the time, these women scattered, often surviving on a pension from the new revolutionary government. Some of them traveled north of Leuven and accepted yet another reform, the so-called Reform of Limburg, from which grew the convents of Dongen (1801), Etten (1820), and Roosendael (1835). These women, cousins of the once-flourishing Grey Sisters, established a new congregation in 1835 and survived into the twentieth century.

But again, Bethlehem itself is gone, its buildings, grounds, and cemetery vanished. Today the space it once occupied, on the corner of the Penitentienenstraat and Mechelsestraat, is the site of a brewery, subsidized housing, and a café named Oh! Champs Elysees! where you can go sip on a Spa or a Stella and wonder just exactly where a couple of nuns named Margaret Smulders and Adriana Truis waged battles of life and death, or what a confessor named Joos looked like coming around the corner from St. Gertrude's to visit.

ACKNOWLEDGMENTS

Thanks to the National Endowment for the Humanities, the University of Idaho Research Council, and the History Department and Women's Research Institute of Brigham Young University for financial support of this project. It was while working on another project, under a research grant from the American Philosophical Society, that I found and began to study the documents on which this book is based.

I have incurred more than the usual debts to a host of archivists and librarians, most notably the extraordinary Professor Dr. Constant van de Wiel, who has worked so tirelessly to bring the rich collection of the Archdiocese of Mechelen-Brussels into order, as well as the other (and volunteer) staff members of this archive, including Pater Joseph Coutennier, Mr. J. De Vos, and Mr. A. Jans. I thank as well Brother Joseph Baetens, now at the Franciscan archive in Rome but then head of the Franciscan provincial archive in St. Truiden, his kindly assistant Mr. Alfred Perry, Pater Jean-Pierre Tytgat of the Capuchin archive in Enghien, and the staffs of the Algemeen Rijksarchief in Brussels, the Rijksarchief in Gent, the Rijksarchief in Antwerp, the archive of the Cathedral chapter of Our Lady of Antwerp, the Stadsarchief of Leuven, the Stadsmuseum of Leuven, the Royal Library in Brussels, and the Koninklijk Kunstpatrimonium in Brussels.

I feel undying gratitude to both Professor Dr. Michel Cloet of the Catholic University of Leuven, who for so long in word and deed has encouraged my efforts, and Dr. Eddy Put of the State Archives in Brussels, whose comments on a late version of the manuscript saved me, as usual, from many errors—and these are the smallest of their kindnesses toward this foreigner. Also benevolent in my home-away-from-home have been Dr. Guido Marnef of the University of Antwerp, Professor Dr. Walter Prevenier of the University of Gent, Dr. Marc Therry of the State Archives, and Dr. Georgi Verbeeck, Dr. Hans Storme, and Dr. Marie-Juliette Marinus of Leuven, all of whom not only answered tedious questions about archives and research but tactfully instructed me in the finer points of modern Belgian culture and the Dutch language, often as a result of my embarrassing mistakes.

Somewhat closer by, Jodi Bilinkoff, Tom Brady, Kent Hackmann, Martha Howell, Sherrin Marshall, Theodore Rabb, Carlos Schwantes, Bob Scribner, and James Tracy have contributed in various ways to the making of this book. I owe much to Louis Perraud, least of all for his expertise in the subtleties of ecclesiastical Latin. Special thanks to Rudolph Bell, Herbert Rowen, and Walter Simons, whose readings of the manuscript encouraged and chastened me at the same time; even when we did not agree, all of the people listed here caused me to think harder about what I wanted to say. I am grateful as well to my agent, John Ware, for taking on the manuscript, and to Tom Cahill, Rob Radick, Trace Murphy, and others at Doubleday for helping to make it much better.

Thanks to Andrew, Jonathan, and Kate, for traveling willingly but inconveniently to foreign places, and for making life richer; they pushed me to keep perspective and to try to keep my touch light with their regular question, "Why do you like to study about nuns?" And thanks most of all to Paula, who understands the answer not only to that small mystery, but many others far more intricate.

BIBLIOGRAPHICAL NOTES

LIST OF ABBREVIATIONS

Libraries and Archives

AAM, CA	Aartsbisschoppelijk Archief Mechelen, Collection Archiepiscopalia
AAM, CK	Aartsbisschoppelijk Archief Mechelen, Collection Kloosters
AAM, CM	Aartsbisschoppelijk Archief Mechelen, Collection Mechliniensia
ARA, GR	Algemeen Rijksarchief, Brussels, Geheime Raad
ARA, KAB	Algemeen Rijksarchief, Brussels, Kerkarchief Brabant
ARA, RSA	Algemeen Rijksarchief, Brussels, Raad van State en Audiëntie
BAA	Bisschoppelijk Archief Antwerp
Greys	Aartsbisschoppelijk Archief Mechelen, Collection Kloosters, Grey Sisters of Leuven
KAM, CA	Kapittel Archief Mechelen, Collection Archiepiscopalia (housed at the AAM)
RAA	Rijksarchief Antwerp
RAG, CB	Rijksarchief Gent, Collection Bisdom
SAL	Stadsarchief Leuven

Periodicals and Reference Works

AHEB	*Analectes pour servir à l'histoire ecclésiastique de la Belgique*
AHN	*Acta Historiae Neerlandicae*
AL	*Arca Lovaniensis*
ARG	*Archive for Reformation History/Archiv für Reformationsgeschichte*
BCFF	*Bulletin de la Comité Flamand de France*
BIHBR	*Bulletin de l'Institute historique belge de Rome/Bulletin van het Belgisch Historisch Instituut te Rome*
BMGN	*Bijdragen en Mededelingen Betreffende de Geschiedenis der Nederlanden*

BIBLIOGRAPHICAL NOTES

CB	*Cahiers Bruxellois*
CHR	*Catholic Historical Review*
CM	*Collectanea Mechliniensia*
DHGE	*Dictionnaire d'histoire et de géographie ecclésiastiques*
DS	*Dictionnaire de Spiritualité*
FL	*Franciscaans Leven*
FR	*Franciscana*
HKKM	*Handelingen van de Koninklijke Kring voor Oudheidkunde, Letteren en Kunst van Mechelen*
HLN	*Het Land van Nevele*
NAGN	*(Nieuwe) Algemene Geschiedenis der Nederlanden*
NBW	*Nationaal Biografisch Woordenboek*
NF	*Neerlandia Franciscana*
OGE	*Ons Geestelijk Erf*
RQ	*Renaissance Quarterly*
SCJ	*Sixteenth Century Journal*
TG	*Tijdschrift voor Geschiedenis*

In preparing this book I decided to keep the narrative free of footnotes, but at the same time I wanted to reveal my sources, discuss problems, and explain how I reached this conclusion or that. The method I settled upon was to write one big note for each chapter. Each note is arranged so as to shadow the basic structure of the chapter itself, but if something is murky, I will be glad, through correspondence, to attempt clarification.

Readers interested in my approach, or in general background to monasticism and the Age of Reformation, will probably find the General note and the long note to the Foreword most helpful. Other notes focus more on the particular topics raised in a given chapter. So that the reader need not page through the entire bibliography to find the full citation of a book or article, be aware that full citations are given the first time a source is listed in any chapter.

General

Most of the manuscript documents for this study may be found in the Archive of the Archdiocese of Mechelen-Brussels, in the substantial collection called "Kloosters"; this contains eleven bundles of varying thickness on the Grey Sisters of Leuven. Inventories for some collections in the archive have recently been published serially in journals; that for the Grey Sisters can be found in the third installment of C. van de Wiel, "Franciscaanse Archiefbronnen in het Aartsbisschoppelijk Archief te Mechelen," *FR* 31 (1976): 9–35; 32 (1977): 39–58; 33 (1978): 129–42. Also useful in this archive were the papers of Archbishops Hovius and Boonen, collected under "Archiepiscopalia," which was recently inventoried and published by Van de Wiel as *Archivalia over de Aartsbisschoppen van Mechelen vanaf de oprichting van het aartsbisdom tot en met de Franse tijd (1559–1815)* (Leuven, 1990), and in the separate Chapter Archive ("Kapittel") housed at the AAM; of further use at the AAM were various documents in the collections "Mechliniensia" (bound registers of episcopal decrees and decisions of episcopal councils) and "Vicariaat" (loose papers of the vicars and their councils).

Other manuscript sources came from collections of the Algemeen Rijksarchief in Brussels, especially the collection "Raad van State en Audiëntie—Briefwisseling" and the mammoth "Kerkarchief van Brabant"; the Provincial Rijksarchief in Antwerp, collection "Kerkarchieven," parish of Mol; the Bisschoppelijk Archief Antwerp, collection "Parochialia," parish of Mol; and the Stadsarchief of Leuven. In all these archives, I consulted as well, for background, manuscripts not specifically about the Grey Sisters; also useful in this regard was the Provincial Rijksarchief in Gent, which contains numerous files on the old Archdiocese of Mechelen. Finally, I used the collections of printed devotional works from the sixteenth and seventeenth centuries in the Royal Library in Brussels and especially those in the provincial archive of the Franciscans in St. Truiden.

Approaches to religion and culture that I have found helpful in developing my own story of the Grey Sisters include G. Le Bras, *Introduction à l'histoire de la pratique religieuse en France,* 2 vols. (Paris, 1942–45); P. Burke, *The Historical Anthropology of Early Modern Italy* (Cambridge, 1987); R. Chartier, *Cultural History* (Ithaca, NY, 1988); P. Mack Crew, *Calvinist Preaching and Iconoclasm in the Netherlands, 1544–1569* (Cambridge, 1978); R. Darnton, *The Great Cat Massacre* (New York, 1984); N. Davis, *Fiction in the Archives* (Stanford, 1987), "From 'Popular Religion' to Religious Cultures," in S. Ozment, ed., *Reformation Europe: A Guide to Research* (St. Louis, 1982), and *Society and Culture in Early Modern France* (Stanford, 1975); W. Frijhoff, "Van Histoire de l'Eglise naar Histoire religieuse: De invloed van de Annales-groep op de ontwikkeling van de Kerkgeschiedenis in Frankrijk en de perspectieven daarvan voor Nederland," *Nederlands Archief voor Kerkgeschiedenis* 61 (1981): 113–53; C. Ginzburg, *The Cheese and the Worms* (Baltimore, 1980); L. Hunt, ed., *The New Cultural History* (Berkeley, 1989); J. Obelkevich, ed., *Religion and the People, 800–1700* (Chapel Hill, 1979); E. Muir and G. Ruggiero, eds., *Microhistory and the Lost Peoples of Europe* (Baltimore, 1991; translated by E. Branch); E. Muir and G. Ruggiero, eds., *Sex and Gender in Historical Perspective* (Baltimore, 1990; translated by M. A. Gallucci, M. M. Gallucci, and C. C. Gallucci); S. Ozment, ed., *Religion and Culture in the Renaissance and Reformation* (Kirksville, MO, 1989); D. Sabean, *Power in the Blood* (Cambridge, 1984); K. Thomas, *Religion and the Decline of Magic* (New York, 1971); and C. Trinkaus and H. Oberman, eds., *The Pursuit of Holiness in Late Medieval and Renaissance Religion* (Leiden, 1974).

Foreword

The meaning and process of Reformation have become major issues and given birth to many terms. One can begin with John O'Malley, *Catholicism*

in Early Modern History: A Guide to Research (St. Louis, 1988) and S. Ozment, ed., *Reformation Europe: A Guide to Research* (St. Louis, 1982). J. Bossy
has much to say on Catholic reform especially, in *Christianity in the West,
1400–1700* (Oxford, 1985) and "The Counter-Reformation and the People
of Catholic Europe," *Past and Present* 47 (1970): 51–70. There is also the
famous essay by H. O. Evennett, *The Spirit of the Counter-Reformation*
(Cambridge, 1968).

On the Dutch "Closer" Reformation of the late sixteenth and early seven-
teenth centuries, one might start with H. A. Enno van Gelder, "Nederland
Geprotestantiseerd?" *TG* 81 (1968): 326–34, 405–64, and his *Getemperde
Vrijheid* (Groningen, 1972). Jean Delumeau, *Catholicism Between Luther and
Voltaire* (London, 1977; first French edition Paris, 1971) made famous the
concept of the "Christianization" of Europe during the period after the
Reformations, while Robert Muchembled systematized the "acculturation"
of society by an imposing elite in, among other works, *Popular Culture and
Elite Culture in France (1400–1750)* (Baton Rouge, 1985; first French edition
Paris, 1978); this was countered most directly by J. Wirth, "Against the
Acculturation Thesis," in *Religion and Society in Early Modern Europe,
1500–1800,* ed. K. von Greyerz (London, 1984), 66–78. John O'Malley points
out the emphasis of the famous German historian, Hubert Jedin, on the
"application" of Trent in an article called "Catholic Reform," in Ozment,
ed., *Reformation Europe.* "Confessionalization" usually refers to what Protestant and Catholic religious movements had in common, especially their
desire after 1550 to tighten up confessional identity through the discipline
of visitation, education, and courts; those who study this process also assess
the consequences of reform, especially how church discipline promoted
growth of the state and secular discipline; see R. Po-Chia Hsia, *Social Discipline in the Reformation* (New York, 1990), who on the latter point discusses
the important work of Heinz Schilling; see also W. Reinhard, "Gegenrefor-
mation als Modernisierung? Prolegomena zu einer theorie des konfessionellen Zeitalters," *ARG* 68 (1977): 226–52, and "Zwang zur Konfessionali-
sierung? Prolegomena zu einer theorie des konfessionellen Zeitalters,"
Zeitschrift für historische Forschung 10 (1983): 257–77; further V. Press, "Stadt
und Territoriale Konfessionsbildung," in *Kirche und Gesellschaftlicher Wan-
del in deutschen und niederländischen Städten der Werdenden Neuzeit* (Cologne, 1980), ed. F. Petri, 251–96. "Confession-building" and "Confessionalism" have more to do with the internal development of a specific religion
after 1550, or as Hsia puts it in *Social Discipline,* "the formation of religious
ideologies and institutions in Lutheranism, Calvinism, and Catholicism."

Specific works that illustrate the variety and complexity of putting Catholic reform alone into practice (because of cultural differences, bureaucratic
limitations, or rivalry between church and state) and thus that also help to
refine the meaning of reform include F. J. Baumgartner, *Change and Conti-
nuity in the French Episcopate: The Bishops and the Wars of Religion, 1547–
1610* (Durham, 1986); P. Benedict, *Rouen During the Wars of Religion* (Cambridge, 1981); J. Bilinkoff, *The Avila of St. Teresa* (Ithaca, NY, 1989); W. A.

Christian, *Local Religion in Sixteenth Century Spain* (Princeton, 1981); S. Nalle, *God in La Mancha: Religious Reform and the People of Cuenca, 1500–1650* (Baltimore, 1992); E. Cochrane, *Florence in the Forgotten Centuries, 1527–1800* (Chicago, 1973), and "New Light on Post-Tridentine Italy: A Note on Recent Counter-Reformation Scholarship," *CHR* 56 (1970): 291–319; D. Fenlon, *Heresy and Obedience in Tridentine Italy: Cardinal Pole and the Counter Reformation* (Cambridge, 1972); J. Ferté, *La vie religieuse dans les campagnes parisiennes, 1622–1695* (Paris, 1962); A. N. Galpern, *The Religion of the People in Sixteenth-Century Champagne* (Cambridge, MA, 1976) plus numerous other studies of French dioceses; K. von Greyerz, ed., *Religion and Society in Early Modern Europe, 1500–1800* (London, 1984); C. Harline, "Official Religion—Popular Religion in Recent Historiography of the Catholic Reformation," *ARG* 81 (1990): 239–62; P. T. Hoffmann, *Church and Community in the Diocese of Lyon, 1500–1789* (New Haven, 1984); R. Po-chia Hsia, *Society and Religion in Münster, 1535–1618* (New Haven, 1984); G. Levi, *Inheriting Power: The Story of an Exorcist* (Chicago, 1988); T. M. Safley, *Let No Man Put Asunder: The Control of Marriage in the German Southwest* (Kirksville, MO, 1984). On the Protestant side, works are legion, but one might look first at G. Strauss, *Luther's House of Learning* (Baltimore, 1978), for a provocative argument of the difficulties of implementing Lutheran reform in Germany, or J. Spaans, *Haarlem na de Reformatie: Stedelijke cultuur en kerkelijk leven, 1577–1620* (The Hague, 1989), on the difficulties of imposing uniformity in the Dutch Republic.

In studying Catholic reform in the Spanish Netherlands, one should begin with a most useful introduction in English by James D. Tracy, "With and Without the Counter-Reformation: The Catholic Church in the Spanish Netherlands and the Dutch Republic, 1580–1650," *CHR* 71 (1985): 547–75; beyond that, there is in Dutch and in French a multitude of specialized studies on the state of Catholic reform in the area, to a significant extent the work of Michel Cloet and his students at the Catholic University of Leuven. Some examples: K. Bergé, *Kerkelijk leven in de landelijke dekenij Deinze (1661–1762)* (Leuven, 1981); R. Castelain, *Kinderen en hun Opvoeding in de Kasselrij Oudenaarde, 1500–1800* (Oudenaarde, 1979); P. Claessens, *Histoire des Archevêques de Malines* (Leuven, 1881); M. Cloet, *Het kerkelijk leven in een landelijke dekenij van Vlaanderen tijdens de XVIIe eeuw: Tielt van 1609 tot 1700* (Leuven, 1968), which is condensed as "Religious Life in a Rural Deanery in Flanders During the Seventeenth Century: Tielt from 1609 to 1700," *AHN* 5 (1971): 135–58; Cloet, "Antoon Triest, prototype van een contrareformatorische bisschop, op bezoek in zijn Gentse diocees (1622–1657)," *BMGN* 91/3 (1976): 394–405; and Cloet, *Karel Filips van Rodoan en het Bisdom Brugge tijdens zijn Episcopaat, 1602–1616* (Brussels, 1970); A. Lottin, *Lille: Citadelle de la Contre-Réforme (1598–1668)?* (Paris, 1984); M.-J. Marinus, *Laevinus Torrentius als tweede bisschop van Antwerpen (1587–1595)* (Brussels, 1989); E. Put, *De cleyne schoolen. Het volksonderwijs in het Hertogdom Brabant tussen Katholieke Reformatie en Verlichting* (Leuven, 1991); M. Therry, *De religieuze beleving bij de leken in het 17de-eeuwse bisdom Brugge*

(1609–1706) (Brussels, 1988); J. Toussaert, *Le sentiment religieux en Flandre à la fin du Moyen Age* (Paris, 1960). For many more titles, the interested reader can turn to a recent historiographical summary in M. Cloet and F. Daelemans, eds., *Godsdienst, Mentaliteit en Dagelijks Leven: Religieuze geschiedenis in Belgie sinds 1970* (Brussels, 1988).

There is now a modest body of historical literature on female monasticism after 1500, but this is slight compared to the massive corpus on monasticism's medieval Golden Age. For the important medieval background, one might consult such surveys as L. Eckenstein, *Women Under Monasticism* (New York, 1963); D. Knowles, *From Pachomius to Ignatius: A Study in the Constitutional History of the Religious Orders* (Oxford, 1966); C. H. Lawrence, *Medieval Monasticism* (New York, 1984); Eileen Power's classic *Medieval English Nunneries, c. 1275 to 1535* (Cambridge, 1922); and more recently P. D. Johnson, *Equal in Monastic Profession: Religious Women in Medieval France* (Chicago, 1991); M. M. McLaughlin, "Looking for Mediaeval Women: An Interim Report on the Project, 'Women's Religious Life and Communities, A.D. 500–1500,'" *Vox Benedictina* 6 (1986): 129–51; and L. T. Shank and J. A. Nichols, eds., *Medieval Religious Women. II. Peaceweavers* (Kalamazoo, MI, 1987). More specialized studies of use are E. Koch, "Entry into Convents and the Position on the Marriage Market of Noble Women in the late Middle Ages," in *Marriage and Social Mobility in the Late Middle Ages,* ed. W. Prevenier (Gent, 1989), 51–68; volume 11 of *Word and Spirit: A Monastic Review* (1989), entitled "Women in Monasticism." For both medieval and early modern monastic life, I simply note the existence of a mountain of literature on the closely related topic of mysticism, such as J. de Vinck's broad introduction, *Revelations of Women Mystics: From the Middle Ages to Modern Times* (New York, 1985); clearly this is an important topic but not one in which the Grey Sisters of Leuven were expert or heavily involved.

Despite increased attention to early modern female monasticism, evident in the number of works to be listed, and despite mountains of documents, countless specialized journals, and learned reference works, our picture of the professional religious in that age has only begun to be sketched and integrated. One should start with such overviews as J. Irwin's "Society and the Sexes," in Ozment, ed., *Reformation Europe,* K. Norberg's "The Counter-Reformation and Women, Religious and Lay," in O'Malley, *Catholicism*, 133–46, and F. E. Weaver's "Women and Religion in Early Modern France: A Bibliographical Essay on the State of the Question," *CHR* 67 (1981): 50–59. As Norberg points out, we have yet to establish some very basic things, such as exactly how many nuns and convents there were in early modern Europe and how those numbers changed over time. The abundant journals of individual orders help to answer such questions for specific areas—typical in Belgium are *Franciscana* and *Augustiniana*—as do specialized studies, such as R. R. Post, "De roeping tot het kloosterleven in de 16de eeuw," *Mededelingen der Koninklijke Nederlandse Akademie van Wetenschappen, Afd. Letterkunde,* Nieuwe Reeks, 13/2 (Amsterdam, 1950): 31–76, and plentiful big histories of individual orders, such as M.-C. Gueudre, *Histoire de l'ordre des Ursulines en France,* 2 vols. (Paris, 1963). Fat reference books are also valuable, including *Monasticon Belge,* 7 vols. and more (Maredsous, 1890–1984); F. Herve-Bazin, *Les grands ordres et congrégations des femmes* (Paris, 1889); K. J. Beloch, *Bevölkerungsgeschichte Italiens* (Berlin, 1939, 1961), especially volumes 2 and 3; and the still-growing Italian publication edited by G. Pelliccia and G. Rocca et al., *Dizionario degli istituti di Perfezione* (Rome, 1974–). These works tend to reveal more about the foundational ideals of monasticism than how the ideals were worked out in the living. Representative of a traditional and important topic, the constitutional basis of monasticism after Trent, is R. Lemoine, O.S.B., *Le Droit des Religieux, du Concile de Trente aux Instituts Séculiers* (Paris, 1973).

Perusal of the literature on female monasticism as well as of the literature on female religiosity more broadly reveals another tendency: We have more in-depth knowledge about the scandalous and saintly and noble few than about the "ordinary" many, largely because of the nature of documentation, partly because of curiosity among outsiders about the mysterious side of conventual and private life. (A focus on this side has been typical of novels and dramas, plausible or sensationalist, since especially the Enlightenment, including the recent *Mariette in Ecstacy* by Ron Hansen [New York, 1991] or J. Faolain, *Women in the Wall* [New York, 1973]; a nonsensationalist but suitably illustrative title comes from a Belgian television program of 1961, "Wat doen zij daar achter die muren?" [What Are They Doing Behind Those Walls?], printed in book form, Brussels, 1961). Recent historical titles of this nature would include G. S. Daichman, *Wayward Nuns in Medieval Literature* (Syracuse, 1986); R. Bell, *Holy Anorexia* (Chicago, 1985); J. Brown, *Immodest Acts: The Life of a Lesbian Nun in Renaissance Italy* (Oxford, 1986) and Bell's response with Brown's rejoinder, "Renaissance Sexuality and the Florentine Archives: An Exchange," *RQ* 40/3 (Autumn 1987): 485–511; C. W. Bynum, *Holy Feast and Holy Fast* (Berkeley, 1987); L. Ciamitti, "One Saint Less: The Story of Angela Mellini, a Bolognese Seamstress (1667–17[?])," in *Sex and Gender in Historical Perspective,* E. Muir and G. Ruggiero, eds., (Baltimore, 1990; translated by M. A. Gallucci), 141–76; R. L. Kagan, *Lucrecia's Dreams: Politics and Prophecy in Sixteenth-Century Spain* (Berkeley, 1990); P. Scrouet, ed., *Isabel de los Angeles, Mother, 1565–1644* (Paris, 1956); R. E. Surtz, *The Guitar of God: Gender, Power, and Authority in the Visionary World of Mother Juana de la Cruz (1481–1534)* (Philadelphia, 1990); E. Arenal and S. Schlau, *Untold Sisters: Hispanic Nuns in Their Own Words* (Albuquerque, 1989), full of detail but more self-consciously autobiographical, more about the inner mysteries of the soul than Margaret's writing; Fulvio Tomizza's *Heavenly Supper: The Story of Maria Janis* (Chicago, 1991; translated by Anne Jacobsen Schutte), an intricate look at spirituality by a novelist working here as historian; F. E. Weaver, *The Evolution of the Reform of Port-Royal* (Paris, 1978); and of course numerous works on St. Teresa of Ávila, starting with Bilinkoff, *Avila.* The question of studying the few rather than the many is an old debate in historiography. See for recent twists in the discussion the works cited in the earlier general note and J. Van Engen, "The Christian Middle Ages as an Historiographical Problem," *American Historical Review* 91 (1986): 541–44, or Marie-Elisabeth Montulet-Henneau, "Cisterciennes flamandes et wallonnes," in M. Sabbe et al., *Bernardus en de Cisterciënzerfamilie in Belgie, 1090–1990* (Leuven, 1990), 261.

For the study of "ordinary" monastic life (a problematic phrase in itself, since monastic life was by definition extraordinary), the historian working before the eighteenth century is often left no choice but to rely heavily on (1) officially generated sources, including normative decrees and visitation reports, which provide often informative glimpses into life within the convent; and (2) documents revealing socioeconomic conditions, such as the assiduously maintained registers of temporal holdings in most convents and local notarial files. The latter are best at the establishment of broad patterns and worst at getting at the spiritual or personal experience of commonplace nuns. The former are one-sided, and always leave me wondering whether the nuns saw things the same way. Such broadly based studies treat many of the same topics that I do, and treat them very well, but in a different manner. The most helpful have been G. A. Brucker, "Monasteries, Friaries, and Nunneries in Quattrocento Florence," in *Christianity and the Renaissance: Image and Religious Imagination in the Quattrocento,* eds. T. Verdon and J. Henderson (Syracuse, 1990), 41–62; R. Devos, *Vie Religieuse Féminine et Société: L'origine sociale des Visitandines d'Annecy aux XVIIe et XVIIIe siècles* (Annecy, 1973); C. Dolan, *Entre Tours et Clochers: Les gens d'Eglise à Aix-en-Provence au XVIe siècle* (Sherbrooke, 1981); W. Gibson, *Women in Seventeenth Century France* (New York, 1989); M. Marcocchi, *La riforma dei monasteri femminili a Cremona (1599–1606)* (Cremona, 1966); E. Rapley, *The Dévotes* (Montreal, 1990); G. Reynes, *Couvents des femmes. La vie des religieuses contemplatives dans la France des XVIIe et XVIIIe siècles* (Paris, 1987); N. Rubinstein, "Lay Patronage and Observant Reform in Fifteenth-Century Florence," in Verdon and Henderson, eds., *Christianity and the Renaissance*, 63–82; F. Schrader, *Ringen, Untergang und überleben der katholischen klöster in den Hochstiften Magdeburg und Halberstadt von der Reformation bis zum Westfälischen Frieden* (Munster, 1977); E. Weaver, "Spiritual Fun: A Study of Sixteenth-Century Tuscan Convent Theater," in *Women in the Middle Ages and the Renaissance*, ed. M. B. Rose (Syracuse, 1986), 173–206.

A final tendency of studies about female religious life during the period after Trent is to focus on new "active" orders, supposedly more characteristic of spirituality in this age than traditional "contemplative" monasticism. Several of the works just listed treat this topic, but one could add Evenett, *The Spirit of the Counter-Reformation*, which may have canonized the idea; C. Jones, *The Charitable Imperative: Hospitals and Nursing in Ancien Regime and Revolutionary France* (New York, 1988); R. P. Liebowitz, "Virgins in the Service of Christ: The Dispute over an Active Apostolate for Women during the Counter Reformation," in *Women of Spirit*, eds. R. Ruether and E. McLaughlin (New York, 1979), 131–52, as well as numerous surveys of women or monasticism in this age, such as O. Hufton and F. Tallett,

"Communities of Women, the Religious Life, and Public Service in Eighteenth-Century France," in *Connecting Spheres: Women in the Western World, 1500 to the Present*, eds. M. J. Boxer, J. H. Quataert, and J. W. Scott (Oxford, 1987); M. Wiesner, "Nuns, Wives and Mothers: Women and the Reformation in Germany," in *Women in Reformation and Counter-Reformation Europe;* S. Marshall, "Protestant, Catholic, and Jewish Women in the Early Modern Netherlands," in *Women in Reformation and Counter-Reformation Europe*, ed. S. Marshall (Bloomington, 1989); W. Monter, "Protestant Wives, Catholic Saints, and the Devil's Handmaid: Women in the Age of Reformations," in *Becoming Visible: Women in European History*, 2d ed., eds. R. Bridenthal, C. Koonz, and S. Stuard (Boston, 1987).

Just as studies of the exceptional are important, so are studies of new active orders—but again one must beware of distortion. In the first place, many active orders were founded before Trent, as is well known, but what seems less known is their continued importance afterward, at least in areas such as the Spanish Netherlands. Thus, when active orders after Trent tried to avoid cloister by taking simple vows in order to be of practical service, they were trying an old idea. Further, it is doubtful that the development of new active orders after 1565 necessarily lessened the significance of traditional contemplative orders, as is usually suggested; it may turn out to be an accurate assertion, but it has not yet been proven. From my reading, it seems we must remember that even while some early modern women championed the active form and while the hierarchy remained almost universally opposed to them, other women became champions of cloister. My impression at the moment is that in both medieval and early modern periods, active and contemplative nuns existed side by side, with some women preferring to enter one form, some the other. I am currently preparing an article that treats this issue in detail, and suggests directions for research; it's tentatively titled "Actives and Contemplatives: The Female Religious of the Low Countries Before and After Trent."

Specialized works on the religious of the Spanish Netherlands are numerous enough if one reads Dutch or French. One useful English-language work is M. J. Ramsey, ed., *English Benedictine Nuns in Flanders, 1598–1687. Annals of Their Five Communities* (London, 1909). Much valuable work is of the traditional sort, tending to focus on a particular order without wider context in the monastic or outside world, such as J. M. Canivez, *L'Ordre de Cîteaux en Belgique des origines (1132) au xxe siècle* (Forges-les-Chimary, 1926); M.-E. Montulet-Hennaut, *Les Cisterciennes du Pays Mosan: Moniales et vie contemplative à l'époque moderne* (Brussels, 1990), an important study on more prestigious nuns than the Grey sisters; Ph. Schmitz, *Histoire de l'ordre de Saint-Benoît* (Maredsous, 1948); P. Hildebrand, *De Capucijnen in de Nederlanden en het prinsbisdom Luik*, 11 vols. (Antwerp, 1945–56); M-.J. Juvyns, "La Communauté des Riches-Claires de Bruxelles de 1585 à 1796," *CB* 10 (1965): 181–239; J. Corstjens, "De Franciscanessen van het klooster OLVrouw-Ter-Rivieren te Bree (1464–1797)" (ms., Licentiaatsverhandeling, Leuven, 1984); H. de Backer, "Het Arme Clarenklooster te Mechelen, vanaf 1500 tot de Opheffing in 1966" (ms., Licentiaatsverhandeling, F. van der Berghe, J. van den Heuvel, and G. Verhelst, *De Zwartzusters van Brugge, Diksmuide, Oostende, Veurne, en Brazilië* (Brugge, 1986); K. Baert en J. Dauwe, *Zwarte Zusters van Sint-Augustinus te Aalst* (Aalst, 1975); J. Okeley, *De Gasthuiszusters en hun ziekenzorg in het Aartsbisdom Mechelen*, 2 vols. (Brussels, 1992); D. Laureys, "Het Elzenklooster te Zichem: Een Slotklooster van Reguliere Kanunnikessen van Sint-Augustinus (1660–1797)" (ms., Licentiaatsverhandeling, Leuven, 1987); or it focuses on devout individuals, such as R. Baetens, "De Bibliotheek van een Geestelijke Dochter uit de XVIIe eeuw te Antwerpen," *OGE* 44 (1970): 213–26. Reference books and overviews are also characteristic, as in other countries. S. Dirks, *Histoire littéraire et bibliographique des Frères Mineurs de l'Observance de St.-François en Belgique et dans les Pays-Bas* (Antwerp, 1885), was helpful for some questions of Franciscan life. E. Persoons, "Panorama van de reguliere clerus in de 17de eeuw," in *NAGN* 8 (*1980*): 383–92, is an informed short survey, which includes a more detailed bibliography. Two surveys of religious life with helpful introductions to the religious are E. de Moreau, *Histoire de l'église en Belgique*, 5 vols. (Brussels, 1952), vol. 5 (1559–1633), and A. Pasture, *La Restauration Religieuse aux Pays Bas sous les Archiducs Albert et Isabelle (1596–1633)* (Leuven, 1925). More detailed, and also of great interest, are C. van de Wiel, "Bibliotheekinventaris van de Priorij Blijdenberg te Mechelen in 1743," *OGE* 47 (1973): 170–202, "De begijnhoven en de vrouwelijke kloostergemeenschappen in het aartsbisdom Mechelen, 1716–1801," *OGE* 44 (1970): 152–212, 241–327; 45 (1971): 179–214; 46 (1972): 278–344, 369–428; and E. Persoons, "De bewoners van de kloosters Bethlehem te Herent en Ten Troon te Grobbendonk," *AL* (1976): 221–40. For works about the Grey Sisters specifically, see the note for chapter 2.

The notion that contemplative orders of numerous monastic families might profitably be studied together as a type was confirmed in my mind while reading the sections about female branches in W. A. Hinnebusch, *The History of the Dominican Order, Origins and Growth to 1500* (New York, 1966); L. J. Lekai, *The Cistercians: Ideals and Reality* (Kent, OH, 1977); and J. Moorman, *A History of the Franciscan Order, From Its Origins to the Year 1517* (Oxford, 1968). Clearly what united female contemplatives of whatever monastic family was the ideal of cloister and the attention to the Divine Office. There may have been differences in the regime of each order, differences in favorite saints, in size of houses, in the social status of the members, and in matters such as color of habit and feast days. But the walls meant similar inner dynamics, and the prayer-oriented schedule meant similar lifestyles.

The best maps of early modern Leuven, located at the Stadsmuseum, include Fr. Hogenberg, 1580 (LP/3bis); J. van der Baren, 1604 (LP/43); Paolo A. and Gerard A., 1635 (LP/5a); Janssonius, 1657 (LP/7bis, which is virtually a copy of Hogenberg), C. Merian, 1659 (LP/48); and maps by De Wit and De Blaeu, 1649 (LP/4 and others). Only the last two and Van der Baren contain identifications of prominent buildings. Van der Baren mentions everything but the Grey Sisters' convent, and the last two name it but assign it the wrong location.

Estimates of the number of female religious in the Middle Ages are given in Post, "De roeping," *Tussen Heks en Heilige: Het vrouwbeeld op de drempel van de moderne tijd, 15de/16de eeuw* (Nijmegen, 1985), and Marshall, ed., *Women in Reformation and Counter-Reformation Europe.* See Gibson, *Women in France,* who also reminds us of the label female religious had in France: the "devout sex." The phrase "garden-variety" nun is from my colleague Jodi Bilinkoff.

The long-held idea of the monastery as microcosm is repeated in the introduction to the Brucker article, "Monasteries, Friaries, and Nunneries." An excellent example of the relationship of the monastery to the outside world, especially in regard to pious bequests, is Dolan, *Entre Tours et Clochers*; Rubenstein, "Lay Patronage and Observant Reform," is a good example of lay concern for piety behind the walls, for reform of this monastery in Florence was begun not by the monks or the order, but by the city's rulers.

The universality of Trent is disputed by Cochrane, "A Note on Recent Counter-Reformation Scholarship." A favorite debate of mine was one that raged for four hundred years among Augustinians in Milan and that involved some of the best minds in Europe—at issue was the proper habit for a statue of their patron saint; see Kaspar Elm, "Augustinus Canonicus-Augustinus Eremita: A Quattrocento Cause Célèbre," in Verdon and Henderson, eds., *Christianity and the Renaissance,* 83–107.

On some other approaches to reform, and on the *debate* over the meaning of reform, see especially D. Sabean, *Power in the Blood* (Cambridge, 1984), and N. Davis, "Some Tasks and Themes in the Study of Popular Religion," in C. Trinkans and H. Oberman, eds., *The Pursuit of Holiness in Late Medieval and Renaissance Religion* (Leiden, 1974). Brucker, in "Monasteries, Friaries, and Nunneries," also notes that the question of reform involved not only abstract decrees but the personalities and ambitions of the players, administrative structure, and relationships with outsiders. In addition, he notes the ambiguities surrounding the terms "reform" and "renovation" in the church, ambiguities that have led such scholars as Simoncelli to conclude that there was no such thing as a Catholic Reformation at all; see E. Gleason's comments in *RQ* 45/1 (Spring 1992): 155–57. The meaning of reform is discussed further in chapter 10.

John O'Malley makes convincingly the point that not all Catholic religious life after 1565 revolved around the notion of reform, in "Was Ignatius Loyola a Church Reformer? How to Look at Early Modern Catholicism," *CHR* 77/2 (1991): 177–93.

Chapter 1

My scenario of Margaret preparing for the visitation in her room is based on impressions built up from many sources. Margaret's visitation letter itself, in

Greys/3, gives clues as to how it was put together, especially the fact that it was written over numerous sessions. During session 3, which came after two long entries composed over an unknown period of time, Margaret noted that Henri Joos had visited since she began writing and that his visit had occurred the Monday before Pentecost. Pentecost fell between mid-May and early June, and the episcopal visitation occurred on June 19, suggesting that the letter was at least weeks, perhaps a month, under construction.

What Margaret ate for lunch is inferred from her 1628 visitation letter as well, when she describes in session 1 that between Easter and Pentecost they usually had at lunch potage and an egg, and at night some milk. Since we know that Catharina was Margaret's liaison with the convent, I've assumed that it was Catharina who brought the meal, and also that it was at this time of day that Catharina broke the news about visitation. Certainly Catharina was friendly with Margaret and would not have tried to withhold this news from her. Besides Catharina, a likely conduit of information for Margaret was the troublesome lay sister named Joanna Schoensetters. In the visitation of 1633, a couple of sisters mentioned that Joanna and Margaret gossiped in the kitchen (Joanna was culinaria, or kitchen sister) about the foibles of the other sisters, a thought that must have made many nuns shudder; see visitation of October 14–15, 1633, Greys/3; interview summary of Joanna Outhagen.

Margaret's motivation to tell the foibles of her sisters I deduce from her past history, the subjects of chapters 2 through 9. Her reluctance to put words on a page is built up from numerous signs of hesitation among many letter-writers—including her own—in this study, who often allude to holding things back and then promise to tell the rest in person.

Margaret expresses her lack of hope for forgiveness in a letter of February 3, 1628, Greys/8, addressed to Bouckaert. The unnamed confessor's refusal to comfort Margaret is mentioned in numerous letters between 1626 and 1628, as well as the visitation summary of 1624, cited in full in the notes to chapter 8. Her delinquent Jesuit confessor she mentions herself, in the letter of February 3, 1628.

Just exactly where Margaret was allowed within the convent is inferred from various documents; she speaks herself of "coming back from the choir" in her visitation letter of 1628. And Boonen's decree to allow her back into the cloister in 1635 notes the places and privileges from which she had been barred; see in Greys/8, "Heymelijcke Instructie" (dated July 10, 1636), "Secreta Instructio Matris," and "Jacob byder gratie Godts."

On Maria Petyt, see A. Deblaere, *De mystieke schrijfster Maria Petyt* (Gent, 1962).

I've assumed that Catharina, as Margaret's caretaker, was the one who brought the paper. She requested the relic mentioned and the picture of Joseph from Bouckaert in the letter of February 3, 1628, and I have assumed that he sent them. She also asked Boonen for relics, such as a piece of the cross.

The faults of other sisters mentioned here are all contained in Margaret's visitation letter of 1628.

The metaphor of the lonely sparrow is from Psalms 102:7, part of the fifth penitential psalm.

Chapter 2

I've assumed Margaret's profession date from her interview of April 1606. At that interview she also stated her age, as best she knew it, her place of origin, and the names of her parents—AAM, CK, Generalia, contains a register of women interviewed for profession around Leuven; see the entry of April 13. Other candidates in Bethlehem, interspersed with candidates for other convents, are also listed in this valuable little book. Margaret's annuity of 6 florins she mentions in later correspondence about her pilgrimage to Scherpenheuvel; Greys/8, March 27, 1624, Margaret to Archbishop Boonen. It could be that she brought more than this when she entered the convent and that the amount diminished by 1624.

Forced entries were a notorious though not universal part of monastic life before Trent. E. Power, *Medieval People* (London, 1924), shows one interesting case, and discusses the problem more in her *English Medieval Nunneries, c. 1275 to 1535* (Cambridge, 1922). An excellent example of a cruel uncle occurred under Archbishop Hovius, in AAM, CK, Generalia, documents dated from October 1 to 10, 1614, in regard to Genoveva Schafts, who as a teenager was forced to enter, then left the convent soon afterward to marry. Around age fifty she was being pestered by the dean to leave her husband and return.

The difference between marriage dowries and convent dowries is well known. J. Brown, *Immodest Acts: The Life of a Lesbian Nun in Renaissance Italy* (Oxford, 1986), notes for instance that a marriage dowry in seventeenth century Pescia was 1,500 scudi, while to get a young woman into a *prestigious* convent there cost a paltry 400. At Our Lady Ter-Rivieren in Bree, the sisters paid a dowry of between 1 and 200 florins between 1465 and 1515, while by 1641 it became the custom that no one was accepted who brought in less than 1,000 florins; J. Corstjens, "De Franciscanessen van het klooster OLV-Ter-Rivieren te Bree (1464–1797)" (ms. Licentiaatsverhandeling, Leuven, 1984), 50, 51, 72. The Rich Clares of Brussels paid by the mid-seventeenth century on average of 3,500 florins, an exceptional amount; see M.-J. Juvyns, "La Communauté des Riches-Claires de Bruxelles de 1585 à 1796," 10 (1965): 206–7. The amount paid by the Grey Sisters is almost never mentioned; but since with the possible exception of the Joos cousins none of the women bore prominent family names, since their temporal situation was always precarious, since their convent was not a prominent one physically or otherwise, and since I could find few clues on the subject in the municipal archives, I must conclude that like so many nuns in this age, they were undoubtedly in the middle of the social ladder. They weren't insignificant, since by definition nuns belonged to an elite, since some of the "greater women" of Leuven were told to quit hearing confession from the new confessor of Bethlehem in 1616 (AAM, CM, 10 [Hovius journal], July 26, 1618), and since they did have as one patroness a woman called Van Heetvelde, who probably lived near the convent and who may well have been a relative of Archbishop Boonen. (His mother was from the wealthy Van Heetvelde family.) W. Gibson, *Women in Seventeenth Century France* (New York, 1989), uses the term "romantic motives."

There are many examples of gifts, or de facto dowries. A Grey Sister of Isegem paid a 1,200 florin entry gift a few decades after Margaret's entry; P. Hildebrand, "Le Couvent des Soeurs Grises à Iseghem (d'avant 1486 jusqu'en 1796)," *NF* 2 (1919): 8–55. One Carmelite novice in Leuven in the eighteenth century brought 326 florins a year in addition to curtains and furniture; see ARA, Collection Notariaat Leuven, 13023. More typical in Bethlehem, no doubt, was the pattern of modest and irregularly given dowries at the comparable Black Sisters convent in Leuven, discussed in the detailed article by L. van Buyten, "Kwantitatieve bijdrage tot de studie van de 'Kloosterdemografie' in het Leuvense: De priorij 's-Hertogeneiland te Gempe, het zwartzustersklooster en de communauteit van het Groot-Ziekengasthuis te Leuven (16de-18de eeuw)," *AL* (1976): 241–76. Ph. Schmitz, *Histoire de l'ordre de Saint-Benoît* (Maredsous, 1948), gives various figures of dowries paid in that order, 246–47. Juvyns, "La communauté des riches-claires," 204–5, points out a pattern in that community by which half of the dowry was given six weeks before the clothing and half six weeks before profession. Juvyns's note that in the mid-seventeenth century the average dowry in this community was over 3,500 florins deserves to be mentioned again, it was so steep.

On the number of women seeking entry in Pescia, see Brown, *Immodest Acts,* 32–37. E. Weaver, "Spiritual Fun: A Study of Sixteenth-Century Tuscan Convent Theatre," in *Women in the Middle Ages and the Renaissance,* ed. M. B. Rose (Syracuse, 1986), 173–206, also contains estimates on the number of religious in Florence. K. J. Beloch, *Bevölkerungsgeschichte Italiens* (Berlin, 1939, 1961), gives figures for many cities in Italy. The geographical origins of the sisters in Bethlehem are usually indicated in the interview for profession, mentioned at the beginning of this note: Between 1605 and 1640 or so one was from Stalle, one from Chamont, five were from Brussels, two from Tienen, two from Balen, four from Leuven, one from Schiedam (in the Dutch Republic).

Two small bits of evidence from later controversies confirm that patronage could matter in Bethlehem. When the women from Mechelen moved to Leuven, an heir of one of the founders of the first convent vigorously defended his inherited right to nominate four places in the new house. Second, at least one sister was introduced into the house by a beguine from Brussels. See Greys/6, 1587 letter to Archbishop Hauchinus, and a letter from Barbara van Herssen to Boonen, Greys/8, discussed further in chapter 9.

The origins of the Grey Sisters of Leuven are made most clear in "Le couvent des soeurs grises de Louvain," *AHEB* 7 (1870): 213–17, which includes the text of Laurent de Vroede's will. The continued history of the house comes partly from short summaries in E. van Even, *Louvain dans le passé & dans le présent* (Leuven, 1895), R. van Uytven, ed., *Leuven: de beste stad van Brabant* (Leuven, 1980), vol. 1, and C. van de Wiel, "Franciscaanse Archiefbronnen in het Aartsbisschoppelijk Archief te Mechelen," *FR* 31 (1976): 9–35, 32 (1977): 39–58, 33 (1978): 129–42, and from assorted manuscript documents. On the physical growth of convents, see among others an account in SAL, 4262–4263, on how the Clares started in 1513 in Leuven in the home of a deceased widow, then grew into a formal monastic complex. The physical layout of the convent of the Grey Sisters is inferred from numerous letters by the sisters, such as a plea to the Council of State found in ARA, GR, 1125, dated August 10, 1594, and its response, September 10, and especially in the same source a stack on the Greys of Leuven starting with documents dated 1665 and going until 1669, and SAL, 4278, on the same topic in 1666, in all of which the sisters had to describe their living conditions in an effort to win sympathy and money from outside sources to rebuild.

Jodi Bilinkoff's *The Avila of St. Teresa* (Ithaca, NY, 1989), includes a nice discussion on the foundation of monasteries in that city, a pattern that was similar to the rest of Europe.

Works on the Franciscans include J. A. Moorman, *A History of the Franciscan Order* (Oxford, 1968), which contains discussion of the third order, as do the order histories by Hinnebusch (Dominicans) and Lekai (Cistercians). On mendicant orders, see W. Simons, *Bedelorde kloosters in het graafschap Vlaanderen . . . voor 1350* (Brugge, 1987). For the Grey Sisters specifically see "Cession du couvent de Louvain aux Soeurs Grises de Malines," *AHEB* VII (1870): 217–19; J. de Cuyper, "Het 'Susterhuys' van Kortrijk: Het klooster van de Grauwe Zusters in de 15de en 16de Eeuw," *De Leiegouw* 24 (1982): 3–15; G. van de Castele, "Grauwe Zusters of Penitenten-Rekollektinen te Nevele: 1502–1784," *HLN* 9 (1978): 155–247; J. Grauwels, "Een lijkbaarkleed der Grauwzusters," *Limburg* 62 (1983): 189; Abbé Léon-L. Gruart, "Les Soeurs Grises de Comines," *BCFF* 14 (1951): 53–87; P. Hildebrand, "Le Couvent des Soeurs Grises à Iseghem"; H. Lemaître, "Les Soins Hospitaliers à Domicile, donnés dès le XIVe siècle par des Religieuses Franciscaines, Les Soeurs Noires et Les Soeurs Grises," *Revue d'histoire Franciscaine* 1 (1924): 180–208, and "Statuts des Religieuses du Tiers Ordre Franciscain dites Soeurs Grises Hospitalières," *Archivum Franciscanum Historicum* 4 (1911): 713–31; A. Roeykens, "Het Onstaan van het Klooster der Grauwzusters te Edingen in het Begin van de 16de Eeuw," *FR* 27 (1972): 51–90; H. Roggen, "Le Tiers Ordre Séculier et Régulier," in *DHGE* 18 (Paris, 1977), cos. 965–71; G. Schoonaert, "Onderwijsstructuren in de 16e eeuw te Poperinge: de graeuwe susteren alleenelyck dochterkens leerende," *Aan de Schreve* 14 (1984): 28–31. For the rule of Leo X, I relied on the Grey Sisters' own manuscript copy, in Greys/1. Keep in mind that the "hospital" function of some Grey houses had a broad definition in this time and before; it usually included taking in lodgers and travelers as well. The Hospital Sisters were often popular with local secular authorities who felt that the presence of religious would help to curb the "rudeness, burden, and unseemliness" that often characterized the guests. Some of these studies show that some formerly active Grey houses, but not all, were cloistered after Trent, especially Gruart, "Les Soeurs Grises de Comines."

By the mid-seventeenth century, about one hundred of the hospital-version Grey Sister houses had been established in Flanders and northern France, according to Lemaître, "Les Soins Hospitaliers"; over fifty existed in the Spanish Netherlands alone by this time (Lemaître, "Statuts Soeurs, Grises"). E. de Moreau, *Histoire de l'église en Belgique* (Brussels, 1952), tome supplementaire, lists nearly 300 female houses by 1559 in the Low Countries, a figure that has been added to steadily by researchers but that suggests the numerically significant proportion represented by the Greys; E. Persoons, "Panorama van de reguliere clerus in de 17de eeuw," *NAGN* 8 (1980): 383–92, also tells us that in the early seventeenth century there were 105 houses of Grey Sisters, Black Sisters, and Hospital Sisters together, another significant figure.

The history of the convent in Mechelen is summarized in G. Marnef, *Het Calvinistisch Bewind te Mechelen, 1580–1585* (Kortrijk, 1987); further details are revealed in AAM, CK, Black Sisters Mechelen/57, an extract from the account books of that house but showing many dealings of the Grey Sisters as well, reinforcing my impression that Greys and Blacks in Mechelen had close connections; and AAM, CM/2, fol. 55, February 7, 1586; CM/7, fol. 21, October 10, 1606 and CM/6, fol. 182, same date, all show their efforts to sell old houses. The document of transfer to Leuven is in Greys/11, undated, but done by Archbishop Jean Hauchinus in 1588. Information on the early house in Leuven is scattered, but see a document at the Provincial Archive of St. Truiden, folder "Documenten Grauwsusters Leuven, Mechelen," which notes that the church was consecrated January 28, 1595 by Bishop Gijsbrecht Maes of Den Bosch; it also briefly describes the altars and relics of the church.

What Margaret brought with her I infer from a fascinating list of things needed in Bethlehem—a list that does not specify whether it is for postulants, novices, or new nuns, but that obviously included items necessary to all three—in Greys/11, in Adriana's hand. It's undated and modified by crossings-out over the years. Certainly much of it would have applied to the time of Margaret's entry as well. It included four wimples of high-quality grey material, two yards of grey cloth for a work bodice, three black petticoats (*onderrocken*) lined with thick wool, a grey petticoat lined with "half-woolen" material, a coat, 18 good shirts, 3 dozen cloths, 3 pair of linen sheets, 15 yards of cloth destined to be made into a kind of pajama (*nacht-doeken*), coifs (*huyven*), and "*spansels*" (woven head or neckbands), 3 dozen "nose cloths," 18 small handkerchiefs, 8 pillow cases, 6 blue aprons, 4 work aprons, 6 black veils, a yard and a half of veil material for small veils, a mattress of 12 florins (crossed out later on), a red woolen blanket, 2 good pillows, 2 woolen sheets, a silver spoon (crossed out later), a beer pot (crossed out), a tin cup, a plate (crossed out), two small bowls (crossed out), an oil cup, a wicker stool, a cushion (crossed out), a vessel for consecrated water (crossed out), two wooden chairs (crossed out), a candlestand (crossed out), a "broom for cleaning," a "fire kettle" (crossed out), a bedframe (crossed out), a dish closet, a small table, two breviaries (one for summer and one for winter), 1 diurnal (part of the breviary), a psalter (3 florins apiece), a piece of leather to cover the books, stockings and shoes according to need until after profession. The document also reminded the entrants that the convent must be fed and provided for, by the nun in question, during the three days of merriment after her profession.

My account of Leuven's terrain, streets, climate, and appearance is based heavily upon Van Even's classic *Louvain dans le passé & dans le présent*; A. Meulemans, *Atlas van Oud-Leuven* (Leuven, 1981); and Van Uytven, ed., *Leuven: "de beste stad van Brabant"* vol. 1, "de geschiedenis van het stadsgewest Leuven tot omstreeks 1600." The demographics of Leuven are discussed in each work, but the data in Van Uytven seemed most reliable, along with those in H. van der Wee, ed., *The Rise and Decline of Urban Industries in Italy and in the Low Countries (Late Middle Ages–Early Modern Times)* (Leuven, 1988).

The monastic population of Leuven, which was probably male-heavy because of the university, consisted of about 365 male religious and secular priests in 1600 and 308 female religious, according to Van Even's edition of W. Boonen, *Geschiedenis van Leuven* (Leuven, 1880); but E. Persoons, in *Leuven: "de beste stad,"* reckons the total figure of vowed religious and beguines slightly lower, at around 530. Persoons also lists the known population of individual houses.

In addition to the errors in maps noted already, another clue about the obscurity of the Grey Sisters of Leuven, compared to other orders in the city and subgroups within the Franciscan family, is given by P. Carolo van Coudenhove, OFM, *Provinciae Germaniae Inferioris Compendiosa Descriptio* (n.p., 1680), when he wrote that none of the great Franciscan historians had any information about the origins of this house: "De hoc cenobio nihil habet Sedulius, multo minus Gonzaga aut Waddingus, nec scitur quando fundatum." Archivist Jozef Baetens in St. Truiden looked in vain for a list of confessors for this house, a list that usually existed for other houses in the province.

The relics of St. Renildis and her history are related in Greys/7, September 26, 1603, letter from the Archiepiscopal palace; Pétin, ed., *Dictionnaire Hagiographique* (Paris, 1850), vol. 2, col. 872; O. Wimmer and H. Melzer, *Lexikon der Namen und Heiligen* (Innsbruck, n.d.), 705; and a letter by Anna Vignarola to the archiepiscopal palace, Greys/10, February 25, 1661. See Gruart, "Les Soeurs Grises de Comines," on the famous relics there. The populations of Hertogendael and Beaupré are given by J. de Brouwer, *Bijdrage tot de Geschiedenis van het Godsdienstig Leven en de Kerkelijke Instellingen in het Land van Aalst tussen 1550 en 1621 volgens de verslagen van de*

Dekenale Bezoeken (Aalst, 1961), 256. Populations of individual convents are contained in almost every study on the subject, but no grand average has ever been made. My impression is that twenty-plus was an average figure. Heavy recruitment in St. Ursula's and St. Monica's is evident in the interview books of the deans, AAM, Collection Dekenale Verslagen, L1, and AAM, CK, Generalia, a "Catalogus virginum quae in regione Lovaniensi examinata sunt ad professionem anno 1605" (which continues to other years). Grey Sisters who like other zealous nuns established branches are discussed in Gruart, "Les Soeurs Grises de Comines," while S. Axters discusses the growth of Annuntiants in *Geschiedenis van de vroomheid in de Nederlanden,* vol. 4 (Antwerp, 1960). Bilinkoff, *Avila,* shows the not uncommon presence of the great of society in convents. On the illuminator St. Ida of Zoutleeuw (or Gorsleeuw), see C. Henriquez, "Quinque prudentes virgines (1630)" in M. Sabbe et al., *Bernardus en de Cisterziënfamilie in Belgie, 1090–1990* (Leuven, 1990). The work of Fra Angelico is discussed by W. Hood, "Fra Angelico at San Marco: Art and the Liturgy of Cloistered Life," in T. Verdon and J. Henderson, *Christianity and the Renaissance* (Syracuse, 1990). On mystic visions and knowledge of Latin, see W. A. Hinnebusch, *The History of the Dominican Order* (New York, 1966), chapter 13. Bits about traffic on the Dijle river are from SAL, 3825–27, Dijle, and Margaret's visitation letters of 1628 and 1633.

The two stages of probation are found in the rule of Leo X and the house statutes of 1626. Earlier sets of statutes, which applied to Margaret at the time of her profession, would on this point probably have provided for the same two stages of probation. The article by Van Buyten, " 'Kloosterdemografie,' " shows that in fact most of the postulants and novices in his sample went through the entire year of each stage. The "common cloth" for novices is in the rule of the order. Many other specifics of the clothing and the profession are not contained in the statutes for Bethlehem; thus I have relied on other useful sources. For instance, reservation of the scapular and the cord for professed nuns only was a requirement laid down by Petrus Marchant in his summa of the third-order rule, *Den Reghel der Derder Orden van S. Fransoys* (Gent, 1626) and then later in his *Af-beeldinghe Des waerachtigh Christen Mensch, Naer het voor-beelt vanden Reghel der derder Ordre Van den Godt-salighen Vader S. Franchois* (Gent, 1639), both of which may have expressed customs in Margaret's house as well. Note that Margaret was not interviewed to be a novice, but after 1610 such a requirement was in effect, according to P. F. X. de Ram, *Synodicon belgicum,* 4 vols. (Mechelen, 1828–1858), vol. 2, 492; the additional interview is also reflected in the book of interviews noted at the beginning of this chapter note.

The training of postulants and novices undoubtedly varied in theory and in practical quality from place to place, but the practices mentioned would not have been unusual. Some of these suggestions are contained of course in the Greys' own statutes, but since these are not laid out in detail I have supplemented them with AAM, CM, 8, statutes of the Hospital of Ninove in 1609; and the Dutch version of Bonaventure's *Spieghel der Goeder*

Manieren veur de Novitie, dat is, Proef-ionghers der Minder-broeders Ordene (Antwerp, 1605). Stories about straying novices abound in Cartusianus, *De Leere der Religieusen* (Brussels, 1626). The interviews for profession of all the sisters in Bethlehem (and some interviews for the novitiate) are found in the source cited in the first paragraph of this chapter note. The required questions to be put at the time of this interview are recorded in De Ram, *Synodicon,* vol. 2, 492. A colorful example of a response that went beyond the standard question and answer is that of Perynken Prissens, who wished to enter the Black Sisters convent of Mechelen because she hoped to attain her salvation in this house and wouldn't be bothered by those who eschewed the rule, "for she takes for her mirror the best, and not those who do ill"; AAM, CK, Black Sisters Mechelen/42, August 1623. For negative responses, or the fear involved in resisting the will of parents, see G. Reynes, *Couvents de femmes* (Paris, 1987), 41–45. The story of Clare fleeing her brothers and then being protected by Francis is recounted by, among others, Moorman, *Franciscans,* 33. See Reynes, *Couvents de femmes,* 50–51, on young Anne-Bathilde, who must have received a dispensation to profess at such a young age.

The ages of the women in Bethlehem were given or at least estimated at the interview for profession. In chronological order, from 1604 to 1640: Joanna de Vorster was 23; Anna Coninxloo, 26; Adriana Truis, 16; Lesken Nijns, 22; Margaret Smulders, 23; Joanna Outhagen, 26; Maria Joos, 20; Lesken Joos, 21; Anna Servranx, 26; Francisca Sannen, 20; Maria de Smet, 21; Margaret Leiniers, 30; Joanna Schoensetters, 27; Anna Vignarola, 19; Margaret Geraerts, 23; Elisabeth de Haen, 26; Barbara Leunens, 21; Josijn-ken Senken, 20; Cecilia Vaes, 24; Catharina Croisaert, 40; Catharina de Grove, 25; Joanna Heusdens, 25.

Distress caused by the delay of the profession ceremony is reflected in a letter from Anna Vignarola years later, to the archbishop, Greys/4, October 22, 1671. The custom of leading the aspiring nun to the door of the choir is mentioned by M. Hereswitha, "Reguliere Kanunnikessen van het Heilig-Graf," *OGE* 50/4 (December 1976): 401–2. All details of the profession ceremony in Bethlehem are again not specified in the house statutes, but some are, and others were probably similar to what occurred in other convents. Those recorded here are from the rule and statutes; from Greys/11, letter by General Caraffa, January 19, 1647, on profession; Marchant, *Afbeeldinghe*; RAG, CB, M242/22, "Forma vestitionis et professionis monialium in hospitali Gerardimonten." The requirement of a subdued profession feast is recorded in De Ram, *Synodicon,* vol. 1, 322.

Chapter 3

The visitation summary of 26 September 1616 may be found in Greys/3. Though there is no question list for the visitation, nor any letters from the sisters themselves, I have inferred from the structure of the interview summaries that the vicar-general's chief purpose in going was to address the issue of what should be done with Margaret. As for how long Margaret was out, Anna Vignarola wrote in 1672 that the troubles started "soon" after profession, thus around 1606—but we still don't know when the troubles grew so serious that they forced her to leave; see Greys/8, December 29, 1672.

On the relationship of animals to witchery, and animals as disguised witches, see F. Vanhemelryck, *Heksenprocessen in de Nederlanden* (Leuven, 1982), 110; J. Sumption, *Pilgrimage: An Image of Mediaeval Religion* (Totowa, NJ, 1975), 16; K. Thomas, *Religion and the Decline of Magic* (New York, 1971), 481; and J. Klaits, *Servants of Satan: The Age of the Witch Hunts* (Bloomington, 1985), 110.

The account of the apparition in Comines is noted by Abbé Léon-L. Gruart, "Les Soeurs Grises de Comines," *BCFF* 14 (1951): 60. The sentiment that Bethlehem became haunted during the exile to Cologne in the 1580s is brought up by Anna Vignarola in her 1672 short history, just cited.

My summary of common views of the otherworld, witchery, and women in this age relies on a number of provocative, highly readable works: *Tussen Heks en Heilige: Het Vrouwbeeld op het drempel van de moderne tijd* (Nijmegen, 1985); *Helse en Hemelse Vrouwen* (Utrecht, 1988); Thomas, *Religion and the Decline of Magic;* F. Vanhemelryck, *Heksenprocessen;* W. Christian, *Local Religion in Sixteenth Century Spain* (Princeton, 1981); Klaits, *Servants of Satan;* Th. Penneman, "Processen en Moeilijkheden wegens Toveren en Onttoveren in het Land van Waas tijdens de XVIde en XVIIde Eeuw," *Handelingen van het XLIe Congres, Federatie van de Kringen voor Oudheidkunde en Geschiedenis van Belgie* 2 (1971): 221–40; L. T. Maes, "Un procès de sorcellerie en 1642, évalué à la lumière de récentes études européennes et d'après la législation et la théorie du droit du XVIIe siècle," *HKKM* 79 (1975): 243–68.

The activity of spirits mentioned by H. C. Erik Midelfort is found in his "The Devil and the German People: Reflections on the Popularity of Demon Possession in Sixteenth-Century Germany," in S. Ozment, ed., *Religion and Culture in the Renaissance and Reformation* (Kirksville, MO, 1989). This article and D. P. Walker's *Unclean Spirits: Possession and Exorcism in France and England in the Late Sixteenth and Early Seventeenth Centuries* (Philadelphia, 1981), give much insight into possession as distinct from witchcraft, though in writing about the one it is hard for any author not to treat the other at least briefly as well. Lottin writes about conventual possession and witchery in his *Lille: Citadelle de la Contre-Réforme (1598–1668)?* (Paris, 1984), citing the Brigitines of Lille and the Cistercian nuns of Verger near Douai; his discussion of the contagiousness of scandals is on 177. Other famous scandals at this time are noted by Vanhemlryck, *Heksenprocessen,* 57. More is said about cases of possession in chapters 5 and 6 and their notes, below.

On the varieties of witchcraft, Muchembled alleges that the kind we probably know best is rural witchcraft; that of cities and of nunneries may have had their own peculiar characteristics, which need studying as well;

"The Witches of the Cambrésis: The Acculturation of the Rural World in the Sixteenth and Seventeenth Centuries," in J. Obelkevich, ed., *Religion and the People, 800–1700* (Chapel Hill, 1979).

Based on Vanhemlryck, *Heksenprocessen*, Margaret would have entered Bethlehem just after the height of executions for witchcraft in the Low Countries. The last witchburning in Leuven happened in 1612, but reduction of the punishment didn't mean people had stopped believing or that trials had stopped.

The case of Marie Everaerts has been written about in several brief articles or mentioned briefly in some big books. See L. Maes, "Un procès de Sorcellerie en 1642," who mentions her case as background; also Maes, *Vijf eeuwen stedelijk strafrecht: Bijdrage tot de rechts- en cultuurgeschiedenis der Nederlanden* (Antwerp, 1947), 211; and especially R. Foncke, "Mechelsche Folklore: Een heksenproces ten jare 1602," *Mechlinia* 4 (1925): 121–32. In these, Marie's status is vague: Most guess that she was either a religious, probably a Black Sister because of her imprisonment at that house, or at least had close ties with religious. The key document in establishing Marie's identity as a Grey Sister is in AAM, Collection Vicariaat, V/11, undated. Other helpful primary documents in the Everaerts case were AAM, CM, 3/ fols. 253–55 and 6/fol. 58vo. and 174vo., and Greys/5, which contains Marie Switten's testament to the house, made in 1597. Also important in these is that the Greys of Leuven supported Marie in jail in Mechelen with an annuity of 42 florins a year, which they hardly would have done had she not been one of their own.

Mater Barbara Noosen's comment about the "old history" in Bethlehem is in a letter to Boonen, March 28, 1624, Greys/8; it's unsigned, but I'm sure it is in her hand. The rumors by other sisters about the infected houses are suggested by Anna Vignarola's 1672 brief history, Greys/8, cited earlier.

The difficulty of distinguishing between witchery and demonic possession is mentioned by Klaits, *Servants of Satan* 111; and Midelfort, "The Devil and the German People," at least outside of legal circles, where he feels the distinctions were fairly clear, 116.

Chapter 4

Margaret's assertions of her reasons for leaving Bethlehem are mentioned most clearly in a letter by Johan Evangelista, Greys/8, February 23, 1624, to Boonen; this is discussed in more detail toward the end of this chapter and in chapter 6.

Women as spiritual advisors are mentioned by D. Herlihy, *Opera Muliebria: Women and Work in Medieval Europe* (New York, 1990), 118–19, among other sources, while K. Norberg, "The Counter-Reformation and Women, Religious and Lay," in J. O'Malley, ed., *Catholicism in Early Modern History* (St. Louis, 1988), 133–46, discusses the problems that arose from not being able to say Mass. Jodi Bilinkoff's "Confessors, Penitents and the Construction of Identities in Early Modern Avila," in *Culture and Identity in*

Early Modern Europe: Essays in Honor of Natalie Zemon Davis (Ann Arbor, forthcoming), considers the attractions of confessing holy women. The problems perceived by contemporary males in confessing women are reviewed more in chapter 8.

J. Brown, *Immodest Acts* (Oxford, 1986), 38, notes the dawdling friars who served Santa Chiara. The problems of the convent in Nevele may be found in G. van de Casteele, "Grauwe Zusters of Penitenten-Rekollektie-nen te Nevele, 1502–1784," *HLN* 9 (1978): 155–247, which reviews the 1614, 1643, and 1644 visitation reports, the potential for scandal because of familiarity with the superior, and the complaints of some girls who attended school at the convent. The loose-talking confessor of Aarschot is accused in AAM, CK, Begijnhof Aarschot/2, visit by Bouckaert, September 7, 1628, and March 29, 1629, while the jealous confessor of the Black Sisters of Leuven is in AAM, CK, Black Sisters Leuven/32, 1689, and the rapid confessor of Bethanie is in AAM, CK, Bethanie Brussels/4, 1590 visitation. Archbishop Hovius recorded numerous problems with confessors in his agenda and journal, one of the best having to do with a convent in Zichem: AAM, CA, Hovius/12, December 1618; see on the latter C. Harline and E. Put, "A Bishop in the Cloisters: The Visitations of Mathias Hovius (Malines, 1596–1620)," *SCJ* 22/4 (Winter 1991): 611–39.

Materials on Joos and St. Gertrude's are drawn from largely manuscript sources. An important account book of Joos is located in the ARA, KAB, 10752, a "manuale" of receipts of Joos from June 24, 1604, to 1624. AAM, CK, St. Gertrude's Leuven/8, includes two other account books compiled by Joos. Number 9 in the same collection is a visitation report of September 17, 1666, that clarifies the long-standing relationship between the vicar and the abbot, especially the financial agreements. The visitation about the scandals in Gertrude's is found in the same collection in number 2, November 10, 1631, by Dean Paridanus, while the candelabra-swinger's case is in an unnumbered file, with the notarial act recording it dated February 27, 1635. Number 8, June 8, 1624 act contains the acquisition of the benefice of the Three Kings Altar by Joos. AAM, Collection Dekenale Verslagen/L1, contains the dean's visitation reports of the church and its vicar. A book he compiled after leaving Leuven for Mol is located in RAA, Kerkarchieven, Mol/82.

An example of a charitable confessor who never received any fees for his labor was Laurent Nagelmaecker of Blijdenberg in Mechelen, noted in AAM, CK, Blijdenberg/72, a register that contains various details on the history of the house. Joos's activities representing the Grey Sisters are reflected in a request to sell an orchard, Greys/5, December 30, 1610; SAL, 7334, fol. 388v and 487, where in February of 1609 he transferred an annuity and is called their "confessor." Favorable opinions of Joos among the sisters of Bethlehem are reflected in their continued alliance with him over the years, even after his dismissal, also the 1616 visitation report, cited in the note to chapter 3, and explicitly in the account of Anna Vignarola of 1672, Greys/8.

The story of Lesken Nijns is drawn almost entirely from the journal of Archbishop Hovius, AAM, CM, 10. Her name comes up only once in all the documents composed by the sisters themselves, but without that single mention (made by Margaret) I would never have been positive of the connection. The most important entries for the affair with Lesken and the question of confessors (all in 1618) are: June 22; July 4, 6, 7, 8, 14, 17, 19; August 8, 11, 25, 26, 27, 28, 30; September 2, 7, 11, 16; October 20, 27, 30; November 3, 5; December 4, 9; and March 5, 1619. The entries dealing obviously with Margaret (there are other possibly related entries as well) are July 14, August 1, September 20, October 18–20, November 23, and December 12. The question of handing jurisdiction over to the Leuven Franciscans is noted February 10, 1619. Joos's dismissal from Bethlehem is in Greys/5, July 5, 1618.

Dhollander must have gone to Mechelen with Lesken's permission, or even at her request, for the secret of confession was supposed to have been so strict that "even if the whole world depended on it, [the confessor] should not reveal the least sin he has heard." See C. Leutbrewer, OFM, *Gulde biecht-konste om op den tijdt van min als twee uren sich te bereyden tot een generale biechte van heel syn leven, sonder peryckel van eenighe doodt-sonden achter te laten* (Brussels, 1646).

Hovius's reputation for strictness rested on such events as his rebuke of a nun who had supposedly visited a tavern. It turned out that she had not, but the chastisement was so severe, said her sisters, she became ill anyway and died; AAM, CK, Roosendael/Chronicle, fol. 68.

Remember that Margaret's assertions about Joos's advances are from Evangelista's letter of February 1624. The part of Evangelista's letter that contains Margaret's own opinions is torn in a crucial place; it excises enough words that those remaining cannot all be put together with certainty. It may be no coincidence that the document is torn just at this point, for in most documents on the subject either the name of Joos or the suspicious events are mentioned, but rarely the two together. The "carnal affection" is clear, but Joos is identifiable only by the "s" at the end of a name, and the subsequent, crucial phrase "who had care of the convent at that time"— referring to the time of Margaret's first exit in 1616.

On the idea of possession being *inflicted* by a human agent, see K. Thomas, *Religion and the Decline of Magic* (New York, 1971); H. C. Erik Midelfort, "The Devil and the German People," in S. Ozment, ed., *Religion and Culture in the Renaissance and Reformation* (Kirksville, MO, 1989), 109; A. M. Walker and E. H. Dickerman, " 'A Woman Under the Influence: A Case of Alleged Possession in Sixteenth-Century France,' " *SCJ* 22/3, (1991): 535–54. On the possessed seeing their tormentor, Thomas, *Religion and the Decline of Magic;* 489, or conversing with the devil, D. P. Walker, *Unclean Spirits* (Philadelphia, 1981), 8.

The Spadens case may be found in AAM, Collection Vicariaat, V/11 (Toverye), February 27, 1627. F. Vanhemelryck, *Heksenprocessen in de Nederlanden* (Leuven, 1982), notes the meeting in Antwerp: 52. The case of the

Capuchin exorcist is contained in AAM, Collection Vicariaat, V/11, October 5, 1616, document signed by Frater Guilielmus.

J. Sumption, *Pilgrimage* (Totowa, NJ, 1975), 17 on sexuality and possession. A. Lottin, *Lille: Citadelle de la Contre-Réforme (1598–1668)?* (Paris, 1984) also cites numerous cases of conventual possession with a strongly sexual element, especially 178. The example of St. Anthony is from *Helse en Hemelse Vrouwen* (Utrecht, 1988). The Sánchez case is in S. Nalle, *God in La Mancha: Religious Reform and the People of Cuenca, 1500–1650* (Baltimore, 1992), 19–20. The Aix-en-Provence case is cited by J. Klaits, *Servants of Satan* (Bloomington, 1985), 113–14, and G. Reynes, *Couvents de femmes* (Paris, 1987), 160, along with others; the famous cases in France are continued by Thomas, *Religion and the Decline of Magic,* 478–81. Another recent case in France involved a woman who during the very public exorcisms cried out, "Kiss me, Canon," and in fact she "forced him to kiss her and was not able to go to sleep unless he laid his cheek against hers or held her in his arms." See Walker and Dickerman, " 'A Woman Under the Influence,' " 549. The case of Loudun has been studied by among others Michel de Certeau, *La possession de Loudun* (Paris, 1970). The Spanish examples comes from J. Bilinkoff, "A Spanish Prophetess and Her Patrons: The Case of María de Santo Domingo," *SCJ* 23/1 (Spring 1992): 21–34.

The account by Anna Vignarola, written in 1672, is in Greys/8. It's significant on the matter of the charges against Henri Joos because: (1) it links the three main players (Margaret, Lesken, and Henri Joos); (2) ties Lesken to the problem of possession and confirms that she too had private sessions with Joos; (3) establishes that soon after the removal the sisters came to know or suspect who had made the charges against Joos; and (4) establishes that the sisters were soon telling tales, since Anna professed in 1624 only and must have had her knowledge of the events of 1616 to 1618 from the other sisters—perhaps she even had information from Joos himself, who continued to visit Bethlehem after his dismissal.

The death of Judoca, the election of a new Mater in Bethlehem, and the attempt to transfer jurisdiction are all in Hovius's journal, February 1–2, April 30, May 21–23, 1619; note that in 1592, though the convent in Mechelen had been obliterated, the cathedral chapter on October 23 issued a proclamation that the "sisters-in-exile" in Leuven were now free to return—despite the seeming finality of the archbishop's transfer of the sisters back in 1588, and even though the women had no convent to which they could return, the cathedral would not give up the fight; see the Franciscan Provincial Archive in St. Truiden, Documents in the folder "Grauwsusters Leuven, Mechelen."

To learn Joos's fate after Leuven one can start with R. Knaepen, *Mol—Baelen—Desschel, 1559–1795: De oude Keizerlijke Vrijheid en haar Voogdijdistrict* (Mol, 1982), especially 71–89. More detailed documentary evidence for this post-Leuven period is contained in the BAA. Some highlights: a letter of support for his nomination to Mol notes his twenty years of "laudable service" in St. Gertrude's (BAA, Parochialia Mol/XI, November 21, 1623);

in a notarial act Joos stated that after long years of praise by his parishioners in Leuven, he wished to return to Mol not for any sinister motives, not compelled by anyone, but only stirred by his soul (Parochialia Mol/XIII, dated ca. November 6, 1623); see Joos expressing to his new patron, the local *seigneur*, unbridled joy, "thanks in the eternities and in this life," perpetual and faithful service, and an invitation to dine at the home of his brother (Parochialia Mol/XIII, September 16, 1623); Joos was buttressed in his nomination to Mol, over the other two candidates, by several Jesuit acquaintances called in to opine on the case (Parochialia Mol/XIII contains numerous letters on the respective candidates); things became so unsatisfactory for Joos at one point that he threatened to give up the nomination altogether, which "amazed" the seigneur since Joos had been so eager before (Parochialia Mol/XIII, March 20, 1624). But after more wrangling, the seigneur was won over, persuaded by magistrates and probably the bishop and the archdeacon. Yet protests from other candidates came in even after Joos began office on June 24. Moreover, after only a few weeks on the job we find Joos lamenting that he was already on bad terms with the seigneur (Parochialia Mol/XIII, July 13, 1624, Joos to Delien). One of his first acts was to put the books and accounts of the church in order, but he discovered that all documents and benefices had been borne away by the bishop or his archdeacon, so he wrote meekly to ask for a copy of them, to be made of course at his own expense (Parochialia Mol/XII, June 29, 1624, to Bishop Zoes).

Chapter 5

St. Gillis, a third-order saint, asked for another brother to sleep in his room to help ward off demons; recorded in C. Thielemans's *Heylighen van S. Franciscus Oirden* (Den Bosch, 1620). The letter from the dean of Leuven: Greys/8, January 16, 1624, Peter Lucius to Boonen. The noises and disturbances characteristic of such cases are discussed further in chapter 6. One later example worth noting here, which practically duplicated Margaret's description, is cited in Maes, *Vijf eeuwen stedelijk strafrecht* (Antwerp, 1947), in a 1642 trial, where the victim also testified that the disturbances happened especially when she was being exorcised.

Margaret's letter to Boonen reviewed here, in Greys/8, is one of the few undated pieces in the file of the Grey Sisters, but given the contents, and the known chronology of events from other dated sources, I think it was written before her attempted suicide on January 17.

Mater Barbara's short note, which includes mention of Margaret's attempted suicide, was written the "27th" but does not give a month; St. Paul's conversion, however, was celebrated January 25. Catharina's short letter does not give a date, either, but she notes that the suicide attempt was on the night of January 17 or 18, which, together with the description in Mater Barbara's letter, along with the haste and brevity of each, makes the scenario I describe in late January as plausible. I think they were all sent on January 27, the same day as the petition. (See two paragraphs below.)

The ritual for installing a new mater, like the profession ritual, varied from house to house but some elements were basic. Those described here are from M. Cloet, ed., *Itinerarium visitationum Antonii Triest, episcopi gandavensis (1623–1654)* (Leuven, 1976), September 21, 1623, Brigitines of Dendermonde, and from AAM, CM, 5/fol. 99, where a ceremony at the hospital of Roosbeek is described in more detail.

The petition from the sisters is dated January 27, Greys/8, and my description of the scenario surrounding its composition is derived from careful study of the document and knowledge of relationships and hands drawn from other documents (especially the 1624 visitation on which each sister signed her name or X after the interview). Boonen's sentiments about private letters vs. public petitions are revealed in a letter he wrote to the dean of Leuven, January 2, 1625, in Greys/5. The devil's urging religious women to tear up their religious clothing fits well into his well-known array of blasphemous acts; a nun of Loudun years later would tear at her veils "and such of my sisters as I might lay hand on," trampling underfoot and chewing as well; see J. Klaits, *Servants of Satan* (Bloomington, 1985), 116.

The sketch of Boonen is drawn primarily from P. Claessens, *Histoire des archevêques de Malines,* vol. 1 (Leuven, 1881); J. Lefèvre, "La Nomination des Archevêques de Malines sous l'Ancien Régime," *HKKM* 63 (1959): 75–92; L. Ceyssens, "Jacobus Boonen," in *NBW,* vol. 2 (Brussels, 1966), cols. 74–89; L. Jadin, "Procès d'information pour la nomination des évêques et abbés des Pays-Bas, de Liège et de Franche-Comté d'après les Archives de la Congrègation Consistoriale (1637–1709)," *BIHBR* (1929): 133–38, 148–55, especially helpful for the opinions other ecclesiastical figures held of him; G. de Munck, "Het bisdom Gent van 1609 tot 1621: Carolus Maes (1609–1612), Franciscus van der Burch (1613–1616), Jacobus Boonen (1617–1621)," *Collationes Gandavenses* 14 (1927): 40–45, helpful for his years in Gent. Boonen's later years and his trouble with Jansenism are noted in the afterword. The comparison of Boonen to Moses is made by Michel Zachtmoorter, *Thalamus Sponsi, oft t'Bruydegoms Beddeken* (Antwerp, 1623), preface. The comparison of Boonen to Borromeo is from KAM, CA, Boonen/73 (Bewind, Varia), from a printed program for a drama entitled *Tragicomedie, Isaacus Angelus Comnenus, Empereur de Constantinople, Pris de Baronius, et Nicetas Choniates Secretaire et Chamberlain du mesme Empereur* (Mechelen, 1628).

Two manuscript examples, of which there are many in Boonen's fat papers, of pastoral involvement among the female religious are AAM, CK, Aarschot Begijnhof/2, visitation 1631; AAM, CK, Mechelen Leprozije/1, 1632 statutes, which include his hand in the marginal notes. Boonen's skilled phrasing in making requests for people is evident in nearly every letter to the political bodies, but see as one fine example ARA, RSA, 2041/1, March 21, 1625. Complaints about the clergy are plentiful in Boonen's own agenda, AAM, CA, Boonen/186. Those I have noted are from January 12, 1622, January 20, May 10, and October 5, 1623. Ignorance of Jesus Christ is noted on April 27, 1622; people suspected of magic on May 10, 1622; overvisiting Dominicans in Leuven on October 26, 1622; students of the seminary on January 11, 1623; confessors and arguing among sisters on February 4, 1623; the temptress in Brussels on May 20, 1623; reforms among his household on July 9, 1623; and the bishop of Arras on December 26, 1623. Isabella also asked Boonen to intervene at the beguinage of Brussels, about which she had heard unsettling tales, in ARA, RSA, 2041/1, September 12, 1622; and he was petitioned to help a female prisoner win release so that she might return to Spain—in the same file, a letter dated December 31, 1622.

The ideal bishop is discussed by P. Broutin, *Le Réforme Pastorale en France au XVIIe siècle*, 2 vols. (Paris, 1956), and *L'évêque dans la tradition pastorale du xvie siècle* (Brugge, 1953; Broutin's French adaptation of H. Jedin, *Das Bischofsideal der Katholischen Reformation*).

The pressing problems cited are from 1624; see the agenda just cited and also AAM, CA, Boonen/157–58 (Smeekbrieven), 223 (loose notes and memoranda). These sources, especially the agenda, also reveal Boonen's movements and activities during this time, such as his meal with the abbot of St. Gertrude's (Agenda, January 5, 1624).

That Boonen had already written to Margaret is noted by Catharina Rijckeboer, who wondered why he hadn't answered Margaret's most recent response, since he had answered so expeditiously previous ones; Greys/8, March 14, 1624. This correspondence and the visitation of 1623 by his vicar-general form the basis for my conclusion that by January 1624 he was probably familiar with the case, though perhaps not with every detail of its past history.

Boonen's modification of the Pastorale is noted by L. Malherbe, "Le Pastorale de Malines: son histoire," *CM* 28 (1939): 369–88. J. Lacnen, "Heksenprocessen," *CM* 7 (1913): 181–91, 239–47, 407–18, 459–80, 537–60, notes that eight suspected nuns were sent before the archbishop. The famous scandals of Lille and Aix-en-Chapelle are noted in A. Lottin, *Lille: Citadelle de la Contre-Réforme (1598–1668)?* (Paris, 1984), 170 ff. The opinion of the vicar-general on women and witchery is drawn from F. Vanhemelryck, *Heksenprocessen in de Nederlanden* (Leuven, 1982), 53.

Chapter 6

Background on the Capuchin order and the convent in Leuven is from P. Hildebrand, *De Capucijnen in de Nederlanden en het prinsbisdom Luik*, 11 vols. (Antwerp, 1945–56), especially vol. 5, 71–78. The learned chronicler who wrote the account of the stricken woman was no less than Jacobus Baius, a theologian and the nephew of the more famous, controversial theologian of the same name. Helpful articles on Evangelista include P. Leonardus, "De Capucijn Joannes Evangelista van 's-Hertogenbosch: Zijn betekenis als geestelijk schrijver," in *FL* 43 (1960): 172–83; P. Gerlachus, "Onze Ascetische Schrijvers: P. Joannes Evangelista van 's-Hertogenbosch (1588–1635)," *FL* 14 (1931): 73–83; Hildebrand, *De Capucijnen*, vol. 5, 115–31, vol. 6, 558, vol. 7, 11, 397, vol. 9, 389–93; Fr. Clarentius, "Pater Joannes Evangelista van 's-Hertogenbosch," *OGE* 8 (1934): 369–97; S. Axters, *Geschiedenis van de Vroomheid in de Nederlanden,* vol. 4 (Antwerp, 1960), 47–56, 135, 302–4; "Jean-Evangèliste de Bois-le-Duc, capucin, 1588–1635," *DS* 8 (Paris, 1974), cols. 827–30. As several of these authors point out, though Evangelista's tracts were published only after his death, they were certainly in his mind and in manuscript during the 1620s and '30s.

The letter that Evangelista wrote here, which is the basis of the scenario and contents of this chapter, is dated February 23, 1624, Greys/8.

J. Klaits, *Servants of Satan* (Bloomington, 1985), chapter 5, on possession and suggestion; also K. Thomas, *Religion and the Decline of Magic* (New York, 1971), offers many insights on the subject. D. P. Walker, *Unclean Spirits* (Philadelphia, 1981), is devoted entirely to possession rather than the more commonly studied witchcraft. The case of the French woman, named Marthe, is cited in another informative article, A. M. Walker and E. H. Dickerman, " 'A Woman Under the Influence:' A Case of Alleged Possession in Sixteenth-Century France," *SCJ* 22/3 (1991): 535–54; most of the criteria I list are from this article and Walker, *Unclean Spirits.* The example of the power of suggestion is from AAM, CK, Begijnhof Aarschot/2, 1629 investigation. A sister in Bethanie in Brussels heard from another nun that the dean of St. Gudule in that city had heard the confession of the Mater of St. Elizabeth's, that the session lasted three or four hours, and that after it Mater retired to bed, obviously ill (AAM, CK, Bethanie Brussels/4, 1590 visitation).

Margaret's inability to meet with Evangelista is mentioned not by the Capuchin but in a letter by Mater Barbara to Boonen, March 28, 1624, Greys/8.

Teresa's early diagnosis is discussed in J. Bilinkoff, *The Avila of St. Teresa* (Ithaca, NY, 1989), 119. Matters to consider in diagnosing possession are included in the pastorale of the archdiocese, first issued by Hauchinus but reedited by M. Hovius, *Pastorale ad usum romanum accomodatum . . .* (Antwerp, 1598, 1608), especially 177. Other helpful sources that discuss melancholy and possession include Walker, *Unclean Spirits*, especially 8–13, where he writes that melancholy, hysteria, epilepsy, and possession were sometimes indistinguishable and sometimes one caused the other, and *Helse en Hemelse Vrouwen* (Utrecht, 1988), which notes that "witches suffered from melancholy." As several authors note, the connection to melancholy is also made in the famous *Malleus Maleficarum* and in the paintings of Lucas Cranach. The despair of Catherine Janssens is noted in Maes, *Vijf eeuwen stedelijk strafrecht* (Antwerp, 1947), 727. The predilection of older nuns to be "dry" is from H. C. Erik Midelfort, "The Devil and the German People," in S. Ozment, ed., *Religion and Culture in the Renaissance and Reformation* (Kirksville, MO, 1989), 109. F. Vanhemelryck points out the susceptibility to possession of persons in debt, *Heksenprocessen in de Nederlanden* (Leuven, 1982), 146. The devil's craftiness in switching the tables and concealing possession by tempting doctors to diagnose natural symptoms such as melancholy is discussed by Klaits, *Servants of Satan;* 110, and Walker, *Unclean Spirits,* 11.

The causes of possession—to punish disobedience or ultimately to promote the glory of God or one's particular religious confession—are discussed in Walker, *Unclean Spirits,* 6, and Midelfort, "The Devil and the German People," 111. The case of the possessed girl in Mechelen may be found in P. Croon, *Onse Lieve Vrauwe van Hanswyck . . .* (Mechelen, 1670), 162–63. Anna's assessment is from her brief history, written in 1672, Greys/ 8. Psychological explanations of witchcraft and possession are discussed by most of the authors—cited in the note to chapter 3 and here—who have written on the topic; most helpful again were Thomas, *Religion and the Decline of Magic,* 480–81; Klaits, *Servants of Satan,* 111; and Walker and Dickerman, " 'A Woman Under the Influence.' "

The formulas of exorcism referred to here are from the archdiocesanal *Pastorale,* 183–86. The champion handbook of the time, brought to my attention by Eddy Put, was probably Maximilian van Eynatten, *Manuale exorcismorum* (Leuven, and other cities, numerous editions). Evangelista may have used an exorcism of his order, but again the spirit of exorcisms, if not the specific content, was similar enough that I feel safe using the approved *Pastorale* as an example. The more elaborate methods noted are from D. P. Walker, *Unclean Spirits,* 46.

Two of Evangelista's three posthumous publications were intended first for religious but also for the "average" devotional reader. These were *Het Ryck Godts Inder Zielen oft Binnen U Lieden* (Leuven, 1637), and *Het Eeuwigh Leven, Qui manducat meam Carnem, et bibit meum Sanguinem, habet vitam Aeternam . . .* (Leuven, 1644). Capuchin tendencies in devotion are discussed by Axters, *Geschiedenis van de Vroomheid.* The quote about sniffing dogs comes from Evangelista's *Ryck Godts,* 3v; see also especially 3–6v, 75–76. The thought about lazy religious comes from Leonardus, "Joannes Evangelista," 174.

In Leuven there was a case involving a certain Margareta Smit, whose purported *magus* was a blacksmith. See AAM, Collection Dekenale Verslagen/D3, 1620.

Catharina Rijckeboer's letter in Greys/8, dated March 14, 1624. On loose-lipped confessors there are legions of examples. A beguine in Aarschot in 1629 complained that she was being expelled from the place by the confessor because of a secret she had revealed in confession that he had in turn revealed to someone else above him who now wrote to a fourth party that the woman should be expelled for this confessed sin (AAM, CK, Begijnhof Aarschot/2, May 2, 1629, testimony of Christina Deckers). An investigation in 1590 into problems with a confessor in the convent of Bethanie in Brussels revealed that several sisters were accused of telling others to be careful of the confessor, for he demanded that they "should reveal all their secrets"; AAM, CK, Bethanie Brussels/4.

Boonen's discharge of the debt is reflected in Margaret's letter of March 27, 1624, in Greys/8. His revelation to Mater and Catharina of the plan for a pilgrimage is from Mater's letter of March 28, 1624, in Greys/8.

Chapter 7

Mater's letter on the sister who wanted to go on pilgrimage to Laken is undated, but given the dean's and archbishop's responses to the case around early January, this request must have been made in December 1624 (the dean's letter in Greys/8, January 8, 1625; Boonen's in Greys/5, January 2; Catharina Rijckeboer's response to the same case is in Greys/8, January 14, 1625). Hovius's rejections are in his journal, AAM, CM, 10; June 29, 1618, he turned down a magistrate of Antwerp writing on behalf of his daughter who was a religious in Vorst, and during 1618 and 1619 he turned down numerous requests by the troublesome sisters of Groot Bijgaarden to leave for various reasons.

P. Numan, *Historie vande Miraculen die onlancx In grooten getale ghebeurt zyn, door die intercessie ende voorbidden van die Heylighe Maget* (Leuven, 1604), was one of the most popular summaries of the miracles at the shrine, but the scholar Lipsius also busied himself with this kind of miracle-recounting. The account of the possessed girl in Mechelen is in P. Croon, *Onse Lieve Vrauwe van Hanswyck* . . . (Mechelen, 1670), 162–63.

Margaret's response to Boonen is dated March 27, 1624, in Greys/8. Mater's response is in the same file, dated a day later. When she wrote about the scandal that might befall the convent "once again" if Margaret went to the shrine, Mater may have been alluding to Margaret's earlier departure from Bethlehem, back around 1615, at which time she could have visited Scherpenheuvel. Anna Vignarola's history of 1672 suggests that Margaret had gone twice to Scherpenheuvel, though she gives no clear chronology of the trips, only that both took place before 1626. Since Anna was not in the convent during Margaret's first exile, the dating may be in doubt, especially since Anna wrote fifty years after the fact. But perhaps this trip of 1624 was Margaret's second; if so, then the scene I describe would have occurred first years before, with much modification, since eight or nine years earlier construction of the shrine was even further from completion.

On the publicness of exorcisms, see D. P. Walker, *Unclean Spirits* (Philadelphia, 1981), and especially the recent A. M. Walker and E. H. Dickerman, "'A Woman Under the Influence:' A Case of Alleged Possession in Sixteenth-Century France," *SCJ* 22/3 (1991) 535–54. People did often know about what went on inside convents, so a nun outside was especially easy to learn about. In Greys/10, a 1662 document shows the concern that the friars of Leuven had if the archbishop released them from their management of Bethlehem—their reputations would suffer. Thus Mater Barbara's worries about public exhibit of Bethlehem's problems were hardly unfounded.

Fear of bandits is noted by J. Sumption, *Pilgrimage* (Totowa, NJ, 1975), 175, while fear of out-of-the-way places and the woman who became infested on the road to Scherpenheuvel are reviewed by F. Vanhemelryck, *Heksenprocessen in de Nederlanden* (Leuven, 1982), 105. The length of Catharina's stay in Diest is inferred from her letter of December 6, when she notes the "three months" she had been back in the convent. Margaret's stay at the hospital of Diest is mentioned in several letters written after her return by Bouckaert and by the sisters of Bethlehem, who were trying to send her back there (Greys/8).

The connection of remote places to the devil is mentioned by J. Klaits, *Servants of Satan* (Bloomington, 1985), 62, and Vanhemelryck, *Heksenproces-sen*, 114. Miracles on remote mountains and bold miracles near heretics are recorded by Numan, *Historie*, 16, 23. The everyday familiarity of the urban parish is discussed by W. A. Christian, *Local Religion in Sixteenth Century Spain* (Princeton, 1981), in his chapter on chapels and shrines, which also discusses the attractions of otherness and distance related to a shrine. Christian further notes the general abilities of Mary, points out the connection between grace and place, and reviews what was needed to make a shrine widely famous; especially 93–94, 98, 123. Sumption also treats how a shrine grew in reputation; *Pilgrimage*, 149 ff. Peter Burke discusses the extraordinary nature of the pilgrimage journey, and the different rituals that might have been engaged in; "Rituals of Healing," in *The Historical Anthropology of Early Modern Italy* (Cambridge, 1987).

Sumption, *Pilgrimage*, has much to say on the powers of shrines, while K. Thomas, *Religion and the Decline of Magic* (New York, 1971), notes their powers to heal the physically as well as the spiritually ill. The sketch of Scherpenheuvel is drawn not only from Numan, *Historie,* but also A. Boni, *Scherpenheuvel: Basiliek en gemeente in het kader van de vaderlandse geschiede-nis* (Antwerp, 1953), and T. Morren, "Bastion op de 'scherpenheuvel,' " in *Spectrum Atlas van Historische Plaatsen in de Lage Landen,* eds. A. F. Manning and M. de Vroede (Utrecht, 1981), 125 ff. For the tale of another shrine, the Miraculous Virgin of Halle, who fended off enemy troops and cannonballs, though outnumbered 10,000 to 200, see Balduinus Iunius, *'t Huys der Wijsheyt* (Antwerp, 1613).

My sketch of Bouckaert is drawn from Boni, *Scherpenheuvel*; P. Declerck, "De priesteropleiding in het bisdom Ieper (1626–1717)," *Handelingen van het Genootschap voor Geschiedenis te Brugge* 105 (1968): 56–59; L. Jadin, "Procès d'Information," 30–32; L. Ceyssens, "Joost Bouckaert," in *NBW* (Brussels, 1966), vol. 4, cols. 97–99; W. Verleyen, *Dom Benedictus van Haef-ten, Proost van Affligem, 1588–1648* (Brussels, 1983), 191–92; and from manuscript sources. Bouckaert's rather sparsely recorded visitations as dean may be found in AAM, Collection Dekenale Verslagen/Diest, in the years after 1616. His complaints about reluctant donors may be found in ARA, RSA, 2042/1, while his work against the heretical image-makers and on confirming the miracles at the shrine is in 1947/2. Bouckaert's family even had connections to the Grey Sisters, noted by P. Hildebrand, "Le Couvent des Soeurs Grises à Iseghem," *NF* 2 (1919): 8–55, and in AAM, CK, Diest Greys/1.

The devotional works I discuss were not chosen at random, but represent those that I thought had at least a good chance of being read by a nun of Margaret's standing and learning. A glance through the *Bibliotheca Catho-*

lica Neerlandica Impressa, 1500–1727 (The Hague, 1954) reveals that between 1605 and 1648 (Margaret's years in the convent), there were 5,208 printings or editions of Catholic works, many in the vernacular, and this list is certainly incomplete. There were more in the vernacular toward 1650, but before that time there were still plenty to choose from. This figure suggests how difficult it is to speculate what someone might have read and what thoughts might have moved her. The Greys left no library inventory, which still offers no guarantee of what any individual read, so I had to rely on those which were written or translated into the vernacular, which seemed directed at religious specifically or to the religious as well as lay public, which may have belonged to a house of nuns or been written for them, and which give some evidence—such as multiple printings—of at least some popularity. I also chose many that had a Franciscan connection—though it will be recalled that Margaret did not get along with her Franciscan confessors and it's possible that she avoided reading anything by someone of her order.

Those included are P. van Alcantara, OFM, *Instructie om wel te mediteren, met meer andere Gheestelycke leeringhen ende devote gebeden* (Mechelen, 1618; at least eleven Dutch printings to 1707, dedicated to the Clares of Mechelen, and owned at one time by a seventeenth-century beguine named Catharina); Bernardin de Balbano, OFM Cap, *Theylich Mysterie Van die Gheesselinghe ons heeren Iesu Christi. Ghestelt in seven Meditatien, voor elcken dach vander weke* (Leuven, 1607; four Dutch editions by the early seventeenth century); Fulvius Androtius, SJ, *Een Devoot Memoriael, Van die heylighe Mysterien vander doot ende Passie ons Salichmakers ende verlossers, Jesu Christi* (Leuven, 1607); F. Vervoort, OFM, *De Woestijne des Heeren, leerende hoe een goet kersten mensche, Christum d'licht der warheyt sal navolghen in dese duyster Woestijne des bedroefder wereldts* . . . (Antwerp, 1613; twelve Dutch printings by 1650; this one belonged to the infirmary of the Small Beguinage, city not specified, and before that to a certain widow); Alphonsus van Madrid, OFM, *Een gulden Boecxken ghenoemt De Conste om Godt Oprechtelyck te Dienen* (Leuven, 1607; five Dutch editions in the seventeenth century); G. Spoelberch, OFM, *Sommighe Meditatien ende Devote Oeffeninghen, opde merckelijckste Poincten vande goetheyt Godts* . . . (Leuven, 1615; one other Dutch printing); C. Thielemans, *Cort Verhael van het Leven der Heylighen van S. Franciscus Oirden met Haer Levende Figuren wt Diversche historie scryvers genomen* (Den Bosch, 1620); for the other books by Thielemans see B. de Troeyer, OFM, "De Brusselaar P. Cornelius Thielmans: Reanimator van het Franciscanisme Tijdens de Contrareformatie," *FR* 43 (1988): 143 ff.; J. Ferraria, OFM, *Vande dry gheloften der Religien, alle Religieuse personen seer oerbaerlyck* (Mechelen, 1618, two other Dutch printings); L. Pinelli (Carthusian), *Den Costelycken Spieghel der Religieuse Volmaecktheydt, Leerende hoe een iegelijc Religieus verbonden is daer toe te arbeyden* (Antwerp, 1605; mostly published in French or Latin); *Contemplationes Idiote, overgheset by Jan van Alen OFM, Pater van die Claren Susters Antwerp* (Antwerp, 1607). Bonaventure's ABCs are appended to his *Soliloquium oft Alleen-*

spraecke des H. tSeraphischen Leeraer Bonaventure (Antwerp, 1624). Margaret's need to steel herself in all three vows is reflected in the 1625 statutes of the Grey Sisters of Diest, probably written by Bouckaert and approved by Boonen, which were copied in AAM, CK, Greys Zoutleeuw/1, no. 1. The excerpts quoted from the penitential psalms are from Psalm 6:2–3, 6 (part of the first), Psalm 38:4 (part of the third), and Psalms 38:19 and 102:8 (part of the third and fifth).

Other contemporary devotional works that helped me greatly in trying to re-create a piece of the mental world of the time include Marchant's works for the third order, cited toward the end of the note to chapter 2, Evangelista's tracts, cited near the end of the note to chapter 6, I Balsamo, *Onderwys om Wel te Bidden ende te Mediteren, met Treffelycke Leeringen tot een Volkomen kloosterlyck leven* (Antwerp, 1607; mostly French editions); J. van der Putte, OFM, *Claren Spiegel der Waerachtiger Christelijcker Maechden* . . . (Antwerp, 1608; seven Dutch printings 1550–1608): Andreas de Soto, OFM, *De Schole van de Eenicheydt des Menschs met God* (Antwerp, 1616; dedicated to the abbess of the Poor Clares in Madrid); Bonaventure, OFM, *Spieghel der Goeder Manieren veur de Novitie, dat is, Proef-ionghers der Minder-broeders Ordene* (Antwerp, 1605); F. Vervoort, OFM, *Bruydegoms Mantelken, vanden inwendigen navolghen des levens ende des Cruycen ons Liefs Heeren Jesu Christi* (Antwerp, 1607; nine Dutch printings, and belonging to the Clares of Brussels "to read at the table," a note written in a late seventeenth- or eighteenth-century hand); B. de Canfeld, OFM Cap, *Den Reghel der Volmaecktheyt* (Antwerp, 1622; two other Dutch printings, but a famous work); *De Leere der Religieusen Eerst ghemaeckt door den Godt Saligen Dionisius ghenoemt Cartusianus* (Brussels, 1626; dedicated to Maria Taye, Abbess of Vorst); A. de Guevera, OFM, *Leeringhe der Religieusen ende Godtvruchtighe Oeffeninghen van Deughdelijcke Menschen* (Antwerp, 1627; four Dutch printings, dedicated to an Abbot of Ninove); J. Raps, OFM, *Het Leven vanden H. Vader Franciscus ende der vernaemste Heylighen Salighen, ende Godtvruchtighen van sijnen derden Reghel* (Brussels, 1655; one other edition, but of interest because this man was once the confessor of Bethlehem; dedicated to two lay women of the third order); B. Iunius, OFM, *'T Huys der Wijsheyt* (Antwerp, 1613; the author was confessor of the third order in Antwerp); a few others will come up as well in discussion of subsequent topics.

In a later letter Bouckaert noted that Margaret had not communed since she left for Bethlehem from Diest, thus implying that while in Diest/Scherpenheuvel Margaret had in fact confessed and taken the Eucharist; December 28, 1624, Greys/8. The plan to allow her to stay in Diest is inferred from letters written around the late summer of 1624, when there was talk of Margaret's returning to Bethlehem; see Greys/10, visitation of August 20, 1624; also Mater Barbara's letter in the late summer that Margaret was healed, and her suggestion that Margaret stay in Diest; Greys/8, undated, but I put it around August or September, when Catharina came back to Bethlehem, and since there was no other mention of Margaret's status between August and November.

The famous image of furiously raging together is from the book of Isaiah.

Chapter 8

The sworn testimony of Barbara Beli, recorded in the hand of Archdeacon Peter van der Wiel and very shakily signed by Beli herself (as if she had learned to write her name but nothing else), may be found in Greys/8, dated June 5, 1624. It's not clear whether Beli and Van der Wiel were in the same room for this interview—probably not. In most cases, discussion between nun and interviewer would have occurred at the grille. The 1613 statutes of the Regular Canonesses of the Holy Sepulchre specified that the nuns were to confess through a covered grille, so that confessor and penitent couldn't even see each other (M. Hereswitha, "Reguliere Kanunikessen van het Heilig-Graf," *OGE* 50/4 (December 1976): 401–2, 395). Serious matters, such as exorcism, were of course performed with the parties in the same room, and perhaps grave interviews might have been as well—the visitors could enter the cloister, under extraordinary circumstances, as long as they were accompanied by other nuns.

Catharina Rijckeboer's assessment of Beli is contained in her letter of November 7, 1624, Greys/8; also December 6, 1624. That Beli was allowed to take the habit is inferred from her interview for the novitiate on July 13, 1624, AAM, CK, Generalia, "Catalogus virginum quae in regione Lovaniensi examinata sunt ad professionem anno 1605."

Guardian Johan Cranendonck's June 25 letter to Mater Barbara is contained in Greys/10. Background to the tradition of being reluctant to confess women is plentiful. As with the study of witchcraft or possession, one should begin with attitudes toward women in general. One stunning example of the sometimes bloody consequences of unflattering attitudes about women, held even by women themselves, is discussed by J. T. Schulenburg, "The Heroics of Virginity: Brides of Christ and Sacrificial Mutilation," in *Women in the Middle Ages and the Renaissance,* ed. M. B. Rose (Syracuse, 1986), 29–72. More specific attitudes on the confessing of women are found in most order histories, many of which I cite near the end of the notes to the foreword. The examples of women as temptresses are discussed in *Helse en Hemelse Vrouwen* (Utrecht, 1988). Borromeo laid down specific, strict requirements for confessing women, reviewed in F. Vanhemelryck, *Heksenprocessen in de Nederlanden* (Leuven, 1982), and J. Delumeau, *Sin and Fear: The Emergence of a Western Guilt Culture* (New York, 1990; translated from the French), 164–65.

Bilinkoff's argument about the desire of confessors to be identified with Holy Women is in her "Confessors, Penitents and the Construction of Identities in Early Modern Avila," in *Culture and Identity in Early Modern Europe* (Ann Arbor, forthcoming), as well as her "A Spanish Prophetess and Her Patrons: The Case of Maria Santo Domingo," *SCJ,* 23/1 (Spring, 1992): 21–34.

The decoration of the Franciscan convent of Leuven has been uncovered by S. van Ruysevelt, "De Franciskaanse Kerken: De stichtingen van de dertiende eeuw (vervolg): IX. Leuven," *FR* 27/3 (1972): 107–21, and J. Baetens, "Minderbroederskloosters in de Zuidelijke Nederlanden, Kloosterlexicon: 44. Leuven," *FR* 42/2 (1987): 81–105 especially. For the tasks of the Franciscan house in Leuven, one can read Baetens, "Kloosterlexicon," and B. De Troeyer, "Bio-bibliografie van de Minderbroeders in de Nederlanden, 17de eeuw, Voorstudies: 3. Arnold Ab Ischa (Aert van Overijse)," *FR* 32/1–2 (1977): 3–38.

One possible motivation for a confessor to take on the service of a house—namely, a good fee—was not operative in the case of Bethlehem. The friars knew they could not expect the kind of 200-florin annual fee that was paid, for instance, to the confessor of the Cistercian nunnery in Aarschot; in AAM, CK, Aarschot St. Niklaasberg/7, notes of 1631, 1635. Hovius's requests to the friars are cited in the note to chapter 4, but to review, they are from his journal on July 26 and November 5, 1618, and January 3, 1620. The annual rotation practiced by the Leuven Franciscans in Bethlehem is inferred from a 1624 letter by Mater Barbara (Greys/8, undated but from the contents this is clearly from 1624), in which she states that they had had six confessors in six years (since the time of Joos's fall). It may be that the figures are coincidental, but I think not. Mater Barbara's 1622 letter about early problems with the system in Bethlehem is dated June 14 and contained in Greys/10. On the back are various doodles, made by someone at the episcopal palace who needed scratch paper.

Benedict XV's declaration about the need for confessors of nunneries to be approved by the local bishop is discussed with other pertinent issues in H. L. De Boer, "De Verlening van de Biechtjurisdiktie in de Germania Inferior van de 17de en 18de eeuw," *FR* 28/1 (1973): 63–125. This particular bull was not allowed to be proclaimed in Spanish territories and thus was not enforceable in the Low Countries, but its spirit must have frustrated the friars, among other orders, and is reflective of the controversy during the seventeenth and other centuries over the rights of the male orders versus those of the bishops.

Mater Barbara's letter telling Boonen the news of the reluctant confessors is dated July 18, 1624, in Greys/10. Boonen's willingness to hear the opinions of the sisters on jurisdiction is inferred from the two letters by Maria Joos and Anna Marcelis, which have all the looks of invited responses (Maria's letter is dated July 1624, and Anna's is undated but is about precisely the same issues—both in Greys/10), and from his sending of a visitor to Bethlehem in August to discuss the question. The visitation summary of August 20, 1624 is contained in Greys/10 as well. The negative response of the two potential confessors is noted by Lucius, August 21, 1624, Greys/10.

News of Margaret's healing probably came to Boonen from another source, but Mater Noosen repeated it anyway in her undated letter of 1624. This letter also contains the sentiment that Margaret needed to have a good penance. The petition of the sisters is in Greys/8 and is dated August 21,

1624, the day after the visitation and the same day as Dean Lucius's written report to Boonen, to which he attached his visitation summary. Bouckaert's efforts are revealed in a letter from him to Boonen, dated September 27, 1624, in Greys/8.

Chapter 9

Description of the road between Diest and Leuven is taken largely from G. Hanegreefs, *De steenweg Diest-Leuven (1777–1797)* (Leuven, 1980), which provides background on conditions before 1700 as well.

Margaret's feelings just before her return are disclosed in part by her friend Catharina Rijckeboer in a letter to Archbishop Boonen, December 17, 1624, Greys/8, in which she noted Margaret's sensation of "inward sweetness." Much of the rest of this scenario is my creation, from synthesis of various sources. On how Margaret was able to arrange the trip to Leuven, and the discussion of money by Bouckaert, see his letter to Boonen of November 6, 1624, in Greys/8. Margaret's probable rituals at the sounding of a bell or the hearing of certain words—rituals not confined to her order—are inferred from the statutes of her house, found in Greys/1.

For the age of portresses, see specifically here R. Weemaes, *Visitationes omnium ecclesiarum, monasteriorum, hospitalium et aliorum locorum ruralium institutae per Reverendissimum dominum Carolum Masium (1609–1612)* (Gent, 1987), 65, Sister Judoca Maps. That Aleidis was portress in Bethlehem is my guess, based on the fact that in the 1616 visitation she held that office, that she was still capable of doing so by 1624, and that Maria Joos, the next known portress, was not yet in office. The description of events at the moment of Margaret's return are in another letter from Catharina to Boonen, November 7, 1624, Greys/8. She noted, among other details, that Margaret arrived at the convent "in the evening."

The practice of ringing the bells three times after Complines in honor of the Virgin was, according to C. Thielemans's *Heylighen van S. Franciscus Oirden* (Den Bosch, 1620), begun by Bonaventure and was by Margaret's time done "all over the church."

Joost Bouckaert's letter to Boonen is dated November 6, 1624, Greys/8. Catharina's letter is from November 7, Greys/8. Margaret's letter is undated, but given the contents and the—even for Margaret—unusually overwhelming sense of grief, I date it in early November 1624, soon after her return.

Lucius's letter to Boonen is dated December 18, 1624, Greys/8. Two other letters of Catharina's, besides the November 7 response, are dated December 6 and 17, Greys/8; they are used in various parts of the chapter. On recluses, for a third-order example named Elisabeth de Honsem, see J. Cruls, *Le S. Sacrament* (Liege, 1881), 186–87. Requirements for the life of a recluse are contained in the statutes issued for that "order" by Hovius, in AAM, CK, Generalia, Kluizenaers, undated (before 1620).

Mater wrote several letters in this period, also used in various parts of the chapter: November 13, December 13, the specially requested December 17 letter, and another on December 30. Bouckaert's account of his visit with Margaret is from December 28, 1624, Greys/8. Margaret wrote two undated letters to Boonen at this time, probably between December 15 and 31, given the events described. She also wrote to Bouckaert on December 26, to express her usual concern that one of her earlier letters to Boonen had not reached its destination, for she had received no speedy response. These are all in Greys/8.

I should note here, in discussing Margaret's distress and where she might have turned, that Mater speaks in one December letter (December 17) of Margaret and "her brother the Jesuit," but nowhere else in any of the documents is he mentioned and if it was true, he was a very indifferent brother; Margaret always complained about being alone, gave the impression that no one visited her, and implied that she relied for financial or emotional support upon Boonen and Bouckaert alone. It may well be that Mater used the "brother" phrase figuratively, or even derisively, since many Maters disliked outside confessors and since she discusses this "brother" Jesuit in the same letter that mentions a Jesuit confessor who failed to show for his appointment with Margaret.

The letter of Barbara Beli's patroness, Barbara van Herssen of Brussels, is in Greys/8; it is undated but given the events described, it must have been written in November or December of 1624.

On the question of poor health—Catharina herself had a cousin not allowed to profess in Bethlehem because of illness; letter to Boonen, September 23, 1626, Greys/1. Boonen's response to these various crises is contained in a letter of January 2, 1625, addressed to Dean Lucius, Greys/5.

The petition of the sisters to Boonen has not survived. That it was sent is inferred from Boonen's letter; that about half the sisters were involved is inferred from the struggle around Barbara Beli. Lucius commented as well on Margaret's resolve to leave, in his letter of January 8, 1625, in Greys/8.

The practice of changing Maters or of Maters volunteering to resign is discussed in many sources, including C. Vleeschouwers, "Joes van Dormael's Kroniek der Hervorming Binnen de Brabantse Cistercienserinnenabdij Hertogendal (1488), *OGE* 47/2 (June 1973): 173–220, especially 192. M. Cloet, ed., *Itinerarium visitationum Antonii Triest, episcopi gandavensis (1623–1654)* (Leuven, 1976), contains many examples of Maters being removed or moved.

Catharina wrote two letters criticizing Mater Barbara, one from December, the second dated January 16, 1625, in Greys/8.

Barbara does not seem to have been ill before—as late as January 22 she sent off a routine letter to the archbishop; and Catharina, writing on January 16, would never have chastised so harshly had Mater already been seriously sick. No doubt the stress of her position—especially during the past two months—affected her. Bouckaert's letter on Mater's last hours and the state of the house is from January 24, 1625, Greys/8. Barbara's final letter is dated January 22, 1625, Greys/8.

Chapter 10

The sense of "burden" as a message of doom is from various texts in Isaiah, such as 13:1.

For elections and shifts in power at the uppermost echelons of the church, I was struck by L. Von Pastor, *History of the Popes,* 40 vols. (London, 1932–50), and L. Von Ranke, *History of the Popes During the last Four Centuries*, 3 vols. (London, 1913). The pattern was imitated at such small places as Bethlehem.

That Adriana appointed her three friends to office is revealed by Margaret in her letter of February 3, 1628, Greys/8. On possible motives for voting for this candidate or that, see C. B. De Ridder, "Les Élection Abbatiales dans les Pays-Bas avant le dix-neuvième siècle," *AHEB* 5 (1868): 315–28. At an election held among the Black Sisters of Mechelen, in AAM, CK, Black Sisters Mechelen/4, January 9, 1629, one sister cast her vote for another because she knew "no one else who could read and write so well," another voted for a candidate because she was "kindly rather than choleric," a third because she was impartial and "for the common good," while one named a sister who was "somewhat inconstant" and who, it was hoped, would improve much through the holding of office. Another named a woman who since the last visitation had "corrected herself in regard to drinking and irritability." Some sisters might not have voted at all: "that simply doesn't interest me," said one nun more than once over the years. One Grey Sister who wouldn't vote, named Maria van den Laer, is mentioned in AAM, CK, Grey Sisters Diest/2, 1652 election; she did the same thing the next time around. An account of another interesting election may be found in AAM, CK, Begijnhof Aarschot/2, September 7, 1628.

Van der Wiel's assessment of Margaret is in Greys/8, May 17, 1626, probably addressed to Boonen. Boonen's visit with Margaret is recorded in Boonen's agenda, AAM, CA, Boonen/186, June 9–10, 1626. See Greys/1 for the statutes of Bethlehem and the rule of the Grey Sisters.

For treatment of the problem and history of reform, see especially the notes to the foreword. But also, on different meanings of reform, see Vleeschouwers, "Kroniek der Hervorming" (cited at the end of the note to chapter 9), on the Cistercian monastery of Hertogendael, 173. Jodi Bilinkoff, *The Avila of St. Teresa* (Ithaca, NY, 1989), 37, treats the notions of rebuilding and endowing monasteries as aspects of Reform. N. Rubinstein, "Lay Patronage and Observant Reform in Fifteenth-Century Florence," in *Christianity and the Renaissance,* eds. T. Verdon and J. Henderson (Syracuse, 1990), 64, reviews the sense of reform as going back to something. The same article focuses on the frequent lay impetus behind monastic reform. J. C. Olin, *Catholic Reform* (New York, 1990), treats reform as a return to primitive religion. Ph. Schmitiz, *Histoire de l'ordre de Saint-Benoît* (Maredsous, 1948), 238, notes that from the twelfth century on, any serious monastic reform for women included *clausura*. The first formal vow of *clausura* was taken, ironically enough, by the Clares in 1263, and other orders began to incorporate such a vow as well. Some of the monastic reforms of Trent that would have sounded familiar, at least in concept, to medieval religious were the call for renewed visitations, avoiding gifts from friends, and improving the keeping of accounts, all present in the works of Eckenstein, Power, and Lawrence, cited in the review of medieval studies in the note to the foreword. Again, the key difference with previous periods of reform may have been the general extent of reform in the air and the emphases of Trent. These included the provision of an extraordinary confessor two or three times a year, absolute freedom of profession, enforcement of canonical ages of abbesses and novices and profession, an interview for profession, the institution of a firm novitiate, a prohibition against cutting hair until profession (to promote freedom to leave), and so on. The biggest emphasis of course was on *clausura,* either in reinstituting or in establishing for the first time. The 1607 Council of Mechelen pronounced a dismal assessment of the observation of *clausura,* recorded in P.F.X. de Ram, *belgicum,* 4 vols. (Mechelen, 1828–1858), vol. 1, 254.

If Bethlehem possessed a set of statutes previous to 1626, which it probably did, it has not survived. We must assume that not all particulars changed, but some important items clearly had.

Catharina's letter on Margaret's mood: Greys/11, September 23, 1626, and December 6, 1627. Mater's is from Greys/9, March 15 or 19, 1628. Boonen's note on his attempts to procure Evangelista is in AAM, CA, Boonen/186, Agenda, November 12, 1627. P. Hildebrand, *De Capucijnen in de Nederlanden en het prinsbisdom Luik,* 11 vols. (Antwerp, 1945–56), vol. 5, chapter 8, tells us that Evangelista went to Tervuren at the time, thus explaining why he couldn't be counted on to help Margaret once more. Her request to Bouckaert for a picture of Joseph is in the letter of February 3, 1628. Knowledge of Joseph's special powers was widespread, and made more so by De Soto's *Life of Joseph* (Brussels, 1615; 2d edition 1628), which discusses Joseph's gifts at withstanding temptations of the flesh. Teresa took Joseph as her special patron and claimed that he saved her from many perils of her honor. Gerson said that his control was so perfect that the spark and prick of fleshly desire was completely bound within him, from the time he married the Virgin. His control was not the result of old age, as often supposed, said De Soto, for he was the most handsome person alive after Christ and the Virgin. He was also exceedingly patient, which Margaret would have valued.

That Margaret could not write when she entered the convent is evidenced in her signing a wobbly "X" to her profession statement in 1606, cited at the beginning of the note to chapter 2.

Chapter 11

Perhaps the best general survey of many of the topics discussed in chapters 11 through 14 is to be found in G. Reynes, *Couvents de femmes* (Paris, 1987). Some of the conditions she discusses are unique to France, but many were widespread.

Margaret's letter of 1628, the letters of the other sisters in chapter 16, the interview summary of Lucius, and Van der Wiel's notes on them all are in Greys/3. See the notes to chapter 1 for an estimate of how long Margaret's letter was in the making. I find forty-three different groupings in the thirty-two-page letter, usually indicated by an abrupt change of topic and physical break. For the sake of convenience I've called each a "session," though this may be grandiose, since some may have been divided by minutes rather than hours or days. Besides the two long opening sessions in which she presented her basic complaints (nearly eight pages), only three others approached one or two pages; the rest were less than a page, sometimes as short as a few lines. Margaret reveals this method herself well into the letter (session 8): "That which I haven't written well or have written too long, please forgive me." Then the explanation: "I write a bit here and there, and don't have the time to go back and check what I've already written."

Margaret's suggestion that Adriana was very young when appointed bursaress is confirmed by a copy of a document in ARA, KAB, 15307 (an eighteenth-century *cartularium*), which Adriana is said to have signed in 1613 as bursaress, making her no older than twenty-four at the time.

Mater's obligations in Bethlehem are set out in chapter 2 of the house statutes. The obligations of the sisters toward Mater are discussed in chapter 3 of the statutes. The analogy to Noah's ark is from A. de Guevera, OFM, *Leeringhe der Religieusen ende Godtvruchtighe Oeffininghen* (Antwerp, 1627).

The sisters were to meet weekly in chapter and receive instruction and discipline from Mater. This is detailed in chapter 19 of the statutes. After prayers all fell prostrate to the ground and kissed it and made a common confession of guilt, received a common penance from Mater, and then listened to any announcements or thoughts of Mater. Mater would then hand out individual punishments and ask that person to kneel where seated or in certain cases to come to the middle of the floor and kneel in front of the whole community. Ferraria's comments on obedience are from his *Vande dry gheloften der Religien, alle Religieuse personen seer oerbaerlyck* (Mechelen, 1618). The last quote on obedience is from AAM, CK, Thabor Mechelen/4, April 28, 1600, ordinances by Hovius on obedience and reverence.

Teresa's fears in J. Bilinkoff, *The Avila of St. Teresa* (Ithaca, NY, 1989), 131; and A. Lottin's in *Lille, Citadelle de la Contre-Réforme (1598–1668)?* (Paris, 1984), 110. The severity in Mechelen of violation of impartiality is discussed in C. Harline and E. Put, "A Bishop in the Cloisters: The Visitations of Mathias Hovius," *SCJ* 22/4 (Winter 1991), especially in table 2, showing that this was the topic most often tied to strict language or specific punishments. Boonen and Van der Wiel on factions: AAM, CK, Thabor Mechelen/4, *determinatio* of 1632.

Examples of generational differences in the divisions around Mater may be found in AAM, CK, Black Sisters Mechelen/41, visitations of 1615 and 1618, and AAM, CK, Bethanie Brussels/4, visitation of March 1590. See J. Brown, *Immodest Acts* (Oxford, 1986), 89, on the importance and perpetuation of social relations inside the convent, and 90, on the concern of authorites for rivalries and favorites.

The title "Mother Martha" is from Marchant's statutes of 1626 for third-order women; "Co-Mother" is from Catharina herself, in her 1625 letter on Barbara Noosen. Chapters 6 and 8 of the Bethlehem statutes contain the instructions regarding novices. See Brown, *Immodest Acts,* 89–90, on the knifewielder.

The tasks and status of the vicaress are treated in chapter 4 of the house statutes. One manuscript source that cites the not-uncommon rivalry between Mater and Co-Mater is AAM, CK, Black Sisters Leuven/32, visitation of 1583.

Tasks and status of the lay sisters are discussed in chapter 18 of the house statutes of Bethlehem.

M. Hereswitha, "Reguliere Kanunnikessen van het Heilig-Graf," *OGE* 50/4 (December 1976): 424, notes the horrible things awaiting those nuns who died in possession of property. Boonen declared in 1626 that a weakness among the Black Sisters of Mechelen was private property: AAM, CK, Black Sisters Mechelen/39, 1626 ordinance, which notes that private property was outlawed by Hovius in 1592. Chapter 2 of the 1626 house statutes of Bethlehem discusses briefly private property there, which wasn't much different from the requirements elsewhere.

On income: Lesken Nijns's annuity, AAM, CM, 6/234–234v, September 10, 1608. Susanna Haecht's gift, Greys/6, October 13, 1628, in Catharina Rijckeboer's hand. AAM, CM, 8/fol. 144–45, recounts the erection of a new monastery for English nuns at St. Monica's in Leuven, and for their support, the 12 nuns received annually 1,100 florins, a figure perhaps higher than in many places, though whether this included communal expenses or not (such as paying a confessor) is unclear. Later in the seventeenth century 150 florins in grants for three unnamed sisters were made to Bethlehem; see Greys/5, undated sheaf of papers—account book is too glorified a term. And see RAG, CB, M211, Begijnhof Aalst, Account of 1619, for the 100-florin annuity that served as an entry fee of that establishment. The Rich Clares of Brussels brought lavish dowries for the convent, but always private annuities for themselves, usually around 50 florins; M.-J. Juvyns, "La Communauté des Riches-Claires de Bruxelles de 1585 à 1796," 10 (1965): 207. G. A. Brucker, "Monasteries, Friaries, and Nunneries in Quattrocento Florence," in *Christianity and the Renaissance*, eds. T. Verdon and J. Henderson (Syracuse, 1990), notes the combination of common funds and individual patrimonies in Florence.

Bethanie, AAM, CK, Bethanie Brussels/4, visitation of March 1590, on Sister Lysken. Hovius's decree against private property: AAM, CK, Thabor Mechelen/4, 1592 ordinances. Marie Switten brought to Bethlehem in 1597 any goods that would remain after the death of the widow of her mother's father, but it was an amount no one could guess at; Greys/5, January 22, 1597. Ferraria, Guevera, and Alcantara are cited in the list of devotional works at the end of the note to chapter 7. (Teresa wrote the introduction to Alcantara's work.) L. J. Lekai, *The Cistercians: Ideals and Reality* (Kent, OH, 1977), 368, wrote on their approach to privation. Greys/8, contains a letter from a certain Barbara van Craesbeek, probably from the second half of the seventeenth century, which recounts the big arguments over poverty in the house at that time, the one murmuring, the other taking as she pleased. Bishop Triest also found many complainers about the frugality in convents, which was often considered a motivator to hold private property; M. Cloet, ed., *Itinerarium visitationum Antonii Triest, episcopi gandavensis (1623–1654)* (Leuven, 1976), May 21, 1624, Black Sisters Pamele; April 26, 1627, Black Sisters Oudenaarde; October 18, 1643, Black Sisters Dendermonde.

Chapter 12 of the house statutes of Bethlehem discusses the customs of the refectory, practices that Margaret barely alludes to. In general, there was to have been as much silence and praying as there was eating (though one assigned nun always read a devotional work aloud). The table was to be set in advance with salt, bread, and beer, and the pots as clean "as necessary." The servers were to be sure that no one lacked and that each was served lovingly and kindly. The cook was to be faithful to the convent and promote the common welfare according to her ability, being careful to avoid favoritism but giving each what was needed, without murmuring and with a kind countenance, while in return the sisters were to be content with the common portion.

On the problem of storytelling, see AAM, CK, Bethanie Brussels/4, visitation of March 1590.

Excesses of medieval monks who went from factionalism to violence are discussed by J. E. Sayers, "Violence in the Medieval Cloister," *Journal of Ecclesiastical History* 41 (1990): 533–42.

Chapter 12

On the elusive question of how much of the house's income came from which source, see R. Devos, *Vie Religieuse Féminine et Société. L'origine sociale des Visitandines d'Annecy aux XVIIe et XVIIIe siècles* (Annecy, 1973), 13, who notes that in Annecy dowries made up the vast bulk of support in convents, given the want of alms received from outsiders. The situation may have been the same in Bethlehem, but here it appears that as much effort was spent on recruiting the goodwill of all kinds of benefactors, blessed with daughters or not.

P. Hildebrand, *De Capucijnen in de Nederlanden en het prinsbisdom Luik,* 11 vols. (Antwerp, 1945–56), vol. 5, 332, discusses the strictness of the Capuchins in regard to fixed incomes and foundations. Most of the works on the Franciscan Grey Sisters, cited in the note to chapter 2, discuss the poverty—voluntary or not—of these women in the early modern period.

For a long list of expenses, see AAM, CK, St. Niklaasberg Aarschot/ Register of Anna Maria Pelmans, especially the list from 1634; RAG, CB, M211/Beguinage Aalst, Account book of 1619. Mass expenses at Bethlehem are from Greys/5, undated account book, in a hand from the second half of the seventeenth century. Expenses of St. Gertrude's are in AAM, CK, St. Gertrude's Leuven/9, for 1607. On the comparison of the Grey Sisters of

Isegem to St. Gertrude's, see P. Hildebrand, "Le Couvent des Soeurs Grises à Isegem," *NF* 2 (1919): 40, and the file on Gertrude's.

The examples of ruin and poverty are from G. van de Castele, "Grauwe Zusters of Penitenten-Rekollektinen te Nevele, 1502–1784," *HLN* 9 (1978): 179; AAM, CK, Rosendaal Cistercianessen, volume containing chronology; B. De Troeyer, "Bio-bibliografie van de Minderbroeders in de Nederlanden, 17de eeuw, Voorstudies: 6. Andreas de Soto," *FR* 37/3 (1982): 73.

On poverty in Bethlehem, note that by 1626 the Greys made almost exactly the same plea to the Privy Council as they had in 1594, claiming that their house was "threatening ruin" and that they needed 8,000 florins at least, according to construction estimates. The sisters in fact received 36 florins after the 1594 request, but this was a pittance; ARA, GR, 1125, dated August and September 1594; the 1626 plea, ARA, GR, 1125, October 2, 1626.

Bethlehem's list of services may be found in Greys/7, undated list but composed in the hand of Catharina Rijckeboer and undoubtedly accompanying a letter of 1630 by Adriana on the topic. From this one major clue to their economic standing before 1645, it's clear that the Greys had no gift for management. In most cases the capital endowment for a given service was unaccounted for or sharply reduced—partly because of emergency needs, certainly thanks to poor records. Complaints about poor record keeping in convents are frequent, such as in Bishop Triest's account: M. Cloet, ed., *Itinerarium visitationum Antonii Triest episcopi gandavensis (1623–1654)* (Leuven, 1976), April 18, 1627, Black Sisters Dendermonde, and May 20, 1640, Black Sisters Oudenaarde. The nearly violent sisters of Our Lady-Ter-Rivieren are in J. Corstjens, "De Franciscanessen van het klooster OL-Vrouwe-Ter-Rivieren te Bree (1464–1797) (ms., Licentiaatsverhandeling, Leuven, 1984), 33, an incident of 1542.

Ferraria believed that a religious should either be praying or working with her hands, to help her control her thoughts. The warning to avoid heavy work is from AAM, CK, Grey Sisters Zoutleeuw/1, statutes of 1625. Sisters in Poperinge, Isegem, Veurne, Wervik, Comines, Berchem, St. Truiden, Hasselt, and Tongeren participated in the activities listed. See the studies on Grey Sisters in the note to chapter 2; especially Schoonaert, Hildebrand, Van de Castele, Gruart, and Grauwels.

Among the cloistered orders, the Benedictine convent of Chiamsee harvested grain for itself, but sold wine, beer, and hard liquor to outsiders by 1575, always a controversial business given the tax-exempt status of monasteries. The Benedictine tradition of charity and care for the poor gave rise to hotels among these cloistered religious as well, though this was discouraged toward the seventeenth century; Ph. Schmitz, *Histoire de l'ordre de Saint-Benoît* (Maredsous, 1948), 254–55. The Annunciation Sisters of Leuven washed for the local Capuchins around 1625, a task that the women of Bethlehem would in future years imitate; P. Hildebrand, "De Kapucijnen te Leuven," *NF* 3/3 (1920): 245. A sister in Bethanie (Brussels), however, washed for a certain Mr. Bruegel without permission, and against the will of Mater, which landed her in trouble; AAM, CK, Bethanie Brussels/4, visitation of March 1590. The babysitting of White Ladies of Leuven is from ARA, RSA 1947/1, from 1618. The Sisters of Blijdenberg in Mechelen, even after being cloistered in 1620, ran the increasingly common conventual school for girls, but several nuns wanted to close it because not enough girls attended and because it disturbed the routine of the choir; the Augustinian Canonesses of the Holy Sepulchre had a similar means of supporting themselves; AAM, CK, Blijdenberg/8, visitation of 1621; M. Hereswitha, "Reguliere Kannunikessen van het Heilig-Graf," OGE 50/4 (December 1976): 390. Economic activities of the Grey and Black Sisters of Mechelen are combined in a single file, AAM, CK, Black Sisters Mechelen/57—the example of the boarder there is from 1586; also KAM, CA, Hovius/Processen Algemeen, the trial of Canon Pussius, 1599; the burning down of Velzeke, Van de Castele, "Grauw Zusters te Nevele," 169. Margaret mentioned in her letter that the Greys of Bethlehem also assisted in childbearing, but it's unclear whether any fee was received.

On the numbers of women in a convent and the attempts at reduction, a figure of two dozen nuns in a house was not unusual, perhaps slightly on the small side of average. AAM, CK, Thabor Mechelen/4, shows eighteen veiled and ten lay sisters in this house, assuming the interview list was complete. Cistercian houses in the Middle Ages had twenty to thirty nuns and fifteen lay sisters; three at their height in Brabant had sixty nuns and forty lay sisters; see M. Sabbe, et al., Bernardus en de Cisterziënfamilie in Belgie, 1090–1990 (Leuven, 1990), 288. Hovius reduced the women of the prominent abbey of Vorst from fifty to thirty in 1615 and took similar measures on numerous occasions; see the index to the ARA, KAB, vol. 3, 201, and many more reductions can be found in the files of the AAM, CK.

Mater's charge over things temporal may be found in chapter 3 of the house statutes, under "Obedience." The bursaress is discussed in chapter 5.

Some balance sheets for some years for some convents remain. The women of St. Niklaasberg in Aarschot took in 765 florins in 1626, though give no overall summary of their expenses versus income; AAM, CK, St. Niklaasberg/1625–26 register on income. The Grey Sisters of Leuven possessed scores of annuities and fields scattered around Brabant and drew much of their income from them; but they also owed much. See ARA, KAB, 15307, a huge eighteenth-century cartularium that contains copies of earlier documents—it reveals eleven annuities from Mechelen between 1460 and 1637, twelve from Leuven between 1522 and 1658, and one to two in ten other cities that were founded before 1650. Most of these yielded 3 to 12 florins annually, hardly a huge amount (one was for 37), which made each of them important to the aggregate; also Greys/5, February 13, 1631, shows a typical annuity from the chapter of St. James's in Leuven—the Greys gave them 300 florins and received 18 florins 15 stiver per year. Another sheaf of paper in Greys/5 (undated, but in a seventeenth century hand) lists over 100 separate annuities coming in, and fourteen big annuities going out, including one for 100 florins a year on capital of 3,000 florins.

Another book of excise taxes and annuities owed is in ARA, KAB, 15306. This book, measuring approximately 6 by 9 inches, "covers" the years 1682 to 1749 but lists some annuities of earlier origin.

No account books reveal incomes and expenses before 1645. One book reveals at least the "bottom line" for the two decades after 1645. Between 1645 and 1654 the average annual income was 3,721 florins, with expenses at 3,707. During the next seven years the income went up to 5,000, and expenses to 4,951, while the last four years saw a figure between these, with slightly more spent than received. This expense book of 1645 to 1666 is in Greys/5.

Schmitz, *Saint-Benoît,* 254, makes the plainest statement on female poverty in the Middle Ages. "The majority of female monasteries existed in continual discomfort . . . and sometimes in real poverty," again beyond the canonical version. E. Power, *Medieval Women* (Cambridge, 1975), 91, reminds us, however, that some convents were almsgivers.

On women collecting alms, the Grey Sisters of Berchem sent one of their own on a "begging trip" in 1592 through Artois, Hainaut, and Flanders, but a town secretary along the way, typically, found the idea of a begging woman scandalous. Thus more and more after Trent, a female convent would hire a representative to collect alms in its name, as the women of Bethlehem did in 1626. See J. de Brouwer, *Bijdrage tot de Geschiedenis van het Godsdienstig Leven en de Kerkelijke Instellingen in het Land van Aalst* (Aalst, 1961), 25; AAM, CM, 4/fol. 70; ARA, GR, 1125, October 1626.

The good deeds at Vilvoorde: AAM, CK, Gasthuis Vilvoorde/9. The problems in Bethanie are, as usual, from AAM, CK, Bethanie Brussels/4, visitation of 1590.

The 1627 decree on food and drink also contained several controversial points on *clausura*, most of which had already been defined by statute but not strictly followed. See Adriana's correspondence on the issue in Greys/9, February 3, 1628, and March 15 or 19, 1628; Maria Coninxloo, July 1, 1625, in Greys/11; Catharina Rijckeboer, September 23, 1626, in Greys/1; Boonen's apology to Adriana in AAM, CK, Grey Sisters Diest/1, September 19, 1627 (misfiled, for it should be with Leuven documents); his instructions to Bouckaert, Greys/8, September 19, 1627; the special decree from Boonen is in Greys/1, November 17, 1627; a letter from Confessor Martens is in Greys/1, December 1, 1627. A later complaint by Adriana is in Greys/1, December 6, 1627; Catharina's retraction of her earlier position is also dated December 6, 1627, in Greys/11.

Women of Ávila who liked their contact with the sisters may be found in J. Bilinkoff, *The Avila of St. Teresa* (Ithaca, NY, 1989).

In Den Luypaert and Den Soeten Inval (Do Drop In) were the names of the houses around the corner from the convent; see house names in A. Meulemans, *Atlas van Oud-Leuven* (Leuven, 1981). The connection of the former establishment to Henri Joos emerges only in his will, in RAA, Kerkarchieven, Mol/236bis, which lists a financial arrangement with Aegidius Seutens, "habitantem et Bracantem Lovanii *in den Luypaert*"; Bracantem suggests that the man was a brewer or that the house was a tavern. This may also explain why the woman "In Den Luypaert" was often willing and able to give beer to the nuns.

A good example of a charge to a steward is in AAM, CM, 8/fol. 153, concerning the steward of Groot Bijgaarden in 1619. Fees are mentioned in AAM, CK, Gasthuis St. Peter's Leuven/6, June 20, 1652, agreement. In 1652 the steward of the hospital of St. Peter's of Leuven received 150 florins a year, 2 florins 10 stivers per diem if on the convent's business and had to stay overnight, and 35 stivers a day if he need not stay overnight; he was also obliged to come on Mondays and Fridays to the convent at 2 P.M. to discuss and render accounts. Troubles with the steward of Jericho are in AAM, CK, Jericho Brussels/visitation of September 2, 1628, and the 1630 visitation as well.

S. Axters, *Geschiedenis van de Vroomheid in de Nederlanden,* vol. 4 (Antwerp, 1960), 128, discusses the emphasis of the Franciscans on Christ's childhood. E. Arenal and S. Schlau, *Untold Sisters: Hispanic Nuns in Their Own Words* (Albuquerque, 1989), 119, 190, note the prominence of the child Jesus in the paintings and sculpture of Spanish nunneries.

The quote from R. Devos, in the introduction to *Vie Religieuse Féminine et Société* (Annecy, 1973).

Chapter 13

The historical and historiographical surveys of female monasticism cited in the notes to the foreword invariably contain discussion of the tradition of cloister, upon which I have relied for this background discussion. The example of concern for cloister in Florence is from G. A. Brucker, "Monasteries, Friaries, and Nunneries in Quattrocento Florence," in *Christianity and the Renaissance,* eds. T. Verdon and J. Henderson (Syracuse, 1990), and has to do with conditions in 1427. Justifications by Ferraria and the anonymous writer are from *Vande dry geloften der Religien* (Mechelen, 1618), and *Tussen Heks en Heilige* (Nijmegen, 1985), 84. Ph. Schmitz, *Histoire de l'ordre de Saint-Benoît* (Maredsous, 1948), offers one example of the perceptions of Trent about the roots of monastic abuse.

Walter Simons reminds me that the first rule specifically for women was composed by Augustine; see L. Verheijen, ed., *La Règle de saint Augustin* (Paris, 1967). The *emphasis* of cloister for women, however, is discussed in detail in A. de Vogüé, "Caesarius of Arles and the Origin of the Enclosure of Nuns," in *Women in Monasticism,* ed. J. Leclerq, et al. (Petersham, Mass., 1989), 16–29; and Jane T. Schulenburg, "Strict Active Enclosure and Its Effects on the Female Monastic Experience (ca. 500–1100)," in *Medieval Religious Women. I. Distant Echoes,* eds. J. A. Nichols and L. T. Shank (Cistercian Publications, 1984), 51 ff. This last article also convincingly demonstrates the differences in requirements of cloister for male and female religious. Regulations for men were "neither as sweeping, nor as strict" (58). There is good evidence that such differences continued into our period.

Finally, Schulenburg also shows old arguments about the weakness of women, which even nuns were supposedly subject to, especially if outside the convent; 63. The article contains a good bibliography on cloister as well.

One example of the vigorous extramural activity allowed in male orders can be found in T. Morren, *Het kerkelijk leven in het dekenaat Diest tijdens de 17e eeuw (1599–1700)* (ms., Licentiaatsverhandeling, Leuven, 1974), 140, where the author cites statistics revealing that well over half of the pastoral work performed in the deanery was carried out by Norbertine monks.

The two scandals cited, on the new Mother of Velzeke and the Hospital Sister of Berchem, are from J. de Brouwer, *Bijdrage tot de Geschiedenis van het Godsdienstig Leven en Kerkelijke Instellingen in het Land van Aalst* (Aalst, 1961), 255, 260. On ignoring strict cloister, see the Dominican nuns in Regensburg and Nuremburg who set aside quarters in the convent for guests to sleep and eat, while at Gmund the community left the cloister under the pretense of fire hazard. These are just the tip of the iceberg of a single order, including the violations from Lowenthat and Steinheim mentioned. See W. A. Hinnebusch, *The History of the Dominican Order* (New York, 1966), chap. 13. The Benedictine nuns of Groot Bijgaarden are cited frequently enough in the notes to previous chapters; see their file in AAM, CK, and especially the journal of archbishop Hovius. Women like Clare in the thirteenth century or the Visitation Order in the seventeenth, didn't want strict cloister at all, but preferred to carry out good works in towns and villages; J. Moorman, *A History of the Franciscan Order, From Its Origins to the Year 1517* (Oxford, 1968), 36.

Sister Gertrude's story is contained in Harline and Put, "A Bishop in the Cloisters," cited in chapter 11. The complaints in Bethanie revolved around the prior of Affligem and a monk of Grimbergen and included charges of private audiences of both men with a certain Sister Lysken, gifts to her of a silver cross and some sugar, and gifts in return. In 1608 in the same house there emerged complaints about overfamiliarity with men and outsiders, including people who stayed too late at the nuns' table (one lawyer until 11 P.M.). AAM, CK, Bethanie Brussels (Marie Magdalena/4, February 28, 1592, and October 8, 1608, visitation by Dean Vinck. Rules about *clausura* in Bethlehem are in the order's rule, page 10, and the house statutes, chapter 17.

On the dean from the diocese of Gent, see Bishop Triest's *Itinerarium*, cited in the note to chapter 12 and previously, 52, Cruybeke, May 1626. The story of the Cistercian visitor from France is contained in R. de Ganck, "Marginalia to Visitation Cards for Cistercian Nuns in Belgium," *Citeaux* 40 (1989): 236–37—the government insisted that the French superiors not introduce anything "novel," such as insistence on strict *clausura*.

The example of the nuns of Blijdenberg pleading for cloister is from 1616; AAM, CM, 8/130, a visitation done in 1618. See also AAM, CK, Blijdenberg Mechelen, 72, a register containing notes on the history of the house. On the prestige of cloister, see J. Brown, *Immodest Acts* (Oxford, 1986), 114–15, and N. Rubinstein, "Lay Patronage and Observant Reform in Fifteenth-Century Florence," in *Christianity and the Renaissance*. Examples of desire among women for strict cloister could be multiplied; see AAM, CK, Grey Sisters Diest/9, November 28, 1628, pastor to Boonen, on the desire of nuns to include the convent's orchard in cloister.

On the grille more specifically: J. E. Sayers, "Violence in the Medieval Cloister," *Journal of Ecclesiastical History* 41 (1990): 533–42, reviews the practical reasons for grilles, namely the "general level of violence in society that accounted for the emergence of the key, the grille and the wall in the convent." Though grilles became common, they were not always popular. When the sisters of Yerres were given grilles by the bishop of Paris, they took them down and threw them into a river. But by the seventeenth century, they were a well-established fact of life and, like most other institutions or rules that have been around for a time, already had a long set of rules made up about them. Schmitz, *Saint-Benoît* (cited in the note to chapter 12 and frequently), 237, discusses the origin of grilles and the reaction of the sisters of Yerres.

On the spirit of the cloister surrounding the grille, see Ferraria, *Vande dry Geloften,* who noted that it was not enough for a religious to be behind walls, for there were many behind four walls who "come daily to the grille," under the pretext of spiritual works, but in fact were there to murmur or gossip, to recount the internal affairs of the convent, and to urge their friends to visit often. Teresa believed that any kind of contact with family members was damaging and discouraged it; J. Bilinkoff, *The Avila of St. Teresa* (Ithaca, NY, 1989). Chapter 16 of the statutes of Bethlehem reflected these beliefs: If you have visitors, they must be addressed at the grille only; go to the grille with Mater's permission; wear a skirt over the habit, or if called from the workroom at least a cloak, and a long veil; you may never go alone, but must go with a sister assigned to accompany you who will hear and observe all; the only exception to this, as was common, was when a spiritual director needed to talk in private with a nun, and even then the accompanying sister was to remain in sight but not in earshot; if anything must be fetched from within the convent, this must be done by the sister being visited, not her companion; take leave soon, use few words, certainly none that will give cause for scandal among laypeople; no one was to go to the grille during the Office, sermon, meals, and times of silence, nor on communion and confession days, nor after Complines or before Primes; avoid singing songs and kissing any "unlike" persons, something that would have been possible only if the holes in the grille were wide enough to allow it; and of course no food or drink should be served at the grille, much less indulged in by the nuns. The stricter statutes for Grey Sisters by Peter Marchant (Gent, 1626) even stipulated that a single friend could visit the convent at most three times per year, unless it was a "great benefactor" who couldn't very easily "be left at the grille." M. Hereswitha, "Reguliere Kannunikessen van het Heilig-Graf," *OGE* 50/4 (December 1976): 402, reviews exceptions for speaking alone at the grille, with a spiritual director. Marchant's rules were from *Den Reghel der Derder Orden van S. Fransoys* (Gent, 1626).

Given the old resistance to the very existence of cloister and problems of enforcement, given the potential for violating its spirit at the grille, and despite the prestige and ideal of cloister, it's no wonder that Pope Alexander VII in 1666 was still issuing proclamations that cloister should be strict, but this "failed to receive unqualified approval"; or that the Frenchman J.-B. Thiers in 1681 could state in his *Traité de la clôture des religieuses* (Paris, 1681, and cited frequently by G. Reynes, *Couvents des femmes* [Paris, 1987]) that there was no other point in the religious discipline more neglected or ignored. Certainly some convents that by rights should have been cloistered (thus besides the Hospital and Black Sisters) furiously resisted *clausura*, at least up through about 1650; Pope Alexander is cited in De Ganck, "Marginalia," 236.

The requirement for the portress to be watchful is from the statutes of the Grey Sisters of Zoutleeuw, AAM, CK, Grey Sisters Zoutleeuw/1, December 1625, point 11.

Specifications for the church grille at Comines are in Léon-L. Gruart, "Les Soeurs Grises de Comines," *BCFF* 14 (1951): 78. Urban VIII's description is in P. Octave D'Angers, "Le chant liturgique dans l'ordre de Saint François aux origines," *Études Franciscaines* 75/3 (1975): 157–306, with this example on 300. Urban also suggested that it be opened so they could hear Divine Office, being sung by the friars. Perhaps the sisters joined their voices. Escapades of Sister Barbara at Vorst are in AAM, CK, Vorst/3. The example of Triest is from the frequently cited *Itinerarium*, May 16, 1624, Oudenaarde.

Chapter 14

Manual labor in Bethlehem is the subject of chapter 11 in the house statutes. Among other things, we see that work began at 8 or 9 A.M. and that Mater or Vicaress was to supervise the work.

The little altars and shrines are discussed in *Tussen Heks en Heilige* (Nijmegen, 1985), especially 86, and in more detail in "Les Jardins clos et leurs rapports avec la sculpture Malinoise," *Bulletin du Circle Archéologique, littéraire, et artistique de Malines* 22 (1912): 51–114.

The example of the Spanish nun who dished out medical advice is from Arenal and Schlau, *Untold Sisters* (cited at the end of the note to chapter 12), 75–76; Teresa's advice to create religious art is on 134.

The rule in Thabor about less able singers moving to the corner of the choir: AAM, CK, Mechelen Thabor/4, February 15, 1610, Hovius ordinances, and 1632 visitation by Boonen. See on Blijdenberg AAM, CK, Blijdenberg Mechelen/chart. 8, visitation of January 21, 1620. For broader considerations of art and female monasticism, see J. Hamburger, "Art, Enclosure, and the Cura monialium: Prolegomena in the Guise of a Postscript," *Gesta* 31 (1992): 108–34. The entire issue is devoted to women and monastic architecture; my thanks to Walter Simons for pointing this out.

The Hospital Sisters in Gent lamented that they had no time for the

Office because of their work; R. Weemaes, *Visitationes omnium ecclesiarum ... Carolum Masium (1609–1612)* (Gent, 1987), 28–29. See on the superiority of the contemplative state Andreas de Soto, OFM, *De Schole van de Eenicheydt,* and Vervoort, *Bruydegoms Mantelken,* in the list of devotional works in the note to chapter 7.

Chapter 1 of the house statutes laid down the guidelines for worship in Bethlehem. The less-lettered Black Sisters of Leuven are discussed in AAM, CK, Black Sisters/32, undated visitation by Van der Wiel. On the literacy of sisters in Bethlehem, Greys/10, June 20, 1624; and ARA, RSA/receipt 1594 signed with an X by the bursaress. The quote on religious sounds is from F. Tomizza's *Heavenly Supper* (Chicago, 1991), 73. On St. Germain, M. Ultee, *The Abbey of St. Germain des Prés in the Seventeenth Century* (New Haven, 1981). The nuns of Our Lady Ter-Rivieren in Bree argued often over whether to do the Office in Latin or Dutch, indicating that many had the ability; the major obstacle was not so much illiteracy as a shortage of Latin books; J. Corstjens, "De Franciscanessen van OLV-Ter-Rivieren" (ms., Licentiaatsverhandeling, Leuven, 1984), 116. Madeleine de Nivelles was elected Abbess of Kortenberg, a prominent convent, in 1595 because among other things she had a good knowledge of Latin; *Monasticon Belge,* 7 vols. and more (Maredsous, 1890–1984), 4 (1), 262. See Arenal and Schlau, *Untold Sisters,* 95, on the assumption of Spanish Carmelite sisters that the Office was to be done in Latin.

On self-mortification, the penitential nuns in Brugge are discussed by M. Cloet, *Karel Filips van Rodoan* (Brussels, 1970), 190. Pinelli's warning is from his *Costelycken Spieghel der Religieuse Volmaecktheydt* (Antwerp, 1605). See for a more general pattern P. Camporesi, *The Incorruptible Flesh: Bodily Mutation and Mortification in Religion and Folklore,* trans. T. Croft Murray (Cambridge, 1988).

Proper behavior around the fire is discussed in chapter 9 of the statutes, "On Silence." Marchant's suggestions are in his 1626 rule. See also Alcantara's *Instructie om wel te mediteren*; Thielemans, *Heylighen van S. Franciscus Oirden*, on Francis; Guevera's from his *Leeringhe*. Placing oneself with Christ and Mary is from Vervoort, *Woestijne.* Van de Putte, *Claren Spiegel der Waerachtiger Christelijcker Maechden,* offers tips on taking communion. The things to consider in transubstantiation are from Evangelista, *Rijck Godts.* All these devotional works are cited in full in the note to chapter 7. On friars in Bethlehem and their long-appreciated sermons, see Greys/10, Anna to Nuncio, February 28, 1673. A volume of Brugman's sermons has been edited by Am. van Dijk, *Verspreide Sermoenen van Johannes Brugman* (Amsterdam, 1948). Angelina and Mechline are described by Marchant in his 1626 rule.

On festivals and the world upside-down, see the now-classic articles by N. Davis in her *Society and Culture in Early Modern France* (Stanford, 1975), as well as R. Darnton, *The Great Cat Massacre* (New York, 1984). The Mechelen Feast of Fools is from a nice survey by E. van Autenboer, *Volksfeesten en Rederijkers te Mechelen (1400–1600)* (Gent, 1962), 72. E. Weaver,

"Spiritual Fun," in *Women in the Middle Ages and the Renaissance,* ed. M. B. Rose (Syracuse, 1986) details play-writing Italian nuns and the abbess of Barking. Guevera's sentiment is from his *Leeringhe,* chapter 28. AAM, CK, Grey Sisters Diest/1, undated letter from Mater.

Chapter 15

The number of official visits that Archdeacon Van der Wiel made to Bethlehem is suggested in an undated document that he must have drawn up in 1638 or 1639, based on the contents and the events discussed (Greys/10). It lists the dates of visitations made to Bethlehem since about 1616, including those in which he participated and did not. On his zeal in general, Van der Wiel's hand and signature can be found in many files in AAM, CK, as well as numerous other collections of the archive.

On using the visitation for revenge, just recently in Diest a new set of statutes repeated the now-common prohibition. Like other statutes, these especially singled out Maters who commanded sisters on their oaths of obedience to divulge what each had said to the visitor, or to prohibit the disclosure of certain information. Though "a visitor might be deceived, God will not"; AAM, CK, Diest Cellesusters/Statutes 1625, fol. 42. More detailed discussion of the institution of the visitation—its methods, findings, and limitations—may be found in Harline and Put, "A Bishop in the Cloisters." On English prattlers, see E. Power, *Medieval People* (London, 1924), 76.

AAM, CK, Bethanie Brussels/4, 1590 visitation, includes the exchange between Grietken and Lysken. The example of the German convent is from L. Eckenstein, *Women Under Monasticism* (Oxford, 1966), 417. Harsh treatment of the decrees of a bishop of Lincoln on cloister is one of many such examples in E. Power, *Medieval Women* (Cambridge, 1975), 99. Van der Wiel also received an ultimatum from the Black Sisters of Mechelen: They would not obey a particular decree until they were visited. He ordered them to obey it, then he would consider visiting; see AAM, CK, Black Sisters Mechelen/42, December 17, 1637.

Specific questions put to the *Vicariaat* are legion in AAM, Collection Amatus Coriache (a former vicar-general who summarized past decisions of the *Vicariaat* in several volumes); interesting examples are from vol. 3: 62, 215, 217, 221, 223, 226, 227, 229, 296. Problems in Groot Bijgaarden: AAM, CK, Groot Bijgaarden/3, visitation of April 1630. Problems with the beguines: AAM, CK, Beguinage Vilvoorde/2, visitations of April and May 1629. Both episodes occurred after this visitation in Bethlehem, but they were not unusual before either.

Information on Van der Wiel is especially from his numerous visitations. As examples, see his involvement in AAM, CK, Poor Clares Mechelen/1 (profession interviews); AAM, CK, Tienen Kabbeek/1633 visitation; AAM, CK, Beguinage Tienen/1, undated *determinatio,* plus interview summary in bundle 5, October 9, 1630; AAM, CK, Mechelen Leprosy House/3, visitation of November 7, 1624, and 1631; AAM, CK, Brussels Leprosy House/2, visitation of 1632 probably by Van der Wiel; AAM, CK, Mechelen Hospital/ 3, visitation of October 4, 1635, and March 16, 1620; AAM, CK, Bethanie Brussels/4, visitations of March 19, 1613, June 27, 1614, January 29, 1624; AAM, CK, Vorst/3, visitation undated, but after 1626. These are just a few of the documents in the hand of Van der Wiel, or that mention his involvement in visitations. Even when he wrote himself, the notes are always well kept. His standing in for Boonen is recounted in AAM, CA, Boonen/143, November 26, 1621. Van der Wiel's interview book is in AAM, CM, 9.

Lucius's visitation reports are in AAM, Collection Dekenale Verslagen/ L3, where may be found his reports from 1619 through 1629. His experience with the nuns of Florival is in AAM, CK, Florival (filed with Dekenij Leuven). It's undated and unsigned, but is certainly in Lucius's hand, and thus before 1629 or 1630.

Information about the rings is from a letter by Adriana in Greys/9, March 15 or 19, 1628, Greys/1, December 6, 1627, and February 3, 1628. Perhaps the protocol for this visit followed that mentioned in a later visit, in Greys/3, visitation of May 24, 1669: it began at 2 in the afternoon with a common meeting, after which the visitors and nuns retired for individual interviews. This visitation of June 19, 1628 is in Greys/3. The rule of 1626 stated that when the visitation was over, the visitor may not enter the workhouse or any of the other "interior places" of the convent; the visitor will "never again remain alone and separated with any sister."

On resigning Maters, see AAM, Black Sisters Mechelen/4. The election of January 9, 1629 mentions that the previous Mater had "resigned."

The interview summaries, letters from Maria Coninxloo, Catharina Rijckeboer, Adriana Truis, Maria Joos, and Anna Vignarola may all be found in Greys/3. The summary is about seven pages long.

Chapter 16

We must remember that not all sisters in Bethlehem belonged or wanted to belong to a particular faction. Six or seven "neutral" sisters can be detected through their mixed praise and criticism of sisters in each of the unofficial factions, and because no one named them as factional—most obviously Aleidis Doelmans, Jacomyn de la Haye, Maria de Smet, and Anna van den Broek.

Anna's motto "worms for lunch" was probably not an uncommon one. It was taken as well by Catharina van Habroeck, a beguine of the late seventeenth or eighteenth century, who owned Alcantara's *Instructie* and inscribed this motto on the inside cover (copy in possession of the Provincial Archive of the Franciscans in St. Truiden).

Chapter 17

Catharina's letter is in Greys/3. That Van der Wiel followed Catharina's recommendations is evident in his memoriale, in Greys/3 (1628) where he mentions having spoken with the confessor, and then in his assignment to the dean, in the same document, to visit the choir himself. Van der Wiel's other notes on the letters and interviews are in Greys/3 as well. The hand in the margin of the memo is sloppy, but looks very much like Boonen's (which was relatively sloppy to begin with).

Concern for Mater's authority in convents is evident not only in how many *determinatio*s were put together, but in such decrees as in AAM, CK, Grey Sisters Zoutleeuw/1, statutes, point 4, where Mater confessed her sins to no one but God or her confessor, "lest her authority be damaged."

Bouckaert's letter of August is referred to by Boonen in his Agenda (AAM, CA, Boonen), 1628 bis (or the second listing of that year), August 14. Bouckaert's letter of November, in which he mentions several other of his recent activities, is in Greys/11. Margaret's letter complaining of Bouckaert: Greys/8, dated February 3. Catharina's letter: Greys/8, February 5, 1629.

Bouckaert's next and extensive letter: Greys/3, February 5, 1629, probably coincidentally written on the same day as Catharina's. Maria Coninxloo's letter: Greys/8, April 21, 1629. Her complaint at the 1624 visitation is in Dean Lucius's interview summary, Greys/10, August 20. Barbara Noosen's frustration was expressed in three letters in Greys/8, dated December 13, 17, and 30. Dean Lucius's letter of September 1629 is in Greys/11. Boonen's warning of March 4, 1630, is in his Agenda.

G. Brucker, "Monasteries, Friaries, and Nunneries in Quattrocento Florence," in *Christianity and the Renaissance,* eds., T. Verdon and J. Henderson (Syracuse, 1990), 58, describes complaints about reform in that city. The Masses mentioned are in Boonen's Agenda, October 8, 1629; the preacher à la mode in AAM, CA, Boonen/223; circulars from Isabella in AAM, CA, Boonen/170, October 30, 1629; prayers for the armies in the same collection dated June 17, 1631 and later. See KAM, CA, Boonen, Bewind/73, for the proclamation to the pastors and preachers on February 1, 1629, the requests for continual prayers, and letters of reference.

A need to visit the Greys is expressed in his Agenda, 1628 bis, before the entry of June 23 and after June 6, and where he lists several other houses in Leuven requiring visitation. Thus he was certainly aware of the general need of the house.

A 1637 letter from Adriana Truis alleged that a written *determinatio* was never delivered at all to the convent for the 1628 visitation; see Greys/3, March 19, 1637. Triest's happy assessment is in the *Itinerarium,* May 21, 1624, Black Sisters of Pamele: the original full text read "Omnia hic utcunque bene ordinata fiunt et tranquille et exemplariter vivunt."

Chapter 18

Catharina's letter on the bursaress is in Greys/8, August 6, 1629. The account of the election is in Greys/4, dated August 20, signed by Lucius.

The request for a reduction of services is in Greys/7, June 1, 1630, signed by Adriana Truis. The accompanying list was undated and in the hand of Catharina.

Margaret's official visitor is discussed in Greys/8, September 12, 1630. On the authorship of the inquest, the draft was hastily written, but given the nature of the visit and the hand it was likely Bouckaert, though the M's don't match up with his better-written letters. The B's, however, not particularly ordinary, are alike, and the slanting and circularity versus an up-and-down style are also alike.

Exclusion was not an uncommon punishment in house statutes, but the fact that Margaret's was so indefinite and initiated by the sisters must have made her feel it was unjust. Besides brief imprisonment for rising up against Mater, defaming another sister, breaking things, overdrinking, hardneckedness, private property, and so on, went more lengthy expulsions—as long or longer than Margaret's—for still more serious wrongs. Standard punishments for less grave violations included eating on the floor in the middle of the refectory, kissing the feet of the cosisters, asking public forgiveness, reciting a psalm or five Our Fathers while kneeling in the middle of the choir, with arms stretched out, and so on. Expulsion orders may be found in AAM, CM, 140/fol. 189 and 189vo. Other punishments are noted by W. Verleyen, *Dom Benedictus van Haeften, Proost van Affligem 1586–1648* (Brussels, 1983), 195; the house statutes of Bethlehem, chapter 20, AAM; CK, Grey Sisters Tienen/3, December 19, 1624; Tienen hospital, AAM, CK, June 16, 1631, decree and further.

On Boonen and Richelieu, see P. Claessens, *Histoire des Archevêques de Malines* (Leuven, 1881), 277. The departure of the Austin Canonesses from Leuven because of the siege is noted by P. Guilday, *The English Catholic Refugees on the Continent (1558–1795)*, vol. 1 (London, 1914), 383.

Note that Van der Wiel began his visitation summary in Latin but then soon switched to Dutch to avoid the headache of translating while writing.

The best single list of ages and years professed in Bethlehem emerges from a sheet composed by Van der Wiel as part of the interview summaries for 1633, in Greys/3. This is as good a place as any to reproduce it, and it should be cited, for it is from this, and comparisons of it to other less comprehensive sources of ages and years professed, that I have calculated ages and profession years for the women in Bethlehem.

Veiled Sisters

Aleidis Doelmans	76/58	Maria Joos	45/24
Anna Marcelis	51/35	Catharina Rijckeboer	37/16
Jacomyn de la Haye	46/29	Maria van Coninxloo	34/14
Adriana Truis	43/27	Maria de Smet	32/11
Margaret Smulders	49/26	Anna Servranx	37/11
Anna van Coninxloo	54/26	Anna Vignarola	29/9
Joanna van Outhagen	50/26	Margaret Geraerts	28/5
Joanna de Vorster	63/26		

Lay Sisters

Maria van der Meycken	56/37		Francisca Sannen	(not given)
Anna Schaepmeesters	70/32		Margaret Leiniers	(not given)
Magdalena Remmens	50/25		Joanna Schoensetters	38/10
Lesken Joos	43/24			

The letters by Margaret and the other sisters, and the interview summary, all used in this chapter and the next, are in Greys/1 and Greys/3, but those in Bundle 1 may have been moved back to Bundle 3, where they rightly belong.

Van der Wiel assigned the letters A through F to each written report, in order of receipt. But Catharina, who was interviewed first, had an "E" after her letter, with a note to that effect squeezed into the summary, thus suggesting it was delivered later; and Margaret's letter should have been "B," but it was labeled "F," with a note that it *was* delivered the second day. Margaret's submission on the second day doesn't necessarily mean that she composed the whole rapidly. Like her first letter, it gives the impression of having been written over weeks. Perhaps she submitted it on the second day merely to keep it secret from the others, or to hold it as long as possible to add any last-minute items. Also of interest is that Maria Coninxloo submitted one part of her letter at the interview, then submitted a second part the next day, as if during the night she had thought of some more things to say.

On the connection of Henri Joos to the wash, remember that Joos was buttressed in his nomination to the pastorship of Mol, over the other two candidates, by several Jesuit acquaintances called in to opine on the case. See the end of the note to chapter 4.

Chapter 19

See the preceding note for citation of the interview summary and most letters used in this chapter. Note that I've also included in the discussion a letter from Maria Coninxloo to Dean Paridanus, for the sake of convenience and because it's very much in the style of a visitation letter. This letter is undated, but must have been written between August 1630 and the end of 1633—I believe right after the visitation in October 1633. Maria says they'd been doing the Jesuit wash for two years, and that the current contract year would expire soon, in December. In the October 1633 visitation, Catharina said that they started doing the wash "within the past two years," thus since December 1631. Finally, she prayed him to "complete the visitation."

On jurisdiction, the visitor noted briefly that Jacomyn de la Haye (also called Verheyen), Anna Coninxloo, Joanna de Vorster, Maria Coninxloo, Maria de Smet, Anna Servranx, Anna Vignarola, and Margaret Geraerts—a mix of persons from all points of view—were among those who prayed to have the convent set under the Franciscans. The lay sister Anna Schaepmeesters complained about having to run after the friars, presumably because they were unenthusiastic about serving a convent not under their complete control.

Chapter 20

Van der Wiel's random notes on Bethlehem, used here, could be from any year, since they are undated and their topics so common at all these visitations, but they seem most pertinent for 1633. One mentions worries about Henri Joos, eating with outsiders, closing the dormitory at nine in the evening, and so on. The fact that this could be from 1633 or 1637 suggests how common the same themes were.

On the date of the *determinatio*: "We have among ourselves considered the content of the Charter of yesterday," October 20, a date which means again that the sisters heard back very quickly this time from the visitors. Evidence that the women of Bethlehem never got the charter back after returning it to Mechelen is from Adriana, whose comments on the topic are discussed in more detail in chapter 22.

Chapter 21

Pitch to purify the house was burned at least by the English Austin Canonesses of Leuven; see P. Guilday, *The English Catholic Refugees on the Continent,* vol. 1 (London, 1914), 383.

On Catharina's death: no necrology for the house remains, and no other document specifically mentions her death. However, recall her long illness; alternative explanations—that she was transferred or expelled from the monastery—seem most unlikely.

In regard to the number of women, at the 1633 visitation there had been twenty-two sisters listed in the house. (Catharina died, of course, and so did old Aleidis Doelmans, who had seen so much, and who had been the only one to suggest that Margaret be let back into the convent, with limits.)

The votes for Vicaress went as follows: Anna—Mater, Jacomyn de la Haye, Joanna de Vorster, Margaret Geraerts, plus all lay sisters save Joanna Schoensetters (who supported Jacomyn); others for Jacomyn—Margaret, Anna Marcelis, Anna Coninxloo, Maria Coninxloo, Maria de Smet.

The interviewer's notes on the election are contained in Greys/2, dated February 14, 1635. Recall that in Bethlehem itself in 1619 Hovius had appointed the sister of his choice as Mater; thus again, appointment was possible. Paridanus's follow-up letter, dated the next day, is in the same bundle of documents. Van der Wiel was the one who wished that Catharina were still present, in Greys/3, dated March 13, 1637.

Crucial documents on Margaret's return are all in Greys/8. Most of the correspondence is undated, including Bouckaert's draft of a document returning Margaret to her place. But from the language and a couple of dates, 1636 was clearly the key year. Mannarts is probably responsible for the anonymous letter in Greys/8. See also Van der Wiel's letter (April 16, 1636), and Hubert's and Bergaigne's letters (May 23, 1636; and probably addressed to Van der Wiel [Rme. Pr.]); Bergaigne was later bishop of Den Bosch and Cambrai, a frequent legate, like Boonen, to Holland, and a man of great eloquence, who died in 1648 in a monastery in Westphalia with his dear treaty not quite signed; see Schoutens (based on Sanderus) *Martyrologium Minoritico-Belgicum,* 177–81, cited at the end of the note to chapter 21. The documents of return are all in the same hand, which I think is Bouckaert's; they're titled "Heymelijcke Instructie" (dated July 10, 1636), "Secreta Instructio Matris," and "Jacob byder gratie Godts." It would not have been unusual for Bouckaert to draw up specific instructions in Boonen's name, then submit them to the archbishop for approval. Bouckaert was well trusted and was already serving as an official visitor to Bethlehem. On Hovius's and Boonen's delegation of particular official visitors of convents, see for instance AAM, CM, 140/fol. 199v, containing a formula to this end for the convent of Jericho in Brussels in 1616; the same place in 1619, AAM, CM, 8/163, where another commission for someone over St. Ursula's is noted. AAM, CM, 8/fol. 147, is a commission for the Black Sisters of Leuven.

On Margaret's 1624 agreement to stay out of the convent, Bouckaert's (and Boonen's) 1636 document read originally: "not compelled, but willingly did she go, and without guilt, but only at the insistence of Mater and the convent, and at our own strong recommendation as well, which she fulfilled to our satisfaction." On the troubles, the original draft read "supernatural"; the eventual "bodily" is obviously less sinister. The original read "one hoped" that the troubles were gone, but this was dropped for surer language in the final version: "we trusted enough, though no one can ever have sure [modified to absolute] knowledge of this." Originally "legal obstacle" was merely "obstacle" but the "legal" made more clear their right to return her; obviously the sisters' opposition was an "obstacle."

Chapter 22

Boonen's note on the prohibitions put on Joos is in his agenda, March 9, 1637. Mannarts's request is in a letter by Van der Wiel, dated March 13, in Greys/3, posted from Mechelen; Van der Wiel's undated letter is in the same bundle.

Adriana's letter, dated March 19, 1637, is also in Greys/3. Adriana appended to the first letter another thought: that Anna should serve not only as vicaress, but continue as novice mistress, for "in truth I can find no one who has more grace and ability," more "understanding and peacefulness, piety, and other good attributes; to no one is her good spirit and effort more obvious and helpful than to me."

Bouckaert's letters of March 21, April 6, and April 14 are all in Greys/3. Bouckaert learned about Van der Wiel's disposition from another dean, Henry Calenus, another confidant of Boonen's who would go down in defeat with him later on the issue of Jansenism.

On routine elections, let us note a case in Thabor where in 1634 a new subprioress and bursaress were elected, and where in 1637 Van der Wiel returned as scheduled to see whether the sisters wanted these women to continue in their offices. At the Grey Sisters' house in Diest, an election was done in 1652 because the current Mater's three-year term was up—the only justification given. See AAM, CK, Thabor Mechelen/3; AAM, CK, Grey Sisters Diest/2, election 1652. In regard to removal, in the Brigitinne monastery of Gent an abbess and her prioress were not only removed but sent to the Grey Sisters monastery in that city "for grave and weighty reasons"; Bishop Triest's *Itinerarium*, 240, cited abundantly. On Kabbeek, see AAM, CK, Kabbeek Tienen, election of November 16, 1588, done by the vicar of Archbishop Hauchin. W. Verleyen, *Dom Benedictus Van Haeften, Proost van Affligem (1586–1648)* (Brussels, 1983), 188, on the Black Sisters of Aalst, 1623, notes another way to solve difficult messes in leadership: bring in an outsider, supposedly neutral in her feelings. This was suggested at an election here but the visitors decided that though this might give the mater more authority, it also worked against *caritas*.

There were clear disadvantages to regular elections—namely even greater fueling of factionalism—as well as the mater-for-life system. For instance, in a series of elections among the Grey Sisters of Diest, who did hold them regularly, we see that the mater chosen in 1652 received at the subsequent election, in 1657, only two out of thirty votes. In 1660 the mater chosen in 1657 received no votes at all (and she was clearly still alive). See AAM, CK, Grey Sisters Diest. See also AAM, CK, Grey Sisters Zoutleeuw/ 1, Statutes, December 1625, chapter 3, decreed that election of Mater was to be done every three years. In Our Lady Ter-Rivieren in Bree, one woman was elected nine different times as Mater in the early seventeenth century, reflecting the back-and-forth swing typical of in-fighting. Rarely did anyone there serve more than one three-year term in this period; J. Corstjens, "De Franciscanessen van OLVrouw-Ter-Rivierent te Bree (1464–1797) (ms., Licentiaatsverhandeling, Leuven, 1984), 96–100.

Some interesting general items in the *determinatio* included distributing linens among the religious, the refectory table will now be served by all, a half-hour meditation measured by the hourglass, and no accepting new religious unless they had a steady income of 100 florins.

Boonen's continued approval of Bouckaert included a December note in which Boonen happily recorded that Bouckaert was being considered for the vacant see of Bolduc: Agenda, December 10, 1637. A month later the vicar-general of Liège sent a thank you to Bouckaert for coming to visit the Grey Sisters of Hasselt, yet another house out of Bouckaert's ordinary jurisdiction, and reflecting further his reputation as a monastic reformer. See AAM, CK, Grey Sisters Hasselt/4, January 4, 1638.

Chapter 23

The Bishop of Antwerp's report is in C. B. De Ridder, "Rapport adressé au Souverain Pontife, Paul V, par Malderus . . . en 1615," *AHEB*, 1 (1864): 113.

G. Bernanos, *Diary of a Country Priest* (New York, 1986; translated from the French original), 83. The number of parishes and convents fluctuated, usually upward, in the reports by Boonen to Rome. See J. Paquay, *Les rapports diocésains de la province ecclésiastique de Malines et du diocèse de Liège* (Tongeren, 1930), 2–4, 9–10, 14, 23. Boonen's 1623 report said that there were over 400 parishes and 11 deaneries, and in 1675 it was said that there were 700,000 souls in the archdiocese.

Boonen's comment about the Grey Sisters of Diest is from AAM, CK, 1625 statutes. Exploits of the sisters of Groot Bijgaarden were numerous; this example is from AAM, CK, Groot Bijgaarden/3, October 24, 1630. P. Broutin, "Les visites pastorales d'un Evêque au xviie siècle," *Nouvelle Revue Theologique* 71 (1949): 942, gives the example of d'Aranthon. See C. Haigh, *The English Reformation Revised,* ed, C. Haigh (Cambridge, 1987), 209–10. The failure in Tienen noted a bit later, is from AAM, CK, Beguinage Tienen/1.

Van Haeften's opinions are recorded by W. Verleyen, *Dom Benedictus Van Haeften, Proost van Affligem (1586–1648)* (Brussels, 1987), 194–95. Van der Wiel's visit is recounted in his letter in Greys/1, May 27, 1638.

Adriana's letter on the *determinatio*: Greys/10, August 6, 1639. Bouckaert on Adriana's excuse: Greys/10, dated August 19, 1639. On the question of altering decrees: two of the twenty questions put to the Black Sisters of Leuven in a 1689 visit had to do with accusations that certain sisters had made about the dean's falsifying of recent visitation decrees. See AAM, CK, Black Sisters Leuven.

Boonen's letter on jurisdiction is dated April 8, 1639, in Greys/10. His reaction to the English Benedictines is noted by Guilday, *English Catholic Refugees,* cited at the beginning of the note to chapter 21, 263.

For reasons unclear, but probably at Boonen's request, Van der Wiel drew up in 1638 or 1639 a document that showed the frequency of episcopal visitation to Bethlehem over the years. Based on his memory and written records, Van der Wiel noted visitations for 1611, 1616, 1624, 1626, then 1628, 1633, 1637, and 1638. He certainly missed a couple, including a 1625 visit often referred to by others. This survey is in Greys/10, and undated, but certainly after the last-named date in the document, May 19, 1638, and before February 1639, when the formal proclamation from the pope came.

The official letters from Rome are in Greys/10, dated 1638 and 1639; but the documents by the cathedral chapter are in Bundle 73 of KAM, CA, Boonen, full of pieces on jurisdiction, one dated March 30, 1639, another June 8, 1640, and several other extracts that are undated.

The bulls referred to, which insisted that all Franciscan houses be under Franciscan jurisdiction, included those of Leo X and Sixtus IV. The two men on retainer were Alexander van der Laen and Henry Calenus, both of them canons and deans. Léon-L. Gruart, "Les Soeurs Grises de Comines," *BCFF* 14 (1951): 84–85, contains information on the length of tenure among maters in this house between 1481 and 1787. Where data are available, the average tenure was about eight years among the twenty-seven maters known. Several of them quit to lead a new convent; five of them were Mater at two different times (indicating elections were held besides at time of death). One of them was superior for twenty-eight years, between 1582 and 1610. In the Poor Clares convent of Mechelen there were twenty-three abbesses between 1500 and 1783, an average tenure of about twelve years; see H. De Backer, "Het Arme Klaren Klooster te Mechelen, van af 1500 tot de Opheffing in 1966" (ms., Licentiaatsverhandeling, Leuven, 1977), 111. Lengths of tenure varied from house to house, but where a mater was powerful or respected or both, a de facto tenure for life was probably not unusual.

Chapter 24

See the rule of the Grey Sisters and chapter 14 of the statutes of Bethlehem for details on care for the sick and dying. C. Leutbrewer, OFM, *Gulde biecht-konste om op den tijdt vanmin als twee uren sich te bereyden tot een generale biechte van heel syn leven, sonder peryckel van eenighe doodt-sonden achter te laten* (Brussels, 1646), with thirteen editions afterward. J. van Gorcum, *Troost der Siecken* (Antwerp, 1644), with numerous earlier editions. The plenary indulgence is in P. Marchant's *Af-beeldinghe* (Gent, 1639), which contains as well other privileges and indulgences of the Third Order; Marchant is also the one who describes the last hours of Elisabeth of Hungary. The memorial services included the following prayers: Each choir sister was to read fifty Psalms, and the lay sisters fifty Pater Nosters, with Requiem Aeternam, all on the same day, or at least within eight days of the funeral; then for thirty days they read three Pater Nosters every day with Requiem Aeternam, for her soul.

The letter announcing Margaret's death was written by Gerard van Reijden, perhaps dean of Leuven at the time, and dated December 18, 1648. That this letter, which again contained discussion of other topics, should have found its way into the files of the Grey Sisters may have been coincidence, may not have been.

It's true that Bethlehem, like most houses, probably had an obituariam or Necrology in which the deaths of sisters were recorded; however, this book was for in-house use only—the announcement of death was to be done by a dean or some other representative, in writing or orally. Perhaps such was often done orally, but certainly some were written. The obituarium of the Grey Sisters of Nevele, for instance, begun only in 1657 and discussed by G. Van de Castele, "Grauwe Zusters of Penintenten-Rekollektinen te Nevele (1502–1784)," *HLN* 9(1978): 155–247, was nicely organized and fat.

Nuns who seem very similar to Margaret are alluded to in AAM, CK, Black Sisters Leuven/32, undated visitation by Van der Wiel, seventeen sisters interviewed; AAM, CK, Bethanie Brussels/4, 1590 visitation; Triest, *Itinerarium,* 65, 121, 158, 492. Anna's troublesome sister is mentioned in an undated letter from around 1666, in Greys/10.

Afterword

A good example of the broad kind of source that reveals only so much, or that conceals more than it reveals, is the 1634 report to Rome by the Internuncio in Brussels named Lagonissa, in L. van der Essen, "La Situation Religieuse des Pays-Bas en 1634, d'après la relation finale du nonce Fabio de Lagonissa," *Revve d'histoire Ecclestiastique* 24 (1928): 335. He does mention one specific deed, however, namely his pride at successfully expelling the "Jesuitesses" of Mary Ward.

The fates of Joos's successors at Gertrude's are mentioned in documents in AAM, CK, St. Gertrude's Leuven/3-4 (Paridanus's letter to Boonen, September 2, 1634, among others). See also Lucius's 1628 visitation report, noting that Blehen had gone mad—AAM, Dekenale Verslagen/L3, 1628. Joos's papers from his days in Mol are thick in RAA, Kerkarchieven, Mol/ 3-4, 796, 236bis, and BAA, Parochialia Mol, 11–13 (which especially shows him a strong defender of church tithes). Information on his death and tomb is drawn from a serialized article published in the late nineteenth century, T. I. Welvaerts, "Geschiedkundige Bijdragen over de Voogdij van Molle," *Het Kempisch Museum* (1890).

A volume that listed the members of his new parish was suitably titled: Anno 1627 in Junio ab Henrico Joos, Pastore insigne ("distinguished")— which was undoubtedly supposed to have been the usual indigne ("unworthy"), but Joos slipped—RAA, Kerkarchieven, Mol/82. RAA, Kerkarchieven, Mol/3, 4, contains testaments drawn up in his presence. The first is dated 1624 and they are regular until 1636; thus he must have fled soon after this. At the end of the bundle there is one regarding Dimpna Joos, a beguine in Diest, apparently a cousin, since her parents were not the same as Henri's. Thus he may have had both a sister and a cousin in Diest, or perhaps the cousin was misidentified as a sister. The will of Joos is contained in RAA, Kerkarchieven, Mol/236bis. Praise of him by the leaders of Mol is from RAA, Voogdij Mol-Balen-Dessel, 208/1, notice from magistrates of Mol to Ulrich ab Homsbroeck that Joos had died and a replacement was needed. Note that in these many documents Henri's age is never mentioned. But if he began in Gertrude's in 1604 and we assume he had done well in his studies and perhaps had therefore drawn attention to himself that way, he must have been between twenty-five and thirty when he began as confessor, which put him at around thirty-five to forty at the time of Margaret's first scandal, about forty-five to fifty when he left Leuven for Mol, and then about sixty to sixty-five when he died in Diest.

Van der Wiel's retirement as vicar-general is noted in Boonen's agenda, July 22, 1641. Until the end Van der Wiel received and dispatched letters to female religious, as well as other institutions, of course; see AAM, CK, Beguinage Vilvoorde/5, January 4, 1641, for a "troublesome" letter from Johanna de Leener; KAM, Personalia/438 (will); J. Baetens, *Verzameling van Naamrollen betrekkelijk de kerkgeschiedenis van Mechelen,* 3 vols. (Mechelen), 1881; J. Schoeffer, "Archidiaconorum Ecclesiae Metropolitanae Mechliniensis Notitia Chronologica" (ms. 1845 in the AAM). On the wall behind his tomb he wanted on one side an "effigy of myself" and on the other an image of his patron, St. Peter, which he hoped might move lookers-on to pray for his soul. He left some of his vestments to his brothers in the chapter of St. Rombouts and then at last some alms for the seminary of Mechelen, as the deceased archbishop Hovius had asked him to do. In a codicil, he also saw to the care of an Apollonia Lorts, his maidservant, leaving her various household items and an annuity of 100 florins per year as long as she lived, because of the faithful service she had rendered him for so long, and then to Anna van Mechelen, his junior servant.

L. Jadin, "Procès d'information pour la nomination des évêques et abbés des Pays-Bas, de Liège et de Franche-Comté d'après les Archives de la Congregation Consistoriale (1637–1709)," *BIHBR* (1929): 133–38, reviews Bouckaert's qualifications as bishop. It was said of him during the confirmation process in 1642 that he was "most capable of directing a diocese." He was consecrated by three other bishops, Boonen not among them, because of illness so disabling that to travel would have put him in "grave peril," he claimed. Certainly it was not because the two had fallen out, for in 1643 Boonen asked him to carry out a formal visitation to the Oratory of Scherpenheuvel. No doubt, though, such excursions as Bouckaert used to be able to make to Leuven were fewer.

See also J. Philippen, "Joost Bouckaert, Pastoor van Scherpenheuvel, Overste van de Oratorianen Aldaar, Landeken van Diest, Bisschop van Ieper," *Oost-Brabant* 28 (1991): 56–61. Two letters to Bouckaert, from sisters in an unnamed convent, are contained in Boonen's papers in AAM, CA, Boonen/192. These tell us that Margaret would not have been Bouckaert's only challenge: The women pleaded that he would come and redress certain situations in their convent, which despite recent reforms still remained; though it was good that no more drinking of brandy was allowed, the grille should be made higher and smaller, and Mater still did according to her own will, listening to two or three favorite sisters only. She had even accepted a novice from Wallonia, or French-speaking Belgium, who spoke no Dutch. We suspect that the novice's dowry was more important than her linguistic skills—and we know that Bouckaert had heard it all before.

The inscription about Bouckaert, which I have simply assumed copied his tombstone, is in ARA, KAB, 23349—*Ovium suarum verus Pastor, non turpis lucri cupidus, nedum honoris, sed unico hoc lapide contentus, Deo et proximo dives.*

Boonen's miscellaneous concerns and expenses: ARA, RSA, 945; AAM, CA, Boonen, 223, and KAM, CA, 223. The 1636 expenses included: 6,000 florins to the ecclesiastical court, 6,000 for "daily alms," 15,000 for household expenses besides wood and grain, 4,500 to the oratory in Leuven, 960 for the choir in St. Rombouts, 600 for the hospital in Mechelen, dozens of gifts or sums to various individuals, including widows and pastors, 300 for the Irish Franciscans, 100 to an agent in Rome, 100 to the confessor of St. Ursula's, 500 to the English nuns, 300 to the Carmelites of Aalst, plus others that totaled 43,227.

Boonen's call for discipline in worship is in KAM, CA, Boonen/73, August 13, 1644, a large printed page. Church meetings were full of evil, and thus he instructed the pastors during the next three sermons to warn their parishioners sharply against being so proud as to enter the house of the Lord unless they were chastely and honorably clothed; men not in tight, shameful attire, and women not to enter unless their breasts and shoulders were completely covered. Each church was to appoint several "inspectors" to see to it, as well as to the prevention of gossip, especially among people of the opposite sex, during the services. See also L. Ceyssens's compelling "Les dernières années de Boonen, archevêque de Malines," *Augustiniana* 11 (1961): 87–120, 320–35, 564–82. Boonen refused to publish in his diocese the 1643 bull that had condemned the *Augustinius* of Jansen, at least until 1651, when he published it under duress.

Boonen continued with his pastoral labors and distribution of big alms in the two years left to him after the troubles. One of his first acts after reinstatement was the granting to the Grey Sisters of Leuven a license to beg alms in fourteen villages (done on December 3, 1653, in Greys/11), in which he noted their "prudence" and zeal in prayer, fasting, Vigils, and so on. Toward the end he stated his wish to be buried in Rombout's, where like Van der Wiel he had labored for so long. He wanted the "pomp and expenses" of his funeral to be "most modest, not more than 2,000 florins," a sum that was enough to pay the annual wage of about six pastors but which for a man of noble blood like Boonen must have been modest indeed. As was common, he also ordered the distribution of various alms, "in cash and bread," to poor monasteries and families, and the usual wish for hundreds of Masses for his soul. Other property should be disposed of according to the laws that applied to those who died intestate, though he wanted his precious library of 4,000 volumes on numerous subjects to go to his successor and remain in the archdiocese, unless the successor was a buffoon, of course, then the books should be sold and the cash earned used to give alms to the poor and the hospitals. His testament is only three pages long and is contained in KAM, CA, Boonen/74. An inventory of Boonen's library is in KAM, CA, Boonen.

P. Carolo van Coundenhove, OFM, *Provinciae Germaniae Inferioris Compendiosa Descripto* (n.p., 1680), 8. The loose, anonymous document: Greys/10. Steenbergh's letter: Greys/10, October 17, 1646.

Maria Coninxloo appeared in the 1669 and 1671 interview summaries, Greys/3, but none after. All the visitations mentioned are in Greys/3. New statutes of 1664 are in Greys/1. Anna's name appears in document after document between 1635 and 1660 as "Vicaress" in a large eighteenth-century cartulariam in ARA, KAB, 15307, while Adriana was clearly always Mater.

During the 1650s and 1660s, Anna composed most of the extant correspondence from the house (though often it was signed by Adriana), suggesting that Adriana had simply delegated more than in the past or perhaps that she was feeling the effects of her old age (dying at around eighty). A memo dated February 21, 1661 (Greys/10), is one of many examples of a letter in Anna's hand, with Adriana's signature.

Almost all of the letters pertaining to jurisdiction are in Greys/10; see especially those dated during Anna's and Adriana's dual reign, from the 1650s to 1673. Anna asserted, and various letters seem to bear it out, that despite the 1639 switch in jurisdiction Boonen did not yet implement it. Around 1660 King Philip IV of little fame issued a proclamation declaring the 1639 bull to be valid and that the house was to go to the Franciscans. But shortly afterward, Anna was secretly pushing the archbishop to take them back again. By 1672 Anna had changed her mind yet again. This is when she wrote her long history of the house's confessors, in which she recounted for the bishop the laudable services rendered them by the friars, ever since the unjust expulsion of their only permanent, secular confessor ever, Henri Joos. Anna seemed less suave in her old age than she had been as a young woman. In a letter of 1673 the writing was too large, the spelling was bad, and her tone was defensive instead of subtle—where was the noble Anna? In any case, the problem still wasn't solved, and more acrimonious exchanges occurred, including one in May 1673 in which Anna noted that she lay sick in bed. She probably died soon afterward.

The dean noted in his visitation of 1663 that the register called for new elections in Bethlehem every three years, but because of various disturbances and distractions he hadn't thought such regularity expedient.

To illustrate the continuing temporal difficulties, we see in 1658, 1659, 1666 evidence of numerous lawsuits against the female religious of Leuven, including the Grey Sisters, over various properties. In 1663 Anna and Adriana sought permission to borrow 3,000 florins, to be repaid in ten years, for the purpose of repaying numerous debts of the house. Archbishop Creusens granted the request, but in 1680 we find a memo which noted that the sisters had not yet paid back the money, because of serious financial troubles. This was perhaps only exacerbated by Anna's vigorous policy of acquisition, for in 1669 she sought permission from the Council of State to purchase a large adjoining house, since theirs was situated too low and subject to flooding, and since they were out of room anyway. (Two years later she was seeking another loan of 3,000 florins to buy the place.) Thus they had the house, but at what price: for in 1671 a gentleman in Brussels wrote a threatening letter to Anna, promising a suit if he wasn't repaid the money owed him (though he began the letter with tender concern for her health). Evidence of lawsuits is in SAL, 3331, 3332, 4272. Documents generated or received by the Greys about loans and temporal matters are in Greys/5. But documents describing pleas to the Council of State and thus description of the house's physical plant are in Greys/11.

ARA, KAB, 15309, November 7, 1693, Greys/3, October 3, 1693, and Greys/11 contain correspondence and visitation reports on the reform of 1696. Perhaps things improved after the switch, as the women had hoped. A profession deed of 1717 noted that one sister entered with 4,000 florins, probably not typical but a big improvement over anything seen in the place before. A profession announcement of 1793 celebrated the entry of Maria Seraphina into the Order of Penitence, noting that many had ridiculed her devotion, but to prove it she chose no "well-placed" convent but the hardest order of all. The wealthy entrant of 1717 is in SAL, 4279, which also contains the 1793 profession announcement.

The scene with Mater Maria Theresa is in ARA, Dijledepartement, 2035, Sequestration of Goods of Closed Convents; Trente Vendomiaire, neuf heures du matin, Ans 5.

A NOTE ON THE INDEX

I have tried to avoid listing every last monastic establishment mentioned in the text; most are therefore grouped according to order (thus the Black Sisters of Leuven and the Black Sisters of Mechelen are listed simply under "Black Sisters," the Cistercian nuns of Beaupré or of Hertogendael under "Cistercian nuns," and so on). Page numbers in italics refer to illustrations. I have listed material from the notes (designated by an "n" after the page number) in the index only rarely: namely, when that material raised new issues or subjects, or stood almost on its own.

INDEX

images of convents, 23, 119,
128, 131, 141, 142, 152, 158,
161, 168, 169, 184, 190, 192,
216, 230, 273. *See also* Guests,
efforts to please; Public
relations
Laken, church and shrine of, 62,
66
Latin, use of by nuns, 16, 164, 165.
See also Divine Office
Lauds, 164. *See also* Divine Office
Lay sisters, 21, 91, 100, 112, 115,
116, 118, 127, 130, 137, 145,
152–55, 169, 179, 184, 190,
203, 210, 215, 216, 222, 228,
230–32, 235, 236, 241, 242,
250, 257, 273, 274
Lent, 118
Leprosy houses, 176
Leutbrewer (spiritual author), 265
Leuven: city and churches of, 8,
11–15, 18, 82, 83, 177, 205,
259, 268, 270; university, 15,
29, 47, 143, 174
Lipsius, Justus (Netherlandish
scholar), 15, 76
Literacy, among nuns, 17, 45,
71–73, 105, 116, 164–65, 205,
241, 242
Love, impartial, spiritual, and
sisterly, 17, 106–22, 168,
185–88, 207, 224, 234, 252,
260. *See also* Factionlism in
convents
Low Countries. *See* Netherlands
Lucius, Peter (dean of Leuven), 79,
80, 86, 89, 91, 93, 94, 101,
177–80, 196, 198, 199, 201
Luypaert, Women in Den (In the
Leopard), 130–33, 151, 210,
213, 214

M

Madrid (spiritual author), 71
Magic, 48. *See also* Exorcism;
Possession, demonic
Malderus (bishop of Antwerp),
255
Male religious, comparisons with,
123–24, 141, 142, 159, 160,
165
Mannarts (dean of Leuven), 243,
246, 247, 249, 250, 252, 254,
256, 258
Marcelis, Anna (nun of
Bethlehem), 20, 78, 148, 165,
171, 172, 232, 242
Marchant, Peter (reformer of Grey
Sisters), 166
Martens, Johan (confessor of
Bethlehem), 195
Martha (biblical), 164
Mary (or Maria), Mother of Jesus,
3, 19, 66, 69, 83, 84, 109, 158,
159, 164, 267
Mary Magdalene, 166
Mass, 49, 147; in life of convents,
6, 9, 12, 28, 74, 93, 124, 145,
150, 151, 157, 162–65, 168,
192, 216, 217, 231, 232, 268,
270
Mater: office and duties of, 12, 78,
93, 102, 106, 108, 109–10, 120,
170–72, 196–201, 206, 207,
213, 224–25, 226, 228, 233,
235, 242, 256, 269; elections
of, 40, 43, 44, 94, 99, 100,
139–40, 146, 156, 172, 178,
197–98, 242, 247, 248, 251,
253, 257, 258, 264 (*see also*
Elections); dismissals of, 92,
94, 214, 218, 248. *See also*